150

P9-DVA-873

chaucer

AND THE FRENCH TRADITION

—◆—

Lo here, the forme of olde clerkis speche
In poetrie, if ye hire bokes seche.

chaucer

AND THE FRENCH TRADITION

A STUDY IN STYLE AND MEANING
BY CHARLES MUSCATINE

1969

UNIVERSITY OF CALIFORNIA PRESS
BERKELEY AND LOS ANGELES

UNIVERSITY OF CALIFORNIA PRESS

BERKELEY AND LOS ANGELES

CALIFORNIA

UNIVERSITY OF CALIFORNIA PRESS, LTD.

LONDON, ENGLAND

Copyright, 1957, by
The Regents of the University of California
Library of Congress Catalogue Card No. 57-5396
Sixth printing, 1969
Printed in the United States of America

FOR DORIS

acknowledgments

FOR HELP with this book I owe thanks to many: particularly to Helge Kökeritz, "myn owene maister deere," under whose guidance the work was begun; to William K. Wimsatt, Jr., for encouragement and criticism; to Robert A. Pratt, for the benefit of his expert knowledge of Chauceriana; and to the authorities of Yale University, Wesleyan University, and the University of California, for haven, books, and research funds. Conversations with Roy Harvey Pearce, Carl E. Schorske, Norman O. Brown, and Ludwig Edelstein have helped me to see the wider implications of my subject, and also the limitations of the present treatment. In translating and commenting on Old French literature, I have tried to profit by the generous criticism of Ronald N. Walpole. The scholarship and friendship of Elizabeth Beckwith, Katherine Ware, and Doris Cooper Powers aided me greatly during the writing of the manuscript; Harold A. Small and John Halverson have contributed much to whatever clarity and accuracy the final text may have. The illustration for the title page was drawn by Ariel Parkinson.

CHARLES MUSCATINE

Berkeley, California
July, 1956

contents

I

introduction

THIS STUDY takes issue with—or departs from—a number of characteristically post-Victorian assumptions that are usually brought to Chaucer criticism, and it takes up a number of questions which the post-Victorian critics either no longer seem to have answered well or did not ask at all. In these senses, although it depends throughout on the immense scholarly labors of the past seventy-five years, it is an exploratory effort toward a modern criticism of Chaucer.

Specifically, it seeks to determine Chaucer's "meaning" as a complex whole; by giving form and style their due attention as essential, inseparable concomitants of meaning, it will try to balance the traditional preoccupation with "content" alone. It sees realism as a technique and a convention, not as an end in itself, and it sees convention as a potentially powerful tool, not as something to be avoided or rebelled against, or even necessarily to be remoulded. Rhetoric, too, it takes to be an instrument and not a vice. Liberated in great measure by post-Victorian scholarship itself, it does not confine its attention to narrowly textual sources in tracing and using the literary history behind Chaucer, but attempts broadly to explore his stylistic heritage.

The problem of style and meaning is most economically introduced here in connection with literary convention. By a style I mean a particular combination of literary traits, large or small; by a conventional style I mean one that is relatively stable over a period of time.

Most of us will agree that a convention in poetic style, like other conventions, acts as a kind of orientation for the parties to the convention, limiting and even defining an area of expectation or reference or meaning with security and consistency. It can be widely used and understood; it lends itself readily to inferior poets. The conventionalization of a style is usually described as a purely historical, associational phenomenon, the result of (mostly mindless) imitation; it is only partly so. The "meaning" of a conventional style is partly determined by the meanings of previous poems in that style, but also partly—and this too accounts for its conventionalization—by an inherent fitness-to-mean within the style itself. One trait, after all, becomes part of a style and another does not; and one style becomes conventionalized where others disappear, because one is best adapted to the expressive needs of the author, group, or culture using it. If no single stylistic trait can be said by itself to have "significant form" or inherent meaning, one of the functions of the mass testing attendant on conventionalization is to develop stable organizations of traits. In any meaningful artistic organization, such as the individual poem, the various traits of style tend to qualify and to reinforce each other. Correspondingly, the extent to which a combination of traits develops the cohesion and collective endurance that we associate with a conventional style depends partly on the degree to which those traits limit each other in a meaningful direction.

In a sense, this ability of its traits to support a meaning together makes a conventional style independent of historical association. Its inner organization gives it a kind of independent identity within certain broad cultural limits. Thus it is that a sensitive modern reader with a mind *not* stored with the specifically traditional associations of a style can usually come to a respectable, if partial, understanding of many a stylistic situation which the historian would describe as Miltonic or Euphuistic or courtly. And thus the recurrence of a style after a long period of disuse is never *fully* explained as a result of nostalgia for a particular period of the past. It heralds also the discovery that a convention formed in the past provides a set of tools ready-made for some specific use of the present. To recognize this element of independence and integrity in conventional style is to modify the unfortunate post-Victorian tendency to think of convention in organic terms. Lowes speaks of "the plasticity of conventions, while the life still runs in their veins." He adopts the Spenglerian view that styles, like men, die of old age, "harden into empty shells.'" While this organic metaphor is useful as a descriptive device, it too often has the practical effect of prescription. It is too quick—as in most Chaucer criticism—to make of a two-hundred-year-old convention a "dead" form, an "empty shell," and too quick to look for "revolt" where constructive acceptance may be going on. Rejecting the organic view, we are freer to see convention as an ideal instrument for certain purposes, and better stanced to appreciate Chaucer's use of it.

No given conventional style, of course, is expressive of a precise meaning. Style is not poetry. If it were, only one poem would theoretically be possible in any given style. But even under the rather gross definition that I am assuming, style lends itself not only to identification with certain remarkably well-defined areas of meaning, but also to classification according to the relationship of these areas. Rhetoricians, from classical times, have divided styles into the "high," the "middle," and the "low," according to varying principles. And while these rigid principles of literary decorum seem to have passed out of favor, there is a basis of truth in them. We speak of the "grand" style and of colloquial style, of formal or artificial style, and of naturalistic style. We speak of levels of usage in language generally. What is particularly significant in the use of this kind of terminology is that it often immediately implies a logical or social or even philosophical relationship among styles. And a perception of this kind of relationship—whether the styles are managed according to prescriptive rules of decorum or not—is often an additional indication of the meaning-function of the style or styles involved. "High," "middle," and "low" about the twelfth century, for instance, indicated not only a difference in traits but also a relative level of social dignity in the subject matter. What we shall apply to Chaucer is perhaps a more sophisticated scale: that which corresponds roughly to the scale by which we classify the levels of human apprehension of experience. Thus we can say that a style which we instinctively call "elevated" is better adapted than a naturalistic style to support an idealistic attitude toward experience. The non-representational traits of the former—often called the "conventional" traits—are among the best resources open to the poet who wishes to deal with that level of experience not immediately apprehensible to the senses. Conversely, the adoption in a naturalistic style of certain traits from the idiom of common life, representationalism generally, is a sign of the particular potency of this style in the expression of a phenomenalistic attitude toward experience. With the complexity of the gradation from idealism to phenomenalism, and with further refinement of stylistic classifications, we need not be concerned here. Let it

---

[1] For notes to chapter i see page 251.

3

suffice to say that the style-meaning problem in Chaucer involves two basic conventional styles, with their concomitant implications of attitude, having the kind of relationship described above.

These assumptions about style, it will be seen, immediately imply the attitudes toward realism and convention (and rhetoric) indicated at the outset, and lead to some basic questions on Chaucer. If conventional styles are developed to support specific areas of meaning, what are the conventional traits of style in Chaucer? What areas of meaning or attitude were they originally developed to explore? To what degree does Chaucer depend on the historically given formulation of style, on its traditional area of expressiveness? To what extent does he exploit the relationships between styles? This approach will entail careful weighing of the traditional notion of Chaucer's "revolt" from "outworn" convention. In our view it is the meaning, or the culture, not the convention that becomes outworn; the latter is always there, awaiting use, awaiting the poet to whom the meanings it can support are still important. "Old Forms and New Content," Lowes labels Chaucer's early poems;[2] our question is, how far does the "old" form alter or control or compound with the "new" content in the creation of meaning? Lowes memorably cites the introduction of barnyard imagery in Chaucer's formal portrait of Alisoun as an example of the vivification of a dead convention;[3] we shall press further to ask whether such passages would have been so vivid, their meaning so rich, if the "dead" convention had not been used at all. If it is indeed the case that Chaucer does not revolt from conventionalism in any profound sense, we shall have to alter the traditional account of his whole development as a poet.

To offer answers to these questions, I shall first turn to the history of the styles leading to Chaucer, and I must here outline briefly what this history is expected to provide.

Literary history can generally be a powerful aid to critical analysis. If history never, with good poets, reveals absolutely what the work shall be, it gives us signposts to the probable areas of relevance. It helps to prevent gross errors of analysis, such as those that proceed from reading a work by the wrong set of assumptions. History, furthermore, tends to corroborate the results of analysis; among equal possibilities it often denotes the more probable. In the identification and definition of style, particularly in a poet of complex style, as Chaucer, it is particularly useful. It helps us to judge which abstractions and combinations to make, which traits to associate with which in order to see potentially meaningful combinations. It is the only source of answers to questions we have already asked: What are the *conventional* traits of style in Chaucer? What areas of meaning were they originally developed to explore?

4

We are thus asking about the tools that tradition made available to the poet and the uses to which they are purposely adapted. The second question, and probably also the first, requires a kind of history that obviously exceeds the area of Chaucer's textual "sources." Apart from what he read and could copy, how much poetry did Chaucer hear?[4] There is no answer; but the question will do to suggest that the ordinary notion of "sources" is too narrow to accommodate a search for the springs of Chaucer's style, the larger assumptions, the grand matrices that precede and underlie and outlive the minor vogues and enthusiasms.

It happens, for instance, that the tradition of the Troy *story* does not coincide with the tradition of *style* in which Chaucer writes the *Troilus*. In discussing the latter tradition, then, although I shall mention some of the works that Chaucer is definitely known to have read, I am not governed in my choice by the principle of narrow textual similarity, but by the importance of a work as originating or propagating the stylistic tradition in which Chaucer writes. Chaucer's most fundamental historical traits are "medieval," but that is a perspective too broad to be manageable at the outset. His deepest linguistic matrix is English, but if his diction and syntax were English before him, his style was not. The most prominent source of the style of Chaucer's poetry—his literary matrix— is not English, Latin, or Italian; his style is most compendiously and clearly described as stemming from the traditions originated and propagated, in the twelfth and thirteenth centuries, in France.

This is what the obvious biographical facts would suggest. Chaucer was brought up in a court still strongly Norman in its tastes and ambitions, ruled by a French-speaking king who periodically laid claim to the French throne. His schooling, we can be sure, was in French and Latin, not in English,[5] and his earliest extant original compositions are closely modeled after the best contemporary French mode, the pretty, decorative poetry of the school of Guillaume de Machaut.

But one must emphasize what his lifelong use of the *Roman de la Rose* by itself would indicate: Chaucer's French literary heritage goes far deeper than a personal acquaintance with Granson and an early interest in modern poetry. He is, indeed, less a kin of Machaut than of the great poets of the centuries previous. He is a common descendant of Guillaume de Lorris and Jean de Meun, of the great French romancers—Chrétien de Troyes, Gautier d'Arras, the anonymous author of *Flamenca*,—and of the *Renart* poets and their brothers of the naturalistic tradition.

In a large sense, of course, twelfth-century French (with Provençal) was the

5

seminal vernacular literature of the high Middle Ages. It is behind Dante and Petrarch, Boccaccio and Machaut, the *dolce stil nuovo, Minnesang,* and English and German romance. Thus, had Chaucer's French been not so good (it was better than his Latin and Italian), nor his particular social milieu so French, he would still very likely have been writing poetry of a French tradition. The proof of the pudding, however, is that a great deal of what Chaucer *does* with style is what in its primary features was invented or done most memorably in twelfth- and thirteenth-century French. That is, he discovers and in his mature work consistently exploits those nexuses between style and meaning which are characteristic of the two great traditions of this literature, the courtly and the "bourgeois."

Let me here avoid a possible misunderstanding. About a century ago a Frenchman named E.-G. Sandras, in his *Etude sur G. Chaucer considéré comme imitateur des trouvères* (Paris, 1859), attempted to prove that Chaucer was substantially a French poet. Actually, considering the resources then available, he deserved rather better than he received at the hands of later scholars. But granting our present superior knowledge of both Old French and Chaucer, I would not be taken to be perpetuating Sandras's project. I am aware of Chaucer's Englishness, and aware, too, that the convenience of using the French tradition as a yardstick for Chaucer begins particularly to diminish in the vast area of the *Canterbury Tales.* A fully satisfactory study of the style of that work, *mutatis mutandis,* would have to take into account a great part of the other medieval literatures, and it would have to face the monumental problem of the stylistic value of Chaucer's English language *per se.*[6] Neither of these is within the skill or scope of the present work. However, it seems to me that the most promising avenue of limited exploration, the one liable to the least fallacy, is the one adopted here. Earlier English literature tells us very little about Chaucer, and Chaucer himself has very little good to say of it. On the other hand there is a substantial progeny of the French tradition among the styles and genres of the *Canterbury Tales.* Most important, the absorptiveness and influence, the central medievalism of the French tradition, make the terms and concepts that attend its description widely applicable to medieval literature generally. Thus the French dualism of style broadly parallels a similar dualism in Italian and Latin.[7] Looking in the other direction, the "epic" vein in Chaucer, which includes in its tradition Virgil, Statius, Dante, and Boccaccio, can be described in terms of a "high" style that shares many traits with French conventionalism. In this case the same medieval tradition of rhetoric, based on Latin models, is behind the French, the Italian, and the English poetry.[8] I assume likewise a certain stylistic equivalence between French and English naturalism. While I share the conviction of generations of readers that there is nothing so primally English in spirit as the *Canterbury Tales*—and I can follow John Speirs's feeling that Chaucer's genius "is rooted in the English language as it was spoken in his time,'"—I may nevertheless point to an area of literary history in which the naturalisms of both literatures intersect. Thus the few extant English fabliaux are based on French models; and thus while Chaucer made of a mediocre French fabliau his exceedingly English *Reeve's Tale,* in doing so he used for the first recorded time in English a kind and degree of colloquialism that has its nearest literary precedent in the Old French mime. The ultimate advantage of the present approach, then, as far as literary tradition is concerned, is in the priority, the breadth, and the centrality of French literature in the Middle Ages. It is the main example of the Gothic mode which Chaucer assimilates to his English consciousness. Its final decadence, indeed, is a clear index to the nature of Chaucer's strength.

The effect of a stylistic scrutiny of the bourgeois tradition will be, I think, to establish the notion of the conventionality of Chaucer's realism—not in order to minimize it, but to suggest that it is a style, having a meaning outside of and beyond itself. In Chaucer it is not a *summum bonum* laboriously achieved, but a technique gradually perfected and finally subordinated to the requirements of meaning. In addition, this relationship of Chaucer to a *tradition* of realism will help to redefine his historical position. The "Medieval-Modern Conflict" in Chaucer's poetry, with convention as medieval and victorious realism as modern, will have to be discarded. Instead we shall find a more conservative poet than traditional criticism presents, but one more complex and more sensitive. Chaucer, who is so "detached" and so niggardly of contemporary allusions, embodies within his poetry the deepest and most characteristic crisis of his age. He is as "historical" as the author of *Piers Plowman*.

Having said that literary history does not determine absolutely what a poem shall be, and having suggested that Chaucer's poetry accommodates two great traditions of style, is to describe the kind and area of his "originality." Chaucer's "new" style is a mixture of "old" ones, and much of my analysis will be focused on the results and implications of this fact.

If what I have said about style-meaning is right, the extent to which a poet can manage multiple kinds or levels of style is an index to the potential complexity and fullness of the attitudes he can express. This is not to set up a purely quantitative estimate. Two views of experience are not necessarily better than one, but two *related* views can provide a third dimension, a perspective, that cannot be encompassed in a single one. The analysis, therefore, will not end with identification of the traits which go to make up Chaucer's style, nor with the definition of the historical associations that cling to it, but will go on to see how in the individual poem Chaucer's peculiar complexity of style contributes to the results, the meanings and values that make him Chaucer.

Some specific uses of the complex or mixed style are familiar to us through recent study of the Augustan mock-heroics and the Elizabethan double plot. Thus on the latter, William Empson takes up the impression of "reality" given to the heroic sentiments of the main plot by relating them to the concrete and popular elements of the subplot, the general impression of dealing with life completely that a play such as *I Henry IV* creates, the device of anticipating parody to disarm potential criticism, and the capacity of the double plot to satisfy multiple impulses in the reader or audience.[10] This is largely a matter of reader or audience psychology. But, though I am dealing with narrative poetry, where duality of style is usually not underlined by duality of plot, and the effects of such stylistic situations are generally less crude, I shall attempt to study the interplay of style as much as possible from within. Chaucer's style lends the poems particularly well to internal analysis. If the style's conventionality provides a historical basis for description, its complexity provides an inner basis, a remarkably clear and objective set of categories and distinctions, turning on the manner of stylistic adjustment, by which to apprehend his method. We shall find, in general in Chaucer, that mixed style is used in the interest of perspective, and that the meanings supported by conventional styles give each other point and clarity, help define each other. More important, they contribute to the creation of new, compound meanings. Perhaps the best introduction to this phenomenon is an acquaintance with the mock-heroic style, as in Pope. In the *Dunciad,* for instance, the epic vein does more than merely define and limit the realistic one. The two strains go into combination, to produce neither a sharply heroic nor a sharply realistic account, but one qualitatively different from either. Perhaps the most interesting thing about such compounds is that the styles which support them can have various valences, and control of the degree and manner of combination can produce significant differences of tone. Within the class of stylistically compound poems called "mock-heroic" we also find the *Rape of the Lock,* in which Pope uses essentially the same components of style. But in the *Dunciad* the heroic style is adjusted to the realistic most often to exploit its exquisite fitness, in compound, to express pomposity. In the other poem the two styles enter into a perhaps more complex relationship. Pope adjusts them to support both the satirical attitude which we all recognize, and a seriously elevated one also. It is as if the heroic implications were at once negated and supported by the commonplace ones. This stylistic situation supports a compound meaning which, as Cleanth Brooks has urged, "is not exhausted in laughing away [Belinda's] claims to divinity."[11]

Chaucer's poems show an even wider variety of such compound meanings. With essentially the same conventional styles, in varying adjustment, Chaucer produces a mock-epic in the *Nun's Priest's Tale,* the bitter satire of the *Merchant's Tale,* the broad comedy of the *Miller's Tale,* and the pervasive irony of the *Troilus.* A description of the stylistic situation in the last will, I hope, articulately reveal a dimension of the poem that has not yet been brought out, and will show generally how stylistic analysis may be brought to bear on specific critical problems. It sometimes, indeed, reveals distinctions which cannot be as clearly seen in any other way. Follow the surface argument of *Troilus and Criseyde* and Pandarus is Troilus' *frend.* But there is something unsatisfactory about this simple description, and it has become a point of critical controversy. Stylistic analysis of the way in which each of these characters is handled goes an appreciable way toward revealing the meaning of the relationship between them and resolving the controversy. In the same way, I shall try to cast some comparatively objective light on the fatal ambiguity of Criseyde, and on the problem of the poem's ending.

In addition to dealing with specific problems, a stylistic study may contribute to the testing of literary theory. One result of the present study, if it does not necessarily stem from the primary assumptions themselves, will be to support the argument against critical relativism. It will show that variant, respectable interpretations of Chaucer's poems often correspond to varying areas of his style, and thus that besides serving to define shifts of sensibility, variant interpretations are abstractions from the total poem, are actually variant and partial discoveries of meaning. The general questions of the "universality" and the mode of existence of poetry are also involved. This study will provide data toward the theory that the perennial significance of great poems depends on the multiplicity of meanings they interrelate. One generation finds the *Troilus and Criseyde* a grave and serious tragedy. Another prizes it for its delicate comedy. Stylistic analysis will show that both of these attitudes are inherent in the poem, that they compose its irony. Troilus, like Shylock, would not be half so tragic without the hidden substratum of the fool, and without the heroic overtones he would not be half so comic.

Our own generation has necessarily its peculiar sensibility. To use such terms as "irony," "ambiguity," "tension," and "paradox" in describing Chaucer's poetry is to bring to the subject our typical mid-century feeling for an unresolved

9

dialectic. Yet I think that we are thus better able than the post-Victorians to see certain elements in Chaucer. We have a new tolerance of convention. The great scholars who reintroduced Chaucer to the literary world a half-century ago were themselves born in the age of Ibsen and Zola, in a close atmosphere of "realism." Many of them lacked the ability to appreciate convention, just as their favorite moderns lacked the impulse to use it. In this atmosphere even the greatest of the older poets, Shakespeare as well as Chaucer, became half invisible. Contemporary with the interpretation of Chaucer's *Troilus* as a psychological novel is the Bradleyan theory of Shakespearean tragedy—by Butcher's Aristotle out of Ibsen,—similarly engrossed in psychological realism, in motivation, in everything but poetic convention. Brilliant reëxamination of the post-Victorian Shakespeare has already taken place. The whole critical atmosphere of today is propitious for rediscovery of poetry lost and poetic meanings inappreciable to older generations. My notes will record, along with an immense obligation to the older scholarship, some debt to an emergent modern criticism of Chaucer. Meanwhile I shall try to describe the typically medieval dialectic that finds its last great synthesis in Chaucer's capacious poetry.

II

the courtly tradition

MEDIEVAL courtly literature appears first in France in the course of the twelfth century, in response to a set of tastes and attitudes then newly arising in high society. The knights, ladies, and clerks of the provincial courts of the time seem suddenly to have come to a new sense of their social identity, and of the refinement and exclusiveness of their ideals. They draw themselves apart from the heterogeneous, Christian audience of epic and hagiography and call into being an aristocratic, secularized literature. They seem actually to have discovered, or at least radically refashioned, the principal topics of this literature—courtly or romantic love, courtesy, chivalry—and they require from their poets the invention of an appropriate literary style. By the end of the century the attitudes are widely spread, the style is almost completely formed, and there exists a distinct and persistent courtly literary tradition.

The courtly lyric had been long nurtured in the Midi when at mid-century the romance emerged in the North, already half-grown, to become the tradition's most prominent genre. Between the *Roman de Thebes* (*ca.* 1150) and the works of Chrétien de Troyes, scarcely a generation later, romance had reached a respectable degree of thematic and stylistic coherence. By the time of Guillaume de Lorris (*ca.* 1234) its major potentialities as romance had all been fulfilled, and there were already beginning to appear, alongside a comparatively undisturbed main tradition, mutations and hybrids leading in a variety of directions: toward popular debasement, toward mystical, religious sublimation, and toward comic and ironic reconstruction. Some of Chaucer's poetry lies in the main course of the tradition. More, perhaps the more interesting part, flows from it obliquely, but deeply tinged with the color of the parent stream. From the largest considerations of genre to the smallest ones of diction and image, Chaucer's mature work turns on its conventions.

§ I. THE CONVENTIONAL STYLE OF THE COURTLY TRADITION

I shall not attempt to deal with the style of this tradition in all its particulars and variations; detailed discussion would require more space than can be spared. Nevertheless, because of the distinctiveness of the tradition itself, and particularly because of the narrowness of its ideological base, we can, I think, come to some valid and useful generalizations.[1]

At its beginnings, the courtly romance has a daring, experimental flavor. The earliest romances retain much of the epic and historiographic character of more popular contemporary literature, but they are attempts, at least, to imitate *classical* epic. Herein their matter is already more learned, more remote, and more wonderful than that of the *chanson de geste* and the chronicle. And by transforming the social and psychological perspective of these models, their observations are at the same time disturbingly more intimate. The *Thebes* is full of echoes of the *Chanson de Roland*, but it is a romance by virtue of a courtly social aura, the interpolation of a few simple love episodes not found in the *Thebaid*, a taste for marvelous description, and a new verse form, the octosyllabic couplet. The *Eneas* (*ca.* 1155) is even more experimental. It makes Lavinia the heroine of Virgil's epic, and gives unprecedented space to a detailed account of her love affair with Aeneas. Along with this new emphasis it brings together a remarkable assemblage of stylistic devices: much of the armory of clerical rhetoric; elaborate and fantastic descriptions; rapid, stichomythic conversations; long, introspective monologues imitated from Ovid, but peculiarly altered; dialogues within monologues. It adopts a physiology and etiquette of love from Ovid and the troubadours, and can deal with this subject, along with other wonders and miracles, with a length and minuteness which bespeak a nearly insatiable interest on the part of its aristocratic audience.

---

[1] For notes to chapter ii see pages 252–255.

The *Eneas* poet is usually considered the greatest stylistic innovator among the early romancers, but he is still, as artist, only partially successful. It is as if the novelty and the excitement of his new materials had concealed their deeper possibilities, or as if the new style had somehow outstripped the sentiment that brought it forth. Style and sentiment in the *Eneas* are not yet fused around a theme that will make the best of both. Apart from being by turns heroic and erotic, the poem appears to have no theme. The epic has been destroyed and the courtliness is not yet well assimilated. There is no relation between Eneas in love and Eneas at war. The Dido episode, which by itself contains some moving poetry, does not shed its light on the rest of the poem. Benoît de Sainte-Maure, whose vast, influential *Roman de Troie* completes the early trilogy of "classical" romances, falls similarly short of artistic success. Three substantial love stories punctuate his interminable battle scenes. One of these, the desertion of Troilus by Briseida, is in itself a successful *lai,* poetic enough to have launched the Troilus tradition. But his poem is still far from being a coherent whole.

Romance is soon at the point, though, where its style is overtaken by the full development of theme, and thus where style, rather than seeming merely *appliqué,* can have a functional relationship to meaning. Love and adventure are the two large topics of romance, and of those who manage to subsume both topics within a single theme, Chrétien de Troyes is preëminent. In his *Erec et Enide,* his *Yvain,* and his *Lancelot,* love is a cue for adventure, chivalry, and chivalry is a means of deserving love. The general principles of courtly love are clear enough for us to see how neatly they fit the typical action of romance. The Lady is traditionally desirable and difficult, and her favors are not lightly given. Love itself is a humbling and refining passion, open only to the worthy. Chivalry, in the form of difficult adventure, is a means of achieving the respect of the Lady, or, in more complex movements, such as the plot of *Yvain,* to recapture it, often on a higher or deeper level than that on which it was previously held. The most sophisticated interpretations of Chrétien, indeed, ultimately reveal some form of the theme of self-realization in his works.[2] In this view adventure is not so meaningful in itself as in figuring forth the willing submission to the test, the search for the refined, attenuated ideal of conduct that will bring the hero to the highest level of courtly virtue. Love, then, more than just a reward for virtue, is a symbol of virtue itself. Love by itself, or with a minimum of adventure, is the topic of some of the best of the later romances, and finds its most elaborate treatment in the incomparable *Roman de la Rose* of Guillaume de Lorris. Here the field of external vision is acutely narrowed; for the movements of knights, giants, and damsels in distress are substituted the movements of the soul itself, and one's attention is focused, not on a set of defeats and victories in field and bower, but on the minutest events in the progress of a single love affair, rendered through allegory. Yet despite the excision of so much adventure, the underlying movement is the same: the Narrator-Lover moving through courtly life, subjected to trial, increasing in knowledge, moving toward (but not, alas, achieving, since the poem is unfinished) a state of perfect felicity in the possession of a Lady's love. Partly indeed a handbook of love, the *Roman* brings the idealism and subjectivity of the courtly tradition to their most refined expression in French literature.

The style of the tradition from the *Thebes* to the *Roman de la Rose* becomes superbly formed to support or express the narrow idealism of the courtly view. The very diction of romance, in both narrative and direct discourse, is characteristically elegant and pure, the ancestor of our polite conversation. Though the octosyllabic couplet is adaptable to a wide variety of rhythms, the total impression of the narrative style is one of a leisurely and fluid movement. The *esprit gaulois* was already in existence in the twelfth century, and the romancers are ever capable of turning upon their subjects with a realistic wit; nevertheless, their style is in large a conventional one. Designed to evoke ideal and invisible worlds, it reflects an unconcern for naturalism or representationalism that is hard, at first, for the modern reader to appreciate. Yet the literary strategy behind this style is both characteristically medieval and artistically logical. The idealism of romance is in some ways a transposed Christian idealism, and its literature inherits, through a clerkly class of poets, the conventional method, if not the matter, of hagiography and pious legend. If the other Christian style, the everyday, "figural" realism described in Auerbach's *Mimesis,* was available to the early romancers, they did not use it; otherwise, there was no medieval tradition which required realism in dealing with important matters. The courtly audience does not have our advantage (or disadvantage) of two centuries of the realistic novel behind it. Medieval culture as a whole is much more receptive to the production of nonrepresentational art than ours is. The medieval audience is ready and able to see effortlessly beyond the surface representation of form and image to a higher reality, and to see the concrete itself as metaphor and symbol. This capacity is rooted in the Christian-Neoplatonic metaphysics of early medieval culture. It is nurtured further for literature partly by the widespread theological habit of symbolic interpretation, with its concomitant theory of poetry, and partly by the medieval version of classical rhetoric, which recognizes and prescribes, from figure to style, a conventional technique for serious writing.[3] Under these conditions it is economical and logical that courtly idealism, attempting to transcend the limitations of everyday, outward appearances, should freely employ a literary style which can directly represent an ideal world, and can convert even outward appearance to ulterior, poetic-symbolic purposes. Thus the setting of romance is often exotic: sometimes a dreamland outside of time and geography, sometimes ancient Greece, Rome, or Carthage, or Britain. There is in these latter settings little effort at historicity; they are all peopled by medieval figures. But the names of these places, and the marvels that can there ensue serve to lift the stories out of the realm of the ordinary, putting them beyond the local and mundane considerations which the courtly ideal tried to transcend. The land of Gorre, and the somewhat less exotic court of Arthur, supply an excellent setting for adventure in the nearly abstract. Freed from the exigencies of time and place, and from the suspicion of practical allegiances and motives, the hero can concentrate on his courtly quest. To cross over on a sword blade into a land whence no stranger has ever returned—for the love of a Lady—is an act of gratuitous valor that no one can quibble about. If Chrétien did not know the immense mythological import of the stories he was borrowing from the Bretons, he was still not engaged in a mindless or enchanted love of marvels, for he used the Celtic imagery in support of his own mythology.[4]

The romances after Chrétien are often nominally set in "France," and with enough truth to courtly life to provide material for the social historian. On this basis they have even been called "realistic,"[5] but the greatest part of this realism is realism only historically. Poetically, the settings of *Guillaume de Dole* or *L'Escoufle* are no more "realistic" than our own reports of opening night at the opera. French courtly society at its most magnificent, with its tournaments and feasts and hunts, if not partly imitating romance, certainly approached the ideality of it. The minute background "realism" of the romances, then, more often than not supports the noble, idealistic concepts on which the stories rest. On the other hand, commentators have been justly amused by the excesses in the description and genealogy that often appear in the romance. Many romances, particularly the earlier and cruder and the later, popularized ones, pander to an unreserved taste for the marvelous.[6] But with the best poets, such as Chrétien and Guillaume de Lorris, there is ample description of a demonstrably functional order.

The luxuriant otherworldliness of place and description in the romances is most clearly seen in its functional aspect where it coincides with the religion of love, and takes on the organizing structure of an imitated or assimilated Christian cosmos, with its worshipers, its martyrs and angels, its God of Love, and its

Paradise.[7] The courtly attitude is quasi-religious—as is seen in its ready adaptation to overtly religious poetry. Thus the garden in springtime, which is a conventional setting for courtly love, is described in the *Roman de la Rose* in terms of a *parevis terrestre*, "an earthly Paradise,"[8] and the superlatives of the description continually evoke an ideal of beauty consonant with the comparison:

> Trop par faisoient bel servise [661]
> Cil oisel que je vos devise.
> Il chantoient un chant itel
> Con fussent ange esperitel;
> E bien sachiez, quant je l'oï,
> Mout durement m'en esjoï;
> Qu'onc mais si douce melodie
> Ne fu d'ome mortel oïe.

> By note made fair servyse [669]
> These briddes, that I you devise;
> They songe her song as faire and wel
> As angels don espirituel.
> And trusteth wel, whan I hem herde,
> Ful lustily and wel I ferde;
> For never yitt sich melodye
> Was herd of man that myghte dye.[9]

The company in the Garden

> sembloient [724]
> Tot por voir anges empenez.
> Si beles genz ne vit on nez.

> So faire they weren, alle and some; [740]
> For they were lyk, as to my sighte
> To angels that ben fethered brighte.

This identification of the superlative with the heavenly is accompanied by a feeling for fullness and regularity. The garden of the *Roman* is of equal length and breadth, and its trees are planted in happy arrangement, to shade the tender shrubbery. There are trees of all the pleasant kinds, and a plenitude of songbirds, flowers, clear fountains and harmless animals.[10]

> Onc mais ne fu nus leus si riches [480]
> D'arbres ne d'oisillons chantanz . . .

> So riche a yerd was never noon   [492]
> Of briddes song, and braunches grene . . .

The Ideal is not usually subjected to the gross impact of events; accordingly, much of the description in the courtly tradition is static and formal. It is often chosen not for direct use in the dramatic action, but for ulterior significance, which can range from the generally atmospheric to the most minutely allegorical. The frequent catalogues which go with the exhaustiveness of description are generally to be taken as "atmospheric": thus the lists of birds and trees in the *Roman de la Rose*. Often, however, a catalogue will be local and selective enough to admit of a more precise interpretation. The robe of the God of Love is made of flowers, "par fines amoretes," and portrayed all over with lozenges and shields, with birds, lion cubs, leopards, and other animals. He is covered with birds: parrots, nightingales, larks, tomtits. This is splendor of a particular sort, expressing doubtless the breadth and quality of Love's natural dominion.[11] But it is description that despite its peculiarity and specificity tends to remain part of the setting. Even more specific in meaning are the two crystal stones in the well of love, where the seed of love is sown; they have the varicolor of a beautiful Lady's eyes, and indeed that is what they stand for. The rosebush of the garden is carefully described, with the attention carefully narrowed from the many to the one, to express the uniqueness, freshness, fragrance, and youth (as of a young bud) of the object of the lover's aspirations.[12] In descriptions like these latter ones we have reached allegory proper. Finally, there is always, in this literature, the possibility of formal symbolism in description, the keys to which may be found in the bestiaries, lapidaries, encyclopedias, and Biblical commentaries.

The general stasis which envelops the formal description of this tradition is not limited to background material. The reader will recall any number of superficially utilitarian objects—swords for fighting, rings for identification, horses and castles that come into use—which are still described so generously as to exceed the demands of action.[13] Setting, landscape, and paraphernalia, then, tend to be exotic, superlative in quality and economy, and, in the best poetry, generating a meaning by their presence without regard for their practical utility in the action—like the fruits and lucent syrups of Keats's "Eve of St. Agnes," which no one ever consumes.

Idealization and formulation dominate the description of characters as well. The conventional device is the formal portrait, a remarkably stable catalogue of homogeneous traits, described in order from head to toe, as if the poet were following the supposed order of nature step by step.[14] The ideal courtly lady has blond hair, a white unwrinkled forehead, a tender skin, arched (but not plucked) brows, gray (*vair*) eyes, well spaced, a straight, well-made nose, a small, round, full mouth, a sweet breath, and a dimpled chin. Poets who go further than physiognomy favor a rather tall heroine, with smooth, white neck, small, hard breasts, a straight, flat back, and a certain broadness in the hips. A "remenant," "blanc et poli," is often alluded to but usually concealed. The description of the lady's dress will then often follow, and sometimes an itemization of her moral qualities. Within the latitude left for poetic elaboration appear similes still familiar to us. The damsel Oiseuse in the *Roman de la Rose,* who is the most minutely described of the courtly company because she appears first, has a throat

autresi blanche   [545]
Come est la nois desus la branche,
Quant il a freschement negié.

also whit of hewe   [557]
As snowe on braunche snowed newe.

Fresne, heroine of *Galeran de Bretagne,* has a face

blanc com fleur de lis,
Destrempé de couleur vermeille,
A qui rose ne s'aparaille,
Tant epanisse en may matin.[15]

[white as the lily-flower, mingled with a vermilion that no rose could match, opening on a May morning.]

The formality of this description, with the brilliance and illumination of its imagery, suggests that behind it there lies the medieval aesthetic theory of beauty as formal excellence and brightness.[16] The theoretical "resplendence of form" denotes a closeness to the divine Light, and this would accord well with the erotic theology. But the conventional portrait also has mingled with it elements of the refined sensuality that coexists in courtly love with idealism, giving us an ideal of still earthly desirability, another *parevis terrestre.* The use of the portrait with uniformly superlative traits in rational arrangement means that the courtly poet's attention is directed in great measure away from the specific woman, and toward Beauty in woman itself. He has no use for qualification or compromise. His ignoring of personally characteristic features, of dissonances and irregularities, is part of the economy of expressing an idealized attitude toward his subject.

A related feature of the courtly poet's style is his apparent carelessness of realism in representing speech and action. Since the conventions of direct discourse are a crucial symptom of the nature of characterization in romance, it will pay us to examine them carefully. We must recognize at the outset, for instance, that any distinction between monologue and dialogue based on the number of persons present is largely artificial. The courtly poet is licensed to interchange these forms in the interest of certain effects and in despite of strictly dramatic propriety. Indeed, dramatic monologue, which acknowledges in its style a fidelity to both the spoken idiom and the presence of a listener, is virtually never used in romance. Formal soliloquy, however, can emerge at any point in the action, often without the "aside" ("entre ses dens" in the romances) to mark the tenuous dividing line between speech and thought. The *Eneas* in many ways sets the style of speech for the whole tradition. The affair of Eneas and Lavinia includes two great scenes in which Lavinia is interviewed by her mother.[17] After a battle of personalities (to which we shall return later) she is finally made to stammer out the name of her lover. The Queen is enraged and tries vainly to turn her daughter's attention to Turnus. But Lavinia is firm, and the inevitability of her resolution is registered effortlessly in a shift from dialogue to soliloquy as the object of her address shifts from the mother to Amor himself. The style and tone of speech shift likewise. Lavinia begins by arguing with the Queen in terms of the concrete situation:

> —Ge ne puis pas faire cest change.   [8622]
> —Ce que ge voil ne doiz amer?
> —Nel puis an mon cuer atorner.
> —Que t'a forfet?—Moi? nule rien.
> —Car l'aime donc et si t'i tien.
> —Autre ai choisi, ge nel puis faire.

["I cannot make this change." "Should you not love what I wish?" "I cannot so dispose my heart." "What wrong has he done you?" "To me? None at all." "Love Turnus then, and attach yourself to him." "I cannot do it; I have chosen another."]

A little farther on she is discoursing on Love's power in a manner not unusual for one recently introduced to the erotic doctrine:

> "Quel deffanse ai ancontre amor?   [8633]
> N'i valt noiant chastel ne tor,
> ne halt paliz ne grant fossé;

soz ciel n'a cele fermeté
qui se puisse vers lui tenir,
ne son asalt gramment sofrir;
parmi set murs trairoit son dart
et navreroit de l'autre part:
l'an ne se puet de lui garder."

["What defense have I against Love? Neither castle nor tower can protect me, nor high fence nor broad moat; there is no fortress under heaven that can be held against him, nor that could long resist his attack. He would shoot his arrow through seven walls and wound on the other side: there is no way to guard against him."]

The speech ends with the Queen forgotten, in a rhetorical invocation designed to evoke high emotion.

"Amors, ge sui en ta baillie,   [8655]
an ton demoinne m'as saisie.
Amors, des or me clain par toi,
Amors, ne fere tel desroi!
Amors, soëf un po me moine!"

["Love, I am in thy power; thou hast seized me and made me thy possession. Henceforth, Love, I am in thy service; Love, put me not into such distress. Love, deal gently with me a little!"]

Then Lavinia faints.

Another example of this shift from dialogue to what is virtually soliloquy occurs in the scene in which Dido learns of Eneas' intention to depart.[18] The scene is constructed on somewhat the same plan as the one discussed above, with passages of quick dialogue separating long speeches. Here is the last of the dialogue passages:

"Sire, por coi m'avez traïe?   [1749]
—Ge non ai, voir, la moie amie.
—Mesfis vos ge onques de rien?
—Moi n'avez vos fait el que bien.
—Destruis ge Troie?—Nenil, Greus.
—Fu ce par moi?—Mes par les deus.
—Ai ge vos vostre pere ocis?
—Nenil, dame, gel vos plevis.
—Sire, por coi me fuiez donc?

20

—Ce n'est par moi.—Et par cui donc?
—C'est par les deus, quil m'ont mandé,
qui ont sorti et destiné,
an Lonbardie an doi aler,
iluec doi Troie restorer."

["Sir, why have you betrayed me?" "Indeed, I have not, my love."
"Did I ever injure you in anything?" "You have done me nothing
but good." "Did I destroy Troy?" "No, a Greek did." "Was this
through me?" "Only through the gods." "Did I kill your father?"
"No, lady, I assure you." "Why then, sir, do you flee from me?" "It
is not my doing." "Whose, then?" "It is the command of the gods,
who have decreed and destined that I must go to Italy, and there
rebuild Troy."]

Eneas explains at length the nature of his mission, reiterating again and again
that the gods are responsible for his departure. Dido is not satisfied. She begins
her reply with a direct attack on him:

"Onc n'apartenistes as deus,   [1797]
car molt estes fels et crueus . . ."

["You had never to do with the gods, for you are too wicked and
cruel . . ."]

but shortly thereafter she is talking to herself, speaking of him in the third
person:

"Ahi lasse! que di ge mes?   [1807]
Quant ge nel puis avoir, gel les;
por noiant parol, quant ne m'ot,
ne il de bien ne respont mot."

["Alas! What more can I say? If I cannot have him, I give him up;
I speak for nothing when he hears me not, and does not answer with
one kind thing."]

The speech ends fifty lines later without a change of perspective. It becomes a
soliloquy in which the speaker analyzes her feelings, looks over her situation,
and concludes that she cannot live without her lover. This shift is a dramatic
flaw, yet it produces one of the best soliloquies of the romance. It shows in a
marked way the changeability of form possible in medieval discourse We have

seen argument give way to a more rhetorical and undramatic kind of utterance in the final speech of Lavinia. Here, to represent Dido's turning to despair, the author openly neglects Eneas' presence. While such a shift is not usually signalized, as here, by an alteration in the pronoun of address, we find in medieval literature a considerable tendency to neglect the second person in long speeches which are superficially parts of the dialogue.

It is equally possible to convert soliloquy into dialogue. As we shall see, many of the rapid verbal exchanges in the romances occur in the lonely speeches of a single character debating with himself. But this is only one of several other directions in which the speech of the courtly tradition leads away from representationalism.

The courtly poets were from the first capable of great variety within the convention of soliloquy. In Ovid they had models of a form which incorporated a sensitive mixture of reflection and emotion, exposition and inner response, all directly pertinent to the situation at hand. In the soliloquy of Dido referred to above, the *Eneas* poet has taken up this form. His character illuminates from a personal point of view a situation that has already been clearly set forth:

> "Nos sentons molt diversement: [1823]
> ge muir d'amor, il ne s'en sent,
> il est en pes, ge ai les mals;
> amors n'est pas vers moi loials,
> quant ne senton comunalment.
> Se il sentist ce que ge sent,
> qu'il amast moi si com ge lui,
> ne partisson ja mes andui.
> Ses devinailles va disant
> et ses mençonges va trovant,
> dit que li deu li ont mandé,
> porveü ont et ordené
> comant il doit traitier sa vie
> et qu'il s'en alt en Lombardie.
> De ce ont or li deu grant cure,
> molt se travaillent sanz mesure,
> et molt tienent de ce grant plet
> de mander li ce que il fet!
> Mais par ma foi ne lor an chalt
> se il remaint ou s'il s'en alt.
> Quant dit qu'as deus est de lui tant,

22

qu'il ne fait rien sanz lor comant,
por coi l'unt donc tant travaillié,
par mer et par terre cotié?
Ne li failloit nul jor lor guerre,
ainz qu'il venist an ceste terre;
quant ariva an cest païs,
esgarez ert. Que fole fis,
que gel reçui ansanble moi;
or m'en repant, que faire el doi;
tot son talant a de moi fet,
ne remaindroit ci por nul plet.
Quant ge nol puis mes retenir,
alt s'en, moi estovra morir."

["Our feelings are so much opposed: I die of love, and he has no
affection; he is untroubled and I am tormented. Love is unfaithful
to me when we do not feel as one. If he felt what I feel, loved me as
I love him, the two of us would never part. He goes inventing his
lies and repeating his imaginings, and says that the gods have com-
manded him, determined and directed how he must live, and that
he should go to Italy. For this the gods take their great pains, labor
endlessly and lavish their attentions, to tell him what to do! But, by
my faith, they don't care if he stays or goes. If he says that the gods
are so concerned with him that he does nothing without their command, why have they hounded him so, knocked him about on land
and sea? He had not a day of relief from their warring before he
came here; he arrived in this land in distress. What madness it was
to take him to me; I regret it now, for I must act differently. He has
had all his will with me and would not stay here for anything I said.
When I can no longer keep him, let him go away, and I must die."]

The passionate and distracted woman's picture of the situation is touchingly
different from the embarrassed, duty-burdened account given by Eneas. Her
speech gives an insight into the nature of her feelings, and at the same time is
anchored dramatically to what has been and what is to come. It is part of the
plot of the story. This is the function we have come to demand of soliloquy.
Chrétien has at his disposal the same form.[19]

Although dramatically conceived discourse is thus within the poet's reach,
he does not make as much use of it as the modern reader would expect. A good

deal of courtly dialogue falls formally into alternate lines or set speeches, where the form is more of a sign than a reproduction of the nature of the action;[20] and the greater part of courtly monologue is as conventional as courtly description. The immense vogue of it argues an interest in the inner life that is so broad and so axiomatic that it pushes the style in several directions away from the dramatic. Monologue is used to promulgate fashionable psychological theory, to represent the highest reaches of passion, and to magnify and dissect the most private motions of the soul. One motive leads to bare, doctrinal description, another to rhetoric and lyric, and another to allegory.

The analytic form, which is the most characteristically courtly form of speech in medieval poetry, develops directly in response to the need for something with which to describe the workings of the soul in conflict with itself. Based fundamentally on the age-old device of rhetorical question, which was widely available to the courtly poets in Ovid, it soon goes through a typically medieval metamorphosis. We hear the simple self-questionings of the character in the *Eneas*:

> "Lasse . . . que ai gié?   [8083]
> Qui m'a sorprise, que est cié?"

> "Ou est li rasoagement,   [8101]
> la boiste o tot son oignement?"

> "Qu'en puis ge, lasse, se ge plor?"   [8132]

> "Ai ge forfet por ce quel vi?   [8157]
> N'avra Amors de moi merci?"

["Alas! . . . what have I? Who has surprised me? What is this?" . . . "Where is the relief, the box with all its ointment?" . . . "What can I do about it even if I weep?" . . . "Have I transgressed because I saw him? Won't love have mercy on me?"]

And answers follow. This we could have found in Ovid. But in courtly monologue the answers often become detached, to represent not the confused, inquiring ego so much as an alter ego, with a point of view different from that of the first person. Thus in Lavinia's long love soliloquies the "other voice" often begins on a note of reproach, as when Lavinia, after seeing Eneas from her tower window, concludes that she is in love, in spite of her mother's objections:

> —Fole Lavine, qu'as tu dit?   [8134]
> —Amors me destroint molt por lui.
> —Et tu l'eschive, se lo fui!

24

—Nel puis trover an mon corage.
—Ja n'eres tu ier si salvage.
—Or m'a Amors tote dontee.
—Molt malement t'en es gardee.
—Molt m'an ert po gehui matin,
or me fet fere male fin;
ne garrai pas longues issi.
—Por coi t'arestas tu ici?
—Por lo Troïen esgarder.
—Bien t'an peüsses consirrer.
—Por coi?—Ne fu noiant savoir
quel venisses ici veor.
—Maint an i ai ge ja veü,
unc mes de nul rien ne me fu.

["Foolish Lavinia, what have you said?" "Love torments me badly because of him." "Avoid him then, flee from him!" "I cannot find it in my heart to do that." "You were not so wild yesterday." "Now Love has completely conquered me." "You protected yourself very badly." "He meant little to me this morning, and now he will bring me to a bitter end. I will not be cured for a long time." "Why did you stand here?" "To watch the Trojan." "You might well have thought better of that." "Why?" "It was stupid of you to come here to see him." "But I've seen lots of people out there, and before this it never mattered to me in the least."]

The remarks of the alter ego are not confined to this sort of give and take. When a significant course of action is in question, the other voice can deliver a longer address. In a sizable number of romances the opposing voices are given names such as Amor and Honte, and their interaction begins to resemble allegory proper.[21] The formality of this division of voices suggests a relationship with the habit of dialectical exposition now coming into prominence in the schools, and monologue sometimes shares the vices of the scholastic discipline. Mingled with an effort at the clarity and precision in psychological description that this discrimination of voices can serve, there is an unfortunate tendency toward pedantry and preciosity. Thus the analytic monologue sometimes uses the second voice as a mere foil to develop a paradox. Chrétien uses it often in *Cligès* as an intellectual playground, with paradox, anatomical symbolism, and other features of the courtly sophistic.[22]

In addition to leading off into such unrepresentational forms as allegory proper, the very length of the analytic monologue often proclaims its independence of dramatic verisimilitude, and it often forces an unrealistic suspension of the surface action itself. In *Florimont* the hero, Povre Perdu, is already at the bedside as his lady debates the relative merits of taking a rich or a poor lover. In *Lancelot* the knight hears the terrified screams of a lady who is about to be raped. The door to her room is guarded by six armed men. Shall he go to her rescue? Twenty-nine lines of monologue are required for an answer.[23] They display the knight's acute sense of the moral issues here, his ultimate preference of honorable death to a life of shame. To make this point, which is for him the essence of the incident, Chrétien is willing to sacrifice strict dramatic propriety.

Monologue takes a more familiar, though equally undramatic direction, where it comes into close relationship with the lyric. At critical points in the story, where intense feeling is to be evoked, the poet will often subordinate analysis to a more elevated kind of speech. In this he is adapting to romance an already widespread stylistic tradition. The complaint monologue is found in the *chanson de geste;* it appears in Latin as the *planctus,* as the lament in Anglo-Saxon, and indeed can easily be traced in Western literature as far back as the Old Testament. With its equally venerable companion types, the apostrophe and the invocation, it is one of the most common of medieval poetic forms. Later it appears in the vernacular as an independent lyric genre, the complaint. In the later romance it sometimes takes the form of a song.[24]

The lyric monologue of the courtly tradition is particularly "elevated," being set apart from the usual narrative tone by its extra seriousness and marked rhetorical character. We have already heard Lavinia's invocation to Amor. Chrétien's lyric monologue is generally superior by virtue of his being a better poet. One of his best, though not markedly rhetorical, is the speech of Laudine before the burial of her first husband in *Yvain:*

> "Biaus sire! de vostre ame
> Et Des merci si voiremant,
> Come onques au mien esciant
> Chevaliers sor sele ne sist,
> Qui de rien nule vos vaussist!
> De vostre enor, biaus sire chiers!
> Ne fu onques nus chevaliers,
> Ne de la vostre corteisie.
> Largesce estoit la vostre amie,

Et hardemanz vostre conpainz.
An la conpaignie des sainz
Soit la vostre ame, biaus douz sire!"²⁵

["Fair lord, may God so truly have mercy on your soul, as that, to my mind, no knight ever sat in saddle who was your equal in anything. There was never, fair dear lord, a knight of your honor or of your courtesy. Generousness was your friend and courage your fellow. May your soul be in the company of the saints, fair sweet lord."]

Guillaume de Lorris is an accomplished poet, and the whole of his part of the *Roman de la Rose* has a lyric tinge. His Lover-Narrator receives instructions from Amor, among them samples of lovers' complaints, which now and again turn to a lyric theme:

"Deus! verrai je ja que je soie   [2457]
En itel point con je pensoie?
Jou voudroie par covenant
Que je morisse maintenant.
La mort ne me greveroit mie
Se je moroie es braz m'amie."

"Ha! solauz! por Deu, car te heste,   [2501]
Ne sejorne ne ne t'areste;
Fai departir la nuit oscure
E son enui qui trop me dure."

"A, Lord! why nyl ye me socoure?   [2591]
Fro joye I trowe that I langoure.
The deth I wolde me shulde sloo,
While I lye in her armes twoo."

"A, slowe sonne! shewe thin enprise!   [2636]
Sped thee to sprede thy beemys bright,
And chace the derknesse of the nyght,
To putte away the stoundes stronge,
Whiche in me lasten all to longe."

The success of such speeches is of course largely independent of their dramatic value. As the complaint, invocation, and similar forms become increasingly prominent in medieval poetry, their colloquial quality, at best weak in the romances, disappears. Their effectiveness lies not in the reproduction of how a particular character would speak at such a time and place, but in the amount of poetic value the poet can generate in a lyric commentary on the action at that point. The poet represents his characters as having feelings, but it is the nature of the feeling, and not the dramatic probability of its articulation, that claims his interest.

Where monologue serves as a substitute for narrative, description, or direct exposition of courtly doctrine, it comes to a similar reach of conventionalization. All too often, discourse used thus has little aesthetic justification. In the *Eneas* the Queen first instructs Lavinia on the nature of love:

> "Pire est amors que fievre agüe, [7919]
> n'est pas retor, que l'an an süe;
> d'amor estuet sovant süer
> et refroidir, fremir, tranbler
> et sospirer et baallier,
> et perdre tot boivre et mangier
> et degiter et tressaillir,
> müer color et espalir,
> giendre, plaindre, palir, penser
> et sanglotir, veillier, plorer:
> ce li estuet fere sovant
> qui bien aimme et qui s'en sent."

["Love is worse than a piercing fever; there is no course but that you perspire. Often Love makes you sweat and grow cold, quiver, tremble and sigh and yawn, and lose all taste for food and drink, and squirm and shudder, change color and sicken, groan, lament, grow pale and pensive, sob, lie sleepless, and weep. This is what you must often do if you truly love and feel its effects."]

At this point the material is relevant to the dramatic situation. But it is handled like a new toy, so tirelessly reiterated in later scenes that we must assume the motive to be extraliterary: to instruct the audience in the new erotic physiology and etiquette.[26] The medieval poet has a general license—from the tradition of Plato and Boethius—to put up learning in the form of direct discourse, and the pedagogical motive is too strong in this poetry to be ignored. But despite the bad examples there is a sphere in which this convention can be seen to have an important literary function. Without giving license to every kind of digression merely because it is a convention, we can see that many pedagogical and self-

28

descriptive speeches operate functionally on a nondramatic level. They may provide meaningful, if impersonal, comment on the action, and even serve to outline the philosophic basis of the poem itself. Where a Dryden or a Pope would have written preface or footnotes, the medieval poet supplies a speech. Where Milton arranges a pedagogical dialogue, which is medieval enough, or where the modern novelist labors to camouflage his attitudes in realistic conversations between enlightened characters, the courtly poet more simply writes a monologue. The problem of the aesthetic of doctrinal discourse will grow as we examine more philosophic poems, and we shall return to it then.

The generally conventional nature of courtly speech is supported by the movement—the stage business—which accompanies it. Ordinary conduct is dominated by courtly etiquette. Love involves a whole system of behavior, as we have seen above. Extraordinary emotions have their appropriate actions and gestures. Sorrow, for instance, is accompanied by sinking of the head, weeping and sighing, failure of the voice and swooning, and more passionate gestures, as wringing and beating the hands, striking and scratching the face, pulling on hair and beard, ripping garments, and so forth.[27] Again the modern reader must be careful not to look at these apparently crudely described motions for physiological accuracy—though some may be accurate enough, for all we know—or for refined discrimination of tone. When the *Eneas* poet writes, as he often does,

> A icest mot perdi l'aloine
> et pasma soi . . .

[With this her breathing failed and she fainted.]

he is indicating an emotional climax, but we must not expect him to deal with it in realistic, medical terms. Like the poetically elevated speech which often precedes or follows it, this kind of action has only an emblematic relation to the facts of life. It is like the patterned and formal gestures that must have accompanied Greek tragedy, for which the condition of performance would seem to have made naturalistic subtleties of action impossible. The recovery from the swoon in romance is often a matter of little importance:

> A icest mot perdi l'aloine   [8660]
> et pasma soi; sole l'i lait
> la raïne; si s'en revait.
> En autre chambre an est antree.
> Set fois s'est Lavine pasmee,
> ne pot durer ne'n repos estre.

El s'an rala a la fenestre,
la où amors l'avoit seisie.

[The Queen leaves her alone and goes back. She has gone to another room. Seven times did Lavinia faint; she could not stand it nor find peace. She went back to the window, there where Love had seized her.]

That the Queen does not pause to assist her daughter suggests that the swoon functions more as a signal than as a representational fact.

§ 2. THE "ROMAN DE LA ROSE" OF GUILLAUME DE LORRIS

We have thus far made a survey of the larger conventions of the French courtly style. I have purposely suppressed, for the moment, any detailed consideration of other, less "conventional" traits that appear in courtly poems, in order to focus on some of the critical problems that come with conventionalism itself. The major one, that of value, is quickly posed by the modern reader with a developed taste for realism, who is predisposed to identify convention with badness. Another problem, that of distinguishing between different exponents of the tradition, is often raised by historians of ideas or genres. These, not going much farther than we have now gone, tend to lump them all together as all containing, like chemicals, "the courtly love element." Apart from intrinsic interest, the solutions to these problems have a direct bearing on the criticism of Chaucer. It will be well to approach Chaucer with the knowledge that the courtly style is capable of supporting good poetry, and poetry which is only minimally realistic, and further, that realism and dealing with reality are two different things. Moreover, we should see that, apart from aesthetic value, the exponents of the courtly tradition have significant differences of attitude among themselves. We should be able to distinguish the devoted and successful exponent of courtly idealism from the fashionable or mechanical fiddler, and from the latent critic. There is no better approach to such an orientation, on the axes of both value and attitude, than an examination of the *Roman de la Rose* of Guillaume de Lorris. It is coördinately high in value and pure in attitude; there is practically nothing in it that is not conventional. Our approach is made easier by the fact that Mr. C. S. Lewis has cleared the way before us; we shall not need to dwell on those elements of scene and story and meaning that he has described so clearly.[28]

Perhaps the greatest distinction of the poet is that he manages a delicate poise between the *a priori* dictates of courtly idealism and medieval habit, and the

30

push of particular human experience itself. Human experience is represented, though, largely in its invisible forms; of all his *dramatis personae* only two, Ami and "une vieille," besides the Lover-Narrator, have a remotely biological existence. The whole style of the poem is marshaled around the evocation of real but mental states in a setting answerable only to an idealizing imagination. For this perspective the dream, with its heritage of visions of another, paradisal world,[20] is just the right framing device.

The poem is linear in design—"tot vos conterai en ordre," (699)—and its opening is particularly well conceived. The unspoken energy which gives the Narrator his desire to wander out of town is figured in the description of the season, as Chaucer must have noticed. The shrubs and the earth itself are given their own will to dress up:

La terre meïsmes s'orgueille   [55]
Por la rosee qui la mueille,
E oblie la povreté . . .

Lors devient la terre si gobe   [59]
Qu'el viaut avoir novele robe . . .

Li rossigniaus lores s'esforce   [74]
De chanter e de faire noise;
Lors se deduit e lors s'envoise
Li papegauz . . .

And the erthe wexith proud withalle,   [59]
For swote dewes that on it falle,
And the pore estat forget . . .

And than bycometh the ground so proud   [63]
That it wole have a newe shroud . . .

Than doth the nyghtyngale hir myght   [78]
To make noyse and syngen blythe.
Than is blisful many sithe
The chelaundre and papyngay.

This diction looks well into the poem, to the Povreté excluded from the Garden, to the lord Deduit, whose company, magnificently clad, spend their time in enjoyment, *envoiseüre*. Further traits of tone and image generate a susceptible and wistful mood:

Mout a dur cuer qui en mai n'aime,   [81]
Quant il ot chanter sor la raime
As oisiaus les douz chanz piteus.

These lines brought out the best in the translator, Chaucer:

Hard is the hert that loveth nought   [85]
In May, whan al this mirth is wrought,
When he may on these braunches here
The smale briddes syngen clere
Her blisful swete song pitous.

There is, further, a nice mixture in the imagery between a clarity and brightness
which idealize the description and a delicate particularity which keeps it just
within human reference:

Lors trais une aguille d'argent   [91]
D'un aguillier mignot e gent . . .

Clere estoit l'eve e ausi froide   [110]
Come puiz . . .

De l'eve clere e reluisant   [118]
Mon vis rafreschi e lavai . . .

A sylvre nedle forth y drough   [97]
Out of an aguler queynt ynough . . .

Cleer was the water, and as cold   [116]
As any welle is . . .

And with that watir, that ran so cler,   [124]
My face I wyssh.

The portraits of the inhabitants of the Garden perpetuate this mixture, without
ever losing their exemplary character:

Cheveus ot blonz come uns bacins,   [527]
La char plus tendre qu'uns poucins . . .

Li cos fu de bone moison, . . .   [539]
Si n'i ot bube ne malan . . .

Hir heer was as yelowe of hewe   [539]
As ony basyn scoured newe . . .

>
> Hir nekke was of good fasoun . . .   [551]
> Withoute bleyne, scabbe, or royne . . .

The conventional comparison of the complexion of Leece (Gladnesse) with a rose accommodates particularizing detail which in turn heightens the ideality of the whole:

> El resembloit rose novele   [840]
> De la color sor la char tendre,
> Que l'en li peüst toute fendre
> A une petitete ronce.

> She semede lyk a rose newe   [856]
> Of colour, and hir flesh so tendre,
> That with a brere smale and slendre
> Men myght it cleve, I dar wel seyn.

Here we see a further motive, of the diminutive, which without challenging the superlative element in the description keeps it on a manageable plane and underlines the delicacy of the experience that is ultimately being described. Thus of Biauté,

> El ne fu oscure ne brune,   [995]
> Ainz fu clere come la lune,
> Envers cui les autres estoiles
> Resemblent petites chandoiles.

> Ne she was derk ne broun, but bright,   [1009]
> And clere as the mone lyght,
> Ageyn whom all the sterres semen
> But smale candels, as we demen.

The Lover wanders

> Par une petitete sente,   [715]
> Pleine de fenoil e de mente . . .

> Doun by a lytel path I fond   [730]
> Of mentes full, and fenell grene . . .

The God of Love approaches, "les sauz menuz," and secures the heart of the Lover with "Une petite clef bien faite, / Qui fu de fin or esmeré" (2000–01).

The Narrator in this first-person poem is not set at a distance from his material. A certain amount of temporal perspective serves nostalgic reminiscence

33

("Encor l'i sens" [1719]), but his present involvement in the experience is empha-
sized as well: "Deus! com menoient bone vie!" (1295), "Las! tant en ai puis
sospiré!" (1608).[30] The quality of this involvement is continuously colored by
his distinctive character, which, even to the point of a precarious relaxation at
times, suggests a combination of credulity and naïve astonishment, precisely the
right response with which to lead us into an ideal yet imaginable world. Thus
he has repeatedly the tone of a young man whose recital of truism has the air of
revelation about it. Here is a rhetorical complaint, generalization on the Wheel
of Fortune, in the medieval tradition: his treatment by love, he says,

> . . . est ausi con de Fortune,   [3981]
> Qui met ou cuer des genz rancune,
> Autre eure les aplaigne e chue.
> En poi d'eure son semblant mue:
> Une eure rit, autre eure est morne;
> Ele a une roe qui torne,
> E quant ele viaut ele met
> Le plus bas amont ou somet,
> E celui qui est sor la roe
> Reverse a un tor en la boe.
> E je sui cil qui est versez!

> It is of Love, as of Fortune,   [4353]
> That chaungeth ofte, and nyl contune;
> Which whilom wol on folk smyle,
> And glowmbe on hem another while;
> Now freend, now foo, [thow] shalt hir feel.
> For [in] a twynklyng turneth hir wheel;
> She can writhe hir heed awey;
> This is the concours of hir pley.
> She can areise that doth morne,
> And whirle adown, and overturne
> Who sittith hyest, but as hir lust.
> A fool is he that wole hir trust;
> For it is I that am come down,
> Thurgh change and revolucioun!

The conventionally organized portraits of Vieillece and Povreté, and the other
anticourtly vices painted on the wall, evoke much of this personality of response:

34

Ce ne fust mie grant morie   [348]
S'ele morist, ne granz pechiez,
Car toz ses cors estoit sechiez
De vieillece e aneientiz.

Car certes el n'avoit poissance,   [392]
Ce cuit je, ne force ne sen,
Ne plus que uns enfes d'un an.
Neporquant, au mien escientre,
El avoit esté sage e entre,
Quant ele iert en son droit aage . . .

Com povres chiens en un coignet   [454]
Se cropoit e atapissoit;
Car povre chose, ou qu'ele soit,
Est toz jorz honteuse e despite.
L'eure puisse estre la maudite
Que povres on fu conceüz!

Iwys, great qualm ne were it non,   [357]
Ne synne, although her lyf were gon.
Al woxen was her body unwelde,
And drie and dwyned al for elde.

She had . . .   [400]
Ne wit ne pithe in hir hold,
More than a child of two yeer old.
But natheles, I trowe that she
Was fair sumtyme, and fresh to se,
Whan she was in hir rightful age . . .

There lurked and there coured she,   [465]
For pover thing, whereso it be,
Is shamefast and dispised ay.
Acursed may wel be that day
That povere man conceyved is . . .

Perhaps the most intrinsically interesting part of the poem, though it did not
inspire Chaucer's emulation, is the section, toward the end, in which the allegory
narrows and concentrates itself to explore the inner life of the Lady. Here the
subjective, introspective element of the courtly romances is brought to its ulti-

35

mate development, commanding undivided attention, and here likewise the technique becomes unmixedly conventional. The outward appearance of the Lady is never given us. Her favor, in both senses of the term, is evaluated in the description of a rose, and the working of her sentiments and passions is rendered through the interplay of a variety of figures: Bel Acueil and Dangier, Pitié and Honte, Largesce and Peor. The clarity and precision with which the allegory is handled testify to the medieval audience's astounding capacity to see the subjective as objective, as real; and the particular organization of this allegory, around a conception of character, and the finesse with which the emotional life is thereby explored, show us literary convention at its best. Here, faced with the problem of describing an invisible world, and attacking it directly through convention, the poet yet makes his strongest claim to dealing with reality.

Once this is granted—and the reader who does not should ponder Mr. Lewis' fine argument,[a1]—we must observe that the real life depicted through Guillaume's allegory is of a special, limited kind. It is true to life that a lady may be forced by passion into showing more than a mere fair reception to her lover. In Guillaume's terms, Venus may force Bel Acueil to grant the Lover a kiss of the Rose. But of all the possible imaginative representations of Venus, of sexual appetite, Guillaume employs the most refined. It is characteristic of the poet's delicacy that her attack is not abrupt. Her opening words to Bel Acueil are a demand for fair play:

"Por quoi vos faites vos, biaus sire,   [3442]
Vers cel amant si dangereus
D'avoir un baisier doucereus?
Ne li deüst estre veez,
Car vos savez bien e veez
Qu'il sert e aime en leiauté,
Si a en lui assez biauté,
Par quoi est dignes d'estre amez."

". . . Sir, what is the cause   [3726]
Ye ben of port so daungerous
Unto this lover and deynous,
To graunte hym nothyng but a kis?
To warne it hym ye don amys,
Sith well ye wote, how that he
Is Loves servaunt, as ye may see,
And hath beaute, wherthrough [he] is
Worthy of love to have the blis."

36

She mentions his pleasing dress and deportment, then warms only slightly to
point out

> "Qu'il a, ce cuit, mout douce aleine;   [3461]
> E sa bouche n'est pas vilaine,
> Ainz semble estre fait a estuire
> Por solacier e por deduire,
> Car les levres sont vermeillettes
> E les denz blanches e si netes . . ."

> "His breth is also good and swete,   [3743]
> And eke his lippis rody, and mete
> Oonly to pleyen and to kesse.
> Graunte hym a kis, of gentilnesse!
> His teth arn also white and clene . . ."

She closes with the age-old warning:

> "Donez lui, se vos m'en creez,   [3470]
> Car tant con vos plus atendroiz,
> Tant, ce sachiez, de tens perdroiz."

> "The lasse to helpe hym that ye haste,   [3751]
> The more tyme shul ye waste."

Bel Acueil feels the heat of the flaming torch which Venus holds, and promptly
grants the lover the desired kiss. The Lady's sense of fair play, of the irrecover-
able passage of time, and her admiration for the Lover's physical appearance,
as represented allegorically by the speech, are irreproachably true to life. But the
Lady herself is ideally conceived. Venus in her has none of the turbulence and
vehemence that another poet might have given her, and so the speech of Venus
to Bel Acueil is without turbulence of rhythm, and Venus' vocabulary is courtly.

The example of Venus is a model of the general relationship between speech
and concept throughout the poem. The poet substantially achieves what the
God of Love prescribes to the Lover, to speak "Senz dire mot de vilanie" (2412).
Further, that deity commands:

> "Soies entres e acointables,   [2099]
> De paroles douz e raisnables
> E as granz genz e as menues . . .

> Après garde que tu ne dies   [2109]
> Ces orz moz ne ces ribaudies:

37

Ja por nomer vilaine chose
Ne doit ta bouche estre desclose:
Je ne tieng pas a cortois ome
Qui orde chose e laide nome."

"Wherfore be wise and aqueyntable,   [2213]
Goodly of word, and resonable
Bothe to lesse and eke to mare.

    For nothyng eke thy tunge applye   [2223]
To speke wordis of rebaudrye.
To vilayn speche in no degre
Lat never thi lippe unbounden be.
For I nought holde hym, in good feith,
Curteys, that foule wordis seith."

Thus it is with the Lover-Narrator of the poem. His avoidance of bad language is an avoidance of bad thoughts. The repose and purity induced by his limited, elevated point of view do not admit full representation of the conflict, the humor, the occasionally sordid or disgusting aspects of human existence. His voice is not that of a broad, critical spirit. The enchantment of the Garden as seen through this boyish consciousness is enhanced, rather than dispelled, by brushes with common sense and with an only half-seen irony:

    Destroiz fui mout e angoisseus,   [508]
Tant qu'au derrenier me sovint
Qu'onques en nul sen ce n'avint
Qu'en si bel vergier n'eüst uis,
Ou eschiele ou quelque pertuis.

    Il paroit bien a son ator   [566]
Qu'ele estoit poi embesoigniee.
Quant ele s'estoit bien pigniee,
E bien paree e atornee,
Ele avoit faite sa jornee.
Mout avoit bon tens e bon mai,
Qu'el n'avoit soussi ne esmai
De nule rien, fors solement
De soi atorner noblement.

38

For I was al aloone, iwys,   [519]
Ful wo and angwishus of this,
Til atte last bithought I me
That by no weye ne myght it be
That ther nas laddre, or wey to passe,
Or hole, into so faire a place.

Wel semyde by hir apparayle   [575]
She was not wont to gret travayle.
For whan she kempt was fetisly,
And wel arayed and richely,
Thanne had she don al hir journe;
For merye and wel bigoon was she.
She ladde a lusty lyf in May:
She hadde no thought, by nyght ne day,
Of nothyng, but if it were oonly
To graythe hir wel and uncouthly.[32]

One must put by one's bourgeois suspicion of idleness for a moment to see that
the strength of this description lies precisely in its easy vulnerability to irony,
and in the Narrator's artless passing by of it. We are not invited to see better
than he does, but to share the limitations of his point of view, as the capping
"noblement" makes clear. If one is not to read it with a continuous laugh, much
of the best courtly literature must be read in this mood. Indeed, the whole drift of
Guillaume's style precludes irony. There is no hint in the *Roman de la Rose* of
the smirking worldliness that sometimes in the *De Amore* of Andreas makes us
think the author to be either an ironist or a nasty fool.[33] What there is of the
critical in Guillaume is direct. Like every respectable courtly poet, he is ac-
quainted with love's enemies, but he is not seriously concerned with its shortcomings. He makes a brief concession to Raison, then dismisses her abruptly.[34]
Occasionally, as in the description of Richece, he deals with the uglier sides of
court life, the lies, flattery, and hypocrisy; but *icil losengier plein d'envie* are like
the Sir Kays and wicked dwarfs of the romances, uncourtly foils.

There is generally in Guillaume's style much less disturbance and shock,
much less variation and contrast of color, than we shall find in poetry reflecting
a more complex attitude. In psychological allegory the introspective monologue
of the romance is replaced by conversation between personifications, but for this
conversation Guillaume did not follow the available models of colloquial expression. He wrote virtually no rapid dialogue. His whole poem, narrative and dis-

course, is dominated by a delicate and leisurely formality of movement. It epitomizes the style of the courtly tradition in its consistent conventionalism as the refinement of its view bring us to the highest plane of the courtly idealism in secular literature.

We are now, I hope, in a position to see how the magnetic interlinkage of conventional traits within the courtly style defines its peculiar potency. In a poet like Guillaume de Lorris the style seems to have formed itself inevitably, from the most diverse sources—from French and Provençal, from classical and medieval Latin, from lyric, epic, philosophical allegory, and rhetorical textbook[35]— into a congruent and stable organization, superbly equipped to support the elevation and purity of the courtly attitude, and to make visible its imaginary, ideal world. Before we go on to study the alloys and mixtures of it, I must allude to some implications of the style in itself that will bear directly on Chaucer. We have seen that it is by and large a "symbolic" style. At its best, in Guillaume, its poetry is true to the imagination, true to the emotional life. Its greatest weakness, which can be seen plentifully in the imitations of the *Roman de la Rose* down to Machaut and Froissart and beyond, is a liability to lose that ultimate, delicate contact with human concerns that gives it meaning, to reduce itself to a collection of shiny but valueless trinkets, symbols without reference. However, the insuring of this contact is not necessarily to be found in concessions to realism. That is rather to exchange one view of reality for another, and courtly poetry is nowhere more wrongly criticized than when realism is demanded of it.

In Chaucer criticism this issue is most often seen in the discussion of characterization. A style based on exotic setting, formal portraiture, undramatic discourse, and semiotic gesture is palpably not meant to produce the "rounded character," the "individual" of modern fiction. It is designed, indeed, with conscious disregard for the whole world of local pressure and motive, color and particularity, in which a modern "character" would have to be seen. Its characters which are truest to courtly sentiment have only as much local color as will preserve a filiation with imaginative experience. Thus in courtly literature—I may be alluding here to an ideally courtly poetry which was rarely written, but it does not matter—we do have a kind of characterization, but it is a delicate kind, created less through vagrant excursions into realism than through a richness and complication of the symbolic texture itself. For the *Roman de la Rose* the coincidence between an idealizing view of life and a particular interest in psychology is of material significance. The style, designed to evoke invisible worlds, is equally well adapted to describe an earthly paradise and a human soul. The Garden of the Rose is both of these at once. Thus we can have, without breach of style, an ideally conceived heroine whose emotions are so finely analyzed that their very complexity and interrelatedness constitute her concreteness. This is the truest area of "characterization" within the courtly style proper. The heroine of the *Roman* has all the pale but charming individuality that the style could support or that the ideology could afford. The test of other courtly poets, who may not have Guillaume's interest in psychology or his analytic finesse, lies in other directions. Less fully articulated symbols—"type characters" to the modern reader—find their meaningfulness through enmeshment in patterns of relationships, in consequential actions, in themes which are themselves articulated fully enough to figure forth significant human concerns. For medieval literature, as for modern, "characterization" in the ordinary sense is in practice (though perhaps not theoretically) a function of realism.

The *Roman de la Rose* thus exemplifies the strengths of courtly poetry, but by implication also its limitations. The remarkable poise of Guillaume is ultimately not one of rest, but of balanced pressures. There is paradox inherent in the very terms we use in describing the poetry: earthly paradise, sensuous, even sensual idealism. We can broadly see the same paradox in other areas of medieval culture. The individual soul was replacing the cosmos, in mystical theology, as the battleground of good and evil. The limited introspective individualism thus fostered is similarly poised between human and cosmic claims.[36] For literature, the conflict inevitably becomes one of styles. The courtly style is not equipped to sustain a radical alteration in point of view. For this another style was fashioned, finally to become an implement of attack on the courtly position itself.

§3. REALISM AND ROMANCE

By the time of Guillaume de Lorris, the Provençals had already begun, and the Italian poets of the New Style were to follow them, in sublimating the style and idiom of the courtly tradition toward the ends of overtly religious poetry. This was so perfectly natural a branching for the tradition to take that it is difficult, sometimes, to see precisely where it comes.[37] In forming, the tradition had, consciously or unconsciously, assimilated Christian forms of organization and expression and was therefore easily adaptable to the change. By Dante the inevitable conflict between the two traditions was resolved, the passionate elevation of courtly eroticism fusing with religious ecstasy. Beatrice brings her lover to a divine paradise. Something of the same process was going on in the romance tradition with the turning of the Arthurian theme, in Cistercian hands, away from the relatively secular search for personal perfection and toward the search for the Holy Grail itself.[38]

41

The tradition was subject to attack and modification from other directions. On the social level it came up against the morality and economy of the newly forming bourgeoisie; and it clashed ideologically, in the thirteenth century with a potent current of philosophic naturalism. Here there was less a question of reconcilement (though terms could be arranged) than of open opposition; in the literature in which these rival attitudes came into contact there is a shift of style into realism.

Nothing so clearly shows the inevitability of this stylistic conflict, and by implication the great sensitivity to stylistic decorum in the poets we are studying, than the variation of style within the courtly tradition itself. It would be a mistake to assume from the preponderance of convention that these poets are incapable of representationalism. Some readers will recall scenes and passages which seem modern and novelistic in technique. The *Eneas* poet is demonstrably capable of very creditable colloquial dialogue, as the second interview between Lavinia and the Queen shows. Here he not only brings out nicely the interplay of personalities, but also manages to suggest the shading of tone and expression which accompany it:

> —Ja Dé ne place   [8488]
> qu'il m'amor ait! Non avra il.
> —Comant, ne l'aimmes tu?—Nenil.
> —Et gel voil, ge.—Vos l'amez bien.
> —Mais tu l'aime.—Ne m'en est rien.
> —Ja est il biaus et proz et genz.
> —Pou me toche au cuer dedanz.
> —Bien est an lui salve t'amor.
> —Ge ne l'amerai ja nul jor.
> —Et qui as tu donc aamé?
> —Vos i avez trop oblïé
> la premereine question,
> savoir se j'ai ami ou non.
> —Ce sai ge bien, esprové l'ai.
> —Plus an savez que ge ne sai.
> —Ne sez? Ja senz tu les dolors.
> —Donc n'a l'an mal ne mes d'amors?
>
> —Ge ain, nel puis avant noier.   [8550]
> —Donc n'a non Turnus tes amis?
> —Nenil, dame, gel vos plevis.

—Et comant donc?—Il a non E..."
puis sospira, se redist: "ne... ,"
d'iluec a piece noma: "as... ,"
tot en tranblant lo dist en bas.
La raïne se porpensa
et les sillebes asanbla.
"Tu me diz 'E' puis 'ne' et 'as';
ces letres sonent 'Eneas.'
—Voire, dame, par foi, c'est il.
—Se ne t'avra Turnus?—Nenil,
ja ne avrai lui a seignor,
mais a cestui otroi m'amor.
—Que as tu dit, fole desvee?
Sez tu vers cui tu t'es donee?

["May it never please God that Turnus have my love! He shall not have it." "What? Don't you love him?" "No." "But I, I wish it." "*You* love him well." "Love him yourself." "He means nothing to me." "But he is so handsome and brave and well-bred." "Deep in my heart he makes no impression." "In him your love is secure." "I shall never love him." "Then whom *have* you fallen in love with?" "There you have forgotten the first question, whether I have a lover at all." "I know very well you have; I've proved it." "You know more about it than I do." "Than you do? Already you feel the pains." "Then are there none but those of love?"]

["I'm in love, I can no longer deny it." "Isn't your lover named Turnus?" "No, madame, I swear it." "What is it, then?" "His name is E..." Then she sighed, and said "ne... ," then a little later, all trembling, she whispered "as..." The Queen thought to herself and assembled the syllables. "You say 'E,' then 'ne' and 'as'; this makes 'Eneas.' " "Yes, madame, in faith, it is he." "So Turnus won't have you?" "No, I shall never have him for my lord, but I surrender my love to Eneas." "What have you said, mad fool? Do you realize to whom you've given yourself?"]

There is here a connection between the subject of the scene and its literary technique which is general in the courtly tradition. Particularly where the subject is love, there is nearly always difficulty to be overcome, persuasion necessary, to bring the affair to its consummation. Where this difficulty exists in the

43

sensible world, where there is an outsider, or an intermediary, or hostility or inexperience, the courtly poet is likely to draw on some mode of realism to represent the temporary incursion of the alien or extracourtly point of view. One recalls the spirited interchange between Fresne and the hostile Abbess Ermine in *Galeran,* and the proverbially bad manners of Kay, who is usually employed in the Arthurian romances as an uncourtly foil for the virtues of a Gawain or a Lancelot. The social inexperience of the young hero in *Perceval,* and of young lovers in *Cligès,* is recorded by Chrétien in some of his most charmingly natural dialogue.[39] The element of intrigue, which comes into courtly literature through a number of doors, is usually represented (as it virtually must be) in a realistic light and brings with it some of the most colorful figures of romance: confidantes, aged duennas, sorceresses.[40] The result is that minor characters are generally more realistically portrayed than major ones, and occasionally serve to bring out a transient mundanity of appearance in the latter, as we see in Lavinia's response to her mother.

Even the purist Guillaume de Lorris responds so sensitively to vagrant shifts of attitude that the antifeminism of his character Male Bouche evokes a few lines in a singsong, popular rhythm alien to the rest of the poem:

> "Il n'est nule qui ne se rie   [3903]
> S'ele ot parler de lecherie;
> Ceste est pute, ceste se farde,
> E ceste folement regarde,
> Ceste est vilaine, ceste est fole,
> E ceste si a trop parole."[41]

The Middle English catches the meaning, but not the satiric music:

> He wolde seyn, with notes newe,   [4253]
> That he fond no womman trewe,
> Ne that he saugh never in his lyf
> Unto hir husbonde a trewe wyf,
> Ne noon so ful of honeste
> That she nyl laughe and mery be,
> Whanne that she hereth, or may espie,
> A man speken of leccherie.
> Everich of hem hath som vice:
> Oon is dishonest, another is nyce;
> If oon be full of vylanye,

Another hath a likerous ye;
If oon be full of wantonesse,
Another is a chideresse.

In the awakening of Dangier by Honte, the poet again breaks through the
bounds of the courtly cosmos for a moment. The scene follows a climax in the
story, at which, the Lover having kissed the Rose, his enemy Jalosie is aroused.
She berates Bel Acueil and Honte for having neglected their charge. Honte,
a simple, humble, nunlike lady, replies in a temperate, reasonable way. Peor
enters and Jalosie departs. We have, in this part of the *Roman,* a fine account
of the gradual change in the Lady's disposition, at first through outside pressure,
for Jalosie represents the Lady's outraged relatives, and later through the workings of her own feelings, for Peor and Honte are her own sense of fear and
shame. Even after Jalosie leaves, Peor and Honte feel her influence. Two ladies
of hitherto impeccable reputation, maidens, I suppose, and cousins, they band
together to redeem themselves from blame, and decide to pass the burden on
to Dangier.

Dangier, who according to the best interpretation represents "the rebuff
direct, the lady's 'snub' launched from the height of her ladyhood," "pride, distance, and excessive or formidable dignity,"⁴² is not easily aroused, Once fierce,
this inimitable *vilain* has since become tame, and almost courtly. Now, having
found the life of leisure quite satisfactory, he is resting sleepily beneath a haw-
thorn, his head pillowed on a great mound of grass. But Honte, recently meek
and mild, has become forceful. The reasonable, nunlike creature is now an irate
domina, rudely awakening her lazy watchman:

> "Coment dormez vos a ceste eure,"   [3678]
> Fait ele, "par male aventure?
> Fos est qui en vos s'asseüre
> De garder rose ne bouton
> Ne qu'en la queue d'un mouton."

> "Estiez vos ore couchiez?   [3691]
> Levez tost sus, e si bouchiez
> Toz les pertuis de ceste haie,
> E ne portez nului menaie."

> "Why slepist thou, whanne thou shulde wake?" [4008]
> Quod Shame; "thou doist us vylanye!

45

Who tristith thee, he doth folye,
To kepe roses or botouns . . ."

"Art thou now late? Ris up in hy,   [4021]
And stop sone and delyverly
All the gappis of the haye.
Do no favour, I thee praye."

She rouses him from his dream of *cortoisie:*

Il n'afiert pas a vostre non   [3695]
Que vos faciez se enui non.
Se Bel Acueil est frans e douz,
E vos seiez fel e estouz,
Pleins de rampones e d'outrage:
Vilains qui est cortois enrage,
Ce oï dire en reprovier,
Ne l'en ne puet faire esprevier
En nule guise de busart."

"It fallith nothyng to thy name   [4025]
To make faire semblaunt, where thou maist blame.
Yf Bialacoil be sweete and free,
Dogged and fell thou shuldist be,
Froward and outrageous, ywis;
A cherl chaungeth that curteis is.
This have I herd ofte in seiyng,
That man[ne] may, for no dauntyng,
Make a sperhauk of a bosard."

We see in this change in Honte a superb allegorical representation of the Lady's
rising sense of shame. Yet the awakening of Dangier is so colorful a piece of
everyday domestic life that we are for a moment transported out of the dreamland that is the setting of the poem. The artistic justification for this shift of
style is clear. The poet sees the reawakening of the Lady's offishness as a blow
to love, to courtesy, a bar to the fulfillment of his dreams. No wonder, then,
that he awakens the reader from the dream world for a moment, to evoke a real
garden where sleepy watchmen must work, and mistresses become petulant and
sour. Guillaume himself nowhere else achieves this degree of naturalism, but
his feeling for style indicates one direction, obviously, which the anticourtly
attitude could naturally take.

The other direction it could and did take approaches parody; here again the method was divined within the courtly tradition itself, notably in the *Yvain* of Chrétien and in the anonymous, thirteenth-century Provençal romance, *Flamenca*. No scene in French romance equals in brilliance and virtuosity of style the sequence in *Yvain* which leads to the marriage of Laudine to the slayer of her husband.[48] Chrétien manages throughout it a sensitive adjustment of style to the nature and attitude of the actors. Lunete, the lady's confidante and maid, is one of the finest go-betweens in romance and a "fixer," hardly touched by courtly idealism, though willing to operate within its forms. She has an unerring feeling for the motives and disposition of her mistress. Yvain, on the other hand, is consistently the courtly lover. He falls in love at first sight, is timid in the lady's presence, and gives himself completely into her power. Lunete, who brings about the first (and conclusive) interview between the lovers, has to exhort him to speech. Laudine is handled more ambiguously: she is at once the bereaved widow, the practical *domina* who has a magic spring to defend, and the object of Yvain's courtly adoration.

Laudine's initial mood is established by two complaint-like utterances. One has been quoted above. The other, preceded by a plentiful array of gestures denoting sorrow, is more violent:

> "Ha! Des! don ne trovera l'an   [1206]
> L'omecide, le traïtor,
> Qui m'a ocis mon buen seignor?
> Buen? Voire le meillor des buens!
> . . .
>
> [addressing the invisible Yvain:]
>
> Ha! fantosmes, couarde chose!   [1226]
> Por qu'ies vers moi acoardie,
> Quant vers mon seignor fus hardie?
> Chose vainne, chose faillie,
> Que ne t'ai ore an ma baillie!
> Que ne te puis ore tenir!
> Mes ce comant pot avenir,
> Que tu mon seignor oceïs,
> S'an traïson ne le feïs?
> Ja voir par toi conquis ne fust
> Mes sire, se veü t'eüst."

47

["Ah, God! Will we find the murderer, the traitor, who killed my good lord? Good? The very best of the good! . . . Ah, phantom, cowardly thing! How is it that you are afraid of me, when you were so bold with my lord? Worthless, timid thing, why don't I have you in my power? Why can't I lay my hands on you now? How could it ever happen that you killed my lord unless you did it in treachery? If he had seen you, he would never have been beaten."]

Chrétien brings her from mourning to marriage in a comparatively short time, and the entwining of the various strands of her disposition is attended by a complexity of style which continuously brings us to the edge of humor, if not satire.

The stylistic base of the sequence is a series of dramatically conceived dialogues in which the clever confidante brings Laudine around to the idea of remarriage—and with Yvain.

> "Dame! mout me mervoil,   [1598]
> Que folemant vos voi ovrer.
> Dame! cuidiez vos recovrer
> Vostre seignor por feire duel?"
> "Nenil," fet ele, "mes mon vuel
> Seroie je morte d'enui."
> "Por quoi?"—"Por aler aprés lui."
> "Aprés lui? Des vos an deffande
> Et aussi buen seignor vos rande,
> Si come an est poesteïs."
> "Ains tel mançonge ne deïs;
> Qu'il ne me porroit si buen randre."
> "Meillor, se vos le volez prandre,
> Vos randra il, sel proverai."
> "Fui! tes! Ja voir nel troverai."

["Lady, I wonder greatly to see you behave so foolishly. Lady, do you think you can recover your lord by mourning?" "No," she says, "but if I had my way I would be dead of grief." "Why?" "To follow him." "Follow him? God prevent you, and let him in his might grant you another lord just as good." "You have never said such a fantastic thing. He could never give me one as good." "Better, if you will take him; I'll prove that he will." "Go! be still! I shall never meet such a one."]

Lunete then goes on to point out the practical necessities of looking for a new husband: the land is in need of defense; all her knights are not worth a chambermaid; there is not one brave enough to dare mount a horse. Laudine, we are told, has begun to see the justice of these considerations, but continues like a woman to refuse what she really wishes. She dismisses Lunete rudely, but then thinks she has made a mistake which she cannot undo. Lunete is unabashed, however, and renews her argument with characteristic vigor. Much dialogue in the romances is neutral exchange of information. Often the speeches fall into balanced and formal alternation. Here, however, Chrétien achieves a supple irregularity in rhythm and tone which gives the dialogue a particularly realistic quality. In her alternation of exhortation, query, description, and positive assertion we are given a good idea of Lunete's tactical powers:

> "Ha, dame! est ce ore avenant, [1666]
> Que si de duel vos ociëz?
> Por De! car vos an chastiëz,
> Sel leissiez seviaus non de honte.
> A si haute dame ne monte,
> Que duel si longuemant maintaingne.
> De vostre enor vos ressovaingne
> Et de vostre grant jantillesce!
> Cuidiez vos, que tote proesce
> Soit morte avuec vostre seignor?
> Çant aussi buen et çant meillor
> An sont remés parmi le monde."

["Ah, Lady! is it nice to kill yourself with grief like this? For God's sake, now control yourself and give it up, at least for shame. It is not right for such a noble lady to keep up her mourning so long. Remember your honor and your high rank. Do you think that all knightliness died with your lord? There are a hundred as good and a hundred better ones still left in the world."]

In Laudine's response we see a little more than an interest in statistics:

> "Se tu n'an manz, Des me confonde! [1678]
> Et neporquant un seul m'an nome,
> Qui et tesmoing de si prodome,
> Con mes sire ot tot son aé."

49

["If you are not lying, may God destroy me! But nevertheless, name me a single one who could have the reputation of being as brave a knight as my lord had all his life."]

The first line, a trifle overemphatic, and the second, with the long, tentative "Et neporquant" and the short, too precise "un seul," reflect her conflicting desires: to know and to appear not too much interested.

The interviews continue as Lunete, with a delightful air of logic and practical simplicity, points out that Yvain, who has just killed Laudine's husband in combat, is thereby proved the better man. Again the lady loses her temper and again she does some private reconsideration. Here the poet shifts his ground, and, ostensibly as private reconsideration in the romance calls for conventional device, he uses an adaptation of the dialogue-in-monologue. Laudine, herself shifting now to the resources of female logic, is represented as holding court with herself. "Par reison et par droit de plet," Yvain will be judged not guilty. As if he had come before her, she argues thus:

> "Va!" fet ele, "puez tu noiier,   [1760]
>   Que par toi ne soit morz mes sire?"
> "Ce," fet il, "ne puis je desdire,
>   Ainz l'otroi bien."—"Di donc, por quoi?
> Feïs le tu por mal de moi,
>   Por haïne ne por despit?"
> "Ja n'aie je de mort respit,
>   S'onques por mal de vos le fis."
> "Donc n'as tu rien vers moi mespris,
>   Ne vers lui n'eüs tu nul tort;
>   Car, s'il poïst, il t'eüst mort.
>   Por ce mien esciant cuit gié,
>   Que j'ai bien et a droit jugié."

["Go," she says, "can you deny that my husband was killed by you?" "This," says he, "I cannot deny; rather, I fully admit it." "Say then, why? Did you do it to injure me, out of hatred or contempt?" "May I have no delay from death, if I ever did it to injure you." "Then you have injured me in nothing, nor did you wrong him. For, if he could have, he would have killed you. Therefore it is my considered opinion that I have judged justly and well."]

The easy justice of the judge, the courtesy and frankness she attributes to the accused, the simple logic of the argument, and the dispatch with which the verdict is rendered stand in almost satiric contrast to the passionate vehemence of her previous complaints. The preceding dialogues, which have revealed to us the play of her practical motives, cast a humorous doubt over this display of reasonable justice. Finally, although the imaginary dialogue is by no means undramatic in style, the very use of the form in the midst of this realistic sequence is a *tour de force* of narrative structure. It adds a value that strict adherence to representationalism could not have supplied: the humor of a judgment scene in which the judge is prejudiced and the accused entirely helpless, the humor of a form (dialogue) especially well adapted to the contest of personalities used to depict no contest at all, and within a form (monologue) generally the vehicle for elaborate analysis of refined, inner sentiment, where refinement and sentiment are both doubtful.

Another locus of humor is the introduction of Yvain to his lady. There is a nice contrast between the knight's tonguetiedness and the maid's forward manner as she induces him to speak. He finally speaks, "come verais amis," that is, gracefully and humbly, on his knees, with the magnified sense of honor and servitude typical of the courtly style. The declaration of love is the scene's climax, and the discourse leading up to it is the best example of formal sophistication in the dialogue of Chrétien. Having received from Yvain a plea of not guilty, the same plea that she has already found acceptable, Laudine fishes further:

> "Et ce mout volantiers savroie,   [2008]
> Don cele force puet venir,
> Qui vos comande a consantir
> Tot mon voloir sanz contredit.
> Toz torz et toz mesfez vos quit.
> Mes seez vos, si me contez,
> Comant vos estes si dontez."
> "Dame!" fet il, "la force vient
> De mon cuer, qui a vos se tient;
> An cest voloir m'a mes cuers mis."
> "Et qui le cuer, biaus douz amis?"
> "Dame! mi oel."—"Et les iauz qui?"
> "La granz biautez, que an vos vi."
> "Et la biautez qu'i a forfet?"
> "Dame! tant que amer me fet."
> "Amer? Et cui?"—"Vos, dame chiere."

"Moi?"—"Voire."—"Voir? an quel meniere?"
"An tel, que graindre estre ne puet,
An tel, que de vos ne se muet
Mes cuers, n'onques aillors nel truis,
An tel, qu'aillors panser ne puis,
An tel, que toz a vos m'otroi,
An tel, que plus vos aim que moi,
An tel, s'il vos plest, a delivre,
Que por vos vuel morir ou vivre."
"Et oseriiez vos anprandre
Por moi ma fontainne a deffandre?"
"Oïl voir, dame! vers toz homes."
"Sachiez donc bien, acordé somes."
Einsi sont acordé briemant!

["And I should very much like to know where this urge comes from, that commands you to submit to all my desires, without resistance. I acquit you of all wrongs and misdeeds. Now sit down, and tell me how it is that you are so softened." "Lady," he says, "the urge comes from my heart, which cleaves to you; my heart has prompted me in this desire." "And what prompted your heart, fair sweet friend?" "Lady, my eyes." "And what your eyes?" "The great beauty that I see in you." "And how is my beauty to blame?" "Lady, in that it makes me love." "Love? And whom?" "You, dear lady." "Me?" "Truly." "Truly? In what way?" "In such that it cannot be greater; in such that my heart does not stir from you, nor elsewhere will you find it; in such that elsewhere I cannot send my thoughts; in such that I surrender myself wholly to you; in such that I love you more than self; in such, if you please, without reservation, that for you I wish to live or die." "And would you dare to undertake for me to defend my spring?" "Yes indeed, Lady, against everyone." "Then rest assured, we are in accord." Thus they are quickly brought together.]

The ending of this scene, in its remarkable variety of style and pace, perpetuates its ambiguously humorous tone. The neat, sophisticated chit-chat gives way to the rhetorical lyric of love, then to the jarring practical question by Laudine, and finally to the Narrator's brief, prosaic comment on the whole.

Reviewing the style of the scene, we find an artistic consistency in this kind of variety. Since Yvain is the *verai ami,* and there is no suspicion of the practical in his motives (though, to be sure, he wishes to show Arthur a token of his victory in combat), he never descends to the colloquial. His love declaration, with its rather overheavy use of anaphora, is in the rhetorical pattern of the courtly lyric monologue. Lunete, however, is given no lyric and no patterned rhetoric. Her idiom is practical, direct, and persuasive. Besides rapid dialogue, we have from her two biting, satirical comments on the prowess of Laudine's men. But in Laudine the motives are various and mixed, so the poet uses for her a wider range of expression. It is this mixture of styles, the reflection of one on the other, that produces the complexity and humor of her characterization. She is capable of a touchingly tender complaint over her dead husband, yet she is susceptible to love, and she can further cap Yvain's soaring declaration of passion with the practical question of the defense of her spring. Her ready amorousness, and the practicality brought out by Lunete, in turn color her role in the conventional passages. The conventions of the love dialogue and monologue are here used with a half smile, the poet exploiting an incongruity between style and attitude. In the context of the whole scene the facility and patness of the final dialogue approach a parody of courtly love talk. There can be no resistance between an anxious, passionate woman and a lovestruck male. What in a perfectly serious treatment would require a long and protracted wooing, here takes on, through its hasty yet punctilious observance of form, a touch of comedy. Jean de Meun must have felt this a century later as he comically adapted a snatch of it to a definition of love *par amour*.[44] If Shakespeare's Romeo and Juliet can find love in the space of a sonnet without suggesting indecent haste, it is not convention *per se*, then, but convention in an alien context, as here, that generates humor.

One must now note that these complex strains of style and tone are carefully limited in *Yvain* to this scene. We hardly get another glimpse of Laudine as an ambiguous character. Yvain, who dominates the poem, is motivated throughout by the principles of chivalry and courtly love, and is not again seen in this half-comic light. The main body of the poem consists of a series of penitential experiences undergone by Yvain after he breaks a promise to his lady. Laudine, who most of the time is out of sight, represents no more than the object of the knight's desire and the sole source of his eventual pardon. The poem's ending finds them reunited after Yvain, as the Knight with the Lion, has arduously and anonymously earned Laudine's regard. In this light, the brilliant episode we have just examined, with its crosscurrents of realism and humor, is strangely overcomplex, and creates a critical problem. I rather think it is not vagrant misogyny on Chrétien's part,[45] but an attempt to shroud this first union of the

53

lovers with doubt, with incompleteness. *Yvain* has the typically bipartite structure of Chrétien's romances, wherein the second series of adventures caps the first, and brings the hero to a fuller and more mature knowledge of himself." In this light, the treatment of our scene, which is a climax to the first part of the romance, may be artistically justified.

The scene's stylistic insularity, at any rate, is explainable. A more elaborate connection between it and the rest of the poem would have undermined the whole structure of belief on which the courtly romance rests. The courtly heroine is not by our standards a perfect moral specimen: witness Iseut, Fenice, the Dame de Fayel, Guenivere, and any number of the other beautiful but deceptive creatures who occupy the bedchambers of romance. In a literature often devoted to the glorification of secret, adulterous love, we shall not find that a certain smiling, masculine recognition of the ways of women is ultimately damaging to the dignity of the heroine. She is still idealized, still the cause and cure of the hero's suffering. But in *Yvain* humor threatens the heroine in her capacity as an ideal. The theme of the widow who remarries in haste was popular in fable and in antifeminist satire. It is clear that more extensive treatment of the story in this vein would presuppose a modification of the courtly ideal itself. But Chrétien is not yet ready to give us the more complex and realistic view of woman, of love and of society in general, that such a modification would entail. The betrothal episode in *Yvain* illustrates the medieval poet's freedom from the canons of strict consistency of style. Chrétien's stylistic decorum is not an *a priori* matter, as it is in the modern realistic novel. It is not dominated by genre, nor even by the medieval rhetorical precept that style should follow the rank of the personages dealt with." It follows and supports attitude; and as the courtly attitude still prevails, so does the courtly style. Chrétien's parodic-realistic excursion, then, is a device, or at most a temporary vagrancy.

There was not enough of this manipulation of style in later courtly literature to create what we could call an actual tradition leading from the *Yvain* to—as the reader may have guessed—Chaucer's *Troilus and Criseyde*." Courtly poets at the beginning of the thirteenth century, and later, begin a stirring; but wherever we find it, it is usually in relatively obscure poems. There is a mixture of bourgeois and aristocratic tendencies in the romances of Jean Renart, whose *Guillaume de Dole* and *Escoufle* are preserved in unique copies; in *Galeran de Bretagne* there is assuredly something bourgeois, realistic, "nominalistic," though I do not think that it is set against the poem's idealism. It has been suggested that the *Bel Inconnu* of Renaut de Beaujeu, though courtly and symbolic in structure, tends, in its close relationship to its author's private feelings, to point toward a modern kind of individualism.[49] The unique *cantefable, Aucassin et Nicolette,* can be read as a delicate but consistent parody of courtly tradition. While such poems appear to have had little historical influence, at least they testify further to the possibilities of stylistic and ideological alterations within the tradition.

The *Flamenca,* which has come down to us in a single, mutilated manuscript, and which appears never to have been mentioned in the Middle Ages,[50] is the finest and most striking example of all. Its unfailing lightness of touch marks it off from the tradition. Its author is so much at home in courtly literature and courtly society that he can afford a certain amount of cheerful disrespect, even to the King and Queen of France. Compared to the Arthur and Guenivere of earlier romance, the former is something of a playboy, and the latter a jealous, troublemaking shrew. The poet is so much a master of courtly style and situation that he can play with them, to produce a romance to end all romances. Its hero, Guillem, is incredibly handsome, seven feet tall, and as learned in theology as in love. The central action is a single dialogue, so quintessential of the difficulties and stratagems of courtly love that it trembles on the edge of burlesque. Days pass between one speech and the next. Flamenca is so closely guarded by her comic, jealous husband that her only public appearances are in church. Guillem secures the affection of the priest with meals and gifts, and, in order to take over the church clerk's job, sends the boy happily off to Paris for two years' further study. When administering the Peace, he finds time to utter a few syllables to Flamenca, under his breath: "Hai las!" On the next holy day Flamenca replies, "Que plains?" In months they reach an agreement.[51]

Revolving about each of these overburdened, whispered messages is a world of debate and analysis, delicately but too surely overdrawn to be taken in perfect seriousness. On hearing Guillem's "Hai las!" Flamenca is at first in despair at what she takes to be mockery—she could not be worse off with a hostile stepmother,—but at the prompting of her two pleasant and amoral maids she soon enters the courtly fencing match—in two months from now she will know all his intentions—and opens her heart fully to the possibility of love.[52] Something of the poet's lightness of touch appears in the lonely speeches of Guillem, as at every crisis he complains, converses and debates with himself over his relation with the God Amor. At one point he engages in a squabble with that deity:

> Non sai qui donc, Amors, quet val?   [4011]
> Qu'il non s'entremet d'autrui mal.
> —Tort has.—Per que?—Si fai.—Cossi?

55

—Deu! fez ti parlar hui ab si.
—Vers es ab ma dona parliei,
Mas qual pro i hai, ni qu'enanciei?
—Tu si fesist; digas mi quan
Tu enansiest sivals aitan?

["Now, Love, I know what you are worth, you who care nothing for
the hurt of another." "You're wrong." "How?" "Truly!" "Why?"
"Good God! Have I not let you speak with her today?" "Yes, it is
true that I have spoken with my lady, but what good is it to me, and
how am I forwarder?" "You have spoken to her. Just tell me now—
when did you ever have such another bounty?"—Trans. Prescott,
p. 79.]

The convention of the allegorical monologue is even further strained as on a
sleepless night Guillem's anatomy takes over the conversation. Anatomical
personification is common enough in the romances, but here it threatens to
crack under a torsion between outright allegory and a realism that substitutes
for heart and mouth what appear to be a timid, clerical young man and a
profane old dame:

Le cors dis: "Hoc, sol que non falla   [4399]
Merces." Aqui eis la batailla.
Li boca dis iradamen,
E fes un estrain sacramen:
"Per Crist, don cors, fols es quius poina.
A tot home faratz vergoina
Que per vostre sen vos segues
Ni vostre fol desir crezes.
Cors caitius, e per quet rancuras?"
"Deus ajuda! domna, que juras?"

[Then the heart spoke: "Very well, so long as Mercy does not fail,"
and at once the fight began. The mouth spoke angrily, and with a
great oath: "By Christ, Sire Heart, he is a fool who listens to you.
Shame on all those who follow your counsel or trust in your crazy
desires. You coward heart, why are you whining?" "God help us,
lady, what are you swearing for?"—Trans. Prescott, p. 87.]

The device is even more conventional than what we generally find in Chrétien.

Its texture, however, is the reverse, for the allegorical monologue, originally designed to explore the recesses of refined emotion, here becomes the vehicle for an idiom reminiscent of common life. One recalls a similar cadence in Chaucer:

> "Sir Parisshe Prest," quod he, "for Goddes bones, [*MLEp* 1166]
> Telle us a tale, as was thi forward yore.
> I se wel that ye lerned men in lore
> Can moche good, by Goddes dignitee!"
>
> The Parson hem answerde, "*Benedicite!*
> What eyleth the man, so synfully to swere?"

A device which Guillaume de Lorris, roughly a contemporary, uses in 4,000 lines of seriously idealistic verse, is in *Flamenca* tossed off with negligent airiness of spirit.

The *Flamenca* poet is not a critic of courtly sentiment. His humor, which may appear broader than it should in these random examples taken out of context, hardly shades off into satire. His smile is benevolent, not malicious. His poem remains a "romance"; but in the hands of this poet of originality the romance reaches its terminal form as such. It is veined with incongruities between overdeveloped, conventional poses on the one hand and persistent touches of dramatic realism on the other. In both directions, style and structure have been pushed to a limit. It is with this whole poem as with the betrothal episode in *Yvain*. A clearer and more thoroughgoing division between convention and realism would open the way to qualification of the courtly attitude itself; it would, in short, play one attitude *against* the other. Although romances continue for another century to be written in the tradition of Chrétien, and the older ones are continually recopied, we do not meet with a poet able to go beyond the *Flamenca* until Chaucer writes his *Troilus and Criseyde*. The ground was further prepared for Chaucer, but not within the tradition of romance. In the interval between Chrétien and him an attitude and literary style opposed to those of romance had been nourished into vigorous existence by the poets of the so-called "bourgeois" tradition. We now turn to them.

III

the BOURGEOIS tradition

BY THE literature of the "bourgeois" tradition is meant that cluster of genres, some of them stemming in form and theme from the Orient and from classical antiquity, which seems, appearing freshly in the twelfth and thirteenth centuries, to attend the emergence of the new middle class. The commonest and for us the most important genre is the fabliau—the short, humorous verse tale. The tradition also includes the mime, the beast epic, the fable, a miscellany of satiric and comic poems, and some secular plays. In the religious drama, a number of scenes, which break away from Scriptural tradition or religious solemnity, share the style of the bourgeois literature, as do the exempla and anecdotes of the popular sermon.[1]

This literature is traditionally humorous, and lightly didactic. Much of it was produced in the North, in the commercial centers of Artois and Picardy, for the amusement and easy edification of a class of newly rich bourgeois with enough leisure for entertainment but not enough for learning or high sophistication.[2] It originates, thus, in an atmosphere of naïve realism, of commerce and

---

[1] For notes to chapter iii see pages 256–260.

common sense. But its style ultimately overleaps the traditional boundaries, to become an almost independent literary tool, tied less to a specific social class or specific genres than to a characteristic set of attitudes. Jean de Meun, about 1275, makes extensive use of this style in a complex and serious continuation of the *Roman de la Rose*. In this aspect, as one of several tools in the hands of a serious poet, the style has its deepest significance for Chaucer. Chaucer wrote several fabliaux, but even in his most elevated and courtly works the bourgeois tradition has a place and a function. It is a second major contributor to his mature style.

§ 1. THE REALISTIC STYLE OF THE BOURGEOIS TRADITION

The literature of the bourgeois tradition is "realistic" or "naturalistic," but it neither attempts nor achieves the reportorial detail of the modern fiction describable by these labels. It is based, even more clearly than the realism of the novel, on a circumscribedly conventional style. It is full of exaggeration, of caricature and grotesque imagination. It is conventional enough to embrace easily the animal stories of the *Roman de Renart* and the fables. I use the terms "realistic" and "naturalistic," then, loosely—for lack of better ones—to indicate that for the Middle Ages, and particularly in contrast to the courtly tradition, this literature has a remarkable preoccupation with the animal facts of life. It takes, in the ordinary sense, a realistic view of things. It finds its easiest subject in low life, but with high or low it is impartially impolite—and often vulgar and obscene. It has an almost total incapacity for disgust or for pretension. Shrewd, irreverent, and skeptical, it lends itself readily to satire, or rather to less constructive kinds of abuse. Despite the specializations of both vision and expression that this attitude entails, the literature at its best gives the impression of dealing with life directly, with something of life's natural shape and vitality.

The fabliau is the most protean genre of the bourgeois tradition, and will supply us with virtually all of its stylistic traits. Perhaps the commonest (some fabliaux have little else) is a blunt economy of plan and procedure.

> Oiez, seignor, un bon fablel.
> Uns clers le fist por un anel
> Que .III. dames .I. main trovèrent.
> Entre eles .III. Jhesu jurèrent
> Que icele l'anel auroit
> Qui son mari mieux guileroit
> Por fère à son ami son buen . . .   (I, 168)°

59

[Listen, lords, to a good story. A clerk made it about a ring that three ladies found one morning. The three of them swore by Jesus that whichever fooled her husband best, to give her favors to her lover, would get the ring.]

Thus go the opening and an outline of the entire plot of *Des .III. dames qui trouverent l'anel.* The fabliau setting is likewise spare: *en la meson* or *en sa chambre* will do at the outset. Particularizing detail is most often brought in with a view towards practical utility in the action. Where a house is placed by a river, someone is thrown into that river. Where there is an especially cold winter, there is a very hot fire, and the fire is used to heat an implement at the climax of the story. An action set in September, when berries are ripe, involves a hungry priest who gets caught in a berry bush.[4] So it goes with description generally. In sharp contrast to the formal and rhetorical *descriptio* of the courtly and learned styles, which often precedes or halts the narrative, a great deal of fabliau description is brought in as needed, piece by piece, *ad hoc:* "And the agreement was such that she would send for him when her husband was away. Then he would come to the two locked gates of the garden . . ." (I, 118); " 'I will put you secretly into an upstairs room [*solier*] I have the key to . . .' " (I, 120); "Estormi, carrying the load, goes through a secret exit [*fausse posterne*]; he doesn't want to use the front door" (I, 209). We do not hear of garden, gates, *solier,* or secret door beforehand.

The descriptive imagery of the tradition is characterized even more sharply by its quality than by its utility. The fabliau cosmos is defined and limited by the important presence of smoked eels and pieces of lard, of hot irons and frying-pan rings, washtubs, barrels, baskets and chests, bats and clubs, loads of dung and thick, white goose sauce.[5] The same prosaism colors figurative language and comparison, oriented as it is toward the low and the comic. The servant Galestrot runs on an errand for her mistress:

> Cele a escorcié ses trumiaus,
> Qui sont gros devers les talons;
> Onques vache, que point tahons,
> Ne vi si galoper par chaut . . .   (IV, 181)

[She moved her beefy legs, which are thick around the heels; I never saw a cow being pricked by a gadfly in so hot a gallop.]

In the same poem a forester is frustrated in his attentions to a lady:

A cest mot de li se depart,
E il remest plus chaut que brese.
Qui li eüst la teste rese
Sans eve à .i. coutel d'acier,
Ou les cheveus fet esrachier,
Si l'en fust il assez plus bel.   (IV, 170)

[With this she goes away, and he is left hotter than a coal. If you had
shaved his head without water with a steel knife, or had his hair torn
out, he would have been much better off.]

The fabliau world is peopled by a representative collection of characters:
peasants and bourgeois, clerks, priests, nuns, jongleurs, miscellaneous rascals of
all kinds, and, as we shall see, some knights and courtly ladies. Most of them
are busily engaged in one or more of the seven deadly sins. Economically
enough, they tend to fall into types. The triangle of the dull-witted or jealous
husband, the sensual wife, and the lecherous priest or clever clerk reappears so
often as to have almost an *a priori* status. It is introduced with the slightest of
preamble:

Un example vueil conmencier
Qu'apris de Monseigneur Rogier,
. . .
Qui bien savoit ymages fère
E bien entaillier crucefis.
Il n'en estoit mie aprentis,
Ainz les fesoit et bel et bien.
Et sa fame seur toute rien
Avoit enamé un provoire.   (I, 194)

[I want to begin a story that I heard about my lord Rogier . . . who
knew well how to make statues and crucifixes. No apprentice he, he
made them fair and well. And his wife beyond everything had been
loving a priest.]

"Monseigneur" Rogier tells his wife he is going to a market. When he sees her
face brighten, he knows the worst:

Si se pot bien apercevoir
Qu'el le béoit à decevoir,
Si come avoit acoustumé.   (*Ibid.*)

61

Such type characters are most often described briefly, in a formulary way (priests are rich, wives are prétty, clerks are fat, or else courteous and debonair), but when description begins to exceed shorthand it is usually in single traits, as economically chosen as the traits of setting. The romance, we recall, tends to describe its ladies, knights, and *vilains* according to the conventional physiognomy for each group; in contrast the fabliau, where it distinguishes at all, does so sharply, with widely disparate traits dictated by the point of the story. Thus one steward has a big, square head, the better to hide a piece of lard under his cap (I, 113). A priest is plumper than his mistress by four fingers of fat, with a relevance unspeakably crude (II, 81–82). There is a young woman who faints if she hears a dirty word, and a *vilain* who cannot stand the smell of spices (III, 81; V, 40). The courtly *effictio*—the formal portrait with its stable set of traits— is thus rare in the bourgeois tradition. Its closest counterpart is perhaps the kind of stereotyped ugliness of the hunchback in *Des Trois Boçus.*° There begins to be that gratuitous richness of detail which we associate with subtler literary effects, though it hardly transcends caricature, in a glimpse of the squint-eyed, clubfooted peasant Berengier in *D'Aloul* (I, 278); in a more extended description an old *truande,* pathetically smeared with cosmetics, sits hopefully sewing up her rags (V, 172–173). In *Du Prestre et des .II. ribaus* the idea of a skinny, ragged minstrel astride a horse for the first time evokes a comic description:

> Mès trop li sont cort li estrier,
> Quar il ot une longue jambe
> Plus noire que forniaus de chambre;
> Plas piez avoit et agalis,
> Grans estoit, haingres et alis,
> Et deschirez de chief en chief,
> Et li huvès c'ot en son chief
> Sambloit miex de cuir que de toile;
> Dès la cuisse jusqu'en l'ortoile
> N'ot fil de drap, ce vous tesmoing,
> Ne dès le coute jusqu'au poing.   (III, 65)

[But the stirrups are too short, for he has a long leg, blacker than a cookstove; he had flat feet, he was tall, lean, and lanky, and ragged from end to end, and the cap he had on his head seemed more of hide than of cloth; from his thigh to his toe there wasn't a thread of clothing, I assure you, nor from his elbow down.]

A more skillful description is that of the *lecheor* Boivin de Provins disguising himself as a rich peasant to deceive a local madam:

> Vestuz se fu d'un burel gris,
> Cote, et sorcot, et chape ensamble,
> Qui tout fu d'un . . .
> Et si ot coiffe de borras;
> Ses sollers ne sont mie à las,
> Ainz sont de vache dur et fort;
> Et cil, qui mot de barat sot,
> .I. mois et plus estoit remese
> Sa barbe qu'ele ne fu rese;
> .I. aguillon prist en sa main,
> Por ce que mieus samblast vilain:
> Une borse grant acheta,
> .XII. deniers dedenz mis a,
> Que il n'avoit ne plus ne mains;
> E vint en la rue aus putains
> Tout droit devant l'ostel Mabile . . .   (V, 52)

[He was dressed in gray wool, gown and jacket and cloak all of the same . . . and he had a hood of hemp. His shoes are not laced (i.e., not elegant), but are of hard, strong cowhide; and he, who knew plenty about trickery, had left his beard unshaven for a month and more; the better to resemble a peasant he carried a stick in his hand: he bought a big purse, put twelve pennies in it—he had no more nor less—and came into the street of the whores, right in front of Mabile's house . . .]

The poet here is just beginning to exploit the power of the device, using description in the interest of characterization. At the same time, the description is barely kept static. Boivin walks away, stick in hand and money in purse, as if he could stand still no longer. In this he expresses the bourgeois tradition's preference for action.

Action is the greatest source of its vividness, of its appearance of inexhaustible vitality. Even the recitation of these tales was something of a dramatic activity. Its talk often sounds like good material for mimicry, of a piece with the semi-theatrical mimes which make their appearance as a genre in the thirteenth century, and with the miscellaneous "acts" that accompany the *Herberie* mime and the fabliau in one entertainment:

L'uns fet l'ivre, l'autres le sot,
. . .
Aucuns i a qui fabliaus conte,
Où il ot mainte gaberie,
E li autres dit l'*Erberie*
Là où il ot mainte risée.   (III, 204)

[One plays the drunk, another the fool . . . there's one who tells a story, where there was many a joke, and another does the quack doctor, where there was many a laugh.]

The fabliau dialogue, in short, is dramatically conceived. In it we hear very skillfully represented all the shriller sounds of everyday life. Like all speech that is not recorded on the street in shorthand, this is no less an artifact than the patterned discourse of the courtly tradition, but it is based more closely on speech as heard, especially as heard on the street corner and in the kitchen. Its conventionalism, if you will, lies in its avoidance of rhetorical and nonrepresentational form, and in a different specialization of diction and rhythm.

The most striking elements of the diction are its obscenity and its free admission of jargon. The language of the thieves in Jean Bodel's *Jeu de Saint Nicolas* remains partly incomprehensible today.[7] Of the same turn toward specialization, and presenting almost the same difficulties, are speeches in which dialect is used for comic-realistic purposes. In the *Privilège aux Bretons,* a satiric mime, a rude peasant addresses the king in a distorted language evidently based on the actual peculiarities of Breton French. In a piece of the same genre, *La Paix aux Anglais,* as in several other bourgeois poems, we hear mimicry of the vocabulary, construction, and pronunciation of French as spoken by the English.[8]

The rhythm of this style of speech is notable for its turbulence. Based on the salient features of popular expression, it is peppered with interjections, curses, and epithets. Shrill sounds of the domestic squabble are heard all through the bourgeois tradition,[9] and much of the best dialogue appears in dicing and drinking scenes. In the fabliau *De Saint Piere et du jougleur* (V, 65–79), Saint Peter comes down to Hell with some dice, to play for souls with a poor jongleur who has been left by the Devil as watchman. The dialogue is richly elaborated with the lingo of the game, and the hallowed, exclamatory comment on its progress. Similarly in tune with the activity of the scene is the tavern talk in drama and fabliau: the coarse humor of inebriation, the arguments over the reckoning, quarrels and jests in which the tavernkeeper, his servants, and his guests all take part.[10]

The rhythm and sound of the direct discourse, then, supports the representation of *action*—direct, violent, practical—which is one of the chief ends of the whole style. Unimpeded by elaborate commentary, set description, inner monologue, or any of the other nondramatic formalities of courtly style, the bourgeois poet readily sets his subjects in motion, when they are more sharply seen than at rest. Movement and potential energy attract his eye; thus, as I have shown, the preponderance of detail seen for its practical significance, and thus the significant amount of realistic gesture caught in the poetry: a peasant woman licking her fingers after an unauthorized snack of roast partridge (I, 189), a happy squire scratching his posterior (II, 64), a knight wrinkling his nose in anger (I, 182), and a king slapping his thigh in amusement (IV, 45). A lecherous priest sits in his doorway and looks down the street (VI, 11). He sees the church charwoman and waggles a finger at her ("contenciée à son doi"). She can help him in a love affair. She comes over and he bows to her from afar ("de loins la salue"). He voices with exaggerated politeness his wish for a little speech with her: "J'ai grant talant / C'un poi peüse à vos parler." Then he begins to embrace her, but he keeps an eye on the street for fear that someone may see him.

The kind of characterization that emerges from this literature is immediately apprehensible to the modern reader. It has the vividness and concreteness of the picaresque tradition, and of Dickens. With all its traits working in concert the style produces some memorable individuals: the prostitute Richeut,[11] an anonymous widow who must be among the ancestors of the Wife of Bath (II, 197–214), the confidence man Boivin, whom we have seen in disguise above. All these are "types," but are seen in such local and mundane situations that they seem to fulfill our modern, *a priori* demand for "life," that is, for naturalism. And yet, this "life" is no less limited a thing than the life in the Garden of the Rose. Here is a dull-witted *vilain* trying to recapture a mouse in the dark:

"Se ele muert! Sainte Marie!
Ele iert ja noiée et perie
En la fosse, se ele i antre;
Ele en a moillié tot le vantre
Et tot lo dox et les costez.
Ostez, biau sire Deus, ostez!
Que ferai je, se ele muert?"
Li vilains ses .II. poinz detuert
Por la sorriz qui brait et pipe.
Qui li veïst faire la lipe
Au vilain et tordre la joe,
Manbrer li poïst de la moe
Que li singes fait quant il rist.   (IV, 162)

["If she dies! Holy Mary! She'll be drowned and lost in the ditch if she goes there; she has wet all her belly and back and sides in it. Take her out, fair lord God, take her out! What will I do if she dies?" The peasant wrings his two hands for the mouse that cries and squeaks. To see the peasant put out his lips and twist his cheeks would remind you of the face a monkey makes when it laughs.]

The immediacy and economy of this scene are the typical products of the bourgeois style. It has the clarity and liveliness of an animated cartoon. The description is spare but (with the possible exception of the monkey) domestic and familiar, and it is chosen for so direct a sensory effect that it shades over into caricature. It sees, in the dark, a wet mouse, a watery ditch, a pair of hands wrung in anxiety, and a grimace. Its sounds—squeak, exclamation, prayer—perpetuate its familiarity, its vividness, and its animation. But the characterization of the peasant, while it depends partly on a context not explainable here, could well have depended entirely on this description. It encompasses the severely limited number of sharply drawn motives and responses that the character is made of. Neither he, nor the style that brings him before us, is capable of the more intangible reaches of reflection and emotion that Guillaume de Lorris, for instance, can deal with so finely. The peculiar strength of the naturalistic style is, as we should expect, also a limitation. It is a style adjusted to a particular cosmos. Behind the comedy and the caricature there is a spirit of intense practicality, a myopic circumscription of the attention to clock time and local space, a reckoning with tangible force, concrete motive, physical peculiarity. It is a style designed to evoke a naturalistic, material world, and little more.

The conventionality of this style, its status as a literary tool, becomes clearest when we free it, as we must, from the association of social level and genre with which we started. Calling it "bourgeois," the style of the fabliaux, helps explain its origins and character, but does not recognize its free literary currency in the Middle Ages. We know that fabliaux were widely circulated among the aristocracy, and were written by poets from courtly circles, just as, one might add, some courtly literature was written by city bourgeois poets.[12] Furthermore, both styles overflow the boundaries of genre. Bédier (pp. 383–384) cites the contamination of the courtly lyric by the fabliau spirit, and we have seen above something of this mixture in romance. We shall see below some intermixture of courtly traits in the fabliaux. The one constant factor in the appearance of the bourgeois style, however, is its potency to support an attitude, to evoke the particular world I have described above. In the widening area of choice that literary development in the Middle Ages brings, the naturalistic style becomes less and less an unre-flective social symptom, and more and more an implement of artistic strategy.

§ 2. COURTLY TRAITS IN THE BOURGEOIS TRADITION

I have intimated above that there are courtly traits of style in the fabliaux, and I can be brief in dealing with them, for the mixture here does not have even the meaning that it has in romance. It took, apparently, a Jean de Meun, and more than a century of experience with the bourgeois attitude, to see the full potency of the attitude and its literary tools. At any rate, I have suppressed nothing essential to a description of the bourgeois literature by postponing this discussion until now. First of all, the presence of courtly elements in the fabliaux is partly an accident of definition. There are many "fabliaux" which are not realistic in style at all. Thus the *Lai d'Aristote,* which describes the conversion of the dour philosopher to courtly love, is a defense of the system, and employs the descrip-tive technique of romance. Its author is as careful in diction as Guillaume de Lorris.¹³ *Des .III. chevaliers et del chainse* (III, 123–136) is not only courtly; it is almost tragic. We cannot count its choice of actors, its setting, its allegorical dialogue, supporting a concept of exemplary fidelity in love, as procedures of the bourgeois tradition. Nor can we count the generally courtly style, the mono-logue, lyric, formal portrait, and idyllic setting of such poems as *Du Vair Palefroi* (I, 24–69), *Du Mantel mautaillié* (III, 1–29), and *Du Chevalier qui recovra l'amor de sa dame* (VI, 138–146).¹⁴

In the remainder, in poems of mingled style, the courtly elements are most often inoperative artistically, petrified fossils of expression that have been intro-duced for lack of something better. They are neither readily assimilable to the dominantly realistic pattern, nor are they countermarshaled in the interest of parody or irony. To call a bourgeoise "bele et saverouse, / Gaie, envoisie et amourouse" in such a fabliau as *Du Clerc qui fu repus* (IV, 47) is to use courtly diction for lack of anything else. This *saverouse* lady, having to hide one lover at the entry of a second, and the second at the entry of her husband, is no courtly specimen. She is shrill and abrupt:

> "Honnie soit vo gloute geule!
> Alons dormir, il en est tans."   (IV, 50)

[Damn your greedy mouth! Let's go to sleep, it's time.]

Her plan to circumvent supper and get him to bed doesn't work. The climax of the tale comes with the woman forgotten, when lover number one mistakes a gesture of the husband and prematurely comes out of hiding, to reveal the presence of lover number two. The fragment of courtly diction, then, at best explains the presence of so many lovers. It does not work in the interest of idealization; it is at best only palely comic. Similarly, a touch of courtly setting in *D'Aloul* irrelevantly yet unselfconsciously ushers one into a long day and night of ribald adventures.[15] At the opening of the *Dit de la gageure* we are introduced to a knight and his lady. His brother is his squire; her cousin is her lady in waiting. By the end of this short, scurrilous piece, things have taken on fabliau colors. We hear the lady, for instance, addressing her kinswoman:

> Et la dame ly escria
> E hastivement li parla
> Ou grosse voiz e longe aleyne:
> "Gwenchez, gwenchez, guenchez, puteyne;
> Trestresse, Dieu te doint mal fyn!
> J'ay perdu le tonel de vyn."
>
> (II, 196)

[And the lady screamed to her, and spoke to her urgently in a loud voice of great volume: "Squirm, squirm, squirm, you whore! Traitress, God give you shame! I've lost the barrel of wine."]

The choice of characters, then, is fortuitous; it has no controlling influence over the style, nor does the style support any particular commentary on the rank of the characters.

If I have missed a touch of irony here or there in examining the mixing of styles in the fabliaux, the fact remains that this procedure is not an important one for the poetry.[16] The bourgeois tradition is capable of some perspective, and of relatively complex literary effects. Such a piece as *De Saint Piere et du jougleur* is shot through with a light irony at the expense of both parties:

> Dist saint Pieres: "Biauz dous amis,
> Met de ces ames .v. ou sis."
> "Sire," fet il, "je n'oseroie,
> Quar se une seule en perdoie,
> Mon mestre me ledengeroit
> Et trestout vif me mengeroit."
> Dist saint Pieres: "Qui li dira?
> Ja por .xx. ames n'i parra . . ."
>
> (V, 70)

[St. Peter says: "Fair, sweet friend, bet five or six of these souls." "Sir," says the jongleur, "I wouldn't dare; for if I lost a single one my master (the Devil) would abuse me and eat me up alive." "Who will tell him?" says St. Peter; "Even with twenty souls, it won't show . . ."]

Many touches like this underlie its prevailing tone of good-natured, reverent impiety, its satirical but affectionate attitude toward jongleurs. But for all this kind of *esprit* in the best fabliaux (and putting off for a moment our consideration of the *Roman de Renart*), this minor literature of the bourgeois tradition rarely, if ever, presents itself in the very largest social context, as one party in a major cultural conflict.[17] Its anticlericalism is not, ultimately, an attack on the Church, or on religion, but presupposes an orthodoxy against which the abuses are projected. Not dissimilarly, its view of woman comprehends divergencies from the bourgeois standard of a faithful, useful wife, but it does not seriously go beyond this system to examine other versions of Woman, to examine the utility and economy of courtly love, or of courtesy. Its plentiful antifeminism does not, except by remote implication, aim to discredit the central symbol of the other great secular tradition; the quick-witted, sensual, materialistic, sharply seen woman of the fabliau does not cast her reflection, through their common sex, on the palely beautiful, remote, and idolized lady of romance. A fabliau like *Du Prestre et du chevalier,* which runs the whole gamut of the two styles and testifies to its author's dexterity with both, does not begin to convey the breadth of meaning that such a complexity of style could support.

The same things cannot be so easily said of the style and ethos of the great collection of animal tales known as the *Roman de Renart.* Some of them (e.g., VII and XXI) are no more than fabliaux, and answer to the description I have made above. But others, particularly the presumed works of Pierre de Saint-Cloud (II, Va) and the very popular Branches I and XVII, achieve a truly mock-heroic tone, which turns on a continuous contrast between realistic animal imagery and the institutions of feudal society. The feudalism thus parodied has perhaps its closest literary model in the *chansons de geste,* that is, in epic rather than in romance.[18] Yet, to turn our attention to the forms and themes that we have been following, here and there a sensitive critic will see in King Noble, the lion, more of Arthur than of Charlemagne, and there are references throughout the tales that are reminiscent of courtly love. Renart the fox loves Hersent the she-wolf, it is said, "par amors" (II, 1089). Another mistress of Renart (shades of Lancelot and Guenivere!) is the King's wife, "madame Fiere l'orgeillose, / que mout estoit cortoise et bele."[19] The King is touchingly sympathetic toward true love (Va, 425–428), and there is a delicious scene (ed. Roques, I, 291 ff.) when the bier of the murdered maiden chicken Coupee is brought to Court by her grieving relatives, that demonstrates the royal sympathy with distressed maidens. The King has just absolved Renart of guilt in the seduction of Hersent. Now Pinte (who lays big eggs), the sister of Coupee and the favorite mistress of Chantecler, delivers a pathetic complaint and falls fainting, with three of her sisters, on the floor. Chantecler the "bacheler" adds his tears, and all that the righteous indignation of Hersent's husband could not do against the guilty fox is quickly accomplished by this touching scene. Elsewhere there are perhaps echoes of *Tristan* and Chrétien de Troyes.[20] But enough has been said to show that some of the comic effect of the *Renart* poems is based on an exploitation of romance traits or motifs.

The extent to which the best Branches of the *Renart* stand as landmarks in the history of style depends somewhat on what history we are tracing. Their parodic structure seems to support the playing off of one view of life with another. Were we studying the permutations of the epic style, or the forms of liturgy, and the implied commentary in these poems on the values of heroic poetry and public worship, we should have to reckon with the *Renart* at greater length. Where Tardif the snail is standard bearer to the King, and Bernart the ass is archpriest, we should perhaps wish to test more carefully the temper of the poetry. I think that we should not find it any more dissident than the fabliaux or the goliardery of the schools.[21] But be that as it may, it is clear that the particular mixture we are tracing, which is central in Chaucer, is not quite central in the *Renart*. The beast epic is if anything too wide in its scope to claim our immediate attention. Chaucer did not tackle it until he wrote the most complex of the Canterbury tales, that of the Nun's Priest; and there he developed the mock-epic form to an unprecedented fullness, introducing, among other things, what we find only here and there suggested in the French, a comic view of courtly life, or a courtly view of animal life.

At least, however, we may remark that the *Renart* is, for its parodic character, different in style from the general run of "bourgeois" poems, and that so far as epic and romance traits are keyed meaningfully with realistic ones in it, the combination gives it something of the same stylistic promise that we see in *Yvain* and *Flamenca*. Using "language at once familiar, parodic, and stylised,"[22] the *Renart* brings us closer than the fabliaux to the degree if not the kind of complexity that Chaucer's style has.

I have thus far attempted to describe the leading traits of the two major styles we have in French literature from the middle of the twelfth century. The attitudes that these two styles support have been contrasted finely and in detail by Bédier and others,[23] and there is no reason for laboring the comparison here.

We have seen realism in romance, and fragments of romance in the bourgeois poems, and we can sense, particularly in the former, a kind of movement toward rivalry and conflict between these attitudes. Yet by and large they live in the literature—and in the culture and in many a capacious medieval soul—quietly, if somewhat uneasily, side by side, for more than a hundred years. That they collided on a major scale, in a major cultural crisis, is seen by the fifteenth century, when the literature shows them everywhere athwart each other, in ironically grotesque ways, as if the conflict had raged beyond the endurance of both sides. In literature, then, this conflict seems not to have begun in earnest until well into the thirteenth century; the battle lines are clearly drawn in the *Roman de la Rose* of Jean de Meun. The poem was for a long time the center of a historically well-documented doctrinal debate. From our point of view it is preëminently, however, a stylistic monument. Coincident with its doctrinal position is an exploitation of style that raises the bourgeois idiom to a new power in French literature. No longer an instrument of therapeutic laughter, it is marshaled toward the support of a seriously philosophic view of life—and toward a meaningful position *vis-à-vis* the courtly view. In the artistic management of the bourgeois style, then, Jean's poem stands between the fabliaux and Chaucer.

§ 3. THE "ROMAN DE LA ROSE" OF JEAN DE MEUN

That Jean de Meun's continuation of the *Roman de la Rose* contains passages of realistic style has long been noticed. It was for a long time the thing most commonly noticed. What claims our attention here is not the simple fact of realism, with its clear heritage from antifeminist and anticlerical satire, but rather the style's meaning in context, and its special form.

The general effect of context can be illustrated by an example near at hand. The reader of the fabliaux is likely to notice before long that while these poems seem to create a cosmos of their own, they at various points—in description and in statement—have an affinity to the literature of a very different tradition. Antifeminism, with its armory of anecdotes and exempla, is common to the fabliaux and to the asceticism of St. Paul and St. Jerome, and at certain points the ascetic and the fabliau styles actually intersect. It follows that while style in itself seems to have some special potency within a given area of meaning— and certainly there is an area of common cause here between the sinners and the saints—the significance of a style is by no means exhausted by a technical description of it. There is no confusing of the temper of Jerome's *Epistle against Jovinian* with that of the fabliau *De Sire Haine et de Dame Anieuse*. This is to

71

say, with Huizinga, that even when we go beyond the distinctions between selective and detailed realisms, and between the realism reporting fact and that creating fiction, there is an important discrimination between realisms to be made on the basis of ethical force and direction. In the Middle Ages we can actually discern a continuum of realisms: from the ascetic's revelation of the corporeal life that he contemns, to the morally directed observations of satire, to the ethically negative, unselfconscious realism of jest.[24] We might add, toward the middle of the list, the Franciscan and Dantesque realisms, with their ethical yet humane character, their evocation of high seriousness and pathos. In the final analysis, much of this kind of distinction between styles depends on context. Now for his Duenna and Jealous Husband, the main agents of his realism, Jean de Meun draws on textual sources as far apart as Ovid, the ascetics, and the fabliaux. The superficial texture of this material is often so much the same that it is not possible to distinguish, on the basis of specific traits, one set of borrowings from the others. It is almost all traditional material. Yet by and large—in its given context—it supports a view of life palpably different from those of Ovid and the Church Fathers. From the realism of the fabliaux Jean's differs to a similar degree through the fact that the former has usually no literary context but itself, while his has that of a huge structure of erotic and philosophical poetry.

The context of Jean's realism, that is, the whole poem with its complex of styles and attitudes, is uniquely difficult to describe. There are very few paths through medieval life and thought that do not cross here. Modern criticism has dispelled the older notion of the thought of the poem as simple, bourgeois reaction to courtly literature; and its structure has recently been revealed as something more than a bizarre, accidental transgression of Guillaume's delicate allegory. We are in a position to see in it a close filiation with the poem that it continues, and to discern a substantial coherence in its thinking.[25] Yet no one describes this poem except under correction. With its formulations, modern criticism has brought complications; the more we can see in the poem, the harder it is to summarize it, and everywhere it still shows its encyclopedic, didactic character, its author's irrepressible willingness to exercise his remarkable talents for popular exposition. No account of the poem, then, can proceed without oversimplification; in what follows I shall be silently passing over many a divagation and inconsistency.

The procedure of the poem is to perpetuate a thin line of allegorical action—in which the Lover finally obtains the Rose,—but to interrupt it with a series of long, didactic monologues by a variety of characters. These are given so much space that the net effect is to transfer the interest from the allegory to what turns out to be a debate and symposium on love. The completed poem thus incorporates and envelops the slender first part, making the lecture of Guillaume's God of Love the first of a series.²⁶ The speakers in Jean's part are, successively, Raison, Ami, and the Duenna ("la vieille"), who are characters first introduced by Guillaume, and then Nature and her priest Genius, the god of generation. Between Ami and the Duenna there speaks Faus-Semblant, whose long self-revelation is only tenuously related to the subject of love, and must thus be considered among the grosser digressions. The situation is complicated by the fact that the speeches are not addressed to a uniform audience: Amor, Raison, and Ami address the Lover; the Duenna addresses Bel Acueil, who in Jean's scheme represents the Lady of the poem; Nature "confesses" to Genius; and the latter, as does Faus-Semblant, speaks to the God of Love and all his barons. Jean, despite certain technical embarrassments, understood the mechanism of allegory, and there is a certain logic in this variety. But it will save us trouble here to think of the speeches as being addressed to the reader under the Platonic and Boethian license to give philosophical exposition a quasi-dramatic form.

The speakers make rivaling claims on our allegiance, and at the same time present a spectrum of related arguments.²⁷ In the debate, Amor of course represents the courtly attitude. Raison characteristically distinguishes and defines a number of species of love: the sickness of courtly eroticism, friendship and love of neighbors, charity as related to justice, and protective animal love. But she then offers *her* love to the lover; we may thus take her final position to be that of the exponent of philosophy, the love of knowledge. Ami is the sophisticated exponent of love, the doctrinaire, who debases it a little. Jean's presentation of him has some heavy-handed joking to it. Instructing the naïve, pure-minded lover, it is Ami who introduces the notions of hypocrisy and deception in love. His prescription for success in unfaithfulness is given with the same competent assurance as his advice on how to keep the love of one's lady. His effect is always more damaging than his avowed purpose. To advise patient endurance of the lady's defects and whims is at the same time to expose them. The most elaborate joke Jean has with this character is in his illustration of the evils of sovereignty in marriage. Ami illustrates the bad temper of the Jealous Husband with a dramatic monologue, a thousand lines of mingled abuse and complaint. The joke is that the speech reflects less upon the intemperateness of the Husband than on the manifold intractabilities of his wife. This is one of the main loci of satiric realism in the poem. Another, the speech of the Duenna, represents

73

the twin positions of erotic materialism and uninhibited sensuality. She is an ex-prostitute, with a talent for gain and an organic weakness for sex. Finally Jean introduces Nature and Genius. Nature in an eloquent, panoramic description of her realm establishes her position as a servant of God, vicar for Him in His plenitude. Her complaint of man's failure to fulfill his part in the divine plan—his failure to attend to the task of generation that ensures the perpetuation of the species—leads to Genius' exhortation to the barony of Love. This, described by the poet as "la difinitive sentence" (19504), and the only position left unchallenged in the poem, is a recommendation of sexual activity on a highly moral basis: procreation is a duty to God. Attached to this heterodox ethic is an orthodox theology, expressed through an unusually moving description of the celestial paradise. To the good and the faithful in the priest Genius' terms there is open a garden of the Lamb infinitely more real and more beautiful than Guillaume's garden of the Rose.[28]

This vest-pocket account of the poem does no justice to Jean's thought in all its color and energy, but it will do to indicate the variety and range of attitudes he handles. We are plunged into a far wider theme here than in any poem we have thus far discussed. To keep to our tracing of the context of realism, the poem's variety—its character as debate—has a significance which we have been steadily if lengthily approaching. It holds the courtly and the "realistic" views, among others, in something of an ordered opposition to each other. And we must observe that while this juxtaposition existed in the culture long before Jean—Andreas' *De Amore* has it,—it is with him that it first appears overtly within the limits of a single poem, a literary configuration to be perpetuated in various forms through the declining Middle Ages and into the Renaissance. Jean's poem seems to mark, in this, the beginning of a special kind of concentration on the rivalries of courtly love, the conversion of a situation into a problem, a conflict. In his poem the realistic view (to ignore the others for a moment) is the aggressive one. It is self-consciously and unambiguously critical of courtly idealism. It exposes in a merciless way the various possible readings of love that courtly sentiment ignores. It crudely disparts notions that Guillaume de Lorris had finely managed to hold together: paradise and earth, refinement and sensuality. This attack is given a novel force by the context, by the fact that the opposing voices are heard within what becomes in Jean's hands an overt and serious disputation.

The context gives moral resonance to Jean's realism in another way. The whole range of attitudes that he introduces, if we measure it against Christian orthodoxy, is shifted toward naturalism. We have seen that at his most elevated he is still defending procreation, and he glories in the fecundity and variety of nature. Paré has acutely compared the views of Jean with those of Alain de Lille. Alain is one of the prominent poet-philosophers of the twelfth-century school of Chartres, and his *Complaint of Nature* is a well-known "source" for Jean's poem. The Chartres poets are "naturalistic"; they give a new dignity to Nature, and begin to suggest a *modus vivendi* between the moral stringency of orthodox religion and the increasing attractiveness of secular life. Jean borrows the figures, and some of the ideas, of Nature and Genius from Alain. But, as Paré says, "if you consider the spirit that animates each of these texts, what a difference!"

> In sum, the *De Planctu Naturae* of Alain de Lille is an apology for Christian virtues; there Nature condemns the practices that Christian doctrine considers as errors, particularly those opposed to moral virtue. The excommunication by Genius only repeats officially this general condemnation, and it is made, not before the soldiery of the god of Love, but in the presence of virgins symbolizing the virtues.
>
> In Jean de Meun . . . the errors which detain these two characters and against which they fulminate for hundreds of verses are not properly those that in scholastic philosophy are called the sins of the flesh, but [are rather] the practices opposed to reproduction and to what is considered an absolute good of man that each individual must contribute to: the perpetuity of the species. The others are left out. In this context chastity and continence are considered as vices, and it is indeed against continence that Genius' accents are most inflamed.[29]

To affirm that the laws of Nature should guide the moral life, Paré says later on (p. 340), was to perpetuate a common scholastic idea. But when Jean interprets these laws to translate them into specific rules of conduct, he diverges from Alain and from orthodoxy, subordinating the spiritual good proclaimed by the scholastic theologians to a good based on procreation.

In this secular, life-oriented purview, it seems to me, the materialism of the Husband and the Duenna and the latter's unabashed sensuality are easily held in concert with the views dictated by Raison and Nature. The "fabliau" material is not merely brazen and dismissable effrontery, jesting to be put by when the serious thinking begins. Jean, if we can call any view his, does not recommend the "low" view of love; yet he lengthily expounds it as a view that can be held, and his logic or his sympathy lead him to show us this view as involved with the higher ones. There is something in him of the cult of experience. The Duenna is not too distant a relative of Raison.[30]

The quickest way to display their kinship is to remark that it is Raison, in what Lewis calls (p. 149) her "unrepentant grossness," who ironically shocks the Lover by her freedom of diction. The God of Love, we recall, had warned the Lover against the use of bad language. Raison's unambiguous reference to the "coilles" of Saturn (5537) opens the way for Jean to present a defense of directness in language, based on the essential goodness of God's creation and the propriety of the names His servant, Raison, has given them.[31] There is, then, in this part of the poem, a conscious and systematic defense of the kind of language that the Duenna will later use unconsciously and naturally. This is only the most striking of a number of threads which bind together the speakers, from the highest to the lowest, in mutual criticism of the courtly attitude. Raison, indeed, first launches the naturalistic ideas which are passed down the poem to become with Genius a doctrine of procreation and with the Duenna a philosophy of promiscuity.[32] No one will confuse the moral worth of one version of this theme with that of another. Yet it is clear that they have a common element, here elevated and moralized, there popularized and seen with shorter sight. Raison, in this poem, is "natural"; the Duenna is, in her way, and as we shall see, "philosophical."

This shifting of the whole scale of values a little earthward is not Jean's personal peculiarity. The immense popularity of his work, which is hardly accounted for by his poetic talent alone, suggests that it found a responsive element in the culture. It has indeed much of the spirit which historians have found in thirteenth-century politics, art, religion, and philosophy, and which is widely considered to be a second major element in the cultural pattern of the epoch. It is a spirit that in all directions comes up against received authority, confronting the older, transcendental views with realistic, mundane ones.[33] We have already remarked the growth of bourgeois commercialism, and we can thus see increasing room for it as an established way of life alongside the feudal and manorial systems. A related development is the rise of secularism and nationalism in politics, which conflict with the "universalism" of the Papal power, and finally conquer it.[34] A new interest in the natural world (which is related to commercialism through the new medieval technology) did not necessarily conflict with the old supernaturalism. Nature, as in Jean's poem, is servant of God and manifests His boundless variety. Thus the emergence of the pious Franciscan naturalism, and the efflorescence of realism in the foliated capitals and columnar sculptures of an architecture that was still on a larger scale pushing transcendentally upward. The elaboration of religious ceremony and dogma surrounding the consecrated Host in the thirteenth century is evidence for the existence of a new sacramentalism, the essence of which is the seeing and handling of the body of God:

> Superficially the new piety might seem to be a development and ex-
> pansion of the traditional sacramentalism, and as such a buttressing
> of the older symbolic and mediate view of nature. But, as the more
> conservative Eastern Church suspected, this was a sacramentalism of
> a new flavor, suffused with a spirit alien to that of the first Christian
> millennium. It seemed almost that the Latin Church, in centering its
> devotion on the actual physical substance of its deity, had inadver-
> tently deified matter.[35]

The same spirit is evident in the iconography of the Last Supper, the Ascension, the Virgin and Child, and in the form of the crucifix, which show a new dramatic emotionalism in this period. This increasing valuation of direct experience has its philosophical parallel in the thought of Robert Grosseteste and Roger Bacon, who now lay the foundations for empiricism and experimental science. Closer to our subject, in the Paris of Jean de Meun's time Averroism was in the air. It is an Aristotelianism that alongside the orthodox version of Aquinas is naturalistic to the point of heresy; it sets philosophy above theology, reason above revelation, and envisions happiness in this life as the highest good.[36] Jean certainly breathes some of this, and he has been variously "explained" by scholars through it and through other traits of late thirteenth-century culture: he has been described as an academic Averroist, as a radical political thinker, as a spokesman for the bourgeoisie, as a rationalist, and as a scientist.[37] We need not subscribe to any one of these narrow and extreme formulations. We know too much about Jean's wide area of orthodoxy. Yet it is undeniably true that the limits of his view, or his poem's center of gravity, show the shift toward naturalism and materialism that we see in the movement of the culture.

In this textual and cultural context, even Jean's comic realism is less extreme, less purely jest, than it would have been a century before. If the views it supports are still comic and still reprehensible, they are nonetheless more tenable, and this may explain the large space he gives to them. This conversion of comic realism to the ends of more respectable art can be clearly seen if we look a century before Jean, and then beyond him to Chaucer. Perhaps few in Jean's audience would have embraced publicly and wholeheartedly his Duenna's unreserved glorification of sex for its own sake. Yet we may observe a certain progress in the relative sympathy and respectability of the idea over the course of two centuries. In the *Roman de Renart* it is a self-consciously scurrilous feature, propounded by the Fox and the Ass in unvarnished terms. Its vulgarity is all the stronger for its religious context. Renart "confesses" to the priest Hubert the kite his unabashed joy in pure sensuality. The mere recollection of a certain bodily part of his mistress thrills him:

> "Car por seul itant qu'il m'en membre   [VII, 433]
> M'en remuent trestuit li membre
> Et heriche tote la charz ..."

["For when I just think of it all my parts tremble and all my flesh prickles . . ."]

He voluptuously venerates its name, "the most noble in the world" (437). The reader will take no more seriously the "sermon" of the archpriest Bernart the ass in Branche XVII.[38] It is a defense of sexual intercourse as a way of life: this is what the organs were made for. He ends by asking the King to proclaim that those who abstain shall go to Hell. Both of these passages fit into the pattern of vagrant impudence traditionally associated with the "medieval mind." The first is from the grossest poem of the *Renart* cycle. Yet the same doctrine, down to the bawdy reminiscence, the physiological utilitarianism, and even the religious context, we find presented through Chaucer's Wife of Bath with power and sympathy as well as humor. It is not quite so impudent or so vagrant two centuries later. In this perspective the naturalism of the Duenna is transitional, emergently serious, marginally sympathetic. We find in her the same philosophy, the same tremble of satisfaction.[39] Jean is of course not basing his poem on a refurbishment of twelfth-century goliardery. But more than one feature of it shows how, in a cultural atmosphere newly hospitable to naturalism, even the old scurrility could resemble the new seriousness. We find Jean's Nature, at the end of her long confession, seriously promulgating an interdict against chastity and an eternal, plenary pardon for intercourse that are reminiscent of Bernart the ass's mock-sermon; and we have already noted the moral status that Renart's perverse veneration of impolite words has achieved in Jean's poem.[40]

The rhetorical theory of the use of such language also undergoes a revitalization in Jean's hands. Alain de Lille had piously repeated a good principle of diction, but more piously avoided the practice: "Sometimes, no doubt, . . . since speech should be related to the matters of which we speak, deformity of expression ought to be molded to ugliness of subject. But in the coming theme, in order that evil words may not offend the reader's hearing . . . I wish to give to these monstrous vices a cloak of well-sounding phrases."[41] This he does to overgenerous excess. Contrariwise, though Jean defends the "realistic" principle in an apology to the reader, he also practices it. He thus anticipates Chaucer's genial conviction, and probably supplied him the dictum, that

> Whoso shal telle a tale after a man,
> He moot reherce as ny as evere he kan
> Everich a word, if it be in his charge,
> Al speke he never so rudeliche and large,
> Or ellis he moot telle his tale untrewe,
> Or feyne thyng, or fynde wordes newe.
> He may not spare, althogh he were his brother;
> He moot as wel seye o word as another.
> Crist spak hymself ful brode in hooly writ,
> And wel ye woot no vileynye is it.
> Eek Plato seith, whoso that kan hym rede,
> The wordes moote be cosyn to the dede."

These two movements—from prurience in idea and prudery in diction to positions more realistic and humane—are borne partly on the cultural drift itself. Chaucer's Narrator, and his Wife of Bath, had a respectable but warmly sympathetic audience. The relevance of the cultural context to the nature of Jean's comic realism, then, is partly in the relationship of this realism to Chaucer's.

The form of Jean's realism is intimately bound up with its context, as the variety of the style in his poem is roughly coextensive with its variety of thought. Jean is capable of the whole range of vernacular style: ornate rhetorical word play, lyric and formal description, scholastic argument, popular scientific exposition, and dramatic realism. His heavenly park is handled with as much elevation as Guillaume's earthly one was. His satirical passages have as much bite as those of the most vigorous fabliaux. What attracts our attention most is his modeling of the latter to, or at least toward, the invention of the dramatic monologue.

I say "invention" to emphasize the speciality of his achievement, and not to lay claim for him to a dubious absolute priority. Actually, the conditions of recitation in the thirteenth century were hospitable to the emergence of dramatic or mimetic forms, and there are some technical developments of direct discourse in the bourgeois tradition that are comparable to Jean's. We have noted in the preceding section that the minor literature of the bourgeois tradition includes some mimes; they must be counted among the early formulations of the dramatic monologue. The best of them, Rutebeuf's *Herberie*, is based on the patter of a street hawker, in this case a charlatan and seller of herbs. The point of the piece is humorous exaggeration; it is clearly an artistic, not a commercial production. Its realism depends mainly on a special vocabulary, here the trade jargon of the *mire*, distorted for comic effect. A broken rhythm, punctuated with asides, helps keep us aware that the speaker is addressing an audience

"Or m'en creeiz:
Vos ne saveiz cui vos veeiz;
—Taisiez vos, et si vos seeiz—
Veiz m'erberie:
Je vos di, par sainte Marie,
Que ce n'est mie freperie,
Mais granz noblesce.

. . . .

A pou de painne
De toute fievre sanz quartainne
Gariz en mainz d'une semainne,
Ce n'est pas faute;
Et si gariz de goute flautre:
Ja tant n'en iert basse ne haute,
Toute l'abat.
Ce la vainne dou cul vos bat,
Ie vos en garrai sanz debat,
E de la dent
Gariz je trop apertement
Par .i. petitet d'oignement.
Que vos dirai?
Oeiz coument jou confirai,
Dou confire ne mentirai:
C'est cens riote.
Preneiz dou sayn de [la] marmote,
De la merde de la linote . . ."[143]

["Now believe me: you don't know who I am, so be quiet and hang on to your seats, and see my layout of herbs. As the Blessed Virgin Mary herself is my witness, I'm telling you these herbs aren't trash; they're something downright noble. . . . Except for quartan, I can cure any fever in less than a week, and that's no lie. And my herb cures ulcerous gout; no matter how low or how high those ulcers are, it breaks them down, and I do mean down. If your rump vein gets to throbbing, I'll cure that little item too, and no argument. And I'll absolutely cure you of tooth trouble, with a little bit of this ointment I've got right here. How am I supposed to keep talking? Well, listen to how I'll explain; and in telling all, I'll spin you no lies. And I'm saying again there's no argument. Take some marmot grease and linnet dung . . ."]

The fabliau is usually too short-winded to sustain dramatic monologue. But a notable exception is the Picard poem *La Veuve*," a satiric sketch rather than a tale, which finely, if sourly, describes the widow's progress through mourning, recovery, man hunting, and uneasy remarriage. In it there is a substantial monologue of the widow, addressed to a gossip and designed to set circulating the tale of her wealth and situation. It is full of prattle, opinion and confidence, inquiry and pious exclamation, with a kind of incoherence that we must attribute to the lady's mentality, not the poet's:

> "Il avoit molt le cuer onestre,   [256]
> Mais il n'avoit point del delit
> Que li prodome font el lit.
> Tantost con il estoit colciés,
> M'ert ses cus en l'escorç ficiés;
> Ensi dormoit tote la nuit,
> Si n'en avoie autre deduit;
> Si me pooit molt anoier.
> Certes jo nel quier a noier,
> Mes sire ert molt d'avoir sopris
> Ançois que je l'eüsce pris,
> Mais il ert ja trestos kenus,
> Ançois qu'il fust a moi venus,
> Et j'estoie une bascelete
> A une crasse mascelete,
> Et vos estiés uns enfeçons
> Autretele con uns pinçons,
> S'aliés corant aprés vo mere
> Qui a ma dame estoit commere
>
> . . .
>
> Or vos dirai de mon segnor: [278]
> Il savoit molt bien gaegnier
> et asanler et espargnier.

Sen arme soit en grant repos!
J'ai assés caudieres et pos
Et blanques quieltes et bons lis,
Huges, sieges et caelis,

. . .

Mais ne n'ai cure d'anoncier   [296]
Se j'ai ce que Dex m'a donet.
Vos consciés bien Deudonet,
Et si consciés bien Herbert
Et Bauduïn le fil Gobert.
Savees rien de lor afaire?
On m'i velt mariage faire;
Mais c'est mervelle de le gent:
On cuide en tel liu de l'argent
U il n'a gaires de plentet.
Li plusor sont molt endetet,
Et je sui rique feme a force."

["My husband was very good-hearted, but he just didn't take the pleasure that noble men have in bed: as soon as he lay down, his rump was stuck in my lap. There he slept the whole night, and I had no other entertainment. It used to make me very angry. I'm certainly not trying to deny it, my husband was loaded with wealth before I took him, but he was all gray before he came to me, and I was a young girl, with a plump little cheek, and you were a child, just a little nipper; you used to go running after your mother, who was a dear friend of my mother . . . Now I'll tell you about my husband: he was a great one for earning and saving. May his soul rest in peace! I have plenty of kettles and pots, and white mattresses and good beds, chests, chairs and bedsteads . . . But I don't want to broadcast if I have what God has given me. You know Deudonet well, and also Herbert, and Bauduin, Gobert's son. Do you know how they are doing? Folks want me to marry around there; but it's strange about people; you think there is money where there's hardly much; most people are in debt, and I am a rich woman in spite of myself."]

Many touches in the piece suggest a relationship to the monologues of the Wife of Bath and Jean de Meun's Duenna. But the relationship is one of subject and texture, and does not extend to the broader reaches of meaning. In this the

82

monologues of Jean and Chaucer stand a step beyond the fabliau tradition, in a position which reveals a special usefulness of the form.

The Duenna's monologue is long, and self-consciously opinionated. It is, within limits that we shall have to gauge later, naturalistic in style. It purveys a commercial and realistic theory of love and defends animal sensuality. Behind this doctrine and this defense is personal autobiography. Not only is the Duenna an example of her own doctrines; her history gives them motivation. There is in this situation a combined complexity of form and richness of material that is foreign to any of Jean's models.

Of the material itself little need be said. Jean ransacked Ovid and the satirical tradition for the mundane and domestic images that make up the Duenna's world. She discourses at length on dress, make-up, feminine hygiene, table manners, and sex techniques, with all the detail that these subjects comprehend. Her manner of expression is colored by commercial and domestic tropes. A woman has "goods" (*bien*), that she sells "at auction" (*par enchierement*). Her synonym for the flame of love is a "hot bath" (*estuve*). The necessity for providing for oneself brings to her mind a proverb about a mouse. Her former popularity is described through the number of times her door was smashed. Her references to sexual activity are on the same level.⁵

Enveloping this Ovidian, satirical doctrine is a self-consciousness and a history. The Duenna is one of the first doctors of the bourgeois tradition:

> "N'onc ne fui d'Amours a escole   [12802]
> Ou l'en leüst la theorique,
> Mais je sai tout par la pratique:
> Esperiment m'en ont fait sage,
> Que j'ai hantez tout mon aage."

["I never went to the school of Love where they taught theory; all I know is through practice: the experiences I've had all my life have made me wise."]

Her history is revealed in snatches. We glimpse a period of happy and prosperous whoredom, a decline and flight from her old haunts, and her present, respectable employment as a companion and guardian. It never comes to much as a story, but Jean clearly uses it as a matrix for the doctrine that the Duenna propounds. At one point he overtly suggests motivation:

> "A qui m'en puis je plaindre, a qui,   [12876]
> Fors a vous, fiz, que j'ai tant chier?
> Ne m'en puis autrement venchier

Que par aprendre ma doctrine.
Pour ce, beaus fiz, vous endoctrine
Que, quant endoctrinez sereiz,
Des·ribaudeaus me venchereiz ..."

["Who can I complain to, who but to you, cherished son? I cannot get revenge except by teaching my doctrine. So, sweet son, I am instructing you so that when you have learned my doctrine you will avenge me on the lechers . . ."]

This kind of passage, this apparent straining for verisimilitude, is unusual for either doctrinal or satiric literature in the Middle Ages. Jean handles it stiffly. Yet, as a symptom of what the poet is up to here, it is of first importance. Its gratuitousness is of a piece with the much more successful interweaving of the advice in the monologue with personal outcry. The old woman reminds Bel Acueil of the transiency of youth and beauty and of the universal duplicity of men. And she herself sighs with regret at a faded career of passion. She becomes vindictive when she thinks of the rascals who scorned her when her beauty was gone. "Were I young as you," she says to Bel Acueil,

"Savez en quel point jes meïsse?   [12909]
Tant les plumasse e tant preïsse
Dou leur de tort e de travers
Que mangier les feïsse a vers
E gesir touz nuz es fumiers,
Meïsmement ceus les prumiers
Qui de plus leial cueur m'amassent . . ."

["Do you know what I would do to them? By hook or by crook I'd pluck them and take so much that I'd make them eat worms and lie naked in the dung heaps, and very first of all the ones who loved me most . . ."]

But there is something in the monologue even beyond this dramatization of the character's motives for lecturing. There is a gratuitously given complication, an irony and a pathos in her history that more clearly exceed the demands of simple satire or simple doctrinal exposition:

"Mauvais iert, onques ne vi pire,   [14485]
Onc ne me cessa de despire;
Putain comune me clamait
Li ribauz, qui point ne m'amait.

Fame a trop povre juigement,
E je fui fame dreitement.
Onc n'amai ome qui m'amast,
Mais, se cil ribauz m'entamast
L'espaule, ou ma teste eüst casse,
Sachiez que je l'en merciasse."

["He was bad—I never saw worse—and he never stopped despising
me. He called me a common whore, the whoremonger, and never
loved me. Women have very little sense, and I was every bit a
woman. I never loved a man who loved me, but if this lecher had cut
my shoulder or smashed my head, believe me, I would have thanked
him for it."]

These circumstances are by now mournfully familiar in narrative and song, but
their inclusion in the Duenna's monologue is striking. It shows the poet turning
his realism toward a new path, catching into the web of the discourse elements
dictated less by traditional satire than by a sense of the round, complex existence
of the speaker herself. The most resonant lines of her whole speech come in a
transitory awakening of her old, fleshly vigor:

"Par Deu! si me plaist il encores   [12932]
Quant je m'i sui bien pourpensee;
Mout me delite en ma pensee
E me resbaudissent li membre
Quant de mon bon tens me remembre
E de la joliete vie
Don mes cueurs a si grant envie;
Tout me rejovenist le cors
Quant j'i pens e quant jou recors;
Touz les biens dou monde me fait
Quant me souvient de tout le fait,
Qu'au meins ai je ma joie eüe,
Combien qu'il m'aient deceüe."

Here is Chaucer's version:

But, Lord Crist! whan that it remembreth me   [WBProl 469]
Upon my yowthe, and on my jolitee,
It tikleth me about myn herte roote.
Unto this day it dooth myn herte boote
That I have had my world as in my tyme.

85

Another facet of her nature, her dominant appetite for sex, is revealed at some length, and with it we see further that her strengths and weaknesses, impulses and responses, including her doctrines, are part of a single fabric. As her vindictive, commercial theory of love grows partly out of her history of disappointment, so her theoretic championship of animal nature is entwined with her personal recollection of animal pleasure. This phase of her lecture arises in a way typical of Jean's digressive structure: it grows out of the story of Venus and Mars, which is itself suggested by the Duenna's mention of Vulcan, who in turn has been cited as a type of jealous person, a subject arising from her instructions to Bel Acueil on the technique of pretended jealousy. The sexual promiscuity of Venus leads the Duenna to a defense of all promiscuity, based on the laws of nature:

> "Car Nature n'est pas si sote [13879]
> Qu'ele face naistre Marote
> Tant seulement pour Robichon,
> Se l'entendement i fichon,
> Ne Robichon pour Mariete,
> Ne pour Agnès, ne pour Perrete,
> Ainz nous a faiz, beaus fiz, n'en doutes,
> Toutes pour touz e touz pour toutes . . ."

["For Nature is not so foolish that she has Marote born only for Robichon—if we really look into the meaning—nor Robichon for Mariete, nor for Agnes, nor for Perrete; but don't doubt it, fair son, she has made us all for all, women for men and men for women . . ."]

Marriage by law is designed to prevent dissension and bloodshed, and to help in the raising of children. But it takes away a woman's natural freedom, and the rest of her life is spent in attempts to regain it. Nature's power is illustrated by many examples. The caged bird, however well kept and fed, never stops trying to escape. The cat which has never seen a mouse or rat must be restrained when one appears, or there will be mousing. It is the same with a colt and a mare, any mare, and with cattle and sheep,

> "Car de ceus mie ne douton [14082]
> Qu'il ne vueillent leur fames toutes;
> Ne ja de ce, beaus fiz, ne doutes
> Que toutes ausinc touz ne vueillent:
> Toutes volentiers les acueillent.
> Ausinc est il, beaus fiz, par m'ame!

De tout ome et de toute fame,
Quant a naturel apetit,
Don lei les retrait un petit."

["For with these we never doubt that they want all females for their
wives; and for that matter, sweet son, don't doubt that all the females
likewise want all the males: all of them would gladly have them.
And by my soul, sweet son, so it is with each man and each woman
as for natural desire, from which law restrains them a little."]

The fundamental kinship of this doctrine with the created personality of the
speaker is fully demonstrated when the Duenna, in the vein of joyful, boisterous
reminiscence that we have seen before, cites her own experience as an example
of the principle of promiscuity:

"Je le sai bien par mei meïsmes,   [14104]
Car je me sui toujourz penee
D'estre de touz omes amee;
. . .

Ces vallez, qui tant me plaisaient,   [14113]
Quant ces douz regarz me faisaient,
(Douz deus! quel pitié m'en prenait
Quant cil regarz a mei venait!)
Touz ou pluseurs les receüsse,
S'il leur pleüst e je peüsse;
Touz les vousisse tire a tire,
Se je peüsse a touz soufire;
E me semblait que, s'il peüssent,
Volentiers tuit me receüssent,
(Je n'en met hors prelaz ne moines,
Chevaliers, bourgeis ne chanoines,
Ne clerc ne lai, ne fol ne sage,
Pour qu'il fust de poissant aage,) . . ."

["I know it well through my own nature, for I always tried to be loved
by all the men; . . . When those young men I liked so much made
those sweet looks at me (Sweet lord! What pity I felt when one of
those looks came my way!) I would have taken them, all or some, if
they had wanted to and if I could; all would I have wanted, one after
the other, if I had been enough for all; and it seemed that if they had

87

been able, all would have gladly had me (and I don't leave out prelates or monks, knights, burghers or canons, nor clerk nor layman, nor fool nor wise man, providing he was of an age to be capable) . . ."]

Jean gives diatribe and sermon a lifelike shape in two other speeches, the Jealous Husband's and Faus-Semblant's.⁴⁸ Like the Duenna's, the Husband's speech is compounded from satirical, antifeminist authorities; and it is similarly dramatized through a concentration of image and diction, and through elaboration of the speaker's personality and situation. He is represented as a middle-class businessman addressing his wife, and his descriptions of their domestic life—her plainness at home and extravagance abroad, her insolent friends, her scheming mother—are done with acutely realistic detail. The speaker himself is given depth and shape, with a sense of self-pity and a talent for bitter mockery. His changes of tone contribute much to the naturalism of his speech. Here sarcasm alternates with self-pity:

"E quant vois a Rome ou en Frise   [8475]
Porter nostre marcheandise,
Vous devenez tantost si cointe,
Car je sai bien qui m'en acointe,
Que par tout en vait la parole;
E quant aucuns vous aparole
Pour quei si cointe vous tenez
En touz les leus ou vous venez,
Vous responez: 'Hari, hari,
C'est pour l'amour de mon mari.'
Pour mei, las, doulereus, chaitis!
Qui set se je forge ou je tis,
Ou se je sui ou morz ou vis?
L'en me devrait flatir ou vis
Une vessie de mouton.
Certes, je ne vail un bouton,
Quant autrement ne vous chasti.
Mout m'avez or grant los basti,
Quant de tel chose vous vantez.
Chascuns set bien que vous mentez.
Pour mei, las, doulereus! pour mei!
Maus ganz de mes mains enfourmai,
E crueusement me deçui

88

Quant onques vostre fei reçui
Le jour de nostre mariage.
Pour mei menez tel rigolage!
Pour mei menez vous tel bobant!
Cui cuidiez vous aler lobant?"

["And when I go to take our goods to Rome or Friesland, you immediately become so stylish—I know how to find out—that every-
body talks about it; and when anyone asks you why you appear so
elegant wherever you go, you answer: 'Oh! that's for the love of my
husband.' For poor, miserable, wretched me! Who knows if I ham-
mer or weave, or if I'm dead or alive? You might just as well hit me
in the face with a bladder. Why, I'm not worth a button if I don't
change your ways. You've built me a fine reputation boasting of such
a thing. Everyone knows that you're lying. For me, poor, miserable
me! A tight pair of gloves I made for these hands, cruelly I fooled
myself, to believe your vows on our wedding day. For me you lead
such a gay life! For me you live in such style! Who did you think you
were going to fool?"]

The reader will note in his speech the recurrent use of figures and images which,
whether they are traditional or not, give his mentality a materialistic coloration:

"A cui parez vous ces chastaignes?"   [8509]

"D'autre part, nou puis plus celer,   [8527]
Entre vous e ce bacheler,
Robichonet au vert chapel,
Qui si tost vient a vostre apel,
Avez vous terres a partir?"

["For whom are you peeling these chestnuts?" "Furthermore—I can't
hide it any more—you and this young fellow, this Robichonet with
the green chaplet, who comes so fast when you call, do you two have
property to divide?"]

The colloquial rhythm and diction, with the abundant interplay between description of his wife and direct or indirect description of himself, make dramatic
monologue of the traditional satirical tirade. The difficulty of Woman is seen
here from no abstract point of view, but through the saddened eyes of a hard-
working merchant with a strong sense of profit and loss:

"Mais, pour le fill sainte Marie,   [8843]
Que me vaut cete cointerie,
Cete robe cousteuse e chiere,
. . .

Que me fait ele de profit?   [8851]

Car, quant me vueil a vous deduire,   [8854]
Je la treuve si encombreuse,
Si grevaine e si enuieuse
Que je n'en puis a chief venir;
Ne vous i puis a dreit tenir,
Tant me faites e tourz e ganches
De braz, de trumeaus e de hanches . . .

Neïs au seir, quant je me couche, . . .   [8865]

La vous couvient il despoillier.   [8868]
. . .

Les robes e les pennes grises   [8873]
Sont lores a la perche mises,
Toute la nuit pendanz a l'air.
Que me peut lors tout ce valeir, . . .

Car, puis que par jour si me nuisent,   [8881]
E par nuit point ne me deduisent,
Quel profit i puis autre atendre
Fors que d'engagier ou de vendre?"

["Now, for the son of Saint Mary, what good to me is that finery,
that costly, expensive robe, . . . what profit does it get me? For when
I want to make a little love, I find it so awkward, so difficult, such a
nuisance—that I can't get anywhere; I can't even get a decent hold
of you, you do so much twisting and dodging, of arms, of legs, of
hips . . . And even at night, when I go to bed . . . you have to take
it all off. . . . Then the robes and the gray feathers are put on the
hanger, all night hanging in the air. Now what good can all this
be, . . . when they torment me so all day, and at night they give me
no pleasure, what profit can I expect here except by selling or pawn-
ing them?"]

Turning to the monologue of Faus-Semblant, we must divide our attention
between its realism, which is perhaps less marked than in the other two, and a

counterrealistic element. All three speeches, but particularly the last, show open breaks of dramatic consistency in the interest of learned, doctrinal exposition. The Duenna's excursion into philosophy does not jibe well with her professed disregard for *theorique* of any kind. A knowledge of Plato and Horace, and of classical mythology, which turns up here and there in her discourse, does not seem to fit with her social status and background.⁴⁷ The Jealous Husband has a surprising arsenal of books to draw on; to weight his personal outcries he invokes authorities and their exempla.⁴⁸ Faus-Semblant's inconsistency is of a somewhat different kind, and much more serious.

Faus-Semblant and his companion Contrainte Astenance appear in the poem as if spontaneously, after the Lover on Ami's advice practices abstinence from his pursuit and pretends to the world that he no longer seeks the Lady's favor.⁴⁹ For the Lover's "false-seeming" and "constrained abstinence" to be thus allegorically represented is consonant with the theme and machinery of the poem. But the possibilities of wider application proved irresistible to Jean. Soon he converts Faus-Semblant into a personification of hypocrisy in general, getting him up in religious costume and using him as a vehicle for partisan attack on friars. The context of the attack is the controversy between the friars and the Arts faculty of the University of Paris in the 1250's and 60's. Much of the speech of Faus-Semblant is digressive from the overt subject of the poem, though in supplying ammunition for an attack on asceticism and celibacy it harmonizes with Genius' doctrine of procreation.⁵⁰

His speech has the character of a self-revelation. Chaucer used it as a basis for his Pardoner's monologue. It has something of the latter's dramatic flavor. Faus-Semblant is asked to reveal his practices so that his companions will know how to recognize him. The outspokenness of the character, signalized by the dramatic, autobiographical element in his performance, contributes powerfully to the satire. He is, as Chaucer was to see, not only wicked, but cynically, barefacedly so:

> "J'ameraie meauz l'acointance   [11241]
> Cent mile tanz dou rei de France
> Que d'un povre, par nostre dame!
> Tout eüst il ausinc bone ame.
> Quant je vei touz nuz ces truanz
> Trembler sus ces fumiers puanz
> De freit, de fain crier e braire,
> Ne m'entremet de leur afaire.
> S'il sont a l'Ostel Deu porté,
> Ja n'ierent par mei conforté,

Car d'une aumosne toute seule
Ne me paistraient il la gueule,
Qu'il n'ont pas vaillant une seche:
Que donra qui son coutel leche?"

"I love bettir th'acqueyntaunce, [*Romaunt* 6491]
Ten tymes, of the kyng of Fraunce
Than of a pore man of mylde mod,
Though that his soule be also god.
For whanne I see beggers quakyng,
Naked on myxnes al stynkyng,
For hungre crie, and eke for care,
I entremete not of her fare.
They ben so pore and ful of pyne,
They myght not oonys yeve me dyne,
For they have nothing but her lyf.
What shulde he yeve that likketh his knyf?"

In the same vein of frankness the most prominent excesses of the friars are described: their competition with the priests for rich parishioners, their coöperative slander of opponents, their false testimonials, their love for cosmopolitan life while pretending abstinence from it, their blackmailing of sinners and their easy, corrupt confessions. But the pressure to make his point repeatedly overtakes the poet in mid-course, and then his otherwise characterized speaker takes on the voice of Jean de Meun or of Righteousness. Jean either forgets from time to time, or doesn't care, that the promulgation of truth is not the direct concern of the hypocrite, but only an accident of his self-revelation. When Faus-Semblant turns from an indirect warning to a direct one, he is no longer False-Seeming. Thus at verse 11091 his self-revelation abruptly becomes a sermon. A little further on (11135) he addresses the Church in the tones of a prophet. At another point he lectures against begging, he a mendicant.[51] Chaucer, in creating his Pardoner, did not withdraw from this simple inconsistency. He accepted it and made it dramatically operative by drawing it into a secure and complex characterization. In him it becomes a source of pathos. Far short of such envelopment in characterization, the shifts of attitude in Jean's creation represent an abandonment of the literary approach—incomplete dramatization.

There is enough direct didacticism—incomplete dramatization—in medieval narrative to make it a kind of convention. The aesthetic question does not arise, of course, in the multitude of works in which the dramatic setting is a mere scaffold and the doctrine is the substance of the work. Philosophy was widely thought to be more pleasing in dialogue form than in direct exposition.[52] Thus Chaucer's *Melibee*. But the critic has a problem when the work itself proclaims its dramatic nature and seems to depend on dramatic illusion for its effect. Since passages of didacticism, learning, are a major component of Chaucer's poetry, we cannot afford to overlook the issue here. How is the modern reader to take them?

I cannot myself be content with the purely historical view that medieval poetry, following Horace's precept, was intended both to amuse and instruct, and that here we simply have instruction interrupting amusement. It seems to me that we can make a valuable distinction among medieval practices in this regard without condemning most medieval poetry for an incredible obtuseness, and yet without giving license to every kind of digression as "convention." We can, indeed, make a distinction between the examples given by Jean de Meun that will be confirmed by Chaucer's practice.

We have observed that the "philosophy" of the Duenna is of a piece with her nature; it is an extension, in the direction of learned exempla, of what we see symbolized in her person and illustrated by her career. The same relationship to the characterization is to be seen in the "learning" of the Jealous Husband, who cites "Theophrastus," Boethius, Livy, Walter Map's *Valerius*, Virgil, Solinus, and, uneasily, the Abélard-Héloïse correspondence, in amplification of his proper opinions. In both, the character is the vehicle, now discursively, now symbolically, for related meanings. In Faus-Semblant, however, the symbolism of the character is contradicted by much of his discourse. Doctrine is dramatically appropriate from the mouth of a Friar, but here the doctrine, by reversing the speaker's position, seriously weakens the whole dramatic illusion on which a good part of the speech's effect depends.

It is clear that in all three—the Duenna, the Jealous Husband, and Faus-Semblant—the poet is primarily interested in his point, his *sentence*. It would in any case be surprising, in an age in which dramatic realism had not yet become an end in itself, and in which the techniques of masking doctrine under it were thus comparatively undeveloped, to find him straining at all points for verisimilitude. This would not, to his mind, have been economical. He is not likely, either, to have had our acutely conscious sense of the difference between the discursive and the mimetic approaches to meaning. The fiction, in a good deal of medieval theorizing, was held to be a shiny coating over the kernel of truth,[53] and Jean may have felt, in the heat of his antimendicant fervour, that the revelation of hypocrisy *through* the characterization of Faus-Semblant and the affirmation of truth *despite* the characterization came to much the same thing, without considering their relationship. But if characterization is to count at all, we must conclude that the inconsistency in the handling of the Duenna and the Jealous Husband is much less damaging than that in the other monologue. The former disturbs our sense of stylistic decorum; but if it dilutes and flattens, generalizes the meaning of the character, at least it broadens it. The latter, however, so far as we feel a characterization to have been established in the first place, by sharply reversing the current of meaning itself, outrages our sense of logic.[64] Chaucer, as we shall see, often follows the first procedure, ignoring dramatic consistency in a whole class of situations in which philosophical expansion is called for. But he rarely, if ever, reverses the meaning of a character without grounding the inconsistency in the characterization itself.

The relationship between realism and meaning in Jean is not an easy one for modern readers to apprehend. We have seen just above, at the expense of exposing some of Jean's weaknesses, that meaning at any level is primary to him; style is secondary. Yet it is also apparent that in certain situations his feeling for realism as an implement of meaning is very strong. The inconsistencies in characterization that we have just discussed are not half so remarkable as the extent to which the characterizations are in fact realized. This is the more clear in that the poem itself is so big, varied and so little elsewhere committed to representation, even in allegorical form. The doctrinal element perhaps too apparent in these monologues shows that the poet conceives of his characters as having a broad and exemplary significance. This is medieval enough; if it almost excludes *la veuve* and Rutebeuf's *mire,* it includes Albertano's and Chaucer's Prudence, and many another colorless vehicle for wisdom in medieval narrative. But Jean also feels that a particular form is needed to support this significance. What is special about him is that he attempts a realistic portrayal of the speakers at the same time. For direct description of them he does not even use as much as the fabliaux could have taught him. We see the merest touch of the Duenna's costume; we see her scurrying to find Bel Acueil, and laughing and swearing, and that is all.[65] Faus-Semblant is dressed like a Friar. The Jealous Husband, who is himself only an exemplum in the mouth of Ami, could perhaps not have been handily described, though we see him beating his wife after his speech is over. But the main business of the poem is talk; and for their talk Jean uses, in the first place, all the technical resources that the traditions of fabliau and satire could offer. Further, he achieves a specialization of form—the dramatic monologue—beyond the inertia of satiric tradition, and far beyond the demands of traditional doctrinal exposition.

94

The nature of Jean's innovations in dramatic monologue has never been considered very closely. His influence—partly through Chaucer—has been so great that we tend to take the form for granted. But its history has not been written. It has been loosely related to the formal tradition of the confession, and to the *chanson de mal mariée*.[56] Its generation is not quite heralded by either. Nor is the character which emerges from the monologue of the Duenna quite accounted for by Ovid's Dipsas (*Amores*, I, viii) nor by the medieval tradition of *la vieille qui enseigne*, of which the Duenna becomes the most influential example.[57] Something happens to the traditional material in his hands that gives it new shape and new meaning. Ovid's overheard snatch of talk is vastly elaborated. And the old bawds and intermeddlers who drift as needed into and out of medieval stories, though they are drawn upon for this feature and that, have none of them the depth that the Duenna has. In the final analysis it is this, the organization of traits in a lifelike relationship, the keying of past career and present opinion, status and attitude and style of speech into a consistent and natural whole, that Jean begins to achieve with dramatic monologue.[58] He does this out of no general, *a priori* impulse toward increased realism, as his breaches of realism alone would show. His realism is not based on the relentless consistency of style that we have learned to prize, but on the measure of dramatic perspective, which, sufficiently elaborated, will govern our reception of his speaker. His absolute achievement, judged by the standards of another seven centuries of technical practice, is not of the highest, but it is there.

I feel that there is a special pressure on Jean toward this achievement—one that was not present to Ovid, nor to the poets of romance and fabliau. It is suggested by the special context of these dramatic monologues, and by what is to be said with them. And his response is a sensitive one; its nature is suggested by what we have already seen in the best poets of the French tradition, that in them style is an instrument of meaning. In the naturalistic context of his poem and his culture the materialist and sensual attitudes are in a position of new prominence. They have a new substantiality. To support these attitudes formally, to give them adequate expression, Jean invents or feels his way toward a new specialization of realistic style. His dramatized, colloquialized, autobiographical monologue reflects the new self-consciousness, the newly humane and sympathetic elements that can now be sensed in the proponence of natural morality and material good. It is indeed a brilliant stylistic invention, for the form is itself a piece of that tangible, sensory, mundane life whose values it expresses and recommends.

Jean's significance for us is manifold. He is a direct, textual source for

Chaucer; and he influences the form of Chaucer's poetry in very specific places. Thus Jean's conversion of a stock character into a lively doctrinaire lies behind the Wife of Bath's flat-footed delivery of feminist and materialist principles. That Chaucer's character is not even presented to her fellows within a tale, but face to face, that she delivers her speech in full voice and being, that the poet palpably insists on her concreteness and personality—writing for her by far the longest prologue in the *Canterbury Tales,*—we may partly attribute to Jean de Meun's handling of the Duenna. A similar relationship exists between Jean's Faus-Semblant and Chaucer's Pardoner.

Yet for us a second point is more significant, and would have been so had Chaucer never borrowed a line from Jean. The French poet for the first time clearly outlines the configuration of styles that Chaucer was to find most congenial. The matter is partly one of community of genius and temperament, and partly one of history. This configuration—the juxtaposition of realism and courtly convention in a meaningful relationship to each other—implies a broadness of spirit characteristic of both poets. Yet we have seen it in the making in the emergent realism of some earlier romancers. By Jean's time the realistic spirit has become emphatic enough in French culture to be formalized on a serious basis. Individual bourgeois for centuries afterward were to pretend that they were aristocrats, but in Jean's poem realism loses its inferiority complex and·becomes a position to be reckoned with alongside courtly idealism. From his time this configuration, in various versions, becomes a leading trait of European literary style. It runs beyond Chaucer, with its ironic attitudinal implications, to a last great formulation two centuries later in *Don Quixote.*

This point implies yet another, more general one. Jean shows as well as any of the poets we have discussed that the relationship between style and meaning in the French tradition is a functional one. We can see this despite the impreciseness of the terms we must use, despite the variety and complexity of the literature, and without attempting to impose a false, formulary neatness on what is far from neatly presented by history. We can see that the courtly style was brought together in the interest of a particularly idealistic realm of feeling, and that the style of the fabliaux serves a different feeling and a different conception of experience. Jean belongs temperamentally to neither bourgeois nor courtly circles, but is rather a scholarly poet outside of either and able to move within both. He thus demonstrates most clearly the ultimate freedom of these styles from the limitation of social or generic tradition. They are called up or dropped at the behest of meaning. In his poem fabliau realism is enlisted and then elaborated in the interest of serious poetry, and it has thus concerned us at length. But to the extent that his broadness of view and irony of spirit utilizes both styles—and the poem of Guillaume de Lorris is a part of Jean's—he begins to demonstrate the breadth and variety of meaning that sensitive management of both can support. This functionalism of style, which is, after all, a major concern in all art criticism, will be the main theme of our discussion of Chaucer.

IV

chaucer's early poems

THE *Book of the Duchess,* the *House of Fame* and the *Parliament of Fowls,*
Chaucer's earliest important poems, are generally believed to have been written
in that order.[1] Traditional criticism has made much of the progressive technical
accomplishment and the widening sphere of interest, nourished by reading and
observation, that they display. We may safely accept these and focus our attention on a third factor, the development of Chaucer's feeling for the adjustment
between style and meaning. In this light the first poem is in a class by itself. It is
the least accomplished technically and the narrowest in scope, but it is in a
sense the most finished. It is the most homogeneous in style and the clearest in
meaning. Perhaps only hindsight enables us to see in it already the beginning of
that flamboyance of style which erupts in the *House of Fame* and is just brought
under control in the *Parliament.* Seen thus, the early poems show no smooth
progression, but rather ambitious experiment and even artistic failure, before the
control felt in the *Parliament* is brought to the mastery of the *Troilus and
Criseyde.*

[1] For notes to chapter iv see pages 260–261.

The two great ponderables of this experimental stage are the two styles of the French tradition, fertilized by reading in Latin and Italian and by writing in English, but still retaining their distinct, contrasting characters of a conventional style and a naturalistic one. The experiments are in the harnessing of the two, not in the "revolt" from or submergence of the former. The *Book of the Duchess* has been shown to be a combination of borrowings from six or seven French courtly works of the fourteenth century.[2] It signalizes well enough Chaucer's initial dependence on the courtly tradition. Unfortunately, however, it tends to focus the attention on transient models of style, and to mask his deeper, perennial relationship to this tradition; for while Chaucer soon gives up the wholesale borrowing of themes and passages from Guillaume de Machaut and his followers, he does not give up the tradition of conventionalism that he, like them, inherits from the twelfth and thirteenth centuries. Even in this earliest poem we can see him reaching back, beyond the allegorical prettiness of his immediate models, to a feeling for the original potency of the style.

Machaut and his school write in the style of Guillaume de Lorris. But they lose, or perhaps never seek, that technique of organizing the allegory around a consecutive psychic experience which gives the *Roman de la Rose* so much of its authority. Nor do they characteristically present a narrative that compares with older romance in its representation of a consequential, if imaginative, action. Machaut inherits and brings to easy fluency the whole idiom and machinery of love allegory—the dream, the lovely setting, the richly described personifications, and the refined diction,—using them to debate a question of love, to pay a compliment to a duke or king or lady, to provide a vehicle for a collection of lyrics or a tale or two taken from Ovid. This general diminution of theme leaves him with a style too rich to be functional. The poetry thus too often converts device to ornament, making of its materials something trivial and banal. This result is aggravated, if anything, by the poet's self-conscious virtuosity of technique.

But critics, particularly Chaucerians, are wrong when they deduce from the artificiality of Machaut either the poet's constitutional blindness to "life" or the style's inherent incapacity to support meaning.[3] The defect is neither of these. In fact, there is a strain of topicality, of contemporary realism, in Machaut. The *Remede de Fortune* has a notably detailed description of a day in a fourteenth-century château, down to the servants brushing the dirt from their masters' clothes. Contemporary persons appear in the poems: Jean de Luxembourg, Charles the Bad, Jean, Duke of Berry, and most prominently, Guillaume de Machaut himself, poet and intimate (as he was) of these dukes and kings. The poems are generally sprinkled with touches of a shrewd and mundane sort.[4]

Critics have a habit of picking out these touches in Machaut, like raisins from pastry, and attributing to them much of his virtue. Machaut's editor is at some pains to describe this realism as a means of giving to the allegorical fiction an air of verity.[5] Actually it does the reverse. In making himself the narrator of his vision poems, Machaut no doubt obtained some audience interest, and his sophisticated observations of the world around him have their own value. But he loses in this representation of a familiar, knowing self that fine air of receptivity to the wonders of the dream world that Guillaume de Lorris had created with his boyish narrator. When the latter mentions a silver needle, or a basin, little candles, or a ladder for climbing an imaginary wall, it is as if he knew no difference between sensory and imaginative experience. Machaut brings in the familiar, even his own foibles, with a knowing smile—as if to show that he does know the difference. The earlier poet creates in us an astonished belief; the later, with his wink and his knowledge, his little *aperçus,* creates knowing make-believe. The "artificiality" of this poetry, then, is of the poet's, not the style's, making. It depends, indeed, partly on his peculiar linkage of convention and realism.

Nothing could better make this plain than Machaut's *Jugement dou Roy de Navarre,* a love debate and compliment to that noble. It opens with a long diatribe on the times, followed by a graphic description of the Black Death of 1349. Machaut describes the terrible rampage of Death over the world, the corruption of the very air that spread the infection. He seals himself in his house, in terror, and is only called to the window, when the danger has passed, by the celebrant survivors' music. He then emerges, goes riding in the fields, and into the visionary, courtly debate that is the body of the poem.[6]

From the same plague had fled a year earlier the band of ladies and youths who tell the stories of the *Decameron.* In both works the somber introduction serves something of a frank escapism. The terror and the survival of it are equal notabilities, and we can impute to Machaut's design what Boccaccio professes, that the plague scenery will set off the beauty of the palaces and pleasances to come. Yet in Boccaccio there is no ultimate escapism. The successive gardens, the happy choiceness of the members of the *brigata,* serve to fix his point of view with the cultured, the leisured, and the sensitive, and to claim a basis of unchallengeable refinement for his philosophy of sex and nature.[7] From this point of vantage we turn in the tales to a whole world of shrewd, often malicious, observation. Then the *brigata,* for reasons impishly adduced, returns to plague-ridden Florence. In Boccaccio there is thus a certain deep and subtle play with the values of his diverse materials. Machaut lacks this depth. One searches in vain the body and ending of his poem for some hint of a relationship to its beginning. Apart from the elementarily simple contrast, they are merely both there: the plague and the courtly diversion. In juxtaposition the one is horribly, historically real; it makes of the other, with its pretty Lady, and twelve allegorical maidens and (historically real) King of Navarre, a flimsy confection.

The burgeoning vein of realism in Chaucer's early poems, then, is not so much a revolt from the sphere of Machaut as a divergent response to a common endowment of convention and experience—common, too, to Deschamps and Boccaccio and to the whole secular literature of the late Middle Ages. The problematical ambivalence of this endowment is that first fully articulated by Jean de Meun. It is recorded by each of these later writers in his own way. Boccaccio makes the easiest and most graceful compromise, giving up neither phenomenon nor dream, raising the one to polite literature, lowering the other to the edge of profaneness. His is a homogeneous, middle style. The vast, various production of Deschamps reflects the capacity of this fourteenth-century ambivalence to become a chaos; he has all the material—*pièces historiques, amoureuses, badines et burlesques, grivoises et grossières, satiriques, didactiques, relatives aux mœurs et aux usages,* as his editor classifies it,[3]—but there is no ordering, no comprehensive grasp and control. The poet in him is second to the journalist. Machaut, as we have seen, sidesteps the problem. Chaucer's English contemporary, William Langland, wrestles endlessly with it. For him the pull between an apostolically pure moral idealism and a sickeningly vivid sense of the facts of life was too great to control. His style produces a hallucinatory effect, in which the distinctions between abstract and concrete, moral and physical, have all but been lost. But Chaucer's early poems record his discovery, confrontation, and beginning mastery of the problem.

§ 1. THE "BOOK OF THE DUCHESS"

The *Book of the Duchess* is an elegy on the death of Blanche, Duchess of Lancaster. It resembles the *dits* of Machaut in its topicality, in its limitation of theme, in its predominant conventionalism of style, and in a modest tincture of realism. It produces the effect of refinement and restraint of feeling of its models at their best, but except for a few touches of rhetorical exhibitionism it is without the French overelaborateness. The center of the poem is an idealized description of the lady, with a narrative, likewise idealized, of the winning of her by her lover. The part of telling the story and making the description is given to a Man in Black, that is, to her bereaved husband and Chaucer's patron, John of Gaunt. His recitation is in turn framed in a dream of the Narrator, wherein the latter, wandering away from a hunt, accidentally overhears the Man in Black's complaint, but tactfully and sympathetically pretends ignorance of the lady's death so that the other may find relief in pouring out his sorrow. The dream is introduced by a prologue in which the sleepless Narrator relates his reading of the story of Ceyx and Alcyone, and his discovery of the God of Sleep.

The poem's success, as I have said, is partly owing to a conservatism of style, which, in the using of little more than the theme requires, approximates the functionalism of the style of Guillaume de Lorris. Though personification inheres in the diction, no personifications appear as characters in the action. The poem has as its end neither psychic analysis nor moral philosophy, and there is thus an initial wisdom in barring out the conventional figures which, short of some such end, could only be decorative. Chaucer, on the other hand, uses the device of the dream, conventionally and functionally, to exclude those reminders of common life, of business, war, and politics, that would cling to a realistic representation of his subject and thus smudge the purity of feeling proper to the occasion. It opens to him the ideal landscape that is his setting, the exemplarily polite conversation, the high-courtly narrative, the brilliant and elaborate portraiture, and the lyrical utterances that form the body of the poem.

I am loath to attribute the success of this frame to what has often been called Chaucer's "flawless" dream psychology, if by this is meant a kind of factualism.[9] It is difficult to distinguish the surface incoherence of dream sequence from the incoherence of plot sequence that is characteristic of conventional narrative of this kind. Where plot is of the slimmest significance and the essence of the poetry is in action of a nonrepresentational kind, neither poet nor audience will pay much attention to ordinary probability. Thus we never quite learn the fate of the blind man in the *Man of Law's Tale,* though the restoration of his sight is a miracle of much importance; and what becomes of the dwarf in Chrétien's *Lancelot?*[10] Though not in dreams, they both melt into thin air, like the Dreamer's horse in the *Book of the Duchess* and the guide in the *Parliament of Fowls.* Chaucer's problem is not to make his dream coincide with the facts of dreaming (whatever he may have thought them to be), but rather to inweave it with poetic relevance to his theme; in short, to unite the device with a meaning that it can support.

We have excellent appreciation of the poem on this level; we have been shown the exquisite relevance of the Ceyx-Alcyone story to the main body of the dream, the identification and sympathy between the Dreamer and the Man in Black, the believable charm of Blanche's portrait, the sense of well-being that this dreaming of sorrow happily leaves us with.[11] There is a fine, anticipatory fitness in the early steps of the dream, in the ringing chorale of the birds, in the colorful bedchamber with decorations that suggest momentous events yet to come, in the call of the hunting horn through the brilliant, cloudless air. There is a quiet eulogy in the choice of a hunt itself. It leads, for the Dreamer, to unsuspected game; he, with his untrained whelp, finds far more than the Emperor Octavian can with all his skilled retinue. We are led, in this sequence, through progressively wonderful events to a place quite remote from the ordinary course of affairs, but of richly realized idealization, where the elegy may begin.

The realism in the *Book of the Duchess* is comparatively faint, yet in this context it already becomes a source of difficulty. By realism, of course, I do not refer to the fine concreteness of specification in the descriptions. Guillaume de Lorris has it; it is the common property of good poets. When the Narrator remarks of the singing birds that awaken him,

> they sate among   [298]
> Upon my chambre roof wythoute,
> Upon the tyles . . .

we recognize that the description is more Chaucerian, more particular and sensuous, than its models,[12] but it is no less enchanting. It has something of the same deeply ingrained feeling for the materials of house and land that is a constant in Chaucer's English, natural to him. We recognize it in the language of the gentle narrator of the *Knight's Tale:*

> I have, God woot, a large feeld to ere,   [886]
> And wayke been the oxen in my plough.

In neither poem does this strain of imagery by itself work against the idealistic temper of its context.

But the characterization of the Narrator in the *Book of the Duchess* has a realism of attitude about it; it introduces a mild note of comic irony, which is doubtless owing to the poet's position *vis-à-vis* his patron and his audience. The Narrator has a kinship with the Man in Black—they are both disappointed lovers,—but his characterization is such that we cannot take his affairs so seriously. The rhetorical elaboration and formal lyricism of the Man in Black's complaints are designed to evoke the highest reaches of seriousness. The Narrator's opening remarks on his own romantic insomnia, couched in a neutral, conversational style despite the conventional hyperbole of statement, seem in

the shadow of the other's grief almost comically unequal. Chaucer was to develop this inadequacy of his Narrator as lover—or as anything else—in poem
after poem. Here the first movement toward this pose serves to define the distance between poet and patron, between the Narrator and the elevated objects
of his narration. At the same time it creates a discrepancy between the known
sophistication of the poet and the obtuseness of the part he has made for himself. In this perspective the characterization of the Narrator becomes overtly
humorous. He is naïvely ignorant of the classical gods: "For I ne knew never
god but oon" (237); more naïvely, he misses the main point of the Ceyx story—
its tale of bereavement—to fasten on its possible offer of a cure for his insomnia.
To "thilke Morpheus" he makes a comically literal offer of a featherbed, then
throws into the bargain an array of bedroom finery that would do credit to a
mercer's apprentice; for sleep he will pay Juno too.[18] Here are the makings of
him who rimed the tale of Sir Thopas.

The Narrator's prosaism of outlook is most at odds with the dominant tone
of the poem in the Ceyx episode itself. It can be felt tentatively in the command of Juno to her messenger: "Now understond wel, and tak kep!" (138),
an accent that is later given to the goose in the *Parliament of Fowls* (563). It
may be suggested in an awkward literalism in the description of Morpheus and
his crew, "That slep and dide noon other werk" (169). It is astonishingly clear
in the awakening of Morpheus. In Ovid, Statius, and the *Ovide moralisé*, the
effect of the scene turns on the contrast between the dark, deadly somnolence
of the cave of Sleep and the fragile brilliance of Juno's messenger. Iris awakens
the sleepy god with the gleaming of her garments, and delivers her message in
measured, rhetorical tones.[19] Less is made of the poetry of the scene in Machaut's
Fonteinne amoureuse (543–698), but nothing in the tradition of the passage
remotely anticipates the realism of Chaucer's version:

> This messager com fleynge faste   [178]
> And cried, "O, ho! awake anoon!"
> Hit was for noght; there herde hym non.
> "Awake!" quod he, "whoo ys lyth there?"
> And blew his horn ryght in here eere,
> And cried "Awaketh!" wonder hyë.
> This god of slep with hys oon yë
> Cast up, axed, "Who clepeth ther?"
> "Hyt am I," quod this messager.
> "Juno bad thow shuldest goon"—
> And tolde hym what he shulde doon . . .

The metamorphosis of Iris into a male is only less startling than the scene's violence of sound and action, which transports us instantly from the mythical cave to an army camp. The mind behind the narrative tears so bluntly through the finery of the traditional rendering that we need hardly know the tradition to feel the shock of the passage in its context. It is a moment of intense, comic practicality in the midst of conventionalism. Its single-minded insistence on the sleepiness of Morpheus suggests a linkage with the prosaic offer of a feather-bed, and with the further posed obtuseness of the claim (270 ff.) that neither Joseph nor Macrobius could rightly interpret the "wonderful" dream that follows.

In the early steps of the dream, our guide to the dream world has an open, willing, receptive, and sympathetic character that reminds us of the Narrator of the *Roman de la Rose*. His attention is easily led from the bird song to the decorated chamber windows, thence to the hunt, finally to the whelp and the Man in Black. We are led with him unsuspiciously, for this facet of his character harmonizes well with the suggestions of ignorance and simplicity that we have already seen in him. Our mildly ironical superiority over him does not hinder, in the dream, a common receptiveness toward the elevated matters to come. Nor are we surprised by his exemplary tact in the handling of the Man in Black. It is a situation that calls for the finest behavior:

> But at the last, to sayn ryght soth,   [514]
> He was war of me, how y stood
> Before hym, and did of myn hood,
> And had ygret hym, as I best koude;
> Debonayrly, and nothyng lowde,
> He sayde, "I prey the, be not wroth.
> I herde the not, to seyn the soth,
> Ne I sawgh the not, syr, trewely,"
> "A, goode sir, no fors," quod y,
> "I am ryght sory yif I have ought
> Destroubled yow out of your thought.
> Foryive me, yif I have mystake."
> "Yis, th'amendes is lyght to make,"
> Quod he, "for ther lyeth noon therto;
> There ys nothyng myssayd nor do."
> Loo! how goodly spak thys knyght,
> As hit had be another wyght;
> He made hyt nouther towgh ne queynte.

And I saw that, and gan me aqueynte
With hym, and fond hym so tretable,
Ryght wonder skylful and resonable,
As me thoghte, for al hys bale.
Anoon ryght I gan fynde a tale
To hym, to loke wher I myght ought
Have more knowynge of hys thought.

But Chaucer's further development of this motif takes a quasi-dramatic form.
The narrative of the bereaved lover is periodically interrupted by short, colloquial interchanges that are designed to motivate its continuation. Though
the Narrator has overheard in the other's lament that the lady is dead, he tactfully feigns ignorance, and the lover betrays an answering eagerness to tell his
story:

"Why so?" quod he, "hyt ys nat soo.   [742]
Thou wost ful lytel what thou menest;
I have lost more than thow wenest."
"Loo, [sey] how that may be?" quod y;
"Good sir, telle me al hooly
In what wyse, how, why, and wherfore
That ye have thus youre blysse lore."
"Blythely," quod he; "com sytte adoun!
"I telle the upon a condicioun
That thou shalt hooly, with al thy wyt,
Doo thyn entent to herkene hit."
"Yis, syr." "Swere thy trouthe therto."
"Gladly." "Do thanne holde hereto!"
"I shal ryght blythely, so God me save,
Hooly, with al the wit I have,
Here yow, as wel as I kan."
"A Goddes half!" quod he, and began . . .

"And telleth me eke what ye have lore,   [1135]
I herde yow telle herebefore."
"Yee!" seyde he, "thow nost what thow menest;
I have lost more than thou wenest."
"What los ys that?" quod I thoo;
"Nyl she not love yow? ys hyt soo?
Or have ye oght doon amys,

That she hath left yow? ys hyt this?
For Goddes love, telle me al."
"Before God," quod he, "and I shal."

The passages like these create the one difficulty of interpretation. Set in a dream, beside the conventionally rhetorical utterances of the Man in Black, their air of realism is surprising and awkward. The interposition of a realistic perspective produces a confusion in our view of the Narrator; for there is an unfortunate similarity between his feigned ignorance in this colloquy and his comic obtuseness in the prologue to the dream. His having clearly overheard the Man in Black's complaint aggravates this similarity, and many readers, lured by the periodically realistic perspective, have found in both prologue and dream a fatal consistency of characterization. They thus see the Narrator as slow-witted to the point of stupidity; for some, he brings into the most serious part of the poem a tasteless vein of humor, if not a blatantly impossible self.[15]

This interpretation of the Narrator's position in the dream would not have much support were it not, as I have indicated, for the corroborative tone of such passages as the awakening of Morpheus. Whether one takes the characterization to be accident or design, then, there is a basis for it in the materials of the poem. Chaucer inherits a modest device from the French tradition (whether his Narrator is the naïve one of Lorris or the knowingly courteous one of Machaut, or both), and develops it with such verve that it exceeds its function as an instrument of perspective. The characterization calls a shade too much attention to itself, as if the poet were not yet aware of the full power of the device, or could not yet manage his realism with precise control of its effect.

The style of the *Book of the Duchess,* then, shows two concurrent movements in the light of French tradition: one toward a functional use of courtly convention, the other toward a realism that suggests comic disenchantment. The latter movement is, I admit, comparatively faint, and I may have given it more attention here than a balanced reading of the poem would justify. But my object has been rather to trace the emergence of Chaucer's central stylistic problem: this strain of realism in the midst of conventional elevation, with the attendant problem of their mutual adjustment, is the only clue in this competent courtly elegy that such poems as the *House of Fame* and the *Parliament of Fowls* will follow.

§ 2. THE "HOUSE OF FAME"

I have said that only hindsight could see in the *Book of the Duchess* a suggestion of the style of the *House of Fame.* Now, looking at the latter, one still marvels at the violence with which the suggestion was taken up. The minor problem of stylistic management in the earlier poem has here grown to what has been called "nearly a major disaster."[10] Not for nothing did Manly consider the *House of Fame* a prologue to a collection. Technically, it is full of choice and widely prized accomplishments. Structurally, it is most charitably seen as an experiment, wherein the poet's energy and imagination by far outrun his sense of form.

The rhetorical preliminaries exhibit the playful, exuberant inconstancy that informs the whole. The epic machinery of proem and invocation at the opening is undercut at once with the syntactic breathlessness of that fifty-line sentence on the causes of dreams (all to demonstrate the ignorance of the Narrator) and again in the curious self-consciousness of

> But at my gynnynge, trusteth wel,　　　　[66]
> I wol make invocacion . . .

The invocation is oddly mixed; there is a reminiscence of the opening of Dante's *Paradiso:*

> And he that mover ys of al　　　　[81]
> That is and was and ever shal . . .

but, like so much of the Dantean material in this poem, the incipient seriousness of it is swallowed up in the parody of the anathema that follows, introduced with its scrap of nursery rhyme, "dreme he barefot, dreme he shod" (98). The proem to Book II begins with a popular swing to the verse:

> Now herkeneth every maner man　　　　[509]
> That Englissh understonde kan,
> And listeneth of my drem to lere.
> For now at erste shul ye here
> So sely an avisyon . . .

Then it turns, inexplicably, to invoking Venus and the Muses in the high style of the Italians. Only the invocation to Book III is "straight," taken from the *Paradiso*. With regard to the amount of actual play in the poem, one wonders how seriously this and the other reminiscences of the *Divine Comedy* are to be read.

The "story" is of the same motley texture. The main characteristic of the Dido episode is the usual medieval reduction of classical tale to something more mundane and compendious and, withal, more moralized. On the side of mundanity Clemen notes the glimpse of the angry goddess Juno, running and

crying "as [she] were wood" (202), and of Venus "my lady dere, / Wepynge
with ful woful chere" (213–214). The bluntness of the narrative gives it, as
Clemen says, the aura of an ordinary, everyday betrayal. He notes, too, that it
falls now and then into the idiom of popular balladry, with its fillers and tags,
as "Lord and lady, grom and wenche" (206), and ". . . he made hir a ful fals
jape" (414)." But alongside this popular strain one should note the extreme and
awkward conventionalism of the complaints of Dido, in which the formality
of speech actually incorporates the logic and diction of scholasticism:

> "As thus: of oon he wolde have fame   [305]
> In magnyfyinge of hys name;
> Another for frendshippe, seyth he;
> And yet ther shal the thridde be
> That shal be take for delyt,
> Loo, or for synguler profit."

> "Now see I wel, and telle kan,   [334]
> We wrechched wymmen konne noon art;
> For certeyn, for the more part,
> Thus we be served everychone.
> How sore that ye men konne groone,
> Anoon as we have yow receyved,
> Certaynly we ben deceyvyd!
> For, though your love laste a seson,
> Wayte upon the conclusyon,
> And eke how that ye determynen,
> And for the more part diffynen."

The poverty of the versification and the improbability of the diction should not
blind us to the fact that Chaucer will elsewhere use the conventional machinery
of philosophical monologue with good effect. What is confusing is the essential
pointlessness of the device here, where the amplification stands in such grotesque stylistic disharmony with its narrative context.

The moralization of the episode, of which these speeches are a part, is likewise unsteady. Dido is presented first as an exemplary victim of man's duplicity.
Then, as if Chaucer were here first discovering the theme of his poem, she
becomes rather a victim of Fame:

> "O wikke Fame! for ther nys   [349]
> Nothing so swift, lo, as she is!

> O, soth ys, every thing ys wyst,
> Though hit be kevered with the myst.
> Eke, though I myghte duren ever,
> That I have don, rekever I never,
> That I ne shal be seyd, allas,
> Yshamed be thourgh Eneas,
> And that I shal thus juged be . . ."

But then there follow some seven exempla of "untrouthe." We might be surer that this was to be the primary significance of the episode were it not that Eneas is then fully excused of his "grete trespas" (428) and the Narrator leads us out of the temple of Venus, into a desert the meaning of which has not yet been plumbed.

Book II replaces the antique matters of Venus and Dido with Chaucerian autobiography, popular science, and pure comedy. The vehicle for most of this is the golden Eagle, who first appears to the Narrator at the end of Book I. Flown out of the *Purgatorio,* he now descends to earth, to be plucked of his allegorical significance and to serve as the Narrator's conveyance to the house of Fame. The Narrator is "Geffrey" Chaucer, his obtuseness of the *Book of the Duchess* filled out with some of the most personal details the poet has left us. He is already fat, henpecked, and with the labor of his studies and his reckonings (as Controller of Customs) he lives the life of a hermit. The trip, says the Eagle, is Jove's reward for faithful literary service to Love.

But the Eagle is much more than the conventional guide of the love visions. His first word is reminiscent of the awakening of Morpheus:

> Thus I longe in hys clawes lay,   [554]
> Til at the laste he to me spak
> In mannes vois, and seyde, "Awak!
> And be not agast so, for shame!"
> And called me tho by my name,
> And, for I shulde the bet abreyde,
> Me mette, "Awak," to me he seyde,
> Ryght in the same vois and stevene
> That useth oon I koude nevene . . .

Nothing in the poem is more impressive and surprising than the consistently naturalistic perspective in which this character is seen. Even his famous exposition of the theory of sound is subsumed by it:

> "Telle me this now feythfully, [853]
> Have y not preved thus symply,
> Withoute any subtilite
> Of speche, or gret prolixite
> Of termes of philosophie,
> Of figures of poetrie,
> Or colours of rethorike?
> Pardee, hit oughte the to lyke!
> For hard langage and hard matere
> Ys encombrous for to here
> Attones; wost thou not wel this?"
> And y answered and seyde, "Yis."
> "A ha!" quod he, "lo, so I can
> Lewedly to a lewed man
> Speke, and shewe hym swyche skiles
> That he may shake hem be the biles,
> So palpable they shulden be.
> But telle me this, now praye y the,
> How thinketh the my conclusyon?"
> [Quod he]. "A good persuasion,"
> Quod I, "hyt is; and lyk to be
> Ryght so as thou hast preved me."

That the exposition has indeed been a model of clarity is achievement enough. Convention would have admitted it to the poem on a nondramatic level, as necessary indoctrination. Thus Lancelot and Lavinia, Troilus, Anelida and Dorigen, or any of the characters of conventional narrative, can go on at length without the suggestion that they are either learned or fluent. We have seen Jean de Meun, indeed, give such learned material to characters who are otherwise specifically nonlearned. But here, with no exigency of realism at all apparent, Chaucer makes the talent for exposition a trait of the speaker himself. The Eagle is a study for Pandarus. Conceived naturalistically, he cannot deliver a lecture without directing attention to it himself. He is a character: an anxious, learned tourist guide and pedagogue. Much of his lecturing has a structural value in the information it conveys to the reader. Thus the speech on sound is a conceivably relevant introduction to the description of the house of Fame in Book III. Yet the information is ultimately swallowed up in the characterization, and there is at least one exchange which seems to have no

III

other function but local satire. At the end of the Book, the Narrator falls into one of his fantasies, thinking of Boethius on philosophic flight, of Martianus Capella and Alain de Lille on the heavenly bodies. The Eagle, incidentally a mind reader, leaps to the pedagogical opportunity:

> "Lat be," quod he, "thy fantasye!   [992]
> Wilt thou lere of sterres aught?"

The Narrator's reply is comically perverse:

> "Nay, certeynly," quod y, "ryght naught."

The Lecturer is hardly to be daunted, but his formerly docile pupil is firm:

> "And why?" "For y am now to old."   [995]
> "Elles I wolde the have told,"
> Quod he, "the sterres names, lo,
> And al the hevenes sygnes therto,
> And which they ben." "No fors," quod y.
> "Yis, pardee!" quod he; "wostow why?
> For when thou redest poetrie,
> How goddes gonne stellifye
> Bridd, fissh, best, or him or here,
> As the Raven, or eyther Bere,
> Or Arionis harpe fyn,
> Castor, Pollux, or Delphyn,
> Or Athalantes doughtres sevene,
> How alle these arn set in hevene;
> For though thou have hem ofte on honde,
> Yet nostow not wher that they stonde."
> "No fors," quod y, "hyt is no nede.
> I leve as wel, so God me spede,
> Hem that write of this matere,
> As though I knew her places here;
> And eke they shynen here so bryghte,
> Hyt shulde shenden al my syghte,
> To loke on hem." "That may wel be,"
> Quod he.

Chaucer is here in command of an idiom that is only dimly seen in the *Book of the Duchess;* this comic dialogue is one of the great technical accomplishments of the poem.

The deliciousness of the characterization, however, should not blind us to the fact that it has no describable function beyond its intrinsic humor. It is not part of a pattern. The Eagle hardly reappears in Book III, nor does the ironic revelation of his weakness stand in meaningful relationship to either the material he presents or the conventional functions he fulfills. It is a free-floating, gratuitous display of talent and of humor, thoroughly Chaucerian in its quality, but not yet bent to the magisterial control of the mature narrative artist.

The third Book shares the antique, bookish flavor of the first, and its unsteadiness. The description is extremely profuse, as if the poet were pouring out all his lore. There is an artistic economy in its creating the sense of overwhelming richness of sight and sound that we should expect in Fame's house. The many-eared, many-eyed goddess is described as changing wondrously in height as she sits gorgeously and permanently enthroned, surrounded by the Muses and bearing on her shoulders the fame of Alexander and Hercules. Down from the dais runs a double row of metal columns; atop them stand "folk of digne reverence," historians and poets of the great deeds of the world. The patterned management of Fame's nine sets of suitors, displayed with a minimum of commentary, is Chaucer's best piece of self-expressive allegory. But set amidst this splendor and formalism, Fame herself periodically shrinks to the dimensions of a fishwife:

> "Fy on yow," quod she, "everychon!   [1776]
> Ye masty swyn, ye ydel wrechches,
> Ful of roten, slowe techches!
> What? false theves! wher ye wolde
> Be famous good, and nothing nolde
> Deserve why, ne never ye roughte?
> Men rather yow to hangen oughte!
> For ye be lyke the sweynte cat
> That wolde have fissh; but wostow what?
> He wolde nothing wete his clowes.
> Yvel thrift come to your jowes,
> And eke to myn, if I hit graunte,
> Or do yow favour, yow to avaunte!"

This is the idiom suited to the peasant Dangier, rampaging in the Lady's mind to snub presumptuous suitors; it is not intrinsically unsuitable for allegory, nor even for representing the graceless whims of Fame. Yet the mixture of styles is so violent that one wonders, even when the poet makes explicit his modest carelessness of fame later on, whether this naturalization of Fame in so conventional and "high" a context is not caprice rather than irony.

Chaucer at least seems not yet to have got his material into focus. He works at each episode with gusto, then leaves it behind as if forgotten. Eight hundred verses of "this lytel laste bok" are passed when we learn that the house of Fame is, after all, not the place that he has been brought here to see. Then follows the remarkable description of the house of Rumor, and as finally the narrative seems to gather itself to the revelation of some vital piece of news, the poem breaks off unfinished.

In the absence of an ending, there is no possibility of a secure interpretation of any poem; for this poem the matter is worse. It is hard to conceive of any ending at all that could consistently follow from what we have. Perhaps this is why, like the overblown *Anelida and Arcite* of the same period, the poem was left unfinished. The first and third Books are reasonably close in theme and style. They share an otherwordly locus, rich, symbolical description, and an irony touching on pessimism. Bronson's hypothesis, that the poem was to raise someone to bad eminence in a matter of love,[18] is perhaps as close as we shall come to relating these Books. But whoever succeeds in harmonizing them with the second Book will deserve the niche of Colle tregetour himself. The oscillations of perspective that we see in the local progress of the narrative are magnified in the larger sequence of the Books. A strain of irony, largely the product of this oscillation, runs through the poem. But the question here is one of direction. How does the irony cut? The effect of the Eagle's characterization is to break through the curtain of dream and allegory, to reduce the journey to commonplace naturalistic terms. But to what end?

It would be worse than churlishness to comb this fascinating poem for incoherencies, were it not that incoherency is the central fact of its character. In view of its range of subject matter, and its technical facility from passage to passage, we must agree with Kittredge that the poem "is composed, in small and great, with astonishing virtuosity. It is full of spirit and originality, and instinct throughout with conscious power."[19] Yet the virtuosity and the consciousness of power outstrip the artistic judgment. The *House of Fame* is Chaucer's most flamboyant poem, the one most characteristically late Gothic, colorful, varied to extremes, undigested. In this direction it more truly reveals the nature of Chaucer's artistic problem than the *Book of the Duchess* does. Or rather, it does not give the false impression that he is simply trying to find his way out of the conservative embrace of conventionalism. He constructs the Eagle and the fabulous edifice of Fame with equal gusto. He is himself embracing as much as his arms can strain of the cultural and stylistic endowment of the times. But he does not yet know what to do with it. What we find in the later works is not progressively more naturalism, but more control, the subordination of technique to method, the management of these diverse materials in the interest of a coherent pattern of meaning.

§ 3. THE "PARLIAMENT OF FOWLS"

We have, before the *Troilus*, a dramatic instance of the growth of Chaucer's feeling for this management in the second half of the *Parliament of Fowls*. It is a prelude to his maturity, not only in general artistic soundness, but also in the particular configuration which the various elements of his thought and style take. Although like the *House of Fame* it shows Chaucer far afield from French sources and exclusively French traits of style, the "unlikely and disparate materials"[20] of the poem have been variously drawn toward a meaningful polarity of relationship, the idealist-realist, conventional-naturalistic polarity of the French tradition.

The first half of the poem is charmingly and exasperatingly variegated, in the manner of the *House of Fame*. Chaucer, writing now in an athletically flexible rime-royal stanza, again adopts the dream vision as a frame. His Narrator is again an outsider to love but an enthusiastic reader, and he begins his tale with an account of a book he has recently read. It is Cicero's *Somnium Scipionis*. The brief but earnest résumé of the book, with the moral and otherworldly exhortations of Africanus that end it, constitutes the chief variance from conventional love-vision material in this part of the poem, and the chief point of critical difficulty. From here we are introduced to the Narrator's dream, in which, at first guided by the moral Africanus, he comes upon a courtly pleasance, a temple of Venus, and finally to Nature's presidency over a parliament of birds on St. Valentine's Day.

Bronson has well traced the playful oddments of tone that give the first section a lightly ironic flavor: the status of the Narrator as a noncombatant on the field of love; the puzzling invocation to Venus "north-north-west"; the curiously comic adaptation of Dante's legend on the gate of Hell for the gate to this garden of Love; the ambiguous treatment of Venus herself; the mixture, in the garden description, of conventional inhabitants of love gardens with such questionable figures as Flaterye, Messagerye, and Meede.[21] All these, and many smaller touches, suggest that the love vision is not being taken with perfect seriousness. Yet the general presence of irony is not enough to establish a unifying theme. Here, as in the *House of Fame*, there is some doubt concerning how the irony cuts, and some grounds for feeling that all is not under control. The heavy influence of Boccaccio in the description was both for good and for ill. It produces stanzas of unparalleled brilliance,[22] and some of careless and mechanical amplification. It leads the poet into the hothouse closeness of the description of Venus, which, missing the full sensuality of the Italian, hits on a voyeurism that is unique in Chaucer. The whole section, with its exuberant cataloguing of trees and personifications and traditional lovers, has somewhat less relationship to what follows than one would like. If Chaucer had at this point visualized ending his poem with a parliament of birds, would he have been content with the passing description of birds in verses 190–192? With the appearance of Nature (298) the poem seems to begin anew, and if there is an irony in the rejection of Venus for Nature as the goddess presiding over these matters of love, it does not strike us as premeditated, but rather as the happy result of the poet's escape from a set of materials that were too fancy and Italian for his present use. From Boccaccio he turns to the more medieval inspiration of Alain de Lille.

The parliament proper redeems the earlier part, casting something of a retrospective coherence over it, and it draws the *Dream of Scipio* into an orbit related obliquely to its own. Its movement is sequential, if not plotlike. The long catalogue of birds at its beginning is securely related to the action in subject and theme. The personified Nature behaves as she ought, that is, functionally and not decoratively. The poem proceeds to its conclusion with a newly acquired thematic coherence. Perhaps some contemporary event, faded now beyond recognition, gave the poet his original focus here, or perhaps it was simply the St. Valentine's idea itself, which appears suddenly in verse 309. One may guess that here, as with the *Book of the Duchess,* the "occasional" status of the poem has helped the poet to hold his materials together. But both these possible foci have been transcended for a more general theme. I have no hesitancy in following Clemen's and Bronson's lead in identifying it as the comic, contradictory variety of men's attitudes toward love.[23] The bare theme as thus stated has some significance for Chaucer's art. It is Jean de Meun's theme; it is also one of the possible themes of the *House of Fame.* The handling of it is, however, incomparably more significant, for it shows the poet for the first time boldly aligning his style in the pattern of his attitudes, and with his characteristic ironic effect.

The parliament begins when Nature, with the beautiful female eagle on her hand, calls on the birds to choose their mates. The tercel eagle, as the highest in rank and most worthy, speaks first. His is a courtly posture, and his speech is in the high-courtly idiom:

116

With hed enclyned and with ful humble cheere   [414]
This royal tersel spak, and tariede noght:—
"Unto my soverayn lady, and not my fere,
I chese, and chese with wil, and herte, and thought,
The formel on youre hond, so wel iwrought,
Whos I am al, and evere wol hire serve,
Do what hire lest, to do me lyve or sterve;

"Besekynge hire of merci and of grace,
As she that is my lady sovereyne;
Or let me deye present in this place.
For certes, longe may I nat lyve in payne,
For in myn herte is korven every veyne.
Havynge reward only to my trouthe,
My deere herte, have on my wo som routhe.

"And if that I to hyre be founde untrewe,
Disobeysaunt, or wilful necligent,
Avauntour, or in proces love a newe,
I preye to yow this be my jugement,
That with these foules I be al torent,
That ilke day that evere she me fynde
To hir untrewe, or in my gilt unkynde.

"And syn that non loveth hire so wel as I,
Al be she nevere of love me behette,
Thanne oughte she be myn thourgh hire mercy,
For other bond can I non on hire knette.
Ne nevere for no wo ne shal I lette
To serven hire, how fer so that she wende;
Say what yow list, my tale is at an ende."

The female responds with a handsome blush of modesty, and then two other
tercels "of lower kynde" in turn make claim to her hand. One claims greater
length of service, and the other greater depth of devotion. Their speeches are
naturally less courtly than the first, but nothing at this point mars the effect of
genteel, ceremonial order in the procession of their pleas. Chaucer draws out this
effect finely by implicating the Narrator:

Of al my lyf, syn that day I was born,   [484]
So gentil ple in love or other thyng

Ne herde nevere no man me beforn,
Who that hadde leyser and connyng
For to reherse hire chere and hire spekyng;
And from the morwe gan this speche laste
Tyl dounward drow the sonne wonder faste.

Then, with an audacity equaled only by its thumping success, Chaucer introduces the opposite note, full blast:

The noyse of foules for to ben delyvered   [491]
So loude rong, "Have don, and lat us wende!"
That wel wende I the wode hadde al toshyvered.
"Com of!" they criede, "allas, ye wol us shende!
Whan shal youre cursede pletynge have an ende?
How sholde a juge eyther parti leve
For ye or nay, withouten any preve?"

The goos, the cokkow, and the doke also
So cryede, "Kek kek! kokkow! quek quek!" hye,
That thourgh myne eres the noyse wente tho.
The goos seyde, "Al this nys not worth a flye!"

The famous, hugely naturalistic squabble among the lesser fowl follows. It quickly boils over the issue of the tercels into the question of love itself. The goose is for no nonsense: "But she wol love hym, lat hym love another!" She is seconded by the duck, but not before the turtledove has spoken:

"Nay, God forbede a lovere shulde chaunge!"   [582]
The turtle seyde, and wex for shame al red,
"Though that his lady everemore be straunge,
Yit lat hym serve hire ever, til he be ded.
Forsothe, I preyse nat the goses red,
For, though she deyede, I wolde non other make;
I wol ben hires, til that the deth me take."

"Wel bourded," quod the doke, "by myn hat!
That men shulde loven alwey causeles,
Who can a resoun fynde or wit in that?
Daunseth he murye that is myrtheles?
Who shulde recche of that is recheles?
Ye quek!" yit seyde the doke, ful wel and fayre,
"There been mo sterres, God wot, than a payre!"

The "gentil tercelet" abuses this vulgar ignorance of love, then the cuckoo's even deeper pragmatism is criticized by the merlin. Nature brings the squabble to a close with both issues unresolved. The female eagle, given her choice, asks a year's respite. The other birds choose their mates, and the narrative closes in an atmosphere of communal felicity:

> And whan this werk al brought was to an ende,   [666]
> To every foul Nature yaf his make
> By evene acord, and on here wey they wende.
> And, Lord, the blisse and joye that they make!
> For ech of hem gan other in wynges take,
> And with here nekkes ech gan other wynde,
> Thankynge alwey the noble goddesse of kynde.

After singing an exquisite roundel welcoming summer, the birds fly away and the Narrator awakens to his books again.

The "contending lovers" and the "court of love" are the commonly recognized traditional motifs which the parliament is based on, but neither retains much importance under Chaucer's hand. The debate is peppered with scholastic and legal terminology, *ple, juge, parti, preve, verdit, diffyne, termine, argumentes,* for realistic, parliamentary flavor, and not to outline a genuine debate for the audience. The irony of the case, rather than the issues, is the prime consideration. The very inconclusiveness of the outcome shows that the pointed contrast of courtly and bourgeois attitudes is designedly balanced. It produces a comic reflection of one attitude on the other; each is partly admirable, partly foolish. The ending leaves us with no hard feelings.

The parliament scene, with its realism, is the part of the poem most often praised, and one may justly savor for its own sake the deliciousness with which Chaucer can now handle colloquial rhythm and diction. Yet if anything is true of the art of the scene, it is that the realism does not achieve half its effect without the carefully measured stanzas of the courtly idiom that it breaks in upon. The ironic reflection of views is paralleled by an ironic reflection of styles, in which each component is essential to the total effect. The freely given, insular comic realism of the *House of Fame* is here used for a purpose larger than itself, subordinated to a larger complex of style and meaning. The courtly idiom has equivalent status; as we have seen, it is managed with equivalent circumspection. The passage seen large, then, shows Chaucer in a new command of his diverse materials. He is done, here, with the random and nebulous effects of the *House of Fame* and of the first part of this poem. While we shall watch him extend, refine, and modulate this balanced, ironic position to the end of the *Canterbury Tales,* and make a poetry infinitely complex out of it, it will never again be a complexity that borders on confusion, nor an irony that suggests chance.

The clarity and precision of the art of the parliament scene implies a similar quality in the vision of the poet; the scene forecasts in an early and simple form the character of Chaucer's ultimate response to the ambivalence that earthly love and life present so strongly to the late medieval mind. He sees the courtly and bourgeois modes, idealism and practicality, in ironic juxtaposition. He holds them in balance, sympathetically and critically, exploring each for its own essence and for the light it casts on the other. In this he is more tolerant than Boccaccio, more serious than Machaut, and much more in control of his material than Deschamps. He makes, more than any of his European contemporaries, a capacious, comprehensible order out of his legacy of style and meaning from the French tradition. Most of his writing that deals with secular values, then, can be understood in terms of the character of the parliament scene. It forecasts particularly the nature of the local comedy in the *Troilus.*

The parliament scene is not the whole of the poem, however. I am less sure of the meaning of the envelope. The introduction of the Narrator and the long, static description of the *locus amoenus* before the action begins are in the pattern of the *Roman de la Rose,* and very deeply embedded in Chaucer's own sense of structure. Bronson has said perhaps all that can be said for the relevance of the place description to the parliament when he describes the latter as a gathering into sharper focus and precision of the irony which plays intermittently about the poem from its very commencement.²⁴ The problem of the Narrator and his summary of the *Somnium Scipionis* presses for more attention. The last stanza of the poem adverts to this beginning with a suggestion of coherence that is hard to ignore. Furthermore, the content of the *Somnium* seems to create with the parliament scene a second and larger issue in the thought of the poem: that between heavenly and earthly love. If so, it gives the poem the larger philosophical pattern, if not the dimensions, of the *Troilus* and the *Canterbury Tales.*

The poem ends thus:

> And with the shoutyng, whan the song was do   [693]
> That foules maden at here flyght awey,
> I wok, and othere bokes tok me to
> To reede upon, and yit I rede alwey.
> I hope, ywis, to rede so som day

> That I shal mete som thyng for to fare
> The bet, and thus to rede I nyl nat spare.

These lines hark back to two early stanzas; the first introduces the *Somnium Scipionis* and the second introduces the Narrator's dream:

> Of usage—what for lust and what for lore—   [15]
> On bokes rede I ofte, as I yow tolde.
> But wherfore that I speke al this? Nat yoore
> Agon, it happede me for to beholde
> Upon a bok, was write with lettres olde,
> And therupon, a certeyn thing to lerne,
> The longe day ful faste I redde and yerne.

> The day gan faylen, and the derke nyght,   [85]
> That reveth bestes from here besynesse,
> Berafte me my bok for lak of lyght,
> And to my bed I gan me for to dresse,
> Fulfyld of thought and busy hevynesse;
> For bothe I hadde thyng which that I nolde,
> And ek I nadde that thyng that I wolde.

The picture of the Narrator in search of "a certeyn thing to lerne" has prompted interpretations of the poem as serious philosophy, as if Chaucer were in some way trying to reconcile the morality of Cicero's book with the mundane concerns represented by the birds, and by his being himself a love poet. Africanus' command to work for the common weal (74–75) suggests a contrast with the inability of the birds to do so. The dictum that lecherous folk shall be punished in the hereafter (79–81) may refer to the lovers within the garden. The generally otherworldly orientation of the book, recommending heavenly love or true felicity, seems pointedly antithetical to the earthly love and "false felicity" dealt with later.[25] There is tonal support for this in the irony of the description, extending even to the catalogue of birds. Here the vices of secular life are recorded in surprisingly full measure for a valentine:

> The waker goos; the cukkow ever unkynde;   [358]
> The popynjay, ful of delicasye;
> The drake, stroyere of his owene kynde;
> The stork, the wrekere of avouterye;
> The hote cormeraunt of glotenye . . .

There is no doubt that a serious view is involved with the poem, but the poem cannot support the theory that makes of it a sober philosophical tract. The most that can be said here is that the philosophical issue, if raised, is not pursued. The felicity of the birds is not made to feel false, and the best poetry of the poem celebrates sensuous life with undiluted enthusiasm. To bring seriously to bear the idea that this life is a kind of death (54), to bring it to bear on that lively, feathered crowd assembled by Nature on St. Valentine's Day, is too crushing a notion for the poetry to sustain. Granting that the tone must remain ambiguous, I favor a less ambitious reading, on the side that sees the irreconcilability of Africanus and the birds as a comic antithesis, a joke at the expense of the Narrator, for his bookishness.

The *House of Fame* gives us a precedent. Its Narrator is a bookish recluse, divorced from life:

> "For when thy labour doon al ys,   [652]
> And hast mad alle thy rekenynges,
> In stede of reste and newe thynges,
> Thou goost hom to thy hous anoon,
> And, also domb as any stoon,
> Thou sittest at another book
> Tyl fully daswed ys thy look,
> And lyvest thus as an heremyte . . ."

There is a comic fitness in Jove's sending, as guide for this character, the mercilessly pedagogical Eagle; we have seen it dramatized at the end of Book II. The Narrator of the *Parliament* is in a similar state.[26] An indefatigable bookworm, with a touching faith in the power of books to solve problems, he sits absorbedly down to what we are to take to be his usual fare, a moral work in Latin on heaven and hell:

> To rede forth hit gan me so delite,   [27]
> That al that day me thoughte but a lyte.

His perfectly serious summary of its somber content is in character. Who will relish more this *contemptus mundi* than a preoccupied scholar? Each man to his own. The night, that takes animals from their "besynesse," takes him from his book. And if he is to dream, naturally his guide will not be a lady with blonde tresses, but the moral Africanus himself. The stanza on the content of dreams underlines this comic fitness of things, and all goes smoothly, with the possible exception of his awkward invocation to Venus, until the scholar is betrayed by his own guide. Africanus, with some pointed comment on his in-capacities, literally shoves him into a garden of love. Thus does this recluse come to be writing of earthly love; and when his dream is done he goes back, nothing daunted, to his books, still pursuing the profit in them, almost unaware of his betrayal, and of the comic insight into earthly "besynesse" that he has left us with.

This is a gracious and humorous way for a poet with some reputation for seriousness and scholarship to write a valentine. Without complete certainty of its success, one can still see important relationships between this method and that of the *Troilus*. It shows, beneath the perennial joke between the Narrator and his audience, a movement toward bringing the handling of the former into deep involvement with the total effect of the poem. I refer not only to the use of the Narrator's naïve personality to promote imaginative surrender to the dream world, a device that is a constant in the early poems, learned from Guillaume de Lorris; I refer also to the Narrator's vein of *sentence* and doctrine, which in a bolder way now begins to have the kind of relevance to the action that we shall find in the *Troilus*.

A comic treatment of the poem's moralizing does not prevent its prefiguring the larger philosophical pattern of the *Troilus*. The epilogue of the *Troilus* embodies the same moral as the opening of the *Parliament*, and in each this moral is set against the main body of the poem.[27] In both, the local problem of the modes of earthly love is related to the larger problem of earth and heaven. Other things being equal, the materials of both poems are strikingly similar. Yet their ultimate tones differ much. The difference between them, between a comic and a tragic expression of the same problem, is thus much a matter of structure. Not for nothing does the palinode in the *Parliament* come first. The birds break in on its bookish, *a priori* morality with a vivacious assertion of life. In the *Troilus,* experience is examined first, and out of its ironic contradictions the serious moral inevitably grows.

V

tROILUS AND CRISEYDE

TROILUS AND CRISEYDE stands as the focal point in Chaucer's artistic career. It
draws together in full development every talent shown in the early poems, and
has, besides, its own new amplitude. Like the *Canterbury Tales,* it contains a
world. The later work excels it only in particularity of reference, not in control of
form or depth of conception. Like many of Chaucer's (and Shakespeare's) works,
it has a direct "source." Chaucer took for it most of the plot, the content of many
whole stanzas, and even words and rimes from Boccaccio's romance *Il Filostrato.*[1]
Textual comparison shows many ways in which Chaucer enlarged on his model;
thus he added two fairly long sequences that are only suggested in the Italian.
But the nature of his originality cannot be fully understood by subtracting, as it
were, one poem from the other. All of the "source" has been changed by a
change in the large conceptions of form and value that dominate the composition, and this in turn accounts for the addition of the literally "original" parts of
the poem. The nature of the change can be seen in terms both of history and
of style; the two are related, and together they provide a useful index to the
meaning of the *Troilus* itself.

[1] For notes to chapter v see pages 262–266.

Boccaccio's *Filostrato* has a strongly autobiographical cast. The author dedicates it to a "nobilissima donna," and says that he expresses through the story of Troiolo's sorrow his own feelings about his lady's absence from the city. Since much of Boccaccio's biography for the 1330's is read from between the lines of his romances, we can be sure of little. But the tone of this romance lends support to the theory that the lady is Maria d'Aquino, the voluptuous, illegitimate daughter of King Robert of Naples—she was Boccaccio's sometime mistress— and that the poem not only records her absence, but perhaps also forecasts her imminent desertion of the poet.[2] The narrator is in complete sympathy with his hero. The twenty-five-year-old Boccaccio *in propria persona* is both, and the manners of the poem strongly reflect its origin in the sophisticated, prosperous, and licentious Neapolitan court of the time.

Naples under the Angevins was a particularly cosmopolitan part of Italy; Boccaccio was later to import some of its sophistication into his barbaric paternal city of Florence. He had already written, adapted perhaps directly from the French, much of the *Filocolo,* his ornately "classical" and courtly version of *Floire and Blancheflor.* As a basis for the *Filostrato* he took an incident from one of the earliest romances in French, Benoît de Sainte-Maure's *Roman de Troie.* He added to Benoît's story of Briseida's desertion of her Trojan lover an invented account of their previous affair. Writing two centuries later than Benoît, he is able to draw on his knowledge of later romance and on the lyric tradition of the *stilnovisti* to elaborate his story greatly in the direction of courtly love. Thus his treatment is far more detailed and more elevated than Benoît's. But at the same time he creates what few French romances are, an urban poem. Courtly life in Italy is characteristically a version of city life, and Boccaccio himself was and always remained a *borghese.*[3] His courtliness thus has a sensuality and a sauce of cyncism, a realistic knowingness, that is foreign to the French and even more to the English courtliness of the Middle Ages.

Boccaccio's heroine, for instance, is conceived less ideally than French heroines are. Criseida is rather *known* than invented at all. She is beautiful, but also instinctive and calculating, faithful only in her own fashion; she submits to practical events in a purely creatural way. The ambiguity of her feminine responses to her suitors is designedly transparent.[4] The mystery, the reticence, the *dangier* of the French mode are gone, as is the semireligious awe of the French hero. He is a young but already experienced city type. The narrator, one is made to feel, knows women. In his frankly indulgent attitude toward sex he forecasts the philosophy of the *Decameron.*

Yet Boccaccio's realism and sensualism already approach in the *Filostrato* that remarkably graceful compromise with French refinement which is his typical characteristic. The style and structure of the poem reflect this poise of feeling. It is preponderantly lyrical, and rises easily to emotional intensity. It uses much of the rhetorical figuration of the high style. Yet it can bend easily, and in short space, to a relaxed, moderately realistic description, with no suggestion of disharmony between imaginative elevation and realistic immediacy. It is thus much a Renaissance poem. The first stanza describing Criseida rises and falls in an unembarrassed modulation of style:

> Tra li qua' fu di Calcas la figliuola   [I, 19]
> Crisëida, quale era in bruna vesta,
> la qual, quanto la rosa la vïola
> di biltá vince, cotanto era questa
> piú ch'altra donna, bella; ed essa sola
> piú ch'altra facea lieta la gran festa,
> stando del tempio assai presso alla porta,
> negli atti altiera, piacente ed accorta.

[Among whom was the daughter of Calcas, Criseida, in dark dress, who, as much as the rose conquers the violet in beauty, so much was she more beautiful than any other lady; and she alone more than any other made glad the great festival, standing very near the door of the temple, in manner stately, gracious, and agreeable.]

The stanzas describing the undressing of Criseida are similarly curved:

> Lungo sarebbe a raccontar la festa,   [III, 31]
> ed impossibile a dire il diletto
> che 'nsieme preser pervenuti in questa;
> ei si spogliaro ed entraron nel letto,
> dove la donna nell'ultima vesta
> rimasa giá, con piacevole detto
> gli disse:—Spogliomi io? Le nuove spose
> son la notte primiera vergognose.—
>
> A cui Troiolo disse:—Anima mia,
> io te ne priego, si ch'io t'abbi in braccio
> ignuda si come il mio cor disia.—
> Ed ella allora:—Ve' ch'io me ne spaccio.—
> E la camiscia sua gittata via,

nelle sue braccia si ricolse avaccio;
e strignendo l'un l'altro con fervore,
d'amor sentiron l'ultimo valore.

[Long would it be to recount the pleasure and impossible to tell the delight they took together when they had come there; they undressed and got into bed, where the lady, still in her last garment, said to him in a charming way: "Shall I undress myself? The newly wed are timid the first night." To whom Troiolo said: "Soul of me, I pray you do, so that I may have you in my arms naked as my heart desires." And she then: "Look, I am rid of it." And her chemise thrown away, she quickly nestled in his arms; and clasping one another with passion, they felt the uttermost value of love.]

For Boccaccio, love's "ultima valore," which Chaucer translates "grete worthynesse" (III, 1316), has nothing in it so remote and elevated that it cannot dwell with the intimate and closely appreciated detail of sexual play. The playful smile with which the heroine's voluptuousness is regarded does not at all interfere with the high valuing of her.

The whole poem's style is ranged in this manner, between limits that are rarely felt to be far apart.[5] The description is, on the whole, thin; there is no particular effort either to realize a contemporary setting or to fabricate a romantic one.[6] The direct discourse is rich in lyric monologue, but Boccaccio's patent interest in the sentiments of his characters does not impel him far in the opposite direction, toward realistically conceived dialogue. When it comes briefly and naturally into the scenes between Pandaro and Criseida, it has neither the stichomythic formalism of courtly dialogue nor the turbulence of the bourgeois style. The idiom of the narrative, while rich enough in poetic figure—even to epic simile and personification,—has nevertheless been described, in comparison to that of the *Filocolo*, as "simpler and humbler . . . sometimes prosaic."[7]

The narrative itself proceeds in a confident, linear fashion. Troiolo is so much the focus of interest that little space is given to the important interventions of others in his affairs. Pandaro's machinations to arrange the rendezvous with Criseida are told as briefly as possible, and the whole account of her wooing by Diomede occupies only twenty-six stanzas. Considering the elaboration and intrigue characteristic of romance, the poem well merits De Sanctis' description of it as a *novella* under epic appearance.[8]

The Italian city poet in Boccaccio coexists with the *trouvère* in so friendly a fashion that one is actually surprised that they have found so few differences between them. The former has a smiling wit that turns periodically on his heroine and once or twice on himself. The other is bound heart and soul to his lady, takes himself very seriously and, in almost hopeless knowledge of his betrayal, can still defend her *gentilezza* to the world.° Both are Boccaccio, accommodated by a restricted, social idealism that is fairly encompassed in Troiolo's declaration to Criseida:

> "Ma gli atti tuoi altieri e signorili,   [IV, 165]
> il valore e 'l parlar cavalleresco,
> i tuoi costumi piú ch'altra gentili,
> ed il vezzoso tuo sdegno donnesco,
> per lo quale apparien d'esserti vili
> ogni appetito ed oprar popolesco,
> qual tu mi sei, o donna mia possente,
> con amor mi ti miser nella mente."

["... but your stately and elegant manners, your fineness and your courtly speech, your ways more gentle than others', and your pretty, feminine scorn, whereby every vulgar desire and action seemed to you base—such are you to me, O my mighty lady—set you in my mind with love."]

To our less enchanted eyes, indeed, this description seems to apply more to Troiolo than to his mistress. But be that as it may, it is clear that both the light irony and the heavy pathos of the poem are based on a surprisingly narrow conception of good and evil. It is not wide enough to suggest broad reaches of meaning, to sustain either comedy or tragedy. The poem's ostensible moral is its actual one: "Giovane donna è mobile." To the end it is a personal, autobiographical cry, a young man's poem.

The difference between *Il Filostrato* and the *Troilus* follows broadly the differences between the poets and their cultures. Chaucer wrote his poem in an England nagged by an interminable war and beset internally by social, political, and religious turmoil, and in a city with an economy based more on hard-won commerce than on feudal tribute. His whole milieu cannot have approached the leisure, the sophistication, the cultural poise of Boccaccio's Naples of fifty years before. Furthermore, England's culture was still dominated by its French history with a weight that the Italian debt to France did not approach. Italian art had never been so Gothic as English art, and the Italian Trecento, with Giotto, Boccaccio, and Petrarch, was already a "renaissance" century. English politics, religion, art, and social organization were going through a much more protracted and difficult changing; with suppression and regression, England was not to have its own renaissance for another two hundred years. Meanwhile, its problems took shape according to the traditional medieval formulations, growing out of the medieval dualism of culture that I have mentioned before. The contrast between country and city, between courtly and commercial life, between religion and secularism, was becoming actually less sharp. But it is a characteristic of English thinking in this period that practical events are continually cast up against an ever-brightening notion of the receding ideals of the past. We find the same revivalist nostalgia in Wycliffe, in Langland, in Malory, and in Caxton. In each, theory and actuality produce a violent, late Gothic contrast.

Chaucer was temperamentally far better situated than Boccaccio to appreciate the wider meaning of his material. There was no autobiographical impulse behind Chaucer's poem. His stance as a poet had always been one of semidetachment. He was, at forty-six, more capable of both humor and seriousness than Boccaccio was at twenty-five. He had recently translated Boethius' *Consolation of Philosophy*.

The differences between the cultures and the men can be seen at once in the broad characteristics of their poems. There is no telling how Chaucer read *Il Filostrato*, but it is clear that what caught his imagination was neither the simple availability of this new "material" nor the novel, renaissance neatness of it; he had plenty of material at hand, and he made the Italian story less neat. The point of contact is a trait that has already given us a moment's pause: the curiously easy amalgamation in the *Filostrato* of critical wit and naïve devotion, of animal sensualism and romantic idealism. With an English consciousness nourished on the French literary tradition, on medieval Christianity, and on Boethius, Chaucer may have felt that what he was to produce was *in* the Italian poem rather than in the structure of his own vision. But it appears more likely that he gauged to the minutest fraction the age of its nameless narrator, the breadth of his concerns, the depth of his philosophy. He saw, as Boccaccio himself may not have seen, what antithetical values had somehow diminished and coalesced in that youthful, urban, pagan, immoral poem. Then he recast it, perhaps consciously and correctively, objectifying its point of view, setting into bold relief the moral issues it barely suggested, making its private, present pathos something *storial*, a comedy and tragedy of universal and timeless dimensions. Thus Chaucer's poem is neither simple in structure nor homogeneous in style. Rather than being linear in design, it is composed of patterned contrasts, encompassing a great diversity of moods and tones, often abruptly juxtaposed.[10] Its characters, rather than being "all of a piece" (in Legouis's phrase),[11] are complex to the point of bafflement. Its plot is complicated with intricate and difficult maneuvering. Supporting this medieval structure is a very broad range of style, embracing in precisely controlled coördination the two major styles of the French tradition.

C. S. Lewis is the first critic to have grasped the historical significance of what Chaucer did to *Il Filostrato*. His theory of the medievalization of it anticipates (if it did not actually suggest to me) fully half of the view presented here. Chaucer, he shows us, amplified the Italian poem after the manner of the medieval rhetoricians, added much doctrine and *sentence*, and, most importantly, purified its rendering and elaborated its teaching of courtly love. "The majority of his modifications are corrections of errors which Boccaccio had committed against the code . . ."[12] Elsewhere Lewis shows how closely the opening movement of the *Troilus* parallels in narrative form the movement of Guillaume de Lorris' allegory, and he invites us to "regard it as a new *Launcelot*—a return to the formula of Chrétien, but a return which utilizes all that had been done between Chrétien's day and Chaucer's."[13] This "all" is the fine psychological analysis of Guillaume de Lorris, which, Lewis suggests, frees allegory from itself and makes possible the narrative treatment of a love story.

Standing on Lewis' shoulders, we can hope to see a little more. His view is immensely valuable as a corrective to the typical post-Victorian one, which reads the poem only for its "modern" psychological realism. But at the same time he undervalues the medieval realism that jostles courtly convention all through the period and all through the *Troilus*. Although Lewis rightly finds Jean de Meun's Duenna (Vekke) and Ami (Frend) behind Chaucer's Pandarus, he does not take into serious account the achievement of the bourgeois tradition between Chrétien and Chaucer. Medieval love poetry, he writes:

> protects itself against the laughter of the vulgar—that is, of all of us in certain moods—by allowing laughter and cynicism their place *inside* the poem; as some politicians hold that the only way to make a revolutionary safe is to give him a seat in Parliament. The Duck and Goose have their seats in Chaucer's *Parlement* for the same reason; and for the same reason we have satire on women in Andreas, we have the shameless Vekke in the *Rose,* we have Pandarus in the *Book of Troilus* . . . the comic figures in a medieval love poem are a cautionary concession—a libation made to the god of lewd laughter precisely because he is not the god whom we are chiefly serving—a sop to Silenus and Priapus lest they should trouble our lofty hymns to Cupid. When this has been understood (and not till then) we

may, indeed, safely admit that Chaucer had sympathy with the Goose and the Duck. So had every knight and dame among his listeners."

The general observation contained here is wise and sensitive, and deserves a fair representation. But its particular application to Chaucer, and also to Jean de Meun, is questionable. We have seen that there had been in Chrétien himself an impulse to illuminate courtly romance from the direction of comic realism. In *Flamenca* the love poetry had been pushed to its limits as such by a similar spirit. But this realism in medieval love poetry can justly be called temporary vagrancy, "a sop to Silenus," only until the late thirteenth century, until Jean de Meun. Thereafter we must be prepared to reckon with it seriously, on an equal basis, for Jean's poem shows that it has become an equally serious factor in the culture itself. Chaucer was "a court poet of the age of Froissart," but not so much a spokesman for a class as Froissart, whose sympathies are exclusively courtly as only those of a certain kind of bourgeois can be. For Chaucer, with his bourgeois parentage, his Controllership of Customs on wools, skins, and hides, and of the Petty Custom on wines, his commercial-courtly milieu, his temperament, there is no question of minor concessions to popular attitudes, or of merely concessionary realism.

But my argument—that Chaucer medievalized *Il Filostrato* in two directions, not one—finds its major justification in the poem, in what Chaucer does with the French tradition itself. The whole meaning of the poem depends as fully on the style and ethos represented by Jean de Meun as on the values of Chrétien and Guillaume de Lorris. This is to say that its courtliness is not that of the twelfth century, merely raised in technical sophistication; it is a fourteenth-century courtliness, seen in a *context* of deepened naturalism. Jean had shown with what effectiveness naturalism could be appended to romance for the purpose of rounding out the possible views of love, and Chaucer follows Jean's lead, but not directly. He sees, as Jean does, the elements of presumption, of naïveté and of impracticality in courtly idealism, and he admires the wholesome sanity of ordinary life. But, unlike Jean, he also prizes courtly idealism for its very real virtues, for its recognition of nobility, of beauty, and of spirit, and he detects in the incessantly practical pursuits of common life the shadow of futility cast over any human activity in which these higher concerns are neglected. His view, more than Jean's, is continuously complex. It is this very round, very comprehensive view of the values of human experience that is implicit in Chaucer's treatment of the story of Troilus and Criseyde.

Beyond this lies another level of perspective. Chaucer is a spiritual pupil of Boethius. He sees in turn the whole sphere of human experience against eternity. He sees the imperfection inherent in any mode of life—be it practical or idealistic—wherein the end itself is *earthly* joy, and hence wherein the prize may at any moment be washed away by the same tides that brought it in.

These two levels of perspective are intimately related, and this relationship gives the poem a philosophical depth which sets it far above conventional medieval moralizing. To dwell at length on the attractiveness of earthly love and then to repudiate all in a palinode is neither philosophical nor artistic. But to present secular idealism as a beautiful but flawed thing, and to present practical wisdom as an admirable but incomplete thing, to present them, indeed, as antithetical and incongruous to each other, is by implication to present a third view, higher and more complete than either. This philosophical third view hovers over every important sequence in the *Troilus,* and is made explicit in the epilogue.

The stylistic structure of the *Troilus* is coextensive with its meaning. Two equally admirable, equally incomplete attitudes toward life are presented in the poem, and the value of each of these attitudes is communicated in the style specifically developed by tradition for its most effective realization. The negative element, the weakness inherent in each attitude, is presented through the reflection of the one on the other. On a stylistic level, by juxtaposition of scenes and passages alternatingly conventional and naturalistic, with all the attitudinal implications that go with those styles, Chaucer creates a pervasive, literary, structural irony which is at the same time profoundly expressive of the irony of his view of life.

§ 2. TROILUS AND PANDARUS

Because of its particular range of style, the *Troilus* can be called neither romance nor realistic novel.[15] Though it has traits common to both, it cannot even be called both. Viewed in the light of the broadest philosophical assumptions on which these genres are based, it has gone beyond the romance's entertainment of a univalent idealism; it is still far from the confident, univalent realism of the modern novel, which, like realistic philosophy, had to await the climate of much later centuries for its full flowering.[16] The *tertium quid* created by the interplay of these styles and these philosophical positions is best called a genre unto itself, for the result is a qualitative difference from romance or novel that requires a different kind of attention from the reader. It needs what S. L. Bethell in a similar context has called "multiconsciousness," the simultaneous awareness of different and opposite planes of reality." For the fourteenth-century audience, this was a condition of life.

Such a resolution of the problem of genre is particularly relevant for criticism in the area of characterization. It indicates why naturalistic criticism usually comes up with a poem in which the hero is minor as a character, and why critics with a merely academic awareness of convention can make little that is meaningful of him. It casts some light, too, on the difficulty of interpreting the "character" of Criseyde. In this poem, under the generic assumption here presented, "characterization" is a device, not an end; it lies largely in the domain of the poem's heritage of medieval realism, and is used, with that style, to create only one of the several aspects under which the action is seen. The poem's truth to life does not depend on a consistently realistic rendering, any more than Chaucer's view of life is exhausted by his knowledge of phenomena, of local pressures and motives. The "characterization" in the poem participates in a larger symbolic pattern which does seem to figure forth the poet's whole view, and which embraces values that tradition did not teach him to deal with in realistic terms. This is not to deny that the poem has three principal actors, and that much of its meaning is generated through their interaction. But the area of "truth to life" in it is one that does not depend *a priori* on the style; it is an area common to the novel and to romance (if one takes romance at all seriously), and is defined by the symbolic meaning of the action. In this poem, although the actors are created as if of differing materials, and are seen now under an ideal and now under a realistic aspect, their interrelations are consistently kept true, and in this, not in reportorial realism, is the truth of the characterization. The characters demand, then, not an exclusive attention to the conventional assumption of romance or to the realistic one of the novel, but rather a continuous multiconsciousness which will appreciate the playing off of one against the other, which will be able to see the value of a character in himself, and the changed value he takes on in the alien context of another character or another style.

Troilus represents the courtly, idealistic view of experience. While there is nothing mechanical or schematic about Chaucer's way with him, it is clear that he is conceived and constructed almost exclusively according to the stylistic conventions of the courtly tradition. He moves, so far as we can see him alone, in an aura of the courtly style. In this Chaucer handles him functionally; in the insubstantial realm of the idealizing imagination he uses nonrepresentational forms. Troilus is described in conventional, hyperbolical terms. When the minute detail of his look or gesture is given at all, as at the end of the following passage, it rather elevates than corporealizes him:

This Troilus sat on his baye steede,   [II, 624]
Al armed, save his hed, ful richely;
And wownded was his hors, and gan to blede,
On which he rood a pas ful softely.
But swich a knyghtly sighte, trewely,
As was on hym, was nought, withouten faille,
To loke on Mars, that god is of bataille.

So lik a man of armes and a knyght
He was to seen, fulfilled of heigh prowesse;
For bothe he hadde a body and a myght
To don that thing, as wel as hardynesse;
And ek to seen hym in his gere hym dresse,
So fressh, so yong, so weldy semed he,
It was an heven upon hym for to see.

His helm tohewen was in twenty places,
That by a tyssew heng his bak byhynde;
His sheeld todasshed was with swerdes and maces,
In which men myght many an arwe fynde
That thirled hadde horn and nerf and rynde;
And ay the peple cryde, "Here cometh oure joye,
And, next his brother, holder up of Troye!"

For which he wex a litel reed for shame,
Whan he the peple upon hym herde cryen,
That to byholde it was a noble game,
How sobrelich he caste down his yën.

His first utterance as a lover, when he is not feigning an antiromantic attitude
for protection, is in the form of a song (I, 400–420). It stands out in bold relief
from the narrative current; the Narrator takes a whole stanza to frame it. It is a
fine, lyric expression of the paradoxical nature of love. Far from casting about
for a dramatic-naturalistic vehicle for this sentiment in Troilus, Chaucer adapts
a sonnet of Petrarch, a perfect example of rhetorical *contentio*. Right after the
song, Troilus offers up a prayer to the God of Love, "with pitous vois" vowing
eternal service to Criseyde:

"Ye stonden in hir eighen myghtily,   [I, 428]
As in a place unto youre vertu digne;
Wherfore, lord, if my service or I
May liken yow, so beth to me benigne;

134

> For myn estat roial I here resigne
> Into hire hond, and with ful humble chere
> Bicome hir man, as to my lady dere."

His next two speeches are likewise apostrophes. The courtly choiceness of Troilus' idiom is now and then punctuated by a sharpness of rhythm or figure for particular emotional effect:

> He seyde, "O fool, now artow in the snare,   [I, 507]
> That whilom japedest at loves peyne.
> Now artow hent, now gnaw thin owen cheyne!"

but in general the other is his characteristic note, reëchoing through all the thirty-odd lyric monologues that still remain for him. His is the voice of the "highest" style in the poem; he is given much of its "poetry," in the narrow sense. The power with which he is brought to our sympathy is more poetic than dramatic; it depends on how well Chaucer has managed to capture and make his own the freshness and purity of the courtly lyric tradition. On the face of it, the stylistic materials Chaucer is using here put characterization in the naturalistic sense out of the question.

The narration of the poem, and thus the description of the actors, is in the hands of a character who is no less related to the action than were the first-person Narrators of the dream visions.[18] He is indeed a descendant of those others, their naïveté being diluted and softened in him to a broadly human weakness, their qualities of modesty and sympathy passing to him whole. He is of course receptive to imaginative elevation, and his vision of Troilus is unreserved in its hyperbole: "It was an heven upon hym for to see" (II, 637), "It was an hevene his wordes for to here" (III, 1742). Thus in the opening view of Troilus that we have just been discussing, the narrative itself combines with the idiom of the monologues to support a nonrepresentational view:

> . . . sexti tyme a day he loste his hewe.   [441]
>
> By nyght or day, for wisdom or folye,   [452]
> His herte, which that is his brestes ye,
> Was ay on hire, that fairer was to sene
> Than evere was Eleyne or Polixene.
>
> Ek of the day ther passed nought an houre
> That to hymself a thousand tyme he seyde . . .
>
> Thise wordes, and ful many an other to,   [540]
> He spak, and called evere in his compleynte

> Hire name, for to tellen hire his wo,
> Til neigh that he in salte teres dreynte.

But the Narrator is not merely a passive recorder of things. He is also a commentator. He rarely suggests what is not soon to become apparent; and what he sees, he often sees in sympathy with someone else. Yet sometimes he anticipates and sometimes he lags behind the shifting sets of assumptions under which the other characters operate. Chaucer's manipulation of him in this manner is one of the subtlest sources of irony in the poem. Here in the first Book it introduces us to the double valence of the conventional treatment of Troilus. By itself this directly expresses a noble and elevated view of experience. But set in a realistic context it has a contrary meaning. Thus in the last of the quotations cited above, the Narrator tells us, in sympathy with Troilus, that the latter

> called evere in his compleynte
> Hire name, for to tellen hire his wo,
> Til neigh that he in salte teres dreynte.

Then he gives an apparently innocent additional detail:

> Al was for nought: she herde nat his pleynte . . .   [544]

The Narrator has made a similar remark once before. Troilus, he says, performs great feats of arms so that his renown will please his lady all the better,

> But how it was, certeyn, kan I nat seye,   [I, 492]
> If that his lady understood nat this,
> Or feynede hire she nyste, oon of the tweye;
> But wel I rede that, by no manere weye,
> Ne semed it as that she of hym roughte,
> Or of his peyne, or whatsoevere he thoughte.

Small wonder! we say, Troilus has never addressed the lady, except through the lamentably impractical medium of the lyric monologue. But in giving us an opportunity for ironic reflection on the Narrator's apparent obtuseness, Chaucer opens the way, hitherto closed by convention, for the same kind of reflection on Troilus' helplessness. The sympathetic Narrator, by answering the wrong questions, has unwittingly led us to a realistic estimate of Troilus' speech and action. We can immediately see that the stylistic peculiarities which lend themselves so well to expression of the ideal nature of the hero when viewed under the assumptions of convention, lend themselves equally well, when seen in a realistic light,

136

to a revelation of his lamentable weakness. Depending on perspective, Troilus can be viewed as an ideal hero of romance, or as an ancestor of Don Quixote.

It is curious that a certain amount of education toward the background of the poem can actually be a hindrance to appreciating this source of its irony. For we are all taught that Troilus' conduct follows the rules of courtly love, and that these rules are different from ours. "Nothing can be more absurd," says Kittredge, "than to describe Chaucer's Troilus as a 'lovesick boy.' . . . The sufferings of Troilus are in complete accord with the medieval system. Lovers were expected to weep and wail, and to take to their beds in despair. It was likewise an article of the code that they should be afraid to declare their passion. Humility was one of the cardinal virtues of the chivalric system."[19] Even that excellent critic, though he feels the irony pulsing through the poem, can track it down only as far as the poet himself. The fact is, that as medieval romance goes, as the "code" goes, Troilus is *too* perfect a courtly lover. In him convention has taken on the superior purity that is only possible in nostalgic retrospection.

There are several ways in which to see this. It is difficult to think of a single hero of French romance who is quite so prostrated by love, so removed from the actual business of courtship, who depends so completely on an intermediary. We need go back no farther than the *Roman de la Rose,* whose Lover is as refined as any. He has already met Bel Acueil, and through overboldness been repulsed by Dangier, before he turns for aid to Ami. In the second part, where the role of Ami is vastly increased, and the incomparable Duenna is enlisted in the aid of the Lover, it is still observed that if the Duenna be unwilling, there are still many devices open to the Lover by himself. Jean de Meun lists a page of them, which calls up reminiscences of *Lancelot* and *L'Escoufle* and the whole strain of amatory initiative that coexists with that of timidity.[20] But Troilus, far from following the dictates of Jean's Faus-Semblant, does not even, so far as practical action goes, fulfill all of the lovers' symptoms described by Guillaume's God of Love.[21] The comparison with the *Filostrato* shows the same thing. It is perfectly clear that Chaucer's is a more courtly poem and that Troilus is a purer lover. Thus Boccaccio leaves his hero a larger measure of autonomous, practical, impulse and activity. On the other hand, wherever in Boccaccio there is some ironic reflection on the shortcomings of courtly behavior, Chaucer deepens and humorizes it.[22]

Chaucer does not of course completely entrust this strain of irony to so fugitive a character as the Narrator, nor to so uncertain a quantity as his audience's knowledge of the precise shades of courtly behavior. It is built into the structure of the poem with the figure of Pandarus. Yet there is no doubt in my mind that for the fourteenth-century audience, as for us, the pure, gentle, spiritual, courtly Troilus is in essence already a figure of the past. Like Lancelot and Galahad he is respected, perhaps even imitated; but he remains out of this world, almost archaic. Only thus can he represent so fine and yet so untenable an ideal of life. Both the comedy and the pathos of the poem depend on the insufficiency of the courtly vision. Its insufficiency to cope with the here and now, its archaism, is again sympathetically and unwittingly disclosed in the charming proem to Book II:

> Ye knowe ek that in forme of speche is chaunge   [II, 22]
> Withinne a thousand yeer, and wordes tho
> That hadden pris, now wonder nyce and straunge
> Us thinketh hem, and yet thei spake hem so,
> And spedde as wel in love as men now do;
> Ek for to wynnen love in sondry ages,
> In sondry londes, sondry ben usages.
>
> And forthi if it happe in any wyse,
> That here be any lovere in this place
> That herkneth, as the storie wol devise,
> How Troilus com to his lady grace,
> And thenketh, "so nold I nat love purchace,"
> Or wondreth on his speche or his doynge,
> I noot; but it is me no wonderynge.[23]

Pandarus is both a devotee of courtly love and a practical realist. This dualism is already present in the Pandaro of the *Filostrato*,[24] and Chaucer, in stretching that poem, stretched this character on the same form. But the polar qualities in Pandarus are not equivalent. His courtliness is, as it were, superimposed on his realism. The difference is like that between environment and heredity, training and temperament; in medieval terms, between accident and substance. The accidental qualities of the character are those demanded by the outward circumstances of the story. He is a gentleman of noble family, friend to a prince; he is expertly knowledgeable about the forms of social and civil affairs. For himself, he has been carrying on an unsuccessful love affair, in the best courtly tradition, for many years. His more substantial qualities are those built into the grain of his speech and action, into his vision of life. He is a doer, a fixer; he lives in a ponderable, manipulable world.

This dualism in Pandarus works in a characteristically Chaucerian way. Pandarus has in one respect the same function as that of the Narrator of the

Book of the Duchess, who has similarly suffered unrequited love "this eight yeer," but whose fate it is, rather, to minister to the needs of a nobler sorrow."[25] The effect in each case is a light, comic irony which sets off the full seriousness of the other lover's position. But Pandarus is not a purely technical figure, nor a minor butt of the audience. He represents a view as powerful as that of Troilus. A deeper effect of his failure in love is in its reflection on his substantial nature, and thus on the realist position itself. His "joly wo," as he humorously calls it, stands for the unbridgeable gap between realism and high, spiritual passion. "By God," he says, "I hoppe alwey byhynde!" (II, 1107). This realist has superb self-knowledge, and can laugh at his plight himself. There is no question of his sincerity in courtly matters; there is only question of his aptness. He has practised love long and hard, and he knows his theory; but he was not born to play this instrument. Presently we shall hear the correct, tutored, but restless note in his rhetoric.

I have now suggested of Troilus and Pandarus that each sets off and questions, enhances, and detracts from, the values represented by the other. Neither cancels the other out arithmetically. This is possible because both represent positive values; their relationship produces irony, not neutrality. But of the two functions of Pandarus, the critical one should take most of our attention: he provides a view of courtly love under the aspect of realism. This is why Chaucer vastly expands his role in the story, adds two major scenes of Pandaric activity, and broadly extends the style of the poem in the direction of the bourgeois tradition. Pandarus is older, more experienced, more substantial than Pandaro; he is characterized with greater naturalism, and he calls into being the superior dramatic quality of the English poem. The alteration of the characterization is simultaneous with Chaucer's altered conception of the story's moral significance. The greater spirituality of Chaucer's Troilus and the more formidable difficulty of Criseyde are meaningless without Pandarus' deeper realism to test them.

This rendering of the realist in a naturalistic style, and the placing of him in meaningful juxtaposition to a courtly theme, is no small part of the poem's medievalism. Mr. Nevill Coghill has called Pandarus "Chaucer's first creation of a piece of actuality with no model before him but life itself."[26] As an estimate of Chaucer's style and skill in the creation, and of the effect he produces, this is no exaggeration. But one must insist, for the sake of what history can suggest of the meaning of Pandarus, on his long genealogy in literature. The conjunction of the clever intermediary with an aura of practical realism is not far to seek, even in romance. Pandarus is a poetic descendant of Lunete and—so inbred is the family—of dozens of other go-betweens in the French tradition, young and old, male and female, friends of the lover and friends of the lady. (I will not insist on Pandarus' androgyny, but there is great dispute about his age, and he is of course an intimate of both Troilus and Criseyde.) There are many traces of this heritage in the very action of the poem. Boccaccio gives hardly a hint of the complicated comings and goings, the trapdoors and secret exits, of Chaucer's two bedroom scenes.[27] But these, and ingenuity like Pandarus', are common in fabliau, and in romance intrigue. Thus the old woman in *Eracle* comes to the lovesick Paridès and tries to find out the reason for his distress. She lectures him on the virtues of having a friend to confide in. A century before Jean de Meun's Duenna, she preaches on love in the light of personal experience. Then she assures him,

> "Tant sai de barat et de guile, [4199]
> Que vostre buens iert acompliz
> Se çou ert nès l'empereriz."

["I know so much deception and trickery that your good will be brought about even if it is the Emperor's wife."]

It is indeed the Emperor's wife. The old woman comes in on Athanais as she is reading. There is a long eulogy of Paridès (unnamed) before the matter is brought to a point. Athanais smuggles him a letter by the go-between, appointing the time and place for a rendezvous. The lovers meet in the old woman's house. Athanais enters in full view of her jealously watching guards. There is no other entrance, and they see that only the old woman is within. But Paridès has been hidden in a secret chamber, with a secret door. Once within, the lady dismisses her attendants, and joins her lover unsuspected.[28] The fabliau tradition of intrigue is not so much different. Indeed, the bare mechanics of the bringing of Troilus to Criseyde could be constructed from just two fabliaux. In *D'Auberee* the old woman tricks a pretty wife into being her guest for the night, then brings her amorous client in upon the guest. In *Du Prestre et d'Alison* a quick-witted mother pretends to accede to the local priest's desires for her daughter. To the priest, sitting in the main room, it appears that the daughter has gone to bed; but the bedroom, not unlike Pandarus', is equipped with a false door and an adjacent chamber, which enables the daughter to be hidden and the prostitute Alison to be smuggled in instead.[29]

In the *Filostrato*, Pandaro is excluded from the love scenes. This is not so in the *Troilus*, nor in many French romances. The comic intrusion of Pandarus in the most intimate scenes of the poem has a family resemblance to Sipriane's buzzing about the bedroom in *Florimont*.[30] In *Guillaume de Palerne* the confidante Alexandrine is present to urge on Melior pity for Guillaume. Only when the lovers finally embrace does she fade out of the picture, in a manner reminiscent of Pandarus. Later, when Melior is betrothed to the son of the Emperor of Greece, Guillaume falls ill. Melior goes with her people to visit him, but only Alexandrine accompanies her into the sickroom, and into the ensuing love scene, as Pandarus accompanies Criseyde in the feigned illness of Troilus.[31]

Romance and fabliau must thus have contributed to details of Pandarus' activity; but, to return to the main point, Chaucer's use of the intermediary as a vehicle for seriously realistic reflection on courtly life owes most to Jean de Meun. Jean, in synthesizing the whole tradition of friends and intermediaries into Ami and the Duenna, and in putting them into a symposium on Love, gave them a newly dignified significance. Both Ami and the Duenna point to Pandarus' position as friend and pedagogue. Ami is, indeed, what Pandaro's Italian dualism must have called up in Chaucer's mind. Pandaro's service to Troiolo and to Love have been altered in the direction of Ami's professorship; and Pandaro's streak of skepticism becomes Ami's heavily ironic and damaging knowledge of women, itself in turn refined and subtilized into Pandarus' implicit view of Criseyde. For Chaucer is not so crude as to give Pandarus explicitly anticourtly doctrine; even Ami, we recall, had damaged courtly love while defending it. Lewis says that Pandarus plays the Duenna in his scenes with Criseyde.[32] Beyond this dramatic parallelism with the French there is a methodological one. Chaucer in conceiving Pandarus himself under the aspect of realism follows Jean's lead with the Duenna. In both, the exponent of the realistic view is himself a sample of that tangible, sensory life that he lives by. It is the character's symbolic meaning in the larger pattern of each poem that calls up the traits of style which make possible this rich "characterization."

Chaucer's triumph in creating so natural and living a go-between is coincident, then, with the final adjustment between his enormous and fully developed technical powers on the one hand and the design of his poem on the other. He had been preparing for such a character as Pandarus in the early poems:

This messager com fleynge faste   [BD 178]
And cried, "O, ho! awake anoon!"

. . . he to me spak   [HF 555]
In mannes vois, and seyde, "Awak!
And be not agast so, for shame!"

. . . in feere   [TC I, 726]
Was Pandarus, lest that in frenesie
He sholde falle, or elles soone dye;

And cryde "Awake!" ful wonderlich and sharpe;
"What! slombrestow as in a litargie?"

Among these three—Juno's messenger, the Eagle, and Pandarus—the last is the only one in whom the naturalistic style has a completely coherent meaning. It achieves this meaning in a configuration of style and attitude that we have seen growing from *Yvain* and *Eracle* to the *Roman de la Rose* and the *Parliament of Fowls*.

Turning now from generalization to the text, I hardly need to itemize the traits of style that relate Pandarus to the bourgeois tradition, or to the more disenchanted scenes of romance. As in Jean de Meun, there is no physical portrait of the character himself, but his idiom is all-expressive. The rhythm of his speech is turbulent, colloquial, energetic.[33] He is full of the direct, concrete, colorful references that we find in the bourgeois idiom. His stage business is described largely in representational terms. He never swoons; but he leaps and jokes with incessant vigor. He is a perpetual fountain of practical activity. He accounts for most of the naturalistic dialogue in the poem, and this is much more than there is in the *Filostrato*. Virtually everything he says or does has a direct, dynamic, practical color to it. His entrances, to take a convenient index, continually refresh the poem's dramatic movement. Of six entrances in Book II, when he shuttles at high speed between Troilus and Criseyde, five are immediate occasions for rapid, colloquial dialogue:

> This Pandarus com lepyng in atones,   [II, 939]
> And seyde thus, "Who hath ben wel ibete
> To-day with swerdes and with slynge-stones,
> But Troilus, that hath caught hym an hete?"
> And gan to jape, and seyde, "Lord, so ye swete!
> But ris, and lat us soupe and go to reste."

Here, beside the leaping and the japing, we note the reflections, typical of the bourgeois style, of mundane details of scene and action. Pandarus' awareness of sweat is equaled in Chaucer only in the *Canon's Yeoman's Tale*. This naturalistic, Pandaric view of Troilus may be compared with the heroic view of the same battle-worn Troilus—"It was an heven upon hym for to see"—that the Narrator has just previously prepared for Criseyde.[34]

In the three entrances to Criseyde's house we note Pandarus' capacity to turn the subject of love into a game, and a continued naturalism[35] of both dialogue and action:

Quod Pandarus, "Madame, God yow see,   [II, 85]
With al youre fayre book and compaignie!"
"Ey, uncle myn, welcome iwys," quod she;
And up she roos, and by the hond in hye
She took hym faste, and seyde, "This nyght thrie,
To goode mot it turne, of yow I mette."
And with that word she doun on bench hym sette.

With that thei gonnen laughe . . .   [II, 99]

This Pandare tok the lettre, and that bytyme   [II, 1093]
A-morwe, and to his neces paleis sterte,
And faste he swor that it was passed prime,
And gan to jape, and seyde, "Ywys, myn herte,
So fressh it is, although it sore smerte,
I may naught slepe nevere a Mayes morwe;
I have a joly wo, a lusty sorwe."

"Now, by youre fey, myn uncle," quod she, "dere, [II, 1103]
What manere wyndes gydeth yow now here?
Tel us youre joly wo and youre penaunce.
How ferforth be ye put in loves daunce?"

"By God," quod he, "I hoppe alwey byhynde!"
And she to laughe, it thoughte hire herte brest.
Quod Pandarus, "Loke alwey that ye fynde
Game in myn hood . . ."

He seide, "O verray God, so have I ronne!   [II, 1464]
Lo, nece myn, se ye nought how I swete?
I not wheither ye the more thank me konne.
Be ye naught war how false Poliphete
Is now aboute eftsones for to plete,
And brynge on yow advocacies newe?"
"I? no," quod she, and chaunged al hire hewe.

Coming to Troilus with Criseyde's letter,

Pandarus, right at his in-comynge,   [II, 1308]
He song, as who seyth, "Somwhat I brynge,"

And seyde, "Who is in his bed so soone
Iburied thus?" "It am I, frend," quod he.

143

> "Who, Troilus? Nay, help me so the moone,"
> Quod Pandarus . . .

Pandarus delivers no lonely lyric; and Chaucer never entrusts to him the highly conventional philosophical monologue or introspective self-debate that he gives occasionally to Troilus and Criseyde. On the contrary, the most conventional in form of his whole armory of expressions—his learned and doctrinal lectures on love—are carefully enmasked in his characterization. Like the Eagle, Pandarus is conceived dramatically as being learned and sententious to a fault; says Troilus:

> "Frend, though that I stylle lye,   [I, 752]
> I am nat deef. Now pees, and crye namore,
> For I have herd thi wordes and thi lore;
> But suffre me my meschief to bywaille,
> For thi proverbes may me naught availle.

> "Nor other cure kanstow non for me.
> Ek I nyl nat ben cured; I wol deye.
> What knowe I of the queene Nyobe?
> Lat be thyne olde ensaumples, I the preye."

A less obvious but just as secure indication of this naturalization of Pandarus' discourse is his characterization as a tactician. The element of practical contrivance behind his lectures is sometimes explicitly stated: "Thise wordes seyde he for the nones alle."[38] More often it comes out dramatically; we find him saying one thing, meaning and doing another: "Lo, here is al! What sholde I moore seye?" (II, 321). He goes on for another nine stanzas. He has a tactical modesty:

> "I woot wel that thow wiser art than I   [II, 1002]
> A thousand fold . . ."

> "Towchyng thi lettre, thou art wys ynough."   [II, 1023]

Then he tells Troilus how to write it. The tactician is at the height of his powers in the dinner-party scene:

> "Rys, take with yow youre nece Antigone,   [II, 1716]
> Or whom yow list; or no fors; hardyly
> The lesse prees, the bet; com forth with me . . ."

He has the gift of being able quietly to inject into a proposition an assumption beyond what his interlocutor has admitted.[39] But once he is caught red-handed:

> "Ther were nevere two so wel ymet,   [II, 586]
> Whan ye ben his al hool, as he is youre:
> Ther myghty God yet graunte us see that houre!"
> "Nay, therof spak I nought, ha, ha!" quod she,
> "As helpe me God, ye shenden every deel!"
> "O, mercy, dere nece," anon quod he,
> "What so I spak, I mente naught but wel,
> By Mars, the god that helmed is of steel!
> Now beth naught wroth, my blood, my nece dere."

Pandarus often contradicts himself. His very doctrine, we are made to see, is adjusted not so much to his own emotionally secure convictions as to the practical needs of the situation. If we follow carefully his debate with Troilus on whether to abduct Criseyde, this becomes apparent. A collection of Pandarus' statements on Fortune would show it likewise.[38] Pandarus' specific motives for this manipulation, often explained by the Narrator with an air of sympathy, are beside the point for a moment. We may grant that he is fundamentally sincere. He nevertheless operates in a naturalistic world where speech is action. His last words in the poem, signifying complete defeat on his level, are: "I kan namore seye" (V, 1743).

In the context of this characterization, his moments of high style cannot be watched without mixed feelings. It is not that Chaucer represents him as hypocrite, buffoon, or pimp. The self-defensive dialogue with Troilus goes farther than the one in the *Filostrato* to assert the "gentilesse, compassioun, and felawship and trist" of Pandarus in his role.[39] He shares, too, in the sympathetic hyperbole of the Narrator: "This Pandare, that neigh malt for wo and routhe" (I, 582). One does not question the genuineness of his surprise and sorrow as in the later Books his whole contrivance, with his friends' happiness, comes tumbling down.[40] But Chaucer has such fine control of the characterization that in giving Pandarus conventional expressions of high passion he makes us often feel the discrepancy between temperament and training, between the natural practicality and the tutored, "appropriate" posture. At the height of Pandarus' persuasion of Criseyde, it is the magnificent tactical build-up and the stiffness of the rhetoric that cast a questionable light on his outburst and his tears:

> "Wo worth the faire gemme vertulees!   [II, 344]
> Wo worth that herbe also that dooth no boote!
> Wo worth that beaute that is routhelees!
> Wo worth that wight that tret ech undir foote!"

145

Elsewhere this feeling is supported by a word: "Therwith it *semed* as he wepte almost" (III, 64). Most characteristically, the effect is in a juxtaposition of the two responses, the practical action ever elbowing the "proper" sentiment aside:

> Therwith his manly sorwe to biholde,   [III, 113]
> It myghte han mad an herte of stoon to rewe;
> And Pandare wep as he to water wolde,
> And poked evere his nece new and newe . . .

> Fil Pandarus on knees, and up his eyen   [III, 183]
> To heven threw, and held his hondes highe,
> "Immortal god," quod he, "that mayst nought deyen,
> Cupid I mene, of this mayst glorifie;
> And Venus, thow mayst maken melodie!
> Withouten hond, me semeth that in towne,
> For this merveille, ich here ech belle sowne.

> "But ho! namore as now of this matere;
> For-whi this folk wol comen up anon . . ."[41]

One can perhaps be excused for recalling Harry Bailly's equally well-meant lyric flight in the *Manciple's Prologue:*

> "O thou Bacus, yblessed be thy name,   [99]
> That so kanst turnen ernest into game!
> Worshipe and thank be to thy deitee!
> Of that mateere ye gete namoore of me."

Noble friend, gentleman, doctrinaire, Pandarus was no more than Harry born for the courtly style. If Pandarus' action and colloquial idiom represent him as a paragon of practical attainments, if it is a joy to see his "bisynesse," the same attributes color his relationship to courtly convention, casting over it a shadow of restlessness. The dominant style is perfectly attuned not only to the character in his own essence—in this respect alone we could compare the Eagle of the *House of Fame,*—but also to the function of the character in the poem's complex pattern of meaning.

One of the most poignant expressions of the visionary nature of Troilus comes in a dialogue that Chaucer closely adapted from the *Filostrato* (VII, 8–10):

> "Have here my trouthe, I se hire! yond she is!   [V, 1157]
> Heve up thyn eyen, man! maistow nat se?"
> Pandare answerede, "Nay, so mote I the!

> Al wrong, by God! What saistow man, where arte?
> That I se yond nys but a fare-carte."

> "Allas! thow seyst right soth," quod Troilus.
> "But, hardily, it is naught al for nought
> That in myn herte I now rejoysse thus.
> It is ayeyns som good I have a thought.
> Not I nat how, but syn that I was wrought,
> Ne felte I swich a comfort, dar I seye;
> She comth to-nyght, my lif that dorste I leye!"

> Pandare answerde, "It may be, wel ynough,"
> And held with hym of al that evere he seyde.
> But in his herte he thoughte, and softe lough,
> And to hymself ful sobreliche he seyde,
> "From haselwode, there joly Robyn pleyde,
> Shal come al that that thow abidest heere.
> Ye, fare wel al the snow of ferne yere!"

The impractical, almost hallucinatory nature of Troilus' vision is given depth here by the Pandaric eyesight to which it is contrasted. The solid, prosaic cart is almost a symbol of the Pandarus world; it expresses the quality of Pandarus' insight, as well as his eyesight, as compared to Troilus'. There is nothing in the earlier Parts of the *Filostrato* to compare with the pointedness of the comparison here, but in the *Troilus* it is present from the beginning, supported by a contrast in the stylistic traits adhering to the two characters.[42] In the dialogues of Book I a mixed style arises as if spontaneously from the interplay of their attitudes. Pandarus supplements tactical doctrine with violent action in the awakening of Troilus from his "litargie" (729 ff.). The same pattern is repeated as he extracts Criseyde's name from his friends:

> Tho gan the veyne of Troilus to blede,   [I, 866]
> For he was hit, and wax al reed for shame.
> "A ha!" quod Pandare, "here bygynneth game."

> And with that word he gan hym for to shake,
> And seyde, "Thef, thow shalt hyre name telle."
> But tho gan sely Troilus for to quake
> As though men sholde han led hym into helle,
> And seyde, "Allas! of al my wo the welle,
> Thanne is my swete fo called Criseyde!"
> And wel neigh with the word for feere he deide.

The blush, the quaking, and the hyperbolical treatment of Troilus' fear are more strikingly conventional by contrast with Pandarus' naturalness than they would have been by themselves. This stylistic definition of the gulf between them is apparent again in the next respite from Pandarus' lecturing. After a brief invocation to Venus, Troilus expresses some doubt whether Criseyde will listen to Pandarus, for she is his niece, and a question of propriety is involved. Pandarus' reply is explosively colloquial:

> "Thow hast a ful gret care   [I, 1023]
> Lest that the cherl may falle out of the moone!
> Whi, Lord! I hate of the thi nyce fare!
> Whi, entremete of that thow hast to doone!"

Troilus' part in the ensuing dialogue is correspondingly courtly, rising finally to the lyric, rhetorical idiom and the patterned, symbolic business of the high style:

> Tho Troilus gan doun on knees to falle,   [I, 1044]
> And Pandare in his armes hente faste,
> And seyde, "Now, fy on the Grekes alle!
> Yet, pardee, God shal helpe us atte laste.
> And dredelees, if that my lyf may laste,
> And God toforn, lo, som of hem shal smerte;
> And yet m'athinketh that this avant m'asterte!
>
> "Now, Pandare, I kan na more seye,
> But, thow wis, thow woost, thow maist, thow art al!
> My lif, my deth, hol in thyn hond I leye.
> Help now!" Quod he, "Yis, by my trowthe, I shal."
> "God yelde the, frend, and this in special,"
> Quod Troilus, "that thow me recomande
> To hire that to the deth me may comande."

In the culminating scene of the poem, this contrast appears in its most extreme form. With it, all residual notions of reading the poem as either novel or romance must fade, for the alternations between naturalistic and conventional activity are so abrupt and striking as to force on us a unique breadth of attention. Pandarus, we recall, engineers the plot with detective-story efficiency. Criseyde is to be detained in his house overnight by the weather (III, 551). Troilus is to be hidden in a little "stuwe," a closet, adjacent to her bedchamber. Even the detective-story trapdoor is supplied, for Troilus' entry to his lady. When all is well, Pandarus comes to Troilus and tells him to make ready. In the midst of this complicated web of practical activity, in this suffocatingly prosaic setting, crouching in the darkness, Troilus makes invocation:

'Now, blisful Venus, thow me grace sende!   [III, 705]
Quod Troilus, "For nevere yet no nede
Hadde ich er now, ne halvendel the drede."

Quod Pandarus, "Ne drede the nevere a deel,
For it shal be right as thow wolt desire;
So thryve I, this nyght shal I make it weel,
Or casten al the gruwel in the fire."

The colloquial incisiveness of this reply, unfelt by Troilus, sets off even further the remainder of his invocation, to Venus, to Jove, to Mars, to Phoebus, to Mercury, to Diana, and to the Fates themselves:

"Yet, blisful Venus, this nyght thow me enspire," [III, 712]
Quod Troilus, "As wys as I the serve,
And evere bet and bet shal, til I sterve.

"And if ich hadde, O Venus ful of myrthe,
Aspectes badde of Mars or of Saturne,
Or thow combust or let were in my birthe,
Thy fader prey al thilke harm disturne
Of grace, and that I glad ayein may turne,
For love of hym thow lovedest in the shawe,
I meene Adoun, that with the boor was slawe.

"O Jove ek, for the love of faire Europe,
The which in forme of bole awey thow fette,
Now help! O Mars, thow with thi blody cope,
For love of Cipris, thow me nought ne lette!
O Phebus, thynk whan Dane hireselven shette
Under the bark, and laurer wax for drede,
Yet for hire love, O help now at this nede!

"Mercurie, for the love of Hierse eke,
For which Pallas was with Aglawros wroth,
Now help! and ek Diane, I the biseke,
That this viage be nought to the looth.
O fatal sustren, which, er any cloth
Me shapen was, my destine me sponne,
So helpeth to this werk that is bygonne!"

And again, this time with redoubled force, we are wrenched back into the practical world:

> Quod Pandarus, "Thow wrecched mouses herte, [III, 736]
> Artow agast so that she wol the bite?
> Why, don this furred cloke upon thy sherte,
> And folwe me, for I wol have the wite.
> But bid, and lat me gon biforn a lite."
> And with that word he gan undon a trappe,
> And Troilus he brought in by the lappe.

One sees the cloth of destiny; the other sees a shirt.

As the scene shifts from the "stuwe" to the bedchamber, and the atmosphere of the scene gradually becomes less like that of a detective novel and more like that of a romance, we can see a correspondingly shifting effect arise from the mixture of styles. In the dark closet with Pandarus, Troilus is pathetically out of his element; his friend is the master mind. In bed with Criseyde, Troilus is the master; Pandarus, before he finally retreats, becomes something of the Fool.

But getting Troilus into bed is in itself a practical matter. It is obvious that here Chaucer purposely exaggerates even the conventional lovesickness of the romance for one last touch of ironic contrast before his most sustained and unhampered passage on the worthiness of earthly love. The motives of the "stuwe" scene are carried out into the bedchamber. With Troilus invisible in the shadows, Pandarus awakens Criseyde. The scene begins on a superbly naturalistic level:

> His nece awook, and axed, "Who goth there?"   [III, 751]
> "My dere nece," quod he, "it am I.
> Ne wondreth nought, ne have of it no fere."
> And ner he com, and seyde hire in hire ere,
> "No word, for love of God, I yow biseche!
> Lat no wight risen and heren of oure speche."
>
> "What! which wey be ye comen, *benedicite?*"
> Quod she, "and how thus unwist of hem alle?"
> "Here at this secre trappe-dore," quod he.
> Quod tho Criseyde, "Lat me som wight calle!"
> "I! God forbede that it sholde falle,"
> Quod Pandarus, "that ye swich folye wroughte!
> They myghte demen thyng they nevere er thoughte."

The whispered dialogue continues until Criseyde's far from naturalistic mono-

logue on false felicity, which has only an ulterior relevance to the action.⁴³ Then
the superbly Pandaric process of convincing Criseyde continues, and finally
Troilus enters:

> This Troilus ful soone on knees hym sette   [III, 953]
> Ful sobrely right be hyre beddes hed,
> And in his beste wyse his lady grette.
> But, Lord, so she wex sodeynliche red!
> Ne though men sholde smyten of hire hed,
> She kouthe nought a word aright out brynge
> So sodeynly, for his sodeyn comynge.

In the activity of Pandarus about the immobile, kneeling, worshiping Troilus
we begin to see a hint of the clown:

> But Pandarus, that so wel koude feele   [III, 960]
> In every thyng, to pleye anon bigan,
> And seyde, "Nece, se how this lord kan knele!
> Now, for youre trouthe, se this gentil man!"
> And with that word he for a quysshen ran,
> And seyde, "Kneleth now, while that yow leste,
> There God youre hertes brynge soone at reste!"

Criseyde kisses Troilus, and bids him sit down. The master engineer and incipient clown, his work presumably over,

> drow hym to the feere,   [III, 978]
> And took a light, and fond his contenaunce,
> As for to looke upon an old romaunce.

This is a carefully managed, premature pause in Pandarus' naturalistic activity.
The style of the scene immediately mounts in the semilyric, semiphilosophic
monologue of Criseyde on jealousy, and her speech is followed by business that
harks back to romantic convention.⁴⁴ The Narrator throws all his sympathy on
the side of Love's triumph—

> But now help God to quenchen al this sorwe!   [III, 1058]
> So hope I that he shal, for he best may.
> For I have seyn, of a ful misty morwe
> Folowen ful ofte a myrie someris day;
> And after wynter foloweth grene May.
> Men sen alday, and reden ek in stories,
> That after sharpe shoures ben victories

—and the noble, idealistic Troilus is so overcome by grief at his lady's tears, that his state can only be described in nonrepresentational terms:

> But wel he felt aboute his herte crepe,   [III, 1069]
> For everi tere which that Criseyde asterte,
> The crampe of deth . . .

In his grief he thinks that all is lost:

> And therwithal he heng adown the heed,   [III, 1079]
> And fil on knees, and sorwfully he sighte.
> What myghte he seyn? he felte he nas but deed,
> For wroth was she that sholde his sorwes lighte.
> But natheles, whan that he speken myghte,
> Than seyde he thus, "God woot that of this game,
> Whan al is wist, than am I nought to blame."
>
> Therwith the sorwe so his herte shette,
> That from his eyen fil ther nought a tere,
> And every spirit his vigour in knette,
> So they astoned or oppressed were.
> The felyng of his sorwe, or of his fere,
> Or of aught elles, fled was out of towne;
> And down he fel al sodeynly a-swowne.

We have seen swoons before in medieval literature: they signalize a deep, noble, monumental sorrow. Our Narrator tells us, in a modest way,

> This was no litel sorwe for to se . . .   [III, 1093]

But in the same breath:

> Pandare up as faste,   [III, 1094]
> "O nece, pes, or we be lost!" quod he,
> "Beth naught agast!" but certeyn, at the laste,
> For this or that, he into bed hym caste,
> And seyde, "O thef, is this a mannes herte?"
> And of he rente al to his bare sherte . . .

This is the first time in medieval literature that the go-between must go so far as actually to pick up the hero and throw him into the lady's bed. Shortly thereafter, as the action turns again into the region of romance, and Criseyde kisses Troilus, and he speaks to her, Pandarus retreats, saying truly,

> "For aught I kan aspien, [III, 1135]
> This light, nor I, ne serven here of nought.
> Light is nought good for sike folkes yën!"

And he carries the candle to the fireplace. His parting shot, as he goes off to sleep, is:

> "If ye be wise, [III, 1189]
> Swouneth nought now, lest more folk arise!"

Now Troilus is in his element, and the style of the scene rises, unhampered, to what has been called "some of the greatest erotic poetry in the world."[45]

The poem's stretch between the idealized and the practical in sentiment and action is drawn to its farthest limits in this sequence. Particularly, the distance between Troilus and Pandarus is never so great as at the moment of that symbolic-realistic swoon. That the scene does not disintegrate between two opposite poles at this point is one of the clearest examples in all Chaucer's works of his complete control of his medium. Pandarus never quite *becomes* the farcical clown. Troilus never *becomes* impossibly melodramatic. In methodological terms, the scene (and by and large, the poem) operates neither under the exclusive assumptions of romantic convention, nor under those of naturalism, but rather under both at once. The result, then, is a double view of the same situation, producing, where the two views are pointedly contrasted, a double irony.[46] Of Pandarus and Troilus, each works better than the other knows.

§ 3. Criseyde

There are very good reasons why Pandarus and Troilus can coexist, each with integrity, in the scene just described and in the poem as a whole. Where Troilus is concerned, the poem is counterweighted against melodrama partly because his idiom has a double function. In the mixture of the scenes with Pandarus it still retains its original courtly purity, irony or no, and thus preserves our conventional acceptance of and sympathy with him. Similarly, the incipient clownishness of Pandarus never degenerates into farce partly because a thousand details of naturalistic speech and action that precede his entry into the bedchamber of romance show him to be consistently true to himself. But there is another and much more important counterweight than this in both scene and poem, namely, that the situation itself is always sufficient unto both views. Criseyde answers to both estimates. In terms of style, she speaks in both idioms. In terms of the poem's pattern of meaning, she represents the many-sided complexity of the earthly fact whose mixture of qualities provides to each beholder the abstraction that he takes for the thing itself. Seen dynamically, in the alternating dominance and recession of each of her various qualities as surrounding conditions evoke them, she represents earthly instability. She is as the world is and goes as the world goes. If between Troilus and Pandarus the mixed style produces an irony turning on human incapacity to see, within Criseyde it produces an ambiguity turning on human inability to be.

The Narrator is an instrument of Chaucer's strategy; both his sympathy and his occasional ignorance contribute to the ambiguity of Criseyde. Where Boccaccio says quite specifically that Criseyde is childless, Chaucer's Narrator is purposely obscure:

> But wheither that she children hadde or noon,   [I, 132]
> I rede it naught, therfore I late it goon.

Where Boccaccio says on Criseyde's departure that she was *soon* to change, and abandon Troiolo for another lover, Chaucer's Narrator toward the end of the story still does not know:

> But trewely, how longe it was bytwene   [V, 1086]
> That she forsok hym for this Diomede,
> Ther is non auctour telleth it, I wene."

In a portrait of her (imitated from Joseph of Exeter's *Ylias*), he adds gratuitously: "But trewely, I kan nat telle hire age" (V, 826). A host of minor narrative touches contribute to the same end. Thus of Criseyde's response to her early meetings with Troilus the Narrator says:

> So wis he was, she was namore afered,—   [III, 482]
> I mene, as fer as oughte ben requered.

and of Pandarus' fateful dinner invitation to Criseyde:

> Nought list myn auctour fully to declare   [III, 575]
> What that she thoughte whan he seyde so,
> That Troilus was out of towne yfare,
> As if he seyde therof soth or no;
> But that, withowten await, with hym to go,
> She graunted hym, sith he hire that bisoughte,
> And, as his nece, obeyed as hire oughte.

Occasionally he contrives a pointed contradiction between narrative and dramatic action, as when Criseyde sees Troilus returning from the battlefield and exclaims to herself, like Lavinia in *Eneas*: "Who yaf me drynke?"[48] In *Eneas* there is no question of the suddenness of Love's assault, but Chaucer's Narrator complicates the effect:

Now myghte som envious jangle thus: [II, 666]
"This was a sodeyn love; how myght it be
That she so lightly loved Troilus,
Right for the firste syghte, ye, parde?"
Now whoso seith so, mote he nevere ythe!
For every thyng, a gynnyng hath it nede
Er al be wrought, withowten any drede.

For I sey nought that she so sodeynly
Yaf hym hire love, but that she gan enclyne
To like hym first . . .

The dramatic action and the editorial comment together produce a kind of controlled ambiguity that is increasingly apparent as the poem progresses. In the last two Books, when the Narrator speaks of

how Criseyde Troilus forsook,   [IV, 15]
Or at the leeste, how that she was unkynde . . .

his function is to hold in suspense our moral condemnation of her. His loyalty to her, no less than Troilus', mitigates the bare sin of her action, urging us to see in it a weakness that is not so much personal and narrowly reprehensible as pathetic, universally human in its mixture with so much that is good:

Men seyn—I not—that she yaf hym hire herte. [V, 1050]

And if I myghte excuse hire any wise,   [V, 1097]
For she so sory was for hire untrouthe,
Iwis, I wolde excuse hire yet for routhe.

For which Criseyde upon a day, for routhe,—   [V, 1587]
I take it so,—touchyng al this matere,
Wrot hym ayeyn . . .

Between them, the two very different lights that Pandarus and Troilus alternately play on Criseyde create the same kind of ambiguity. The scenes with Pandarus show us Criseyde the woman, pliable and movable. Like Laudine, she is in these scenes so much less the goddess. As Troilus appeals to her highest and most intangible standards of value, Pandarus addresses himself to the widow, the niece, the traitor's daughter, and the lonely female. Troilus brings out her pity and admiration. Pandarus strikes sparks from her practical, self-protective nature. For Criseyde's scenes with him Chaucer creates a purely representational setting, and the action is described with unexampled subtlety and minuteness:

> With that she gan hire eighen down to caste,   [II, 253]
> And Pandarus to coghe gan a lite . . .

> Therwith al rosy hewed tho wex she,   [II, 1198]
> And gan to homme . . .

> She shette it, and in to Pandare gan goon,   [II, 1226]
> Ther as he sat and loked into the strete,
> And down she sette hire by hym on a stoon
> Of jaspre, upon a quysshyn gold-ybete . . ."⁴⁹

In these scenes we find Criseyde meeting Pandarus in his world, on his own terms, fencing with the master in dialogue that has no equal for naturalism in all of medieval literature. Pandarus tells her that he has news five times better than if the siege were over. Then he refuses to tell her what it is. Her response is acutely seen:

> Tho gan she wondren moore than biforn   [II, 141]
> A thousand fold, and down hire eyghen caste;
> For nevere, sith the tyme that she was born,
> To knowe thyng desired she so faste;
> And with a syk she seyde hym atte laste,
> "Now, uncle myn, I nyl yow nought displese,
> Nor axen more that may do yow disese."

They talk "of this and that," and Chaucer underlines the tactical motives beneath the polite conversation by the subtlest exaggeration of its hollow echo of agreement:

> she gan axen hym how Ector ferde,   [II, 153]
> That was the townes wal and Grekes yerde.
> "Ful *wel, I thonk it God*" quod Pandarus,
>
> . . .
>
> "*In good feith*, em," quod she, "that liketh me;
> Thei faren *wel, God save hem bothe two!*"
>
> . . .
>
> "*In good faith, that is soth*," quod Pandarus.
>
> . . .
>
> "*God help me so*, I knowe nat *swiche tweye*."

> "*By God,*" quod she, "of Ector *that is sooth.*"
>
> . . .
>
> "Ye sey *right sooth,* ywys," quod Pandarus.

Then follow three hundred verses of magnificent fencing, with feint and parry and passionate attack on both sides. It can sustain one's closest examination for all the traits that make for great dialogue: the dynamic ebb and flow of advantage, the shading of tone, the dramatic revelation of character and motive. Criseyde is finally no match for Pandarus. Just before she succumbs to his final maneuver, the Narrator tells us sympathetically that she was almost dead of fear, that she

> was the ferfulleste wight   [II, 450]
>   That myghte be . . .

After the masterful display of the currents of force that flow beneath the surface of appearance, we are shown Criseyde's responding to appearance itself:

> and herde ek with hire ere   [II, 451]
> And saugh the sorwful ernest of the knyght,
> And in his preier ek saugh noon unryght . . .

But no less adversary than victim, she thinks to herself: "It nedeth me ful sleighly for to pleie" (II, 462). Then she agrees to make Troilus "good chere," within the bounds of her honor, and finally, in a less guarded mood, she asks, "Kan he wel speke of love?" (II, 503).

This scene contains the seeds of two old theories of Criseyde's character: Criseyde the calculating woman, and Criseyde the innocent seduced by treachery. She is neither, but has rather some proportion of both, ambiguously mixed. What should further be seen, however, is that any traits made apparent in these naturalistic scenes must be essentially of a piece. No concession made to Pandarus alone could reveal her in any aspect but that of the social, practical, and movable woman. Only this much, however skillfully, does Chaucer show us through naturalism, and it by no means exhausts her nature. She can be pushed by Pandarus a certain distance, as far as revival of her naturally feminine interest in love, but it takes other impulses and other scenes to show us the side of her nature through which she is not pushed, but inspired.

This we see in the scenes with Troilus. When Pandarus leaves, Troilus rides by, heroically described, and he speaks directly to the heart. For the first time Criseyde feels love itself, and, as if to signalize the shifting of the action to another plane of reality, Chaucer turns for the first time to the conventional introspective monologue of the French romance. He reviews, with fullness but with no loss of ambiguity, all the factors which enter Criseyde's situation with the onset of love. Some of these are practical, and Criseyde is represented as harboring an inner conflict between hope and fear; but the whole mode of presenting this conflict has left naturalism behind. No longer is she presented as the possibly "calculating" woman, in the realistic sense, any more than the endless inner debates of romance represent their thinkers as calculating.[50] With this monologue the setting shifts; Criseyde passes out of the Pandaric world into the garden of love:

> This yerd was large, and rayled alle th'aleyes,   [II, 820]
> And shadewed wel with blosmy bowes grene,
> And benched newe, and sonded alle the weyes,
> In which she walketh arm in arm bitwene,
> Til at the laste Antigone the shene
> Gan on a Troian song to singen cleere,
> That it an heven was hire vois to here.

Then follow the song, the description of the coming of evening, the singing nightingale, and Criseyde's dream, the sequence in which the poem comes closest to pure romance.

There are several such transitions of Criseyde from one world to another. In the great consummation scene in Book III, Criseyde is seen alternately in a naturalistic light, as she responds dramatically to Pandarus' sudden appearance, and in a conventional light, as the poet gives her nonrepresentational monologue to speak. With the ascendance of Troilus in the action she is correspondingly idealized. A heightened style comes into the description:

> And as the newe abaysed nyghtyngale,   [III, 1233]
> That stynteth first whan she bygynneth to synge,
> Whan that she hereth any herde tale,
> Or in the hegges any wyght stirynge,
> And after siker doth hire vois out rynge,
> Right so Criseyde, whan hire drede stente,
> Opned hire herte, and tolde hym hire entente.

She sings an aubade to match her lover's, and no one can doubt, reading the poetry that Chaucer lavishes on her, that here she mirrors the loftiest conceptions of courtly love. But immediately after this scene, with the lyric cadences of the lovers still in our ears, Pandarus enters again, and again our perspective of Criseyde is reversed:

Pandare, o-morwe which that comen was   [III, 1555]
Unto his nece, and gan hire faire grete,
Seyde, "Al this nyght so reyned it, allas,
That al my drede is that ye, nece swete,
Han litel laiser had to slepe and mete.
Al nyght," quod he, "hath reyn so do me wake,
That som of us, I trowe, hire hedes ake."

And ner he com, and seyde, "How stant it now
This mury morwe? Nece, how kan ye fare?"
Criseyde answerde, "Nevere the bet for yow,
Fox that ye ben! God yeve youre herte kare!
God help me so, ye caused al this fare,
Trowe I," quod she, "for al youre wordes white.
O, whoso seeth yow, knoweth yow ful lite."

Perhaps the highest point in Chaucer's representation of Criseyde in her ideal aspects comes in a declaration which Chaucer transferred[51] to her from Boccaccio's Troiolo:

"For trusteth wel, that youre estat roial,   [IV, 1667]
Ne veyn delit, nor only worthinesse
Of yow in werre or torney marcial,
Ne pompe, array, nobleye, or ek richesse
Ne made me to rewe on youre destresse,
But moral vertu, grounded upon trouthe,
That was the cause I first hadde on yow routhe!

"Eke gentil herte and manhod that ye hadde,
And that ye hadde, as me thoughte, in despit
Every thyng that souned into badde,
As rudenesse and poeplissh appetit,
And that youre resoun bridlede youre delit;
This made, aboven every creature,
That I was youre, and shal while I may dure."

Now and again we can apprehend Criseyde at the very mid-point of her ambivalence. When she enters the bedchamber at the house of Deiphebus, and the suffering Troilus greets her as his "swete herte" and wishes to kneel to her, she is caught between two roles, the lady of romance and the woman in political danger:

Gan bothe hire hondes softe upon hym leye.
"O, for the love of God, do ye nought so
To me," quod she, "I! what is this to seye?
Sire, comen am I to yow for causes tweye;
First, yow to thonke, and of youre lordshipe eke
Continuance I wolde yow biseke."

The scene embodies in a marked way the corresponding ambivalence in the
approaches of the two men. On the one hand there is Pandarus, who "poked
evere his nece new and newe." On the other hand there is Troilus' testament
of love. While dynamic in effect and representational in cadence, it reminds us
of nothing less boyish and elevated than the pure speech of Guillaume de Lorris'
Lover:

"What that I mene, O swete herte deere?"   [III, 127]
Quod Troilus, "O goodly, fresshe free,
That with the stremes of youre eyen cleere
Ye wolde somtyme frendly on me see,
And thanne agreen that I may ben he,
Withouten braunche of vice on any wise,
In trouthe alwey to don yow my servise,

"As to my lady right and chief resort,
With al my wit and al my diligence;
And I to han, right as yow list, comfort,
Under yowre yerde, egal to myn offence,
As deth, if that I breke youre defence;
And that ye deigne me so muche honoure,
Me to comanden aught in any houre;

"And I to ben youre, verray, humble, trewe,[52]
Secret, and in my paynes pacient,
And evere mo desiren fresshly newe
To serve, and ben ay ylike diligent,
And with good herte al holly youre talent
Receyven wel, how sore that me smerte,—
Lo, this mene I, myn owen swete herte."

The doctrine here is perfect and conventional, but it cannot be fairly dissociated
from the style, which embodies the anxious breathlessness, the boyishly literal

completeness of Troilus' devotion to the ideal. The stanzas themselves are grammatically connected, in a single sentence, to give the whole speech a breathless continuity, which is supported by the simple accretion of clauses. It is the sense of passionate purity implied by the style of Troilus that has an effect equal to that of all the machinations of Pandarus on the disposition of Criseyde. Farther on we have from her a superb statement that ties together both worlds:

> "Ne hadde I er now, my swete herte deere,   [III, 1210]
> Ben yold, ywis, I were now nought heere!"

Here is perhaps an ironic reflection on the labors of Pandarus. He, through his stratagems, has delivered the woman in the flesh, but she would not have been there if the woman in spirit had not yielded herself first. The spiritual woman yields to Troilus.

§ 4. THE ENDING

The form of the poem's hortatory epilogue—direct address by the Narrator—grows out of the continuous part that this character plays in the poem.[53] In the final Book his part is gradually increased, so that the ending takes on the nature of a dramatic climax to his participation in the action. His position in relation to the action shifts as well. For a good part of the poem he has been on almost the same plane as the actors, downstage and to the side, so close and so responsive that occasionally he cannot restrain his identification with them; his stance is that of a witness.[54] Our ability to see both him and the actors thus simultaneously makes him, as I have said, a fine instrument for irony. But toward the end of the story, as if belatedly learning from it, he draws back from the action and more into our line of vision. He becomes a storyteller again. He depends more on his "olde bokes." He is now less an occasional victim of irony than, with us, a perceiver of it. There creeps into his still active sympathy a note of detachment:

> Thus goth the world. God shilde us fro meschaunce, [V, 1434]
> And every wight that meneth trouthe avaunce!

> Swich is this world, whoso it kan byholde: [V, 1748]
> In ech estat is litel hertes reste.
> God leve us for to take it for the beste!

Then, moved by Troilus' fate, and as if to compensate for the recency of his discovery of the story's meaning, he steps right before us and announces it in the epilogue, with triumphant rhetoric and movingly eloquent exhortation:

Swich fyn hath, lo, this Troilus for love!   [V, 1828]
Swich fyn hath al his grete worthynesse!
Swich fyn hath his estat real above,
Swich fyn his lust, swich fyn hath his noblesse!
Swich fyn hath false worldes brotelnesse!
And thus bigan his lovyng of Criseyde,
As I have told, and in this wise he deyde.

O yonge, fresshe folkes, he or she,
In which that love up groweth with youre age,
Repeyreth hom fro worldly vanyte,
And of youre herte up casteth the visage
To thilke God that after his ymage
Yow made, and thynketh al nys but a faire
This world, that passeth soone as floures faire.

   The moral of the epilogue is inherent in the poem from its beginning. That the poem is a criticism as well as a celebration of secular life is announced in its very first line. The dramatic irony thus established is early caught up in the Troy background, and in occasional philosophic comments on the action, as Pandarus' on fortune and Criseyde's on false felicity, which take on an increasingly somber meaning as the poem progresses. But the greatest source of irony, for the first four Books, is in the narrative structure, the pattern of characters, and the contrast of styles that we have studied in detail. The genius of comedy, insisted Socrates, is the same with that of tragedy. Nothing proves it better than this poem. For the irony of Troilus' paralysis when compared with Pandarus' lively grasp of affairs, and of the latter's busyness when compared with Troilus' idealism, is easily convertible from comedy to tears. It prepares us for the defeat of each of these figures with the ending of the poem. It has been argued that we are prepared for Criseyde's defection by our knowledge of her weaker traits, her timidity and softheartedness.[85] These are the concrete expressions, it is true, of her involvement in time and tide, and thus they must have a relationship to her change of heart. But they do not explain it. The poetry speaks more deeply and symbolically than this. Our preparation for whatever may befall is rather in the very shimmering ambiguity of Chaucer's rendering, in which we find promise of everything, and assurance of almost nothing but change. Chaucer's handling of the denouement is the acid test of the poem and of all the theories of it; and here there is more support for a symbolic reading than for a psychological one.

In the denouement our view of the action continues to shift, as in the first three Books, between scenes and characters of different quality, but with the beginning of Book IV it takes on a wider swing and a longer focus. We are reminded of the Trojan setting at once in a resumption of the sinewy description of the fighting. Group scenes—of the Trojan Parliament and of Criseyde's sympathetic friends—are introduced as a palpable factor for the first time since Book II, and with Criseyde's departure from Troy our attention is divided over an unprecedented physical space. Where Boccaccio has only two passages adverting to her in the Greek camp, Chaucer has four,[55] and each swing from one locus to the other not only separates, with deepening irony, the lovers from each other, but swallows up their private concerns in the enlarged picture. Furthermore, each series of events, the Trojan and the Greek, is given a tone pathetically faded, as if some of the importance were already ebbing out of the affairs of Troilus and Criseyde. This tone is partly owing to the Narrator's increasing intervention between us and the action, and partly to the comparative spareness of the writing itself, which now deals by stanzas with matters that would earlier have taken pages. But the abbreviation is itself owing to a sense that all these events have been spelled out before. We hear Troilus' prolonged lyricism here as the echoing of his earlier sorrow; and we find Pandarus, his part now muted, still urging his friend to arise from his bed, and still using the old, tactical accusations.[57] There is another exchange of letters. And on the other side, the wooing of Criseyde by Diomede sounds like "an inferior and degraded replica" of her wooing by Pandarus and Troilus. Recognition of this we owe to Speirs,[58] and on the trail of it we find a host of reminiscences. Diomede is Pandarus again in his power of speech and in his tactical sense, in his idiom and in his gesture.[59] And Criseyde responds with the same kind of equivocation, as Speirs suggests. She accords to his suit the same inner debate that she gave Troilus',[60] and finally, "men seyn—I not," the same reward. There is more than an echo of past events in this; Chaucer improvises for this "sodeyn," tactical Diomede the air of a Troilus, too:

> And with that word he gan to waxen red, [V, 925]
> And in his speche a litel wight he quok,
> And caste asyde a litle wight his hed,
> And stynte a while; and afterward he wok,
> And sobreliche on hire he threw his lok,
> And seyde, "I am, al be it yow no joie,
> As gentil man as any wight in Troie."

The time span to which we must now attend is lengthened further, on one side by the sudden reminiscence that even Troilus was not the first:

> "I hadde a lord, to whom I wedded was,   [V, 975]
> The whos myn herte al was . . ."

On the other side there is for Criseyde no ending; she fades out of the poem with time itself: "But al shal passe; and thus take I my leve" (V, 1085). Meanwhile she still retains her old ambivalence of nature, now faded in distance:

> "But syn I se ther is no bettre way,   [V, 1069]
> And that to late is now for me to rewe,
> To Diomede algate I wol be trewe."

The difficulty of assessing the nature of Criseyde is almost proverbial. This in itself seems to me the most promising key to the critical problem she presents.[61] Her ambiguity is her meaning. To see her only as the ideal heroine of romance would be to ignore the strength of her relationship to the phenomenal, realistic world created through Chaucer's naturalism. Criseyde is one of the most "natural" figures in medieval literature. She cannot be understood purely through courtly convention. Yet Chaucer constructs her only partly of naturalistic materials, and she is thus only imperfectly describable by naturalistic criticism. An exclusive view of her as a psychological entity, subject only to the stress of circumstances and analyzable purely in terms of concrete motives, would be to ignore or distort those idealized traits that are exhibited in the scenes with Troilus. In this limited perspective we would have to read the love scenes as something like hypocrisy, and the betrayal as the product of an individual, psychological quirk, be it "fear," "impressionability," or any of the other "tragic flaws" that are used to explain her. While the denouement does indeed perpetuate one's sense of her softness and changeability—she was "slydynge of corage," says Chaucer,—it does not present her with psychological finesse, nor as a psychological entity. To read it thus makes her action grotesque, her significance trivial, the Narrator's sympathy inexplicable. The truth of her characterization is in her consistent ambiguity. The meaning of the poem does not hinge on so fortuitous a fact as Troilus' placing his faith in the wrong woman or in a bad woman, but in the fact that he places his faith in a thing which can reflect back to him the image of that faith and yet be incapable of sustaining it. The rendering of Criseyde's betrayal is rather symbolic than psychological. The whole denouement is a symbolic repetition, seen now in a wider and more impersonal context, of what has been and what, indeed, may be again. Chaucer has dealt with Criseyde naturalistically in certain scenes, then, not in the interest of character analysis for itself, but because such scenes show us one aspect of man's involvement with life, his subjection to the ebb and flow of practical circumstance. Chaucer has succeeded, drawing equally on this and on the idealizing imagination of the courtly tradition, in creating in Criseyde one of his most compelling symbols of secular life:

> thynketh al nys but a faire   [V, 1840]
> This world, that passeth soone as floures faire.

Were the world not fair, it would not have its deep and tragic attractiveness; were it not mutable and passing, it would not be the world. Criseyde's ambiguity is as the world's. Read it one way and you make Troilus' ennobling discovery, and also his error; read it another and you do Pandarus' zestful business, and get his returns. But either way, the world will pass.

The conclusion of the *Troilus* is medieval and conservative, but coming at the end of this poem it has an impressive validity. It is neither the reactionary "conclusioun" of a philosophical recluse nor the conventionally pious retractation of a frightened heretic. Chaucer is astride his world; his conservatism is a critical conservatism that has confronted, felt, and mastered the characteristic experience of his age. This is what the nature of the poem says. The Narrator's stance is such that the story is literally experienced in the telling, and the poem's texture is dense with the interlacing of a wide range of alternative values, tested in themselves and by each other. The style of the poem is similarly medieval and conservative, but developed and deployed with critical energy. Its naturalism is the inherited style made newly acute. It can explore recesses of phenomenal and social experience well beyond the scope of Jean de Meun or Chrétien or the *Flamenca*. Chaucer's conventionalism, in his readiness to test it, is likewise exploratory. His knowledge of it—how much elaboration and how much tension it will sustain, what lights it will reflect, in what modes it can be combined— argues more than a merely received knowledge. Chaucer neither rejects one style nor discovers another. His characteristic achievement, of which the *Canterbury Tales* is another and more grandiose example, is the perception of the ways in which traditional forms can be used to apprehend and organize contemporary experience. His literary maturity comes with the *Troilus,* with the control and subordination of both naturalism and conventionalism to the expression of a coherent pattern of meaning.

VI

the canterbury tales

THOUGH Chaucer completed only a quarter of the projected *Canterbury Tales*, he left a very good idea of its form. This form—a collection of stories framed in the account of a pilgrimage, with the pilgrims telling the stories—has no precise, positivistic source in medieval literature. The framed collection as a genre was already three thousand years old, and had a number of other exemplars in the Middle Ages, but the best and most likely model, Boccaccio's *Decameron,* still lacks certain features that would give it absolute claim to parentage:

> Chaucer's plan differs from Boccaccio's in such general considerations as these: the storytellers represent not one, but many, social classes; the same person presides over the storytelling throughout; in the assigning of tales to individuals, conspicuous attention is given to the appropriateness of the stories to their personalities; the individual pilgrims are made known to us in detail through descriptive and characterizing "portraits"; and the essential element in the frame is a pilgrimage on horseback, in the course of which the stories are told, not at the resting-places, but as the pilgrims travel along the road.[1]

[1] For notes to chapter vi see pages 266–272.

We do not know whether Chaucer had acquaintance with the *Decameron* or not. The form of his work can be approached, certainly, from a number of other directions. It was an age of collections, attended by a scarcity of books and of entertainment generally, by a newly vigorous intellectual culture, especially among laymen, and by a tradition of gathering exempla for moral guidance and for sermons. Countless medieval manuscripts are no more than personal collections of one sort or another. There is in literature, besides the framed collection, a tradition of the intercalation of short tales in longer works, evidenced for instance by Ovid's *Metamorphoses,* the *Roman de la Rose,* Boccaccio's *Filocolo* and *Ameto,* and several of Machaut's *Dits.* Chaucer himself includes subsidiary tales in the *Book of the Duchess* and the *House of Fame;* and he had already begun one collection in the *Legend of Good Women* and perhaps another in the *Monk's Tale.* He could hardly have escaped the notion of a framed collection of stories. The immediate character of his frame—a pilgrimage from Southwark to Canterbury—has long been related to his actual surroundings: he probably lived in Greenwich, on the road to Canterbury, from 1385 until near the end of his life, and must thus have been in intimate contact with the very thing he writes of, pilgrims or travelers telling stories.[2]

§ 1 GOTHIC FORM

This factual and generical account of the origin of the *Canterbury Tales* falls far short of recognizing it as art, however; it is surprising how few critics have been impelled to turn to what one might call the formal tradition behind the work. To do so is to discover relationships that point much more satisfactorily to its aesthetic character. The larger form of the poem can be substantially defined by a common generalization about Gothic art. "The basic form of Gothic art," says Hauser (following Frey, and doubtless with no thought of Chaucer),

> is juxtaposition. Whether the individual work is made up of several comparatively independent parts or is not analyzable into such parts, whether it is a pictorial or a plastic, an epic or a dramatic representation, it is always the principle of expansion and not of concentration, of co-ordination and not of subordination, of the open sequence and not of the closed geometric form, by which it is dominated. The beholder is, as it were, led through the stages and stations of a journey, and the picture of reality which it reveals is like a panoramic survey, not a one-sided, unified representation, dominated by a single point of view. In painting it is the 'continuous' method which is favoured; the drama strives to make the episodes as complete as possible and

prefers, instead of the concentration of the action in a few decisive situations, frequent changes of scene, of the characters and the motifs. . . . Gothic art leads the onlooker from one detail to another and causes him, as has been well said, to 'unravel' the successive parts of the work one after the other. . . .³

This Gothic, sequential procession "through the stages and stations of a journey," a deep-seated general form for the ordering of experience, takes on specific symbolic meaning in its particular manifestations. Edith Kern finds in the *Decameron* journey, the stations of which are successive gardens, a progression "away from society with its sufferings and horrors . . . to the very temple of Venus in the heart of Nature. . . ." The procession of the stages in the English mystery cycle, representing the biographical and historical journey of Man from the Creation to the Resurrection, has a more public and self-evident meaning. The dual procession of Chaucer's travelers and their tales is given such specific moral significance by the conception of a religious pilgrimage. If Chaucer knew the road through Greenwich, he also knew the one through the *Divine Comedy:* "Nel mezzo del *cammin* di nostra vita." The metaphor permeated medieval consciousness. Chaucer adapted his early lyric, *An ABC,* from a poem entitled *Le Pèlerinage de vie humaine.* The idea is expressed nobly in his ballade *Truth:*

> Her is non hoom, her nis but wildernesse:
> Forth, pilgrim, forth! Forth, beste, out of thy stal!
> Know thy contree, look up, thank God of al;
> Hold the heye wey, and lat thy gost thee lede;
> And trouthe thee shal delivere, it is no drede.

The two pilgrimages are specifically related in the Parson's prayer for wisdom,

> To shewe you the wey, in this viage,   [*ParsProl* 49]
> Of thilke parfit glorious pilgrymage
> That highte Jerusalem celestial.

The coördinateness and linearity of Chaucer's form, his "heye weye" through life, with its various juxtaposed versions of experience, is invested with a second typically Gothic quality, the tension between phenomenal and ideal, mundane and divine, that informs the art and thought of the period. The variety of pilgrims and tales is thus ordered between traditionally opposed values. This has been very widely recognized in Chaucer criticism, though usually expressed in terms of dramatic rather than symbolic contrast. The pilgrimage frame, with the prologue and links that define it, is likewise ambivalent; it is both realistic and symbolic. This ambivalence is in the symbolic conception of life as a pilgrimage alongside the concrete existence of the Canterbury road, in the generally symbolic character of Chaucer's later naturalism next to his "good ear" and his keen reportorial eye. It is also in various conventionalizations of form and style which stand in an artistically effective relationship to this naturalism.

Of the "two factors in the Gothic duality," Charles Morey says that "the ideal one is visible only in its ensembles; the other [i.e., the realistic] is revealed in innumerable details of which these ensembles are composed."⁵ While this formula cannot be strictly applied to the poem, it fits closely enough to explain why so much of its character has eluded naturalistic criticism. Fortunately we have two excellent inspections of the "ensemble" of the *General Prologue*. J. V. Cunningham, bringing to it a sophisticated notion of the nature and function of literary tradition,⁶ shows that the form of the opening of the *Tales* is a "special realization" of the form of the dream vision. The setting at a given time of year, the seasonal description, the arrival of the Narrator-actor at a special place, the successive portrayals of the company met there, the introduction of a "guide," and the subsequent initiation of the main action, are the elements and the order of the tradition of the *Roman de la Rose*. In the very largest sense, this dream-vision sequence is itself a modification of the universal medieval pilgrimage, be it in quest of human or divine love, but here it is special enough to show how much Chaucer's seeing still employs the forms of the specifically courtly tradition.

Cunningham has remarked the persistence of the traditional form, but we must go on to investigate its function. It is not a relic; it enters a meaningful synthesis such as we have seen unfolding through the early poems and the *Troilus*. By means of this synthesis, secular love is set in juxtaposition to divine love and, on the other side, to the various profanenesses supported by Chaucer's naturalism. Arthur Hoffman's recent study of the "two voices" of the *Prologue* makes just this kind of observation, so sensitively that I can give in summary only a partial indication of its content. Hoffman shows how the opening description of spring, with its natural, sexual metaphors of regeneration, and then its progress toward the other motive of spiritual regeneration, at once establishes a "double view" of the pilgrimage. This ambiguity is perpetuated in the series of portraits, both between and within them. Thus between the Knight and the Squire there is a pointed dualism:

The Knight's love is an achieved devotion, a matter of pledges fulfilled and of values, if not completely realized, yet woven into the fabric of experience (ideals—"trouthe," "honour," "fredom," "curteisie"). The Squire is a lover, a warm and eager lover, paying court to his lady and sleeping no more then the nightingale. In the one, the acquired, tutored, disciplined, elevated, enlarged love, the piety; in the other, the love channelled into an elaborate social ritual, a parody piety, but still emphatically fresh and full of natural impulse. One cannot miss the creation of the Squire in conventional images of nature . . . comparisons that are a kind of re-emergence of the opening lines of the Prologue, the springtime surge of youthful, natural energy . . . the Knight's pilgrimage is more nearly a response to the voice of the saint.[7]

Within the portraits of the Prioress, the Monk, and the Friar there is tension, in various degrees, between the sacred office and the person, the conventional standard and the individual detail. In the Summoner and the Pardoner it lies in a grimly ironic perversion of the "love" which all of the pilgrims variously pursue. Hoffman's most profound observations come when he shows these tensions ultimately resolved: the Squire bent to the service of his father, and thus to his religious goal; the ambiguous motto of the Prioress, in which secular love is encircled by divine; the Parson and the Plowman, brothers, linking the sacred and the secular in harmony of purpose and relationship. Even the Summoner and Pardoner, who are described last, suggest in their offices, "beyond their appalling personal deficiency . . . the summoning and pardoning, the judgement and grace which in Christian thought embrace and conclude man's pilgrimage . . ."[8]

Chaucer's use of the seasonal description and the portrait series—both of them conventional devices of romance and rhetoric—is part, then, of an artistic synthesis, and has nothing either of mechanical habit or gratuitous invention about it. The formal portrait and its formal arrangement mean—and here I come somewhere between the historical observation of Cunningham and the textual analysis of Hoffman—a formal, *a priori,* ideal ordering of experience, without which the naturalistic detail would have only the barest sociological significance. The portraits of the *Roman de la Rose* and of the fabliaux, as we have seen, are full of such detail. What Chaucer has done to the conventional portrait is to pull the traits out of their formulated, uniplanar arrangement, thus to give them an added dimension. Many of the portraits in the *Roman* come in selected series, as first the Vices painted on the garden wall, then the company of courtly Virtues of the Lord Deduit. Boccaccio has just such a select company in the *Decameron*. Chaucer quite consciously abandons the exclusive classification and the reasoned sequence—"Al have I nat set folk in hir degree"—to produce pairings and contrasts that span virtue and vice, heaven and earth. His modifications of convention both within and between the portraits produce not only the "real life" of naturalistic criticism, but also the tension, detail against form, observed nature against formulated order, that supports his deepest meaning.

The links between the tales are consistently naturalistic, full of noise and horseplay, and severely localized by such references as to the shrews in Greenwich and the mud at Bobbe-up-and-doun. It may seem perverseness to try to find "symbolism" in this. Yet I shall risk suggesting that the very consistency is symbolic in the circumstance that, to approach the obvious deviously, the two processions, of travelers and tales, take in different worlds. The latter comprehends a universe of time and space: ancient Thebes, Asia, Tartary, imperial Rome, modern Flanders, London, Oxford, and the North Country, "as fer as cercled is the mapemounde." The former takes in the constricted circle of the sensorily present. It is the known quantity, the lowest common denominator by which the other is scaled and measured.[9] That Chaucer chooses this denominator rather than the palaces and gardens of Boccaccio's frame is the necessary outcome of everything we have already observed of him and his work. For his temperament, his culture, his literary career, the spectrum of values that he sees, the courtly garden cannot be a *common* denominator. His choice of a pilgrimage and of pilgrims has determined his choice of setting. On what possible road, in what possible sphere, can they all be seen at once? All touch at the public inn and the public road, exist bodily in the present—and even here the scholar is ill at ease, and the Canon-alchemist can hardly abide.

The Host stands as mediator between the two processions, director of both. He is made apt for the job by his trade, by his magnificent presence, and by his choric activity, which, though sometimes imperfectly, links the larger world with the local one. To this end, within the naturalism of the characterization, Chaucer has broadened the Host's consciousness to include at least the verbal edges of a variety of spheres. He is the most explosive swearer on the pilgrimage, yet capable of fine, bourgeois overpoliteness. He has a smattering of Latin (imperfect), medicine, law, and rhetoric. He can invoke Bacchus and sermonize on Time.[10] He personifies the thread of local, human response, various yet always the same, which the naturalistic links constitute as a whole.

The relationship between tellers and tales varies, as everyone knows, from a mechanical inconsequentiality to the full naturalism of the dramatic monologues. It is obvious, after allowing for the incompleteness of the plan and the evident carelessness with which some tales were assigned, that Chaucer did not seek in the tales any reportorial fidelity to the idiom of his pilgrims; nor did he fashion the pilgrims as mere dummies to match narrative material already at hand or in mind.[11] Some of the tales, as the Knight's and the Second Nun's, were very likely in existence before the pilgrims. But nine pilgrims (the forester, the plowman, the five guildsmen, and two priests) are given no tales at all, which suggests that for Chaucer the pilgrims at some point achieved a measure of independence. Both the pilgrims, who are visible images of the contemporary human condition, and the tales, which are the experience of a universe of time and space, are marshaled to express a great range and compounding of attitudes. There need not be a one-to-one relationship between them. Where Chaucer mediated carefully between teller and tale, he sought not an idiomatic but a tonal and attitudinal relationship. No medieval poet would have sacrificed all the rich technical means at his disposal merely to make a story sound as if such and such a character were actually telling it. The *Miller's Tale*, to name but one of many, would have been thus impossible. But Chaucer would, after Jean de Meun, adopt dramatic techniques where this technique would in turn support a particular tone or attitude. Thus for the special versions of realism represented by the views of the Wife of Bath, the Pardoner, and the Canon's Yeoman he uses the special naturalism of their dramatic monologues. The basic narrative idiom, however, is that of Chaucer, or rather, of the Chaucerian Narrator whose figure we have traced from the *Book of the Duchess*. His function as intermediary between poet and audience is now to be shared, under the pressure of an unprecedentedly large task, among some nine-and-twenty others, but the final editorial voice is his.[12]

The reader will already have seen that the scheme of the *Canterbury Tales* is in large part the outgrowth of the long story I have been telling. There is a sense in which Chaucer's pilgrims are descendants—to go back no farther—of the speakers in the *Roman de la Rose* and the *Parliament of Fowls*. The form and meaning of the *Tales* completes on a grand scale and in immense detail Chaucer's solution to the besetting problem of the age. The meaningless luxuriance of the *House of Fame*, with its full discordance between realism and conventionalism, presents this problem. The *Parliament* reveals its susceptibility to ordering. *Troilus and Criseyde*, with its alternation and juxtaposition of style, character, and scene in an ironic balance, shows this discordance under control. And in the *Tales* we have, along with this artistic and moral synthesis, a fuller exploration of the worlds it brings together. By virtue of this larger scale, the

Tales show some elements of meaning in clearer articulation, and some in compounds different from those of the earlier poems. My object is now to investigate some of these versions of conventionalism, naturalism, and the mixed style in the light of their relationship to meaning.

§ 2. TWO VERSIONS OF CONVENTIONALISM

Like the portraits in the *General Prologue,* the tales themselves vary in style. The Knight's tale, like his portrait, is highly conventional, and so are the tales of the Man of Law and the Clerk. The Parson is given, in defiance of the least concern for naturalism, a long prose tract on Penitence. The style of tales such as these is explained by the extremity or the purity of the attitudes they represent. When Chaucer writes at either end of the scale of values, indeed, his style becomes correspondingly extreme. When he writes at the Knight's end of the scale,

> Of storial thyng that toucheth gentillesse,
> And eek moralitee and hoolynesse,

he leans heavily on conventional forms.

One of the most general attributes of Chaucer's conventionalism, and a most convenient point of entry into the critical issues it raises, is rhetoric.[13] It is well known that medieval schools preserved in an unbroken but altered tradition the rhetorical teaching of the ancients. Every medieval student took his rhetoric along with grammar and logic in the lower division of the liberal arts curriculum. Rhetoric was the common property of the literate. As we have seen, it served courtly, erotic poetry. It could and did serve, in the hands of the same clerkly class of poets, every other kind of writing that pretended to more than plain speech. In Chaucer's time there were available a number of standard *artes,* textbooks of letter writing and of poetry, based on a corruption of classical theory and often taking their examples from bad, postclassical models. They are primarily concerned with the amplified, "high" style. This is the style presumably represented by Virgil's *Aeneid,* the style in which to deal with grave or elevated matters, or to address important persons.[14] They deal with composition prescriptively, and list both minor figures of speech and larger forms, most of them mediated by the Latin tradition from the tropes and topics of ancient oratory. Thus the formal portrait and the conventionalized description of grove and garden are recommended by the textbooks as examples of *descriptio.* The lyric monologue is substantially *apostrophatio,* with its various "adornments" *exclamatio, conduplicatio, subjectio, dubitatio.*[15] There are many additional figures, including some of the most useful terms in criticism—metaphor, simile, synecdoche,—and some which lend themselves with fatal ease to bad writing: *digressio, expolitio* (expansion or embellishment), *circumlocutio.*

The late Professor Manly was one of the first to draw attention to Chaucer's use of rhetoric and the rhetoric books; his attitude has unfortunately dominated most of the thinking on the subject. In order to protect Chaucer from the stigma which the term had acquired in the nineteenth century, Manly at the outset identified rhetoric in Chaucer with the bad, "artificial," "rejected" style. This is the style that post-Victorian criticism sees in Chaucer's conventionalism generally:

> To any student of his technique, Chaucer's development reveals itself unmistakably . . . as a process of gradual release from the astonishingly artificial and sophisticated art with which he began and the gradual replacement of formal rhetorical devices by methods of composition based upon close observation of life and the exercise of the creative imagination.[16]

Manly goes to some pains to explain the existence of rhetoric in several of Chaucer's best works, and concludes that Chaucer "came more and more to make only a dramatic use of these rhetorical elements, that is, to put them into the mouths of his *dramatis personae* and to use only such as might fittingly be uttered by them." Fitting are scenes in which "the rhetoric is dramatic, is conformed to the character, and is motivated."[17]

The contention that Chaucer gradually abandoned rhetoric is statistically questionable.[18] More questionable yet is the assumption that rhetoric is automatically bad. It takes only a little reflection to see that the use of forms which the critic can describe as rhetorical is one of the principal characteristics of poetry. The critical problem in Chaucer is not the accounting for the presence of rhetorical (i.e., poetic) forms, but the determination of whether they perform as integral parts of the poem. The fact that Chaucer knew the rhetoric books and used their forms in the manner prescribed has little to do with whether the forms so used have poetic value. The common medieval teaching on poetry, it is true, calls merely for an expression in metrical form, ornamented with stylistic devices.[19] But whatever the state of theory in his time, Chaucer managed to produce a quantity of poetry which far exceeds this simple prescription. Nor is this poetry always dramatic, that is, naturalistic and psychological. The tendency of the post-Victorian critic to submerge the problem of Chaucer's rhetoric within a concept of art as naturalism falsifies the nature of both rhetoric and Chaucer. The function of Chaucer's rhetoric is nowhere more demonstrable than in his most conventional poetry.

i. The *Knight's Tale*

A reasonable sympathy with conventionalism requires our understanding that the experience of the idealizing imagination is no less varied than that of realistic observation, and no less true. If the themes of most of Chaucer's conventional poems seem to converge toward the single point of recognizing supernal values in human affairs, the nature of the pointing differs with each poem. We do not read Chaucer, after all, for his philosophical conclusions, but for his workings-out, his poetry. Similarly, if tradition seems to codify Chaucer's poetry according to a fixed number of general forms in a defined area of style, the particular structure and local style of each poem are unique.

Chaucer's conventionalism should neither be dismissed nor taken for granted. The criticism of the *Knight's Tale* has long suffered from both of these errors.[20] The trouble has been in the kinds of assumptions brought to the poem, in an attention to its poor dramatics rather than its rich symbolism, to its surface rather than its structure. The poem is nominally a romance, adapted from Boccaccio's *Teseida*. The plot concerns the rivalry of Palamon and Arcite, Theban knights, who while they are imprisoned by Duke Theseus fall in love with his fair kinswoman, Emilye. Arcite is released from prison and Palamon escapes; they finally fight for Emilye's hand in a tournament. Arcite wins, but at the moment of victory, in a supernaturally inspired accident, he is thrown from his horse and thereafter dies. After a period of mourning, Palamon marries Emilye. This plot has been taken to be the poem's main feature; but unless we wish to attribute to Chaucer an unlikely lapse of skill or taste, it will not sustain very close scrutiny. The "characterization" of Palamon and Arcite has been widely invoked as a key to the poem. In one view the two knights have quasi-allegorical status, representing the Active Life versus the Contemplative Life. But there is little agreement upon which knight is actually the more "contemplative" or the more admirable: if Palamon, the ending is poetic justice; if Arcite, it is irony.[21] The existence of any significant characterization in the poem has been seriously questioned:

> In the *Teseide* there is one hero, Arcita, who loves and is eventually loved by Emilia, a young woman characterized by a natural coquetry, an admiration for a good-looking young knight, and love and sympathy for the wounded hero. Palemone is a secondary figure, necessary to the plot because he brings about the death of Arcita.

The story is a tragedy, caused by the mistake of Arcita in praying to Mars rather than to Venus. In Chaucer's story there are two heroes, who are practically indistinguishable from each other, and a heroine, who is merely a name. In the Italian poem it is possible to feel the interest in hero and heroine which is necessary if one is to be moved by a story. . . . In Chaucer's version, on the other hand, . . . it is hard to believe that anyone can sympathize with either hero or care which one wins Emelye.

In this approach the lack of characterization is the story's greatest weakness; what remains is merely an elaborate and now archaic game:

> Chaucer saw in the *Teseide* a plot which, with some alterations, could be used effectively to present one of those problems of love which the votaries of courtly love enjoyed considering . . . which of two young men, of equal worth and with almost equal claims, shall (or should) win the lady? Stated in such simple terms, the problem may seem foolish, but to readers who could be interested in such questions of love . . . this problem would be no doubt poignant. . . . Obviously in so far as the ideas of courtly love have passed into oblivion since the middle ages, narratives in which they are basic cannot appeal to modern taste.[22]

Long ago, Root suggested the possibility that the poem was not written under the assumptions of naturalism:

> If we are to read the *Knight's Tale* in the spirit in which Chaucer conceived it, we must give ourselves up to the spirit of romance; we must not look for subtle characterization, nor for strict probability of action; we must delight in the fair shows of things, and not ask too many questions. Chaucer can be realistic enough when he so elects; but here he has chosen otherwise. . . . It is not in the characterization, but in the description, that the greatness of the *Knight's Tale* resides. . . . [It] is preëminently a web of splendidly pictured tapestry, in which the eye may take delight, and on which the memory may fondly linger.[23]

Root's conclusion shares in the general critical distrust of the poem; while recognizing its texture he depreciates its meaning, as if these rich materials could not at the same time be the carefully chosen, well-ordered machinery of serious poetry. Generations of readers have made this the most perennially valued of the *Tales*. But neither Root's nor the naturalistic interpretations begin to suggest the depth and complexity which one would expect to find in a work with such a reputation. Now although it is not always necessary to proceed inductively from style to reach a satisfactory interpretation of a poem, the method is sometimes useful in making clear certain assumptions with which the poem should be approached. In the *Knight's Tale*, furthermore, form and style are so functional that they point directly to the meaning.

The pace of the story is deliberately slow and majestic. Random references to generous periods of time make it chronologically slow. Though Chaucer omits a great deal of the tale originally told by Boccaccio in the *Teseida*, he frequently resorts to the rhetorical device of *occupatio* to summarize in detail events or descriptions in such a way as to shorten the story without lessening its weight and impressiveness. Further, there is an extraordinary amount of rhetorical *descriptio* in the poem, all of which slows the narrative. The description of the lists is very detailed, and placed so as to give the impression that we are present at their construction, an operation that appears to consume the full fifty weeks that Theseus allows for it. The narrator's repetitious "saugh I," and his closing remark, "Now been thise lystes maad" (2089), coöperate to this effect.

We can hardly fail to note, too, that a great deal of this descriptive material has a richness of detail far in excess of the demands of the story. At first glance, at least, many passages appear to be irrelevant and detachable. For example, we have sixty-one lines of description of Emetrius and Lygurge; yet so far as the action of the poem is concerned, these two worthies do practically nothing.

Like the descriptions and narrator's comments, the direct discourse in the *Tale* contributes to its slowness. There is virtually no rapid dialogue. Speeches of twenty-five or thirty verses are normal, and one, the final oration of Theseus, takes more than a hundred. More than length, however, the nondynamic *quality* of the speeches is characteristic of the whole poem's style. Many of them have only a nominal value as action or as the instruments to action. Formal, rhetorical structure, and a function comparatively unrelated to the practical necessities of the dramatic situation are the rule. This is true even where the speech is addressed to another character. For instance, when old Saturn is badgered by his granddaughter Venus to aid her in her conflict with Mars, he replies as follows:

> "My deere doghter Venus," quod Saturne, [2453]
> "My cours, that hath so wyde for to turne,
> Hath moore power than woot any man.
> Myn is the drenchyng in the see so wan;
> Myn is the prison in the derke cote;

> Myn is the stranglyng and hangyng by the throte,
> The murmure and the cherles rebellyng,
> The groynynge, and the pryvee empoysonyng;
> I do vengeance and pleyn correccioun,
> Whil I dwelle in the signe of the leoun.
> Myn is the ruyne of the hye halles,
> The fallynge of the toures and of the walles
> Upon the mynour or the carpenter.
> I slow Sampsoun, shakynge the piler;
> And myne be the maladyes colde,
> The derke tresons, and the castes olde;
> My lookyng is the fader of pestilence.
> Now weep namoore . . ."

And finally, the rest of the speech, a mere eight verses, is devoted to promising Venus his aid. We can safely assume that Venus knows all about her grandfather. The long, self-descriptive introduction, therefore, must have some function other than the dramatic.

Going on now to the nature of the action, we find that while the chivalric aspects of the scene are described with minute particularity, there is very little in the *Knight's Tale* of the intimate and distinctive details of look, attitude, and gesture that mark some of Chaucer's more naturalistic poems. It is replete with conventional stage business. There are swoons and cries, fallings on knees, and sudden palenesses; there is a symphony of howls, wails, and lamentations.

When we look at the form in which these materials are organized, we find symmetry to be its most prominent feature. The unity of the poem is based on an unusually regular ordering of elements. The character grouping is symmetrical. There are two knights, Palamon and Arcite, in love with the same woman, Emilye. Above the three and in a position to sit in judgment, is the Duke Theseus, who throughout the poem is the center of authority and the balance between the opposing interests of the knights. In the realm of the supernatural, each of the knights and the lady has a patron deity: Venus, Mars, and Diana. The conflict between Venus and Mars is resolved by the elder Saturn, with no partiality toward either. In the tournament each knight is accompanied by one hundred followers headed by a particularly notable king, on one side Lygurge, on the other Emetrius:

> In al the world, to seken up and doun,   [2587]
> So evene, withouten variacioun,

> Ther nere swiche compaignyes tweye;
> For ther was noon so wys that koude seye
> That any hadde of oother avauntage
> Of worthynesse, ne of estaat, ne age,
> So evene were they chosen, for to gesse.
> And in two renges faire they hem dresse.

This arrangement of the two companies *in two renges* is one of many details of symmetry of scene and action in the poem. At the very beginning we find a uniformly clad company "of ladyes, tweye and tweye, / Ech after oother" (898). When Palamon and Arcite are found in the heap of bodies at Thebes, they are "liggynge by and by, / Bothe in oon armes" (1011). We find that they are cousins, "of sustren two yborn" (1019).

In the scene following the discovery of Emilye, each offers a lyric on the subject (1104 ff., 1118 ff.). When Arcite is released from prison, each delivers a complaint in which even the vocabulary and theme are symmetrical:

> "O deere cosyn Palamon," quod he,   [1234]
> "Thyn is the victorie of this aventure."

> "Allas," quod he, "Arcita, cosyn myn,   [1281]
> Of al oure strif, God woot, the fruyt is thyn."

In the second part, the narrator divides his attention between them, in alternate descriptions; and in the fight subsequent to their meeting they are evenly matched:

> Thou myghtest wene that this Palamon   [1655]
> In his fightyng were a wood leon,
> And as a crueel tigre was Arcite . . .

Theseus appears, "And at a stert he was bitwix hem two" (1705). He sets the conditions of the tournament in round numbers: " 'And this day fifty wykes, fer ne ner, / Everich of you shal brynge an hundred knyghtes . . .' " (1850–51). In the third part the narrator describes the making of lists, in the same place as where the first fight occurs. The lists are circular in shape, a mile in circumference. They are entered from east and west by identical marble gates. The altars or temples of Mars and Venus are situated above these gates. Northward (and equidistant from the other two, no doubt) is the *oratorie* of Diana. The three temples are described in succession, and each description is subdivided in the same way: first the wall-painting with its allegorical figures, and then the statue of the deity itself.

The symmetry of description continues with parallel accounts of the two rival companies, each containing a portrait of the leading king. (2117–89). Then follow the prayers of the principals: Palamon to Venus, Emilye to Diana, Arcite to Mars. The prayers are made in careful order at the hours dedicated by astrology to those deities,[24] and each prayer is answered by some supernatural event. Internally, too, the three prayers show a striking similarity of design, each beginning with rhetorical *pronominatio* and continuing with a reference to the deity's relations with the opposite sex, a self-description by the speaker, a humble assertion of incompetence, a request for assistance, and a promise to worship. The spectators enter the lists and are seated in order of rank. The combatants, Palamon and Arcite, with banners white and red respectively, enter the field through the gates of Venus and Mars.

After Arcite's death, his sepulcher is described. It is erected "ther as first Arcite and Palamoun / Hadden for love the bataille hem bitwene" (2858–59). This is also where the lists were built.[25] The funeral procession, like the procession to the lists, is characterized by precise order, and the details of the funeral are full of the same kind of ordering:

> . . . the Grekes, with an huge route,   [2951]
> Thries riden al the fyr aboute
> Upon the left hand, with a loud shoutynge,
> And thries with hir speres claterynge;
> And thries how the ladyes gonne crye . . .

Further elements in the poem's symmetry of structure and scene could readily be brought forward.

Chaucer's modifications of the *Teseida* seem to have been made precisely in the interest of the kind of organization I am describing. By selection and addition he produced a poem much more symmetrical than its source. Chaucer even regularizes the times and places of the incidents in Boccaccio. He adds the character Emetrius, the parallel descriptions of Emetrius and Lygurge, and the description of Diana's temple.[26] His crowning modification is the equalization of Palamon and Arcite.

These general and inescapable observations on the nature of the poem make clear how it must be approached. The symmetry of scene, action, and character grouping, the slow pace of the narrative and the large proportion of static description, the predominantly rhetorical kind of discourse—along with a lack of subtle discrimination in the stage business—all indicate that the tale is not the best kind in which to look for either delicate characterization or the peculiar fascination of an exciting plot. Subtle delineation of character is neither called for in the poem's design nor possible of achievement through the technical means Chaucer largely employs. There is neither rapid dialogue, nor psychological analysis, nor delicate and revelatory "business" in the poem. Nor does the *Knight's Tale* amount to much as plot and story interest go. Its value depends little on the traits that make a good story: a swift pace, suspense, variety, intrigue. Its main events are forecast long before they occur.[27] The structure of the poem, indeed, works against story interest. Symmetry in character grouping, movement, time and place, supports the leisurely narrative and description in producing an over-all sense of rest and deliberateness. The general intention indicated by the poem's materials and structure lies in a different direction. Its grouping and action, rather than existing for any great interest in themselves, seem constantly to point to a nonrepresentational, symbolic method. There is a decisive correlation of all its elements on this level.

The *Knight's Tale* is essentially neither a story nor a static picture, but rather a sort of poetic pageant. Its design expresses the nature of the noble life,

> That is to seyn, trouthe, honour, knyghthede,   [2789]
> Wysdom, humblesse, estaat, and heigh kynrede,
> Fredom, and al that longeth to that art . . .

The story is immediately concerned with those two noble activities, love and chivalry, but even more important is the general tenor of the noble life, the pomp and ceremony, the dignity and power, and particularly the repose and assurance with which the exponent of nobility invokes order. Order, which characterizes the structure of the poem, is also the heart of its meaning. The society depicted is one in which form is full of significance, in which life is conducted at a dignified, processional pace, and in which life's pattern is itself a reflection, or better, a reproduction, of the order of the universe. And what gives this conception of life its perspective, its depth and seriousness, is its constant awareness of a formidably antagonistic element—chaos, disorder—which in life is an ever-threatening possibility, even in the moments of supremest assuredness, and which in the poem falls across the pattern of order, being clearly exemplified in the erratic reversals of the poem's plot, and deeply embedded in the poem's texture.[28]

The descriptive sections of the *Tale* support this interpretation perfectly, not only in the long passages that come immediately to mind, but also in the short flights that interrupt the narrative more than is warranted by what little information they add to the mere story. By contributing to currents that run continuously throughout the poem—currents that make up the main stream of the noble life—these superficially "irrelevant" descriptions achieve a secure position in the poem's pattern, and ultimately contribute in an important way to its meaning.

The portraits of Emetrius and Lygurge, for instance, have this kind of poetic relevance although their contribution to the surface narrative is slight. Emetrius has "A mantelet upon his shulder hangynge, / Bret-ful of rubyes rede as fyr sparklynge" (2163–64). Lygurge wears

> A wrethe of gold, arm-greet, of huge wighte,   [2145]
> Upon his heed, set ful of stones brighte,
> Of fyne rubyes and of dyamauntz.

Unlike the portraits in the *General Prologue,* here the imagery is organized around no three-dimensional conception of personality; it is conventional, framed in the flat, to express the magnificence that befits nobility. I have noted that after all the description of these two kings they hardly figure in the narrative. The inference, however, is not that the portraits are a waste and an excrescence, "merely decorative," but that they perform a function that is not directly related to the action and is independent of the question of character. They contribute first to the poem's general texture, to the element of richness in the fabric of noble life. More specifically, Chaucer solves the problem of describing the rival companies by describing their leaders; not Palamon and Arcite, but their supporting kings.[20] Their varicolored magnificence, like Theseus' banner, makes the whole field glitter up and down—black, white, yellow, red, green, and gold. Their personal attributes—the trumpet voice of Emetrius, the great brawn of Lygurge, their looks, like lion and griffin—give both a martial quality that we are to attribute to the whole company. About the chariot of Lygurge run great, white, muzzled hunting dogs, big as bullocks. Emetrius' pet animals are a white eagle, lions, and leopards. The fact that these animals are tame only makes the comparison with their masters the more impressive. And practically every other detail is a superlative, the quality of which contributes to martial or royal magnificence.

In some of the descriptions in the *Knight's Tale,* Chaucer is at his very best as a poet:

> The rede statue of Mars, with spere and targe,   [975]
> So shyneth in his white baner large,
> That alle the feeldes glyteren up and doun;
> And by his baner born is his penoun

> Of gold ful riche, in which ther was ybete
> The Mynotaur, which that he slough in Crete.
> Thus rit this duc, thus rit this conquerour,
> And in his hoost of chivalrie the flour . . .

Even in so short a passage, the power bestowed on this description suggests a function deeper than mere ornament. It links with a score of other passages as an expression of Theseus' preëminence in war and chivalry.[30] For instance the very opening of the poem, with its compressed but powerful description of the conquest of the Amazons and the marriage of Ypolita, is devoted to this end, and the texture of the following incident of the mourning women of Thebes, which acts as a kind of prologue to the *Knight's Tale* proper, widens and perpetuates our notion of Theseus as variously the ruler, the conqueror, the judge, and, not least, the man of pity. Among many subsequent details, the magnificence of the lists and of Arcite's funeral is directly associated with Theseus' dispensations.

The establishment of this preëminence is essential to the meaning of the poem and is carried out in many aspects of it. There is an obvious correspondence between the quality of these descriptions and the position of Theseus as the central figure in the poem's pattern of characters. And like the descriptions, the speeches in the poem have a great deal of metaphoric value. If they do not operate very effectively in the interest of plot and characterization—Theseus has been likened to Polonius!—it is because they serve other and more poetic ends; they too contribute to the pattern of tones and values which is the real substance of the poem. Those of Theseus again show him as representative of the highest chivalric conceptions of nobility. As the most noble human figure he presides over the events and interprets them. His final oration is a masterpiece of dignity. Theseus assembles his parliament, with Palamon and Emilye, to make an end of the mourning for Arcite. The speech is carefully and formally introduced:

> Whan they were set, and hust was al the place,   [2981]
> And Theseus abiden hadde a space
> Er any word cam fram his wise brest,
> His eyen sette he ther as was his lest,
> And with a sad visage he siked stille,
> And after that right thus he seyde his wille . . .

The speech itself is adapted from Boethius. It is a monologue of *sentence* and doctrine in the medieval manner. The progress of it is logical and orderly:

Theseus takes up first principles, then general examples from nature, and finally the matter in hand. Chaucer makes no effort to conceal its scholastic character. As a parliamentary address it is not outside the realm of possibility; but this is the least justification for it. A deeper one is its perfect agreement, in organization and content, with the principle of order which Theseus both invokes and represents throughout the tale. In a sense the representative of Fate on earth, the earthly sovereign interprets the will of the divine one:

> "Thanne may men by this ordre wel discerne   [3003]
> That thilke Moevere stable is and eterne.

> "What maketh this but Juppiter, the kyng,   [3035]
> The which is prince and cause of alle thyng,
> Convertynge al unto his propre welle
> From which it is dirryved, sooth to telle?
> And heer-agayns no creature on lyve,
> Of no degree, availleth for to stryve.
> Thanne is it wysdom, as it thynketh me,
> To maken vertu of necessitee,
> And take it weel that we may nat eschue . . ."

The king is an inveterate enemy to rebellion: "And whoso gruccheth ought, he dooth folye, / And rebel is to hym that al may gye" (3045–46). The principal representative of chivalry espouses a highly idealistic conception of the value of a good name:

> "And certeinly a man hath moost honour   [3047]
> To dyen in his excellence and flour,
> When he is siker of his goode name;
> Thanne hath he doon his freend, ne hym, no shame.
> And gladder oghte his freend been of his deeth,
> Whan with honour up yolden is his breeth,
> Than whan his name appalled is for age,
> For al forgeten is his vassellage.
> Thanne is it best, as for a worthy fame,
> To dyen whan that he is best of name."

The actions and speeches by the central figure are the normative ones in the poem. Those of Palamon and Arcite are lesser and contributory, in the sense that they only provide the questions and the elements of variety which are to be resolved; it is Theseus who expounds the resolutions. The knights' actions are, in fact, exemplary of life as it is lived. In this light, it is important to differentiate carefully between the balance of tone that Chaucer preserves in his treatment of them and the more or less direct evidences of satire and of tragedy which many critics have seemed to find there. Theseus' speech on the loves of Palamon and Arcite (1785–1820), for instance, has prompted the suggestion that here Chaucer revolts against the courtly code which the knights represent.[31] First of all, it must be seen that the poet is not here dealing with courtly love *per se,* but only with love, on a par with chivalry, as one of the persistent facts of the noble life. The tournament is held, we remember, "For love and for encrees of chivalrye" (2184). The emphasis, however, is not as in the courtly allegory, where the inner life is explored and where the action revolves about the pursuit and defense of the lady's rose. The lady in the *Knight's Tale* is merely a symbol of the noble man's desires. And the question of love is never in debate here. We take love in this society for granted, and then go on to discover how faithfully experience in love exemplifies the partial blindness of all earthly experience. Love, we find, can create dissension between sworn brothers; can make a man lament his release from prison; make him forsake safety and native land; and, after unending toll of time and strength, it can leave him bloody and desirous of death. Theseus' speech on love, as his speech on Arcite's death, is normative and judicial; and to the noble, the mature mind, the paradoxically impractical quality of love is both laughable and admirable. The rivalry and consequent exploits of Palamon and Arcite are so impractical, and yet so much a reflex of their knightly spirits, that there is something to be said on both sides. Theseus' speech, therefore, is a mature appraisal, not an adverse criticism, of courtly love; certainly not a reflection of Chaucer's "strong revolt against the code."

The leavening, balancing element of common sense is signalized here, as it is usually signalized in Chaucer, by a lapse of the high style and the introduction of colloquialism:

> "But this is yet the beste game of alle,   [1806]
> That she for whom they han this jolitee
> Kan hem therfore as muche thank as me.
> She woot namoore of al this hoote fare,
> By God, than woot a cokkow or an hare!"

With all this humorous ventilation of the subject, however, the real power of love is not denied:

> "But all moot ben assayed, hoot and coold;   [1811]
> A man moot been a fool, or yong or oold,—

185

> I woot it by myself ful yore agon,
> For in my tyme a servant was I oon.
> And therfore, syn I knowe of loves peyne,
> And woot hou soore it kan a man distreyne,
> As he that hath ben caught ofte in his laas,
> I yow foryeve al hoolly this trespaas . . ."

This kind of balance, if it precludes satire, does not of course rule out the possibility of irony. Indeed, such a tone is consonant with Theseus' maturity and dignity. But the several touches of this sort in the poem, and the tensions within its structure that might also be called ironic, neither point to the moral superiority of one knight nor support a tragic attitude toward either of them. It is true that, while Chaucer equalized the Palemone and Arcita of the *Teseida*, he carefully preserved a certain difference between them. One serves Venus, the other Mars. One prays for Emilye, the other for victory. But it does not appear that by preserving this distinction Chaucer implies any moral preference. As the whole background of the *Tale* shows, the worship of Mars is no less important an aspect of the noble life than the worship of Venus. To Arcite go the honor in war, the magnificent funeral, and the intangible rewards brought out in Theseus' oration. To Palamon goes Emilye; in her are described the rewards that accrue to him as the servant of Venus. That the differentiation between the knights is ultimately a source of balance rather than of conflict can be seen even at the beginning of the poem. Palamon sees Emilye first, but his claim is balanced by Arcite's contention:

> "Thyn is affeccioun of hoolynesse,   [1158]
> And myn is love, as to a creature . . ."

Now this distinction is not clearly carried out beyond the passage in question, although it has been expanded by critics to allegorical and morally significant proportions. And even if it did exist as a sustained and fundamental difference between the knights, it would not create a moral *issue* in the poem.[32]

What further deadens any possibly moralistic or tragic implications in the fate of Arcite is a touch of Chaucer's lightness. Were Arcite's death ultimately attributable to some moral disjointedness of his own, we should expect it to be made abundantly clear. But in a literature in which the advent of death is one of the most powerful instruments of moral exemplum, Chaucer goes far out of his way to stifle any such construction. In describing Arcite's death, he involves the reader not in moral conclusions, but in complicated *physical* data with associations so cold and scientific that no moral conclusion can possibly be drawn

(2743–58). The spirit of moral noncommitment is brought out clearly in the final lines of the narrator's comment, where again we see the leavening, commonsensical element expressed through colloquialism:

> Nature hath now no dominacioun. [2758]
> And certeinly, ther Nature wol nat wirche,
> Fare wel phisik! go ber the man to chirche!
> This al and som, that Arcita moot dye . . .

The critic must be on his guard here not to exaggerate the meaning of this digression, not to convert a deftly administered antidote for tragedy into an actively satiric strain. This would be to mistake Chaucer's balance for buffoonery. Immediately following this passage comes Arcite's most elevated speech. Were the narrator's remarks to be read as a satiric comment on Arcite's death, the whole noble fabric of the speech, and of the poem too, would crumble.

If Palamon and Arcite exemplify legitimate attitudes of equal value, and balance or supplement each other in providing not moral conflict but variety, we must look not at the relationship between them, but rather at their common position in relation to the universe, to find the real moral issue in the poem. And Chaucer expresses this issue not only through a tension between the poem's symmetrically ordered structure and the violent ups and downs of the surface narrative—too plainly to be seen to require elaborate analysis,—but also through a complication of texture, in the weaving of darker threads among the red and gold.

I have already suggested that the poem's speeches, like its descriptions, are largely part of its texture; many of them are less important as pointing to specific psychological characteristics that issue in direct action than as elements in broader organizations, with deeper and more ulterior relevance to what goes on in the poem. Thus we have from Palamon and Arcite a considerable number of lyrics, some of them contributing only to the poem's general background of conventional love and chivalry, and others, more important, in which love lament melts into poetry of a more philosophical kind, and brings us to the heart of the issue. This latter characteristic of the poem's texture supports the view that love, which has been too often regarded as the poem's central theme, is used only as a vehicle of expression, a mode of experience of the noble life, which is itself the subject of the poem and the object of its philosophic questions. Thus, in the magnificent death speech of Arcite the lyric of love merges with the philosophical, the lady addressed becomes part of the speech's descriptive imagery, and the theme of love itself is subsumed in the category of all earthly experience:

"Naught may the woful spirit in myn herte   [2765]
Declare o point of alle my sorwes smerte
To yow, my lady, that I love moost;
But I biquethe the servyce of my goost
To yow aboven every creature,
Syn that my lyf may no lenger dure.
Allas, the wo! allas, the peynes stronge,
That I for yow have suffred, and so longe!
Allas, the deeth! allas, myn Emelye!
Allas, departynge of oure compaignye!
Allas, myn hertes queene! allas, my wyf!
Myn hertes lady, endere of my lyf!
What is this world? what asketh men to have?
Now with his love, now in his colde grave
Allone, withouten any compaignye."

Similarly, the speech of Arcite after his release from prison shifts from personal
outcry to general speculation. Here, although Arcite mentions the paradoxical
nature of men's designs with reference to the irony of his *own* position, he
sounds a note which reëchoes throughout the poem:

"Som man desireth for to han richesse,   [1255]
That cause is of his mordre or greet siknesse;
And som man wolde out of his prisoun fayn,
That in his hous is of his meynee slayn."

The parallel lament of Palamon in prison is a variation on the same theme:

"O crueel goddes that governe   [1303]
This world with byndyng of youre word eterne,
And writen in the table of atthamaunt
Youre parlement and youre eterne graunt,
What is mankynde moore unto you holde
Than is the sheep that rouketh in the folde?
For slayn is man right as another beest,
And dwelleth eek in prison and arreest,
And hath siknesse and greet adversitee,
And ofte tymes giltelees, pardee.
What governance is in this prescience,
That giltelees tormenteth innocence?"

The motive of misfortune and disorder is extended in ever-widening circles of reference in the descriptions of the three temples:

> First in the temple of Venus maystow se　　[1918]
> Wroght on the wal, ful pitous to biholde,
> The broken slepes, and the sikes colde,
> The sacred teeris, and the waymentynge,
> The firy strokes of the desirynge
> That loves servantz in this lyf enduren . . .

On the walls of the temple of Diana are depicted the stories of Callisto, Daphne, Actaeon, and Meleager, all of unhappy memory. In the description of Mars's temple, the narrator is most powerful. He sees

> the derke ymaginyng　　[1995]
> Of Felonye, and al the compassyng;
> The crueel Ire, reed as any gleede;
> The pykepurs, and eek the pale Drede;
> The smylere with the knyf under the cloke;
> The shepne brennynge with the blake smoke;
> The tresoun of the mordrynge in the bedde;
> The open werre, with woundes al bibledde . . .

In this context, the monologue of Saturn is the culminating expression of an ever-swelling undertheme of disaster:

> "Myn is the drenchyng in the see so wan;　　[2456]
> Myn is the prison in the derke cote;
> Myn is the stranglyng and hangyng by the throte,
> The murmure and the cherles rebellyng,
> The groynynge, and the pryvee empoysonyng . . ."[33]

In Theseus' majestic summary there is a final echo, the continuing rhetorical repetition as insistent as fate itself:

> "He moot be deed, the kyng as shal a page;　　[3030]
> Som in his bed, som in the depe see,
> Som in the large feeld, as men may see . . ."

This subsurface insistence on disorder is the poem's crowning complexity, its most compelling claim to maturity. We have here no glittering, romantic fairy-castle world. The impressive, patterned edifice of the noble life, its dignity and richness, its regard for law and decorum, are all bulwarks against the ever-threatening forces of chaos, and in constant collision with them. And the crowning nobility, as expressed by this poem, goes beyond a grasp of the forms of social and civil order, beyond magnificence in any earthly sense, to a perception of the order beyond chaos. When the earthly designs suddenly crumble, true nobility is faith in the ultimate order of all things. Saturn, disorder, nothing more nor less, is the agent of Arcite's death, and Theseus, noble in the highest sense, interprets it in the deepest perspective. In contrast is the incomplete perception of the wailing women of Athens:

> "Why woldestow be deed," thise wommen crye,   [2835]
> And haddest gold ynough, and Emelye?"

The history of Thebes had perpetual interest for Chaucer as an example of the struggle between noble designs and chaos. Palamon and Arcite, Thebans, lovers, fighters and sufferers, through whom the pursuit of the noble life is presented, exemplify through their experiences and express through their speeches this central conflict.

ii. The *Clerk's Tale*

I need not pause to demonstrate the close attitudinal relationship between the Knight and the *Knight's Tale*. It has been well argued by others, even to the suggestion of a common ingenuousness shown by the man in his loyalty to his age and class and by the tale in its purity of view. This tale takes on its relationship to other views by contrast and juxtaposition, particularly to the *Miller's Tale,* which follows.[34]

The *Clerk's Tale* of the patient Griselda is similar to the Knight's in this inner purity, in conventionalism of style, and even in theme. Between them they show the basis of Chaucer's conventionalism in a common sphere of meaning, and also the breadth of that sphere, the variety of the style. If the texture of the *Knight's Tale* is very rich, that of the *Clerk's Tale* is very thin. But thinness has a poetic function in the one as richness has in the other.

The moral of the *Clerk's Tale* goes thus:

> This storie is seyd, nat for that wyves sholde   [1142]
> Folwen Grisilde as in humylitee,
> For it were inportable, though they wolde;
> But for that every wight, in his degree,
> Sholde be constant in adversitee
> As was Grisilde; therfore Petrak writeth
> This storie, which with heigh stile he enditeth.

For, sith a womman was so pacient
Unto a mortal man, wel moore us oghte
Receyven al in gree that God us sent;
For greet skile is, he preeve that he wroghte.

This moral makes so transparently conventional an appeal to Christian piety that it has been a disadvantage to the poem. The *Clerk's Tale* has been very little appreciated, much condemned, and almost never analyzed.[35] It is so transparent as to seem to have nothing in it. But I shall declare at the outset that as poetry it is very good. It does not ultimately depend on mechanical piety, but on a controlled and finely specialized poetic structure that thoroughly supports the special variation of its Christian theme. It is, let it be admitted, a connoisseur's poem. It requires rereading; and with successive readings one's indifference turns to tolerance, then to admiration. Stock response aside, the poem has a fine astringency, an austerity, that will not appeal to the untutored or to the extravagant taste. It is truly the tale of Chaucer's Clerk; sharing his threadbare leanness, it despises ordinary riches for the rarer, more educated pleasure of philosophical morality. It has some of the consequential logic of the Clerk's training, the clean abstractedness of his philosophy. It is a proposition cleared of all but two or three assumptions. And the Clerk brings to its exposition his own talent for obedience:

"Hooste," quod he, "I am under youre yerde;   [22]
Ye han of us as now the governance,
And therfore wol I do yow obeisance,
As fer as resoun axeth, hardily."

The story was first told by Boccaccio at the end of the *Decameron*. Petrarch translated it into Latin prose in 1373–74, at the very end of his life. In France, within a generation or so, his Latin was versified, twice translated into vernacular prose, and thence made into a play. This and the immense subsequent popularity of the story[36] are clearly owing to the variety of themes to which it could answer. Boccaccio's version preserves some of the grotesque curiosity of a hypothetical folk-tale original, but overlays this with the motif of the use of feudal power, personified in its chief character Gualtieri, Griselda's husband. Petrarch overtly Christianizes and moralizes the tale, shifting its emphasis fully to Griselda—"De Insigni Obedientia et Fide Uxoris"—and casting it into the language and rhetorical style that would suit the new dignity of the subject matter. This title reveals yet a fourth focus of interest, already latent in Boccaccio and most overtly advertised later. By the fifteenth century the tale is used as a document in the perennial medieval controversy over women and marriage. Chaucer's version is based rextually on Petrarch and on the more literal of the two French translations. Though the tale is placed by the Clerk's envoy in the context of the controversy over marriage that is stirring in the dramatic frame of the pilgrimage, its inner inspiration, announced by the *Clerk's Prologue* and the concluding moral, is Petrarchan.

Something of the same impulse that led Petrarch to translate into Latin can be felt in Chaucer's casting of his poem into rime-royal stanzas. The stanza is of course not inherently expressive, but in the *Canterbury Tales* it is always an implement of seriousness. Apart from the *Clerk's Tale,* it is used in the pious tales of the Man of Law, the Prioress, and the Second Nun. In the *Clerk's Tale* Chaucer meters out his scenes and speeches in stanzas and blocks of stanzas, and this deliberateness supports the sense of self-containment and restraint felt in the whole poem's rhythm. The high style is severely muted, breaking out in the choric commentary at only three high points of the action.[87]

The restraint of the style is equally evident in a frugal conservation of imagery. There are only four images of color in the entire poem.[38] The description is in general remarkably plain. Where in the *Knight's Tale* we are treated to every kind of feudal magnificence in minute, concrete terms, here almost all is neutral generalization,

swich pompe and richesse   [943]
That nevere was ther seyn with mannes ye
So noble array . . .[39]

In this context only a few items are allowed to stand out with immediate clarity: Griselda at her homely duties, a waterpot, an ox's stall, some sheep, a torn smock, and the like. It is as if the compressed description of the abundance of the land at the opening, and later on the passing mention of Griselda's village— "of site delitable,"—were designed to eliminate rather than raise the question of circumstantial details.

The narrative sequence is clear, articulate, and simple, progressing in measured stages. There is the marriage of Walter and Griselda, the first trial in his pretended murder of her daughter, the "murder" of her son, her dismissal, then the ultimate trial in her attendance on Walter's new wife, and finally his restoration of all. There is no trifling here with large narrative "effects" of the usual kind, no suspense, no dramatic irony. Variety of action and utterance is pointedly avoided by frequent parallelism and repetition.[40] This simplicity is of a piece with the rest; the poem is quite plainly designed in imitation of no "life" in any naturalistic sense, but as something abstract and formulated, essential, pared of "accident" almost to nakedness.

The characterization is minimal. What there is of it serves the purity of the moral. Chaucer's additions to the received text heighten Griselda's submissiveness and deepen the pathos of her situation." But this note serves little to individualize her as compared to what Chaucer was easily capable of. His habitual treatment of the subject of parent and child has a kind of limited, pathetic realism peculiar to itself. Griselda, indeed, shares some specific traits with Constance of the *Man of Law's Tale* and the virgin-heroine of the *Physician's Tale*. Characters of this class owe much in turn to Chaucer's vision of the sorrowing Mary, with whom there is a consciously implied resemblance in Griselda herself." Nowhere did the late medieval poet so easily fall into excess of feeling as in this area. The superfluity of Chaucer's pathos over Petrarch's—like his sentimentalizing of Dante's Ugolino—may well be a mark of the times. But Griselda's emotional response is so framed that, though it trembles on the edge of sentimentality, it does not drown the figurative meaning of the action. As Speirs rightly puts it, "*too* great humanization would have spoiled this particular tale."⁴³

One is likely to smudge the *Clerk's Tale* by the slightest mixing of earth with its pure water. Griselda's deficiency as a mother has been several times deplored; one should on the same basis criticize Abraham's carelessness of Isaac. Chaucer, after Petrarch, makes perfectly plain that Griselda is not a model for wifehood to imitate. She is a model of "vertuous suffraunce," and of nothing more specific. She will wither at the touch of practical realism. Chaucer indicated the human perspective best with a brevity through which pathos cries to be admitted, but is restrained:

> "O goode God! how gentil and how kynde   [852]
> Ye semed by youre speche and youre visage
> The day that maked was oure mariage!"

At the end the flood of maternal response is allowed its fullest run, still framed by conventional gesture and rhetorical form:

> Whan she this herde, aswowne doun she falleth   [1079]
> For pitous joye, and after hire swownynge
> She bothe hire yonge children to hire calleth,
> And in hire armes, pitously wepynge,
> Embraceth hem, and tendrely kissynge
> Ful lyk a mooder, with hire salte teeres
> She bathed bothe hire visage and hire heeres.

O which a pitous thyng it was to se
Hir swownyng, and hire humble voys to heere!
"Grauntmercy, lord, God thanke it yow," quod she,
"That ye han saved me my children deere!
Now rekke I nevere to been deed right heere;
Sith I stonde in youre love and in youre grace,
No fors of deeth, ne whan my spirit pace!

"O tendre, o deere, o yonge children myne!
Youre woful mooder wende stedfastly
That crueel houndes or som foul vermyne
Hadde eten yow; but God, of his mercy,
And youre benyngne fader tendrely
Hath doon yow kept,"—and in that same stounde
Al sodeynly she swapte adoun to grounde.

For the rest, it is the narrator's (our own) exclamations that we hear. These are less a vicarious expression of what Griselda should have said than an index of the difference between her and ourselves.

Griselda's loving of Walter demands no psychological motivation. Like the plot and the description, it is something assumed, "given," felt in other than psychological terms. Walter is even less a character; first he is a symbol of lordship, then of adversity also. The poem's theme is in Job v, 17: "Behold, happy is the man whom God correcteth: therefore despise not thou the chastening of the Almighty." Walter's lack of motivation is an advantage in presenting this theme. This is *pure* chastening, *pure* correction. Griselda's trial is a trial because there is no reason for it. The life of the tale, simplified down to extremity, makes show of the nature of bare virtue itself. The tale attains poetic force through its concerted insistence, in every detail, on naked obedience to the Lord.

In medieval thought, the secular grades of sovereignty, paternal, political, marital, are figures for each other and copies of the divine fatherhood, lordship, spousal. One is made to feel this in the poem. The marital level is the most obvious one on which the theme of sovereignty is worked out. Here, though very little is said of marriage *per se,* is some food for the Wife of Bath. The theme is briefly taken up on the filial level, in Griselda's relationship to her father. But it is on the political level that much of the poem's materials operate, and beyond this on the religious level, from which the others depend. Much of the hierarchical pattern is already in Petrarch's Latin prose. His very opening *descriptio,* which the Clerk in his chasteness abbreviates as "a thyng impertinent" (54), and which the French do not translate at all, is almost religiously symbolic. The picture is of Mount Vesulus (Viso), "mons unus altissimus," its peak above the clouds, thrusting up to the clear aether itself. From its side springs the source of the Po, "fluviorum . . . rex," which, cutting and bounding various lands, descends finally into the sea through many great mouths."

Chaucer picks up the thread of this imagery of lordship and domination in his second stanza:

> A markys whilom lord was of that lond,   [64]
> As were his worthy eldres hym bifore;
> And obeisant, ay redy to his hond,
> Were alle his liges, bothe lasse and moore.
> Thus in delit he lyveth, and hath doon yoore,
> Biloved and drad, thurgh favour of Fortune,
> Bothe of his lordes and of his commune.

The idea of stability and antiquity, that behind Walter lies a long period of rule, is Chaucer's. While his adaptation of Petrarch is very close, his diction at every subsequent turn likewise makes more intense the political aura of the story. Severs notes Chaucer's addition of gestures of subjection." The language of the poem verges on monotone in its semantic restraint. It admits principally terms of necessity, endurance, servitude, sovereignty, and, conversely, of liberty and release. The dialogue is narrowly diplomatic with "assente," "preye," "graunte," "requeste," and the formal imperatives and pronouns. Even the fillers and tags, in the very corners of the poem, share this character, insistently repeating "as hym leste," "myn owne lord," "ech in his degree," "whil that my lyf may dure," and the like.

The characters are bound to each other irrefrangibly by political and spiritual dominion. Even the most minor actions of the poem instance it. Of Walter's "wicked" sergeant, "The lord knew wel that he hym loved and dradde" (523). Dealing with the court of Rome, Walter "enformed of his wyl . . . comaund-ynge" (738 f.). Marriage is a "yok of soveraynetee," (113 f.), and even lordship is a kind of "servitute," which "constreyneth" (798 ff.).

Political dominion is intervolved with, and finally subordinated to, the dominions of death, and of the Lord God. Mortal frailty is dwelt upon first in the Clerk's own reflections (36 ff.), then echoed in the parley of the citizens (122 ff.) and in Griselda's speeches. When Griselda says

> "Deth may noght make no comparisoun   [666]
> Unto youre love"

we are not moved to think of secular love, but to look beyond it. The religious allusion is occasionally overt. It quite frankly brings the poem into the class of Job, the Sacrifice of Isaac, and the Crucifixion:

> "Naked out of my fadres hous," quod she,   [871]
> "I cam, and naked moot I turne agayn. . . ."

This is much like Job i, 21. God, his bounty and his grace, are present throughout: "he may doon as hym leste" (161). Of similar significance are passages like the following, which are not direct allusions, but still suggest to the sensitive reader a religious symbolism:

> "This is my wyf . . . that standeth heere.   [369]
> Honoureth hire and loveth hire, I preye,
> Whoso me loveth; ther is namoore to seye."

> And as she wolde over hir thresshfold gon,   [288]
> The markys cam, and gan hire for to calle;
> And she set doun hir water pot anon,
> Biside the thresshfold, in an oxes stalle,
> And doun upon hir knes she gan to falle,
> And with sad contenance kneleth stille,
> Til she had herd what was the lordes wille.[16]

The homely, pathetic-realistic imagery of the poem clearly evokes an apostolic purity of attitude, a Franciscan piety already detectible in Boccaccio's rendering,[17] and here presented with a disarming candor. It is not to be confused with the realism of material concerns. Janicula's household is the poorest of the village, not out of economic or social design, but for spiritual reasons, just as Walter's realm is "habundant of vitaille" for reasons of the whole sufficiency of lordship.

This religious symbolism and allusion operates functionally in the poem; the moral is generated by the style itself. The whole ordonnance of the poem invites, constrains a symbolic reading. Most of all, the uncompromising plainness of the tale's secularism points to a religious meaning. It is the plainness not of untutored simplicity but of an art that achieves plainness by an effort of thought and feeling. I am not the first whom the tale reminds of Wordsworth. In it there is almost nothing to impede the "intimations," the aura of something miraculous and divine at every step; there is, indeed, nowhere else to turn.

Chaucer appreciated the fragile purity of the *Clerk's Tale* as he revised its ending to link the tale with its dramatic frame. The Clerk's envoy, "for the sake of the Wife of Bath," begins thus:

> "Grisilde is deed, and eek hire pacience, [1177]
> And bothe atones buryed in Ytaille;
> For which I crie in open audience,
> No wedded man so hardy be t'assaille
> His wyves pacience in trust to fynde
> Grisildis, for in certein he shal faille.

> "O noble wyves, ful of heigh prudence,
> Lat noon humylitee youre tonge naille,
> Ne lat no clerk have cause or diligence
> To write of yow a storie of swich mervaille
> As of Grisildis pacient and kynde,
> Lest Chichevache yow swelwe in hire entraille!"

This envoy's aptitude to the dramatic situation has been only too well cele-brated.⁴⁸ We should also note its function as a literary defense. It is an excellent example of "concessionary" comedy. The Clerk admits the opposition pur-posely, so willingly and extravagantly as to make safe from vulgar questioning the finer matter that has gone before. In all, the tale of Grisilda is a latter-day parable:

> This world is nat so strong, it is no nay, [1139]
> As it hath been in olde tymes yoore . . .

It yearns for the naked, simple, uncompromising virtue of original Christianity, in which the divine lordship manifests itself in every corner of life, and in which nobility is humble obedience, not birth or station. It is at once impossibly and hopefully nostalgic. It is thus in many ways similar to the *Knight's Tale*. Boethius and St. Francis in the end make common cause. Yet the immense difference in the ways of Knight and Clerk, in their thought and experience, in the felt temper of their two approaches, makes very different poems. Each in its way is a triumph of Chaucer's conventional style.

§ 3. THREE VERSIONS OF NATURALISM

Chaucer's management of the naturalistic style is historically more striking than his achievement with conventionalism. In the latter he has some very note-worthy peers, but in naturalism his technique is unequalled in medieval times. Every reader will have noticed the sharpness of his descriptions, the lifelikeness of his dialogues. The tales are full of specially realistic effects: animal sounds, belching and snoring, epithets and oaths, and Chaucer can easily register the most minute, revelatory gesture, the finest shading of colloquial discourse. Even so, commentators have tended to overlook two aspects of his practice. The first follows from the fact that naturalism involves a technical discipline which must be learned in the same way that the technique of composing ballades and invocations must be learned. The recording eye and ear are essential to the practice of the naturalistic style, but they are by no means all. The artist never, except for very special purposes, attempts merely to record every grunt and irrelevance of phenomenal experience. What he sees and hears, the selections and combinations he makes, are partly the result of training, much of it literary training. Tradition guides observation. Henry James could not have written before Jane Austen and George Eliot; nor Zola before Balzac and Flaubert. Similarly Chaucer, for all his "good ear," his knowledge and appreciation of ordinary life, could not have written his most naturalistic works without the exploratory work of the fabliaux, the mimes, the popular preachers, and Jean de Meun before him.

This would be no more than a mildly interesting historical observation were it not for a second feature of Chaucer's naturalism. This is that in his mature works the style is not an end, but a method—a convention, in fact, though usage reserves that term for another style,—and that it thus supports values beyond those of mere reporting. It has its own symbolism. And as the bourgeois tradition affords us pointers to Chaucer's technique, it also indicates roughly the area of meaning in which this technique is most efficient. The special naturalism of some of the *Canterbury Tales* thus has a special function. If Chaucer uses conventional style to navigate the insubstantial air of the spiritual world, naturalism serves his soundings of the world of matter.

i. The *Reeve's Tale*

The *Reeve's Tale* will serve us as an example of Chaucer's treatment of the fabliau, and will illustrate the literary functionalism of one of his most purely representational efforts. The tale retains the fabliau skeleton. It has a neat plot, based on physical action. Its setting is resolutely prosaic, securely anchored at the outset in a limited, physical world:

> At Trumpyngtoun, nat fer fro Cantebrigge,   [3921]
> Ther gooth a brook, and over that a brigge,
> Upon the whiche brook ther stant a melle;
> And this is verray sooth that I yow telle:
> A millere was ther dwellynge many a day.

But as the tale proceeds, it takes on a richness of specification, both in tone and image, that is rarely seen in French fabliaux. This is a symptom of Chaucer's typical investiture of the naked fabliau jest with the substance of a rather deeper poetry. In his hands the fabliau becomes an art form. Its materials are no longer the minimum of properties that will serve the action. Not unlike those in the conventional poems, they are knowingly used to create a world and to evoke an attitude.

The most interesting stylistic elaboration in the poem is the naturalistic Northern idiom of the two clerks. Chaucer's rendering of it is not a complete philological transcript, but neither is it a vaudeville version, easily achieved with a few odd terms. It is a convincing artistic imitation, based on the outstanding characteristics of the dialect.⁴⁹ It is the first of its kind in English, and unique in Chaucer. He is never elsewhere so faithful to nature. He tells us that the Friar lisped, but the trait is not suggested in the Friar's speech, nor do the Yorkshire characters of the *Summoner's Tale* have any local peculiarity of dialect.⁵⁰ The mastery of a Northerly dialect perhaps befits the Reeve, a Norfolk man who lets slip a few Northernisms himself. But Chaucer is not to be expected to adjust the idiom of a tale to the native dialect of the teller; the Wife of Bath and the Dartmouth Shipman have no trace of an unusually Westernized accent. It is clear that the special naturalism of speech in the *Reeve's Tale* is owing to some special literary demand, beyond mere representationalism, created by the peculiar nature of the tale itself. J. R. R. Tolkien suggests that with the dialect Chaucer aims only "to give some life and individuality to a *fabliau* of trite sort . . ."⁵¹ But this answer poses another question. If variety is the aim, why in this direction? The meaning of the tale points to a more specific reason for its extreme naturalism.

The *Reeve's Tale* follows the Miller's; it is a variation on the Miller's materials, given a dramatic setting in the personal rivalry between the two pilgrims:

> "This dronke Millere hath ytoold us heer
> How that bigyled was a carpenteer,
> Peraventure in scorn, for I am oon.
> And, by youre leve, I shal hym quite anoon;
> Right in his cherles termes wol I speke."
> [*ReeveProl* 3913–17]

The Miller is a loud, coarse fellow, "a janglere and a goliardeys." He is vulgar in a lusty, openhanded way. The humor of the Reeve is colder and more bitter. The narrow animosity directed at the miller in the *Reeve's Tale* goes well beyond the fabliau's conventional lack of sympathy. The method of the tale is to make of the miller a vessel of preposterously inflated social and intellectual pretension, then to deflate him by the crudest means possible. The naturalistic dialect of the two clerks is a part of this scheme.

The tone of the Reeve's performance is forecast in the *General Prologue* by his physical appearance, or, what is the same thing in great representational art, by his character. His traits already suggest a pointed contrast to the Miller. The Miller is thick, broad, strong. The Reeve is thin, choleric; his legs are like sticks. The Miller has a broad, red beard; the Reeve is close-shaven. The Miller brings the pilgrims out of town with the playing of his bagpipe. The Reeve, Chaucer says, always rides at the tail end of the crowd. The clerical cut of his appearance suggests the ascetic or preacher *manqué*:

> His heer was by his erys ful round yshorn;   [589]
> His top was dokked lyk a preest biforn.

> Tukked he was as is a frere aboute . . .   [621]

The first thing we hear from him is stringent moral rectitude:

> "Stynt thy clappe!
> Lat be thy lewed dronken harlotrye.
> It is a synne and eek a greet folye
> To apeyren any man, or hym defame,
> And eek to bryngen wyves in swich fame."
> [*MillProl* 3144–48]

In the *Reeve's Prologue* the preacher actually takes hold. His rebuke wanders somehow to a sermon on the impotence of the aged, full of timeworn similes, and aping even the preacher's habit of division and enumeration:

> "Foure gleedes han we, which I shal devyse,—   [3883]
> Avauntyng, liyng, anger, coveitise;
> Thise foure sparkles longen unto eelde."

The Host demolishes this vagary—"The devel made a reve for to preche"— and the thin clerical man, deprived of the opportunity for sermoning, turns to an acidly knowing exemplum of "avauntyng, liyng, anger, coveitise."

His narrative is fairly curdled with an unrelenting irony. The opening description of the miller's social pretension is so cutting that the irony sours into sarcasm. The narrator's frustrated clericalism wells up to plague his victims:

His name was hoote deynous Symkyn.　　　　[3941]
A wyf he hadde, ycomen of noble kyn;
The person of the toun hir fader was.
With hire he yaf ful many a panne of bras,
For that Symkyn sholde in his blood allye.
She was yfostred in a nonnerye;
For Symkyn wolde no wyf, as he sayde,
But she were wel ynorissed and a mayde,
To saven his estaat of yomanrye.
And she was proud, and peert as is a pye.

. . .

And eek, for she was somdel smoterlich,
She was as digne as water in a dich,
And ful of hoker and of bisemare.
Hir thoughte that a lady sholde hire spare,
What for hire kynrede and hir nortelrie
That she hadde lerned in the nonnerie.

The ecclesiastical "connections" of the miller provide a continuous blast of comment:

A doghter hadde they bitwixe hem two . . .　　　[3969]
This person of the toun, for she was feir,
In purpos was to maken hire his heir,
Bothe of his catel and his mesuage,
And straunge he made it of hir mariage.
His purpos was for to bistowe hire hye
Into som worthy blood of auncetrye;
For hooly chirches good moot been despended
On hooly chirches blood, that is descended.
Therfore he wolde his hooly blood honoure,
Though that he hooly chirche sholde devoure.

The two clerks of Cambridge are the ones who violate the miller's vessels of "hooly blood." The irony of this sacrilege lies in the fact that throughout the tale their speech represents them to the miller as country bumpkins of no social position whatsoever. We can hardly know as a historical fact what would have been the standard response of a Londoner to this provincial dialect. In the Old French mimes, a century before Chaucer, dialect means social or intellectual inferiority.[53] In the *Secunda Pastorum* of the Towneley Cycle, the incomparable

Mak is accused by the Yorkshire shepherds of putting on airs with his Southern (presumably, then, sophisticated) accent.[53] But even disregarding what analogy would indicate, the emphasis of the *Reeve's Tale* is such that it presumes in the clerks' speech an indication of social inferiority. That the miller's wife and daughter are ultimately *swyved* is comic. But the crude humor derived thence owes little to the fact that the miller is ferociously proud, and his ladies "high"-born. If "the tables turned" exhausts the meaning of the story's denouement, then the extended preliminary account of these characters is an excrescence. The story's outcome, however, has more bite than this; it is securely related to the opening description, and to the special naturalism of the clerks' idiom.

The miller's intellectual deflation is prepared for in the same way. The motif parallels that in the *Miller's Tale,* where the aged carpenter similarly ridicules clerkly ingenuity. Our miller entertains as much pride in his own cleverness as in his wife's lineage. The provincial dialect of the clerks gives them a superficial appearance of rustic simplicity. This the "deynous" miller takes readily as justification for his own conceit. The clerks are young and poor; they come from some obscure town in the North. They arrive at the mill with their bag of grain, and with an air of complete ignorance of practical matters:

> "By God, right by the hopur wil I stande,   [4036]
> Quod John, "and se how that the corn gas in.
> Yet saugh I nevere, by my fader kyn,
> How that the hopur wagges til and fra."
> Aleyn answerde, "John, and wiltow swa?
> Thanne wil I be bynethe, by my croun,
> And se how that the mele falles doun
> Into the trough; that sal be my disport.
> For John, y-faith, I may been of youre sort;
> I is as ille a millere as ar ye."

Here "mispronunciation," "bad" grammar, and the transparence of their strategy merge in the miller's mind to assure him of success: "This millere smyled of hir nycetee . . ." (4046). The tumultuous confusion following the escape of the clerks' horse is supported again by a welter of Northernisms, and again the apparent simple-mindedness of the clerks feeds the miller's self-indulgence. He steals their flour,

> And bad his wyf go knede it in a cake.   [4094]
> He seyde, "I trowe the clerkes were aferd.
> Yet kan a millere make a clerkes berd,

> For al his art; now lat hem goon hir weye!
> Lo, wher they goon! ye, lat the children pleye."

When they beg for a night's shelter, his self-satisfaction can afford the luxury of
open ridicule:

> "Myn hous is streit, but ye han lerned art;   [4122]
> Ye konne by argumentes make a place
> A myle brood of twenty foot of space.
> Lat se now if this place may suffise,
> Or make it rowm with speche, as is youre gise."

The prologue to the events of the night is rounded off by a description of
the miller's family asleep. Here again the narrative tone betrays a special animus
beneath the comedy, sarcasm rather than irony:

> This millere hath so wisely bibbed ale   [4162]
> That as an hors he snorteth in his sleep,
> Ne of his tayl bihynde he took no keep.
> His wyf bar hym a burdon, a ful strong;
> Men myghte hir rowtyng heere two furlong;
> The wenche rowteth eek, *par compaignye.*
> Aleyn the clerk, that herde this melodye,
> He poked John, and seyde, "Slepestow?
> Herdestow evere slyk a sang er now?"

The Reeve's bitter treatment of his subject now needs only the sudden reversal
of fortune for its completion. The miller is defeated in a rowdy, fabliau climax.
A preliminary cut at his social pretension is in Aleyn's lyric farewell to the high-
born daughter. In mock-recognition of her station he plays the courtly lover,
and delivers an *aubade,* significantly marred by the odd-sounding vowels of the
Northern idiom:

> Aleyn wax wery in the dawenynge,   [4234]
> For he had swonken al the longe nyght,
> And seyde, "Fare weel, Malyne, sweete wight!
> The day is come, I may no lenger byde;
> But everemo, wher so I go or ryde,
> I is thyn awen clerk, swa have I seel!"

Any suspicion that a touch of genuine romance resides here is brutally dispelled
by his next speech:

"Thou John, thou swynes-heed, awak, [4262]
For Cristes saule, and heer a noble game. . . ."

But he is in the wrong bed; it is not his friend John, but the miller himself. When the class-conscious Symkyn hears thus of the fate of his heiress-daughter, his outraged response is drenched with the special sarcasm of the narrator, who exploits to the hilt the spectacle of his victim's social vanity:

"Ye, false harlot," quod the millere, "hast? [4268]
A, false traitour! false clerk!" quod he,
"Thow shalt be deed, by Goddes dignitee!
Who dorste be so boold to *disparage*
My doghter, that is come of swich lynage?"

To translate "disparage" simply as 'dishonor' or 'discredit' is to miss the point. In context the word has clearly a strong flavor of the older meaning, "to match unequally; to degrade or dishonor by marrying to one of inferior rank."[54] The miller is chagrined, not at what has been done to his daughter, but that it has been done by someone of lower class!

The ground for this culminating sarcasm is prepared from the first, in the rich but peculiarly acid descriptions, and in the sharp, uncompromising characterizations, of which the clerks' idiom is an integral part. The fabliau, never a vehicle for the idealization of man, is here adapted to the reverse process. The tale's special naturalism goes beyond factual description to contribute to the rendering of a particularly bilious view of life.

ii. The *Wife of Bath's Prologue*

The wise Justinus of the *Merchant's Tale,* in one of Chaucer's most astonishing breaches of literary decorum, reminds his brother January of the Wife of Bath's authority in marriage. "The Wyf," he says, "declared hath ful wel in litel space."[55] There is no disagreement about either the meaning or the value of the Wife's *Prologue,* but I should like to offer some observations on its technique, particularly on the method by which Chaucer creates so much in so little space. The Wife of Bath is the most memorable of his characters, and furthermore, an antagonist in three parallel medieval controversies: she represents practical experience as against received authority, female freedom as against male domination, and unblushing sensuality as against emotional austerity.

In adopting a literary form for the best possible representation of the Wife's attitudes, Chaucer had the precedent of Jean de Meun to go by. The main strength of Jean's Duenna, we recall, is that this representative of philosophic naturalism is herself presented naturalistically. After Jean, indeed, the dramatic monologue becomes almost an inherently expressive form. Its familiar imagery, its scraps of biography and opinion, its colloquial rhythm, and its awareness of a live audience all contribute to relating the speaker to the earth, to the present, and to the practical facts of daily existence. Its adoption for the Wife of Bath seems inevitable.

Chaucer not only learns from Jean; he elaborates on Jean's technique. The Duenna's gift for both joyous and pensive reminiscence reappears and is fully developed in the Wife of Bath. We know a remarkable amount about Dame Alice; both her person and her history are more circumstantially described than the Duenna's.[56] Chaucer also follows Jean, and excels him, in specific poetical procedures. Both use imagery in such a way that the nature of the speaker is as much established through what she incidentally refers to as through what she specifically professes. Jean sometimes adapts to his character's views the homely imagery of popular proverbial sayings:

> "Mout a *souriz* povre secours   [13150]
> E fait en grant perill sa druige
> Qui n'a qu'un *pertuis* a refuige."

Chaucer borrows this and adds an image:

> "I holde a *mouses herte* nat worth a *leek*   [572]
> That hath but oon *hole* for to sterte to."

The imagery of this implied simile is at one with a whole field of denoted things that circumscribe and delineate, each one imperceptibly, the world of the speaker:

> "Therfore I made my visitaciouns . . .   [555]
> And wered upon my gaye scarlet gytes.
> Thise wormes, ne thise motthes, ne thise mytes,
> Upon my peril, frete hem never a deel;
> And wostow why? for they were used weel."

Lowes has shown the force that the demonstrative "thise" has in establishing an extra sense of her familiarity with worms, moths, and mites.[57] But the choice of the images themselves is equally remarkable, if more obvious. In emphasizing the extent of the Wife's activity, Chaucer at the same time suggests her exhibitionism, her vanity, and her feeling for domestic property, and adds a few vivid pieces to his mosaic of her domestic, physical world. It is put together of images like dart, fire, tow, vessel, tree [wood], wheat seed, barley bread, tun, wine, ale, bacon, chough, gnat, horse, mill, sheep, tooth, mouth, tail, flour, bran, grease, shoe, market, ware, bed, blood, gold, legs, feet, and so on. The whole collection is impressive in its unity of connotation.

The Wife's manner of speech, so far as this can be dissociated from what she says, is more distinctive than the Duenna's. It would be extremely difficult to separate the Duenna's digressiveness from the author's. But the large number of parentheses and repetitions in the Wife's discourse, the looseness of construction, may justifiably be associated with her character. At one point (585) the gossip finally strangles the narrative and makes her lose the thread of her argument completely.⁵⁸ She is given to that type of circumlocution in sexual matters which attracts more attention to her subject than bluntness would have done.⁵⁹ She periodically adopts a flatfootedness of assertion that can be heard in the rhythm itself:

"For sothe, I wol nat kepe me chaast in al."   [46]

"He spak to hem that wolde lyve parfitly;   [111]
And lordynges, by youre leve, that am nat I."

"In swich estaat as God hath cleped us   [147]
I wol persevere; I nam nat precius.
In wyfhod I wol use myn instrument
As frely as my Makere hath it sent."

"An housbonde I wol have, I wol nat lette. . . ."   [154]

"As helpe me verray God omnipotent,   [423]
Though I right now sholde make my testament,
I ne owe hem nat a word that it nys quit."

With these, and with a thousand other traits that give her a lifelike individuality, Chaucer creates the embodiment of practical experience, of domestic freedom, and of sensuality.

But though the Wife is possibly the most fully realized character in Chaucer, her characterization accounts for only part of the *Prologue*. The poem derives as much weight from the wealth of doctrine, *sentence,* and exemplum it incorporates. This material is amassed to represent the points of view opposed to the Wife, and only with its assistance does Chaucer achieve depth, and the compendiousness that Justinus recommends. The actual extent of the Wife's "learning," once a scholarly eye pieces it together, is quite astounding:

In the eight hundred twenty-eight lines of her *Prologue* she refers . . .
to Jesus, Solomon, St. Paul, Lamech, Abraham, Jacob, Mark, Ptolemy,

Argus, Job, Metellius, Venus, Darius, Appelles, Mars, Simplicius Gallus, Ecclesiastes, Valerius, Theophrastus, Jerome, Jovinian, Tertullian, Chrysippus, Trotula, Héloise, Ovid, Midas, Adam, Mercury, Eve, Sampson, Hercules, Dejanira, Socrates, Xantippe, Pasiphaë, Clytemnestra, Amphiaraus, Eriphyle, Livia, Lucilia, Latumyus (whoever he is), and Arrius, not to mention the various saints by whom she swears—an average of better than one new literary or mythological reference to every twenty lines.[60]

The assimilation of this mass of material is one of the stylistic triumphs of the *Prologue*. It shows how deeply Chaucer feels the "meaning" of his form, how closely he respects the artistic assumptions behind it. Whereas Jean de Meun had unblushingly put undigested learning into the mouth of his character at every turn, regardless of the detriment to the characterization, Chaucer does everything he can to smuggle it in under a realistic disguise. But his will to keep the realism of characterization inviolate has nothing to do with a general striving for verisimilitude. What wife was ever so learned or so pedantic as Prudence in Chaucer's *Melibee?* How can one defend as verisimilitude Dorigen's learned complaint in the *Franklin's Tale?*[61] The careful naturalization of the Wife's authorities (as compared to the frank conventionalism of the other cases) arises from the fact that the naturalistic style is essential to the symbolism of the Wife's attitudes, but not to Prudence's prudence nor to Dorigen's *sorwe* and *trouthe.* Though the *Prologue* may have been intended to follow the *Nun's Priest's Tale,* and thus to stand in some relationship to the matrimonial matter therein, as we have it there is no link with what goes before. It begins in a vacuum. That this has been little disadvantage (Kittredge thought it began his "Marriage Group" of tales)[62] is testimony to Chaucer's success in developing the controversy from within. The doctrinal authorities extend vastly the sphere of the *Prologue*'s meaning and provide the issues that feed its argument. But they do not usurp the Wife's voice; their inherent disagreement with the Wife's nature is never allowed to weaken the poetry of her own position. Chaucer solved here a problem comparable to Jean de Meun's problem with Faus-Semblant. Jean's patience, or his grasp of the technique of naturalism, was not equal to the delicate operation required.[63] Chaucer's was.

The most obvious means of giving the doctrinal material a naturalistic cast is seen in Chaucer's choice of examples. He drew on a variety of traditional authorities, notably Jean de Meun, the *Miroir de mariage* of Deschamps, the epistle of Jerome against Jovinian with its fragment of Theoprastus' *Liber Aureolus de Nuptiis,* and Walter Map's *Epistola Valerii ad Rufinum.* Antifeminist doctrine is presented in these works in a variety of forms. Chaucer chooses much from what is already cast in familiar, realistic terms. Thus the magnificent immediacy of the following passage of Theophrastus, which was doubtless a prime factor in its attraction for Jean de Meun and Deschamps, presented itself to Chaucer as ideal material for the *Wife's Prologue:*

> Equus, asinus, bos, canis, et vilissima mancipia, vestes quoque, et lebetes, sedile ligneum, calix, et urceolus fictilis probantur prius, et sic emuntur: sola uxor non ostenditur, ne ante displiceat, quam ducatur.[64]

In Chaucer's version the imagery is kept practically intact; it harmonizes closely with the list of common things that we have already seen in the web of the Wife's ordinary speech:

> "Thou seist that oxen, asses, hors, and houndes,   [285]
> They been assayed at diverse stoundes;
> Bacyns, lavours, er that men hem bye,
> Spoones and stooles, and al swich housbondrye,
> And so been pottes, clothes, and array;
> But folk of wyves maken noon assay,
> Til they be wedded . . ."

Jerome quotes the proverb, "Sicut in ligno vermis, ita perdit virum suum uxor malefica," and Chaucer finds it immediately suitable to his purpose:

> "Thou seyest, right as wormes shende a tree,   [376]
> Right so a wyf destroyeth hire housbonde . . ."

Chaucer improves on such material as well. In Jerome's *Epistle against Jovinian,* one of the tracts bound up in the "book of wikked wyves" belonging to the Wife's fifth husband, there is the following version of Socrates' marital misfortunes:

> Quodam autem tempore cum infinita convicia ex superiori loco ingerenti Xantippae restitisset, aqua perfusus immunda, nihil amplius respondit, quam capite deterso: Sciebam, inquit, futurum, ut ista tonitrua imber sequeretur.[65]
> [Once when he opposed Xantippe, who was heaping endless abuse on him from above, she doused him with dirty water. Having wiped his head, he answered with nothing more than, "I knew that rain would follow such thunder as that."]

When it becomes the Wife's turn to pass the story on to her listeners, it has been altered:

> "No thyng forgat he the care and the wo [727]
> That Socrates hadde with his wyves two;
> How Xantippa caste pisse upon his heed.
> This sely man sat stille as he were deed;
> He wiped his heed, namoore dorste he seyn,
> But 'Er that thonder stynte, comth a reyn!' "

The whole incident is made more domestic and more concrete. By a shift of emphasis at the end, the ruefully witty response of the philosopher is converted into a popular proverb, and the philosopher himself becomes more henpecked than ever.

Many of Chaucer's borrowings, and adaptations such as the one just mentioned, are of course only appreciable by scholars, by reference to the textual sources. The fact of such borrowing and adaptation, while it tells us something about Chaucer's method, is not a part of the public meaning of the poem, and is not detectible by ordinary stylistic analysis. But there is another powerful class of naturalizing devices in the surface rhetoric. Even where the doctrinal material is nakedly learned or conventional, it appears in the *Prologue* in an altered guise. The issue in the opening section turns on Biblical authority for remarriage. Chaucer does not go to the trouble of establishing the fact that the Wife is a Biblical scholar before having her cite John iv, 17–18. Rather, he eliminates the problem of verisimilitude stylistically. In the oral recitation of passages like the following, naked textualism is swallowed up by the dramatics of the delivery:

> *"But me was toold, certeyn, nat longe agoon is,* [9]
> That sith that Crist ne wente nevere but onis
> To weddyng, in the Cane of Galilee,
> That by the same ensample taughte he me
> That I ne sholde wedded be but ones.
> *Herkne eek, lo, which a sharp word for the nones,*
> Biside a welle, Jhesus, God and man,
> Spak in repreeve of the Samaritan;
> 'Thou has yhad fyve housbondes,' quod he,
> 'And that ilke man that now hath thee
> Is noght thyn housbonde,' *thus seyde he certeyn.*
> *What that he mente therby, I kan nat seyn;*

> *But that I axe, why that the fifthe man*
> *Was noon housbonde to the Samaritan?*
> *How manye myghte she have in mariage?*
> *Yet herde I nevere tellen in myn age*
> *Upon this nombre diffinicioun.*

Besides the obvious device of attributing the learning to hearsay (9), phrases such as "Herkne eek," typical of dramatic monologue, continually refresh the illusion of an actual speaker and an actual audience.[66] The personal comment and evaluation (14, 20–25), and the repeated, combative querying, as "How manye myghte she have in mariage?"[67] give the textual material a dynamic quality that we do not find in the conventional idiom. They move both speaker and audience to take issue, as the doctrinal passages in the *Knight's Tale,* for instance, do not. And unlike such passages in the *Knight's Tale,* these have a broken, turbulent rhythm which reduces their structural isolation and sweeps them into the current of the Wife's naturalistic chatter.

Chaucer's boldest naturalization of learning comes in the adoption of the exemplary or "sample" monologue. In Jean de Meun, and in Theophrastus and Deschamps, passages of monologue are quoted as exempla.[68] Thus in Jean the tirade of the Jealous Husband is structurally only an example, cited by Ami, of the evils of sovereignty in marriage. Here the full literary possibilities of the device are not exploited, because Ami, who is doing the quoting, is himself lost from view. This is not a serious limitation in the *Roman de la Rose,* because nothing depends on a full characterization of Ami. He is not portrayed naturalistically in the first place. But Chaucer saw in the "sample" speech a needed opportunity for broadly extending his character's remarks without violating her personality. Accordingly, part of the Wife's monologue is quotation of what she could and did say at different times and under far different circumstances.

The first sample Chaucer gives her is familiar to the scholar from the fragment of Theophrastus and its imitations:

> Deinde per noctes totas garrulae conquestiones: Illa ornatior procedit
> in publicum: haec honoratur ab omnibus, ego in conventu feminarum
> misella despicior. Cur aspiciebas vicinam? quid cum ancillula loque-
> baris? de foro veniens quid attulisti?[69]

This Chaucer found immediately useful because the speaker is a woman, a typical shrew, and the material is already in dramatic form. His departure from the traditional technique is to take the quotation from the doctrinaire and give it to her who spoke it in the first place:

"... but herkneth how I sayde: [234]
'Sire olde kaynard, is this thyn array?
Why is my neighebores wyf so gay?
She is honoured over al ther she gooth;
I sitte at hoom, I have no thrifty clooth.
What dostow at my neighebores hous?
Is she so fair? artow so amorous?
What rowne ye with oure mayde? ...' "

Chaucer thus converts exemplum into autobiography. Within the same auto-biographical frame, however, he goes a step farther, widening the scope of the dramatic monologue by also including within the Wife's report what her husbands might have said, or thought they said, to her. The whole process of quoting the masculine abuse of the three old husbands is further dramatized by its being represented as the Wife's *invention* of what they said. In short, it does duty as an example of her aggressive war on them. So, beginning with verse 248 we hear the Wife of Bath quoting herself as she used to pretend to quote her old husbands. The matter attributed to them constitutes a significant part of the traditional antifeminist material that sets off and gives perspective to the Wife's position.

Here again, through rhetorical and stylistic means, the "auctoritees" are naturalized into strict conformity with dramatic consistency. Jean de Meun could not, or would not, have made distinct the separate voices in this complicated pile-up. Only the final voice would have been heard. In Chaucer, however, so much care is taken to preserve the perspective between voices that we never lose sight of Dame Alice beneath her double mask of quotation. The frequent repetition of "thou seist" is a device to distinguish the middle and upper layers of the speech, to separate the Wife's account of actual events from the fabrications she employs within those events. A whole series of epithets and replies similarly stabilizes her account and brings the unfortunate victims of matrimony into concrete existence. The epithets are colorful, if one-sided: "sire olde kaynard" (235), "olde dotard shrewe" (291), "olde barel-ful of lyes" (302), and the like. The formula "thou seist," the epithets and replies, with sidelights illuminating an intimate domestic scene, all mingle with the doctrinal exempla in a single stream of flexible, energetic discourse. Within it the realistic conflict between the old husband and the young wife, and the ideological conflict between traditional authority and boisterous feminism, are presented simultaneously:

> " 'Sire olde lecchour, lat thy japes be! [242]
> And if I have a gossib or a freend,
> Withouten gilt, thou chidest as a feend,
> If that I walke or pleye unto his hous!
> Thou comest hoom as dronken as a mous,
> And prechest on thy bench, with yvel preef!
> Thou seist to me it is a greet meschief
> To wedde a povre womman, for costage;
> And if that she be riche, of heigh parage,
> Thanne seistow that it is a tormentrie
> To soffre hire pride and hire malencolie.
> And if that she be fair, thou verray knave,
> Thou seyst that every holour wol hire have;
> She may no while in chastitee abyde,
> That is assailled upon ech a syde.
> Thou seyst som folk desiren us for richesse,
> Somme for oure shap, and somme for oure fairnesse,
> And som for she kan outher synge or daunce,
> And som for gentillesse and daliaunce;
> Som for hir handes and hir armes smale:
> Thus goth al to the devel, by thy tale.' "

With this much of Chaucer's technique in view we are in a position easily to appreciate the symbolism of the monologue's closing incident. A final gathering of authorities is brought into the poem between the covers of Jankyn's book. Here again Chaucer takes pains to keep the doctrine within its dramatic compartment. Alice mentions the book seven times; sixteen times she says "he redde" or "he tolde me," and she counters the authorities with her own comment. However, the burden of such comment is not here interwoven among the proverbs and exempla; in fitting climax to her tale it is concentrated into a single violent action:

> "And whan I saugh he wolde nevere fyne [788]
> To reden on this cursed book al nyght,
> Al sodeynly thre leves have I plyght
> Out of his book, right as he radde, and eke
> I with my fest so took hym on the cheke
> That in oure fyr he fil bakward adoun."

The scene harks back to the fabliaux in its superficial features, but it is more broadly meaningful than any scene in that literature. In the context of the *Prologue*'s doctrinal material, we behold not only a magnificently natural creature in domestic squabble; she is also the embodiment of experience ripping out the pages of the book of authority, and of militant feminism fetching traditional masculine domination a healthy blow on the cheek. The symbolism of her position could not have been made secure without the naturalistic style whereby Chaucer creates and then protects it.

iii. The *Canon's Yeoman's Tale*

Whan ended was the lyf of Seinte Cecile,   [554]
Er we hadde riden fully fyve mile,
At Boghtoun under Blee us gan atake
A man that clothed was in clothes blake,
And under-nethe he hadde a whyt surplys.
His hakeney, that was al pomely grys,
So swatte that it wonder was to see;
It semed as he had priked miles three.
The hors eek that his yeman rood upon
So swatte that unnethe myghte it gon.
Aboute the peytrel stood the foom ful hye;
He was of foom al flekked as a pye.
A male tweyfoold on his croper lay;
It semed that he caried lite array.
Al light for somer rood this worthy man,
And in myn herte wondren I bigan
What that he was, til that I understood
How that his cloke was sowed to his hood;
For which, whan I hadde longe avysed me,
I demed hym som chanoun for to be.
His hat heeng at his bak doun by a laas,
For he hadde riden moore than trot or paas;
He hadde ay priked lik as he were wood.
A clote-leef he hadde under his hood
For swoot, and for to keep his heed from heete.
But it was joye for to seen hym swete!
His forheed dropped as a stillatorie,
Were ful of plantayne and of paritorie.
And whan that he was come, he gan to crye,

213

"God save," quod he, "this joly compaignye!
Faste have I priked," quod he, "for youre sake,
By cause that I wolde yow atake,
To riden in this myrie compaignye."
His yeman eek was ful of curteisye . . .

The abruptness of the Canon's arrival among the pilgrims, his equally abrupt flight, and the breathless, vehement urgency of his Yeoman's subsequent discourse, have led most critics from the poem to the facts that may have inspired it. Tyrwhitt's conjecture—"that some sudden resentment had determined Chaucer to interrupt the regular course of his work, in order to insert a Satire against the Alchemists"—has not been generally accepted. But scholarship still tends to class the poem as a "current event." If not autobiographical, it is journalistic, and something like biographical interest still lurks in the much-debated question of Chaucer's attitude toward alchemy. Was Chaucer a credulous, medieval dupe, or an initiate into alchemical mysteries, or was he modern, a skeptic? Speculation on questions such as this has robbed the poem of the critical interest due it. The story is widely regarded as a good one, a good piece of realism, and not much more.[70] Let it be admitted that there is hardly another poem of Chaucer's that seems so compact of fact, so little ulterior in its design. Its surface argument is determinedly simple; it is a warning against alchemy. Its materials are so solid as to seem to defy further "interpretation." If there is a philosophical pattern to the *Canterbury Tales,* this seems to be its one unassimilable lump. I am emboldened to present the following rather hypothetical reading partly by the conviction that journalism is un-Chaucerian, partly by the virtual absence of previous literary criticism, and partly by the enigmatic nature of the poem itself. The reader will have to judge how much to allow in it for the peculiar preoccupations of our own age,[71] and how much for my own conviction, already expressed in these pages, that Chaucer's realism is ultimately symbolic.

The poem divides itself into three parts which do not quite coincide with the formal, textual divisions. The first part (the *Prologue* and *prima pars* of the text, i.e., verses 554–971) describes the arrival of the Canon and Yeoman, the Canon's flight, and the Yeoman's revelation of their alchemical activities. Its style is dramatic: all of the *prima pars* is, indeed, dramatic monologue. The second part (*pars secunda* to verse 1387) is the Yeoman's tale proper, of another swindling canon-alchemist. The narrative here, though it contains some rhetorical formalism, is so highly dramatized with interjections and asides that it harmonizes closely with the tone of the first part. In the third part (1388–1481)[72] the stance

214

of the narrator changes. Whereas before he has been represented as unlearned, and his very proverbs are accredited to hearsay,[78] now his voice carries its own authority. He cites Arnaldus de Villanova and the rather mysterious "Senior" without embarrassment, and ends with a sober, philosophical statement that deepens the context of the entire poem. We must recognize here—what we have seen in the *Roman de la Rose,* in the *Troilus,* and elsewhere—the convention of philosophical amplification. The characterization of the speaker is suspended in favor of comment on the wider meaning of his position:

> Thanne conclude I thus, sith that God of hevene   [1472]
> Ne wil nat that the philosophres nevene
> How that a man shal come unto this stoon,
> I rede, as for the beste, lete it goon.
> For whoso maketh God his adversarie,
> As for to werken any thyng in contrarie
> Of his wil, certes, never shal he thryve,
> Thogh that he multiplie terme of his lyve.
> And there a poynt; for ended is my tale.

This philosophical postscript expresses the ruling attitude toward alchemy in the poem. In the light of it, the poem expresses neither credulity nor skepticism, but rather a distinction between false alchemy and true, between men's alchemy and God's. The body of the poem, the first two parts, is an exposure of the alchemy without God, of faith in earth. Its skepticism is that of the believer, not of the scientist, who sees in technology another secular religion, as seductive in its way as the religion of Love:

> This sotted preest, who was gladder than he?   [1341]
> Was nevere brid gladder agayn the day,
> Ne nyghtyngale, in the sesoun of May,
> Was nevere noon that luste bet to synge;
> Ne lady lustier in carolynge,
> Or for to speke of love and wommanhede,
> Ne knyght in armes to doon an hardy dede,
> To stonden in grace of his lady deere,
> Than hadde this preest this soory craft to leere.

The poem's dualism of attitude is conventional. It corresponds to the division of the science between the charlatans and puffers on the one hand, and the philosophers and mystics on the other.[74] Medieval alchemical texts from about the early thirteenth century discuss pro and con the doubts already raised concerning the possibility of transmutation, and the Christian alchemical tradition is full of both practical "skepticism" and the thoroughly orthodox but hardly credulous notion that to God all things are possible.[75]

As with other philosophical poems of Chaucer, we are more interested in the poetry than in the conclusion. The poetry everywhere evokes a profound sense of the futility, the cursedness, of a soulless striving with matter. The trickery of alchemical swindlers, illustrated by the "tale" proper, stands also for the nature of the science itself. The chantry priest is swindled by the alchemist in the second part just as the alchemist is swindled by the science in the first. That the victim is a priest and the alchemists also canons may be owing to current events, for all we know.[76] But the poetic effect is to suggest that their activity is a deep apostasy, a treason, a going over to the devil himself. They are Judases (1003). The falseness of mere deceit is not enough to account for the Yeoman's passionate insistence on "this chanons cursednesse," and the ubiquity of "the foule feend" in the Yeoman's discourse.[77] The following rhetorical invocation to an undistinguished victim can be anticipated only by our seeing something infernal in "this chanoun,"

roote of al trecherie,   [1069]

That everemoore delit hath and gladnesse—
Swiche feendly thoghtes in his herte impresse—
How Cristes peple he may to meschief brynge.
God kepe us from his false dissymulynge!
Noght wiste this preest with whom that he delte,
Ne of his harm comynge he no thyng felte.
O sely preest! o sely innocent!
With coveitise anon thou shalt be blent!
O gracelees, ful blynd is thy conceite,
No thyng ne artow war of the deceite
Which that this fox yshapen hath to thee!
His wily wrenches thou ne mayst nat flee.

Religious overtones are suggested equally by the context. The poem follows the *Second Nun's Tale*. There is perhaps something more than coincidence in the contrast between St. Cecilia, unharmed in her bath of flames, conquering fire through faith, and the blackened, sweating believers in earth, whose fire blows up in their faces. Cecilia, in her retort to the pagan prefect, curiously anticipates the Yeoman's teaching:

"Ther lakketh no thyng to thyne outter eyen [2NT 498]
That thou n'art blynd, for thyng that we seen alle
That it is stoon, that men may wel espyen,
That ilke stoon a god thow wolt it calle.
I rede thee, lat thyn hand upon it falle,
And taste it wel, and stoon thou shalt it fynde,
Syn that thou seest nat with thyne eyen blynde."

Though ye prolle ay, ye shul it nevere fynde. [CYT 1412]
Ye been as boold as is Bayard the blynde,
That blondreth forth, and peril casteth noon.
He is as boold to renne agayn a stoon
As for to goon bisides in the weye.
So faren ye that multiplie, I seye.
If that youre eyen kan nat seen aright,
Looke that youre mynde lakke noght his sight.
For though ye looken never so brode and stare,
Ye shul nothyng wynne on that chaffare.

The extremely naturalistic characterization of the Yeoman serves the conception of alchemy as a blind materialism. He is a simple, unlearned soul. His greatest gift is a dogged sense of the world of matter. There is not the faintest glimmer of spirituality or mysticism about him. Screened through this personality, everything is lost but the world of rocks and stones. Thus his idiom is ruggedly dramatic. His narrative can be trusted to describe the slightest motions in the physical world:

But taketh heede now, sires, for Goddes love!   [1176]
He took his cole of which I spak above,
And in his hand he baar it pryvely.
And whiles the preest couched bisily
The coles, as I tolde yow er this,
This chanoun seyde, "Freend, ye doon amys.
This is nat couched as it oghte be;
But soone I shal amenden it," quod he.
"Now lat me medle therwith but a while,
For of yow have I pitee, by Seint Gile!
Ye been right hoot; I se wel how ye swete.
Have heere a clooth, and wipe awey the wete."
And whiles that the preest wiped his face,

This chanoun took his cole—with harde grace!—
And leyde it above upon the myddeward
Of the crosselet, and blew wel afterward,
Til that the coles gonne faste brenne.
"Now yeve us drynke," quod the chanoun thenne;
"As swithe al shal be wel, I undertake.
Sitte we doun, and lat us myrie make."
And whan that this chanounes bechen cole
Was brent, al the lemaille out of the hole
Into the crosselet fil anon adoun;
And so it moste nedes, by resoun,
Syn it so evene aboven it couched was.
But therof wiste the preest nothyng, alas!
He demed alle the coles yliche good;
For of that sleighte he nothyng understood.

His commentary, on the other hand, is dully repetitive; it is analysis frustrated
and strangled by a limited vision. Blear-eyed, he has come to see only, as his
modern counterpart might put it, that alchemy "don't work":

"We blondren evere and pouren in the fir,   [670]
And for al that we faille of oure desir,
For evere we lakken oure conclusioun."

For alle oure sleightes we kan nat conclude.   [773]

Noght helpeth us, oure labour is in veyn.   [777]

For lost is al oure labour and travaille.   [781]

Al is in veyn, and parde! muchel moore.   [843]

This is to seyn, they faillen bothe two.   [851]

The pot tobreketh, and farewel, al is go!   [907]

    be it hoot or coold, I dar seye this,   [956]
That we concluden everemoore amys.

Beneath the Yeoman's unconscious simplicity, this insistent chorus voices a
frustration beyond that of mere mechanical failure. It registers a failure of vision.
It says that dealing with matter as matter has no end, that is, no teleology.
Medieval philosophical alchemy was nourished on hylozoism, on the feeling
that matter was instinct with life. The Yeoman's recitation, however, evokes

an opposite feeling, of matter spiritless and contingent, of that primordial impurity, "corrupt," "floterynge," from which only God can raise man.[78] To expect an end, a "conclusioun," to the cooking of this hopeless stuff is the real irony of the alchemist's failure.

The technical imagery of the poem is very powerful in evoking the feeling of matter as matter. The Yeoman's recitation is dramatically motivated; now that the Canon is gone he will tell all that he can. The ensuing list of materials and equipment answers to a tradition of inventory in the alchemical writings themselves, but, given certain changes of tone, it answers also to the literary convention of the *parade,* the list of wares or drugs vaunted in the *Herberie* and in the *mercator* scenes of the passion plays.[79] Chaucer read alchemy for the matter. The manner belongs more to the tradition of Rutebeuf. Nowhere else in Chaucer is there such a solid, unspiritual mass of "realism," and nowhere is its artistic function less to be doubted:

> Ther is also ful many another thyng [784]
> That is unto oure craft apertenyng.
> Though I by ordre hem nat reherce kan,
> By cause that I am a lewed man,
> Yet wol I telle hem as they come to mynde,
> Thogh I ne kan nat sette hem in hir kynde:
> As boole armonyak, verdegrees, boras,
> And sondry vessels maad of erthe and glas,
> Oure urynales and oure descensories,
> Violes, crosletz, and sublymatories,
> Cucurbites and alambikes eek,
> And othere swiche, deere ynough a leek.
> Nat nedeth it for to reherce hem alle,—
> Watres rubifiyng, and boles galle,
> Arsenyk, sal armonyak, and brymstoon;
> And herbes koude I telle eek many oon,
> As egremoyne, valerian, and lunarie,
> And othere swiche, if that me liste tarie;
> Oure lampes brennyng bothe nyght and day,
> To brynge aboute oure purpos, if we may;
> Oure fourneys eek of calcinacioun,
> And of watres albificacioun;
> Unslekked lym, chalk, and gleyre of an ey,
> Poudres diverse, asshes, donge, pisse, and cley,

Cered pokkets, sal peter, vitriole,
And diverse fires maad of wode and cole;
Sal tartre, alkaly, and sal preparat,
And combust materes and coagulat;
Cley maad with hors or mannes heer, and oille
Of tartre, alum glas, berme, wort, and argoille,
Resalgar, and othre materes enbibyng,
And eek of oure materes encorporyng,
And of oure silver citrinacioun,
Oure cementyng and fermentacioun,
Oure yngottes, testes, and many mo.

The *Wife of Bath's Prologue,* as we have seen, has a notable collection of concrete, material images. But compared to this, it is spiritual and airy. If art and
not journalism is at work in the *Canon's Yeoman's Tale,* this chaos of matter,
refuse, excrement, represents the universe of technology.

In the context of this kind of interpretation, the headlong entry of the Canon
and Yeoman cannot be read as Chaucer's afterthought. It seems thoroughly,
artistically, premeditated. These men are not introduced with the other pilgrims, because they are not within Christian society. They do not go on pilgrimages; they are not headed for Canterbury, or rather, for the City of God
that it represents. Their entry is dramatically motivated, to be sure. They see
the pilgrims leave town and must therefore gallop to catch up. But Chaucer's
emphasis on the haste and the hot sweat, like the Yeoman's stridency of tone,
seems to call for a more-than-dramatic explanation. It is very well for the sympathetic Chaucerian Narrator to find an earthy zest in it all: "But it was joye
for to seen hym swete!" (579). We must ask, nevertheless, whether the hot gallop
and the high temperature are not at the same time precisely characteristic of
the Canon's way of life, the way of technology. The Canon doubtless intends
to swindle the pilgrims, but this is only one stage in the greater pursuit:

"To muchel folk we doon illusioun,   [673]
And borwe gold, be it a pound or two,
Or ten, or twelve, or manye sommes mo,
And make hem wenen, at the leeste weye,
That of a pound we koude make tweye.
Yet is it fals, but ay we han good hope
It for to doon, and after it we grope.
But that science is so fer us biforn,

We mowen nat, although we hadden it sworn,
It overtake, it slit awey so faste."

The Canon is described as carrying peculiarly little baggage. Dramatically, this is explainable by the traditional poverty of alchemists. Poetically, it says what the Yeoman in a brief moment of reflection says later on:

> I warne you wel, it is to seken evere.   [874]
> That futur temps hath maad men to dissevere,
> In trust thereof, from al that evere they hadde.

The pathetic gravity of these lines suggests that the "al that evere they hadde" is more than money and clothing and a fresh complexion. It is also, perhaps, the spiritual tradition that a community of men takes with it along the way, and that gives purpose and direction to the journey. Marie Hamilton remarks that the Canon was apostate, or else "guilty of that *instabilitas loci* forbidden to monastics."[80] Surely his flight, while it is dramatically motivated by "verray sorwe and shame" (702), poetically symbolizes an apostasy from the human congregation, an instability of place in life. Like the canon of the Yeoman's story, he abides nowhere.

Chaucer could make fun of the complacent ignorance that despises knowledge. The carpenter of the *Miller's Tale* is a victim of this vice:

> "I thoghte ay wel how that it sholde be!   [3453]
> Men sholde nat knowe of Goddes pryvetee.
> Ye, blessed be alwey a lewed man
> That noght but oonly his bileve kan!"

The *Canon's Yeoman's Tale* deals with an ignorance that is less funny: that complacent faith in science that despises God. Dante's Hell has its place for those who "wished to see too far ahead."[81] Chaucer is no less conservative. In attitude the poem is as medieval as the *Knight's Tale*. The dogged refusal to admit the intractability of matter, one of the virtues to which we owe so much of our civilization, is here represented by a group of sooty figures sifting and picking for salvage in a pile of refuse. He who cheers them on is a fool. In the light of later history, indeed, the poem is reactionary. This kind of alchemy gave us chemistry. Yet there is still time to judge whether the poem has not a germ of wry prophecy in it, whether already in the fourteenth century an acute consciousness could not have caught the future of technology in a single line:

> The pot tobreketh, and farewel, al is go!

221

§ 4. THE MIXED STYLE

The *Canterbury Tales* as a whole is an example of the mixed style. Each of the tales, by analogy and by contrast, takes meaning from others. The effect of the larger form, a structure of juxtapositions and tensions, is to place and control the attitudes evoked separately by its parts, to reveal their virtues and limitations in context. Some of this manipulation of attitudes is announced dramatically by rivalries among the pilgrims. The Miller and Reeve, the Summoner and Friar, are at overt personal debate. The Clerk recognizes in his envoy a relationship to the Wife of Bath. The Cook promises a comment on an innkeeper.[82] These dramatic relationships are in turn supported, and nondramatic ones are established mutely but no less powerfully, by the choice and disposition of the literary materials themselves. Thus the Miller's dramatic announcement of

"a noble tale for the nones
With which I wol now quite the Knyghtes tale,"
[*MillProl* 3126–27]

is underscored in his tale by a resemblance to the Knight's in plot and in character grouping. The Reeve's rivalry with the Miller has similar literary support. The Host's implied comparison of the Nun's Priest with the Monk is followed by the Priest's recitation of a "tragedy" which comments on the Monk's collection of tragedies.[83] Criticism has detected (or suspected) a whole web of such relationships among the tales, in genre, subject, plot, characterization, and so on.[84]

It is hard to know where to draw the line between art and algebra in these correspondences. The work is so great as to begin to generate its own relationships. Does the description of the clerk Nicholas in the *Miller's Tale*, with its verbal reminiscences of the Clerk's portrait in the *General Prologue*, announce a comparative study of clerkships? Is Chaucer's Clerk to be compared to the Wife of Bath's fifth husband? Is there a "Marriage Group"?[85] Had Chaucer extended his poem, would the Merchant or the Monk have replied to the *Shipman's Tale*? There are provocative resemblances between the *Miller's Tale* and the *Merchant's*: do they support a philosophical comparison? One could not begin to describe the relational possibilities suggested by Chaucer's language, by phrases repeated—"pitee renneth soone in gentil herte," "allone, withouten any compaignye,"[86]—and by such repeated figures as the rhetorical *comparatio* on the death of Priam, which is used to describe both Constance's departure from Rome and Chauntecleer's abduction from a chicken yard.[87] We need not pause to evaluate all these possibilities. Even what is announced in the gross stylistics of the *Canterbury Tales* shows Chaucer's tireless capacity for definition and comparison. He has a passion for relationships, and the over-all structure of the work, the linear sequence of discrete stories in various styles, meets this passion perfectly.

We are not surprised to find something of the same structure within the individual tales. Many of them can richly stand alone as containing significant measurement within themselves. The dominant attitudes they convey are habitually conjoined with other attitudes, idiosyncrasies with norms, norms with idiosyncrasies or other norms. The perspective is created variously; it is inserted, appended, implied, disguised, or worked plainly into the main pattern of the story. Sometimes it is a matter of plot and circumstance, the irony of a wrong turning that exposes an ignorance and prepares for a defeat.[88] Often it comes with an internal shift of style.

Virtually all the *Canterbury Tales* have some mixture of styles. The poems of dominantly religious inspiration have a realism which, if the poem is successful, as I think the *Prioress' Tale* is, melts symbolically into the conventional frame without conflict or irony. This peaceful stylistic mixture has some of the quality of the religious paradox itself; naturalism and the supernatural make peace in miracle. But in other poems the shifting style brings in whole shifts of assumptions. In poems where one style is heavily dominant, the mixture is enough to comment on, but not enough to rival the dominant attitude; thus the touches of commonsensical humor in the *Knight's Tale*, the scrap of lyricism in the *Reeve's Tale,* and the formal rhetoric in the *Canon's Yeoman's Tale* are relatively minor in effect. The *Wife of Bath's Prologue* swallows up a great mass of learned doctrine without losing its dominantly naturalistic shape. But there are a number of tales in which, as in the *Parliament of Fowls* and the *Troilus,* the mixed style is on display and becomes part of the subject of the poem. These are the tales which seem most "Chaucerian," comprehending in small space, as they do, so much of Chaucer's range.

i. The *Miller's Tale*

In the *Miller's Tale* the alien style contributes importantly to the realization of the theme, but it is not a central feature of the poem. That it is not accounts partly for the mixture's broadly comic effect. The tale does not have the pathos of a *Troilus* nor the bitterness of a *Merchant's Tale,* because the views it presents are so outrageously unbalanced. The courtliness in the *Miller's Tale* is never given full, traditional value. It is never a norm, always an idiosyncrasy; and it is juxtaposed to a naturalism of exceptional force and vitality.

The normal view is perhaps best apprehended in the fact that the Miller's "noble tale" is fabliau at the stage of richest elaboration. All the fabliau features are here so completely realized that the genre is virtually made philosophical. The simple, sequential fabliau plot has become, in the lucidity of this complicated plot's arrangement, an assertion of the binding, practical sequentiality of all events. The pragmatic, prosaically solid imagery of fabliau is here built into an unbroken, unbreakable wall of accepted fact. The fabliau's preference for physical action becomes an ethical imperative. Even the stock triangle of fabliau—the lecherous young wife, the jealous husband, and the clever clerk (here two clerks)—is a self-assertive vehicle for the purest fabliau doctrine, the sovereignty of animal nature. So fully does the tale fulfill its fabliau entelechy that its working-out is attended, as Tillyard says, by "feelings akin to those of religious wonder."[89]

The poem's dominant style is of great intrinsic interest, and, having passed it by in my discussion of naturalism *per se,* I must notice it here in a rather elaborate preface to the main topic. Let me observe, then, that in no other naturalistic poem of Chaucer is practical circumstance so closely tended, and practical detail so closely accounted for. We are given the name of the town and of the neighboring town, the names of all the characters (Nicholas, Absolon, Alisoun, John, Robyn, Gille, Gerveys) save one (the cloisterer, 3661), a close knowledge of the architecture and plan of the house:

> And broke an hole an heigh, upon the gable,   [3571]
> Unto the gardyn-ward, over the stable . . .

We have a scrupulous accounting of days of the week and of the hours of the crucial day. The description is rich with an expressive superfluity of specification:

> "Clepe at his dore, or knokke *with a stoon.*"   [3432]
>
> hente hym *by the sholdres* myghtily . . .   [3475]
>
> *His owene hand* he made laddres thre,   [3624]
> To clymben *by the ronges and the stalkes*
> Unto the tubbes *hangynge in the balkes* . . .

The great mass of such given detail achieves an extraordinary solidity—beyond that of the *Reeve's Tale* or the *Wife of Bath's Prologue*—because so much of it is given specific antecedents or consequences. Where the typical fabliau brings in properties and explanations only as needed, the *Miller's Tale* seems to explain everything. That the town is Oxford explains—overpoweringly explains—the presence of a clever clerk. That Absolon is named Absolon "explains" his blond beauty and his femininity.⁹⁰ That John the carpenter is made a "riche gnof" in the very first statement explains his securing a pretty, young wife. That Absolon offers her rich gifts, later on, is a link in this chain of explanations. That the carpenter "gestes heeld to bord" in the second verse prepares for the boarder Nicholas in verse four. The boarder's two days' self-confinement is silently prepared for in the eighteenth verse (3204); he rooms "allone, withouten any compaignye." Before Robyn the knave can peek in through Nicholas' door we are told that

> An hole he foond, ful lowe upon a bord,   [3440]
> Ther as the cat was wont in for to crepe . . .

Besides generally poetic consequence on the one hand (the board and the cat for solidity and animality), and practical consequence on the other (the hole for Robyn to peek through), many details through sheer recurrence achieve what I can only call a psychological consequence. Nicholas' door is not only peeked through; it is first cried and knocked at, then heaved off its hinges, then prayed by, then shut fast. That this door is at best only a minor factor in the action is symptomatic of the care with which the "naturalness" of the poem is contrived. The very smallest scraps of image and action are handled thus consequentially, even where they are entirely unnecessary to the gross plot. The cat image cited above is already the second such image in the poem. The hole image twice reappears later. The kinesthetic effect of its lowness is repeated with the carpenter's window (3696). The whole denouement, coming when it does, is by virtue of a mass recurrence of images given an air of utter probability. The nocturnal visit of Absolon to the carpenter's house has first a dress rehearsal that seems inconsequential—"This passeth forth; what wol ye bet than weel?" (3370)—except to familiarize us with this action, with such details as the wall and the hinged window, and with such minute facts as that the window can be heard through (cf. 3744). Similarly, the cockcrow, the knocking, the (sweet-smelling) mouth, the stone (I am citing items consecutively from verse 3675), the coal, the forge, the nobles, the cough, the knocking again, the haunch bone, the flatulence, bread and ale, the cry of "out" and "harrow," the neighbors, the carpenter's arm, the gaping and staring, the carpenter's madness—are all prepared for beforehand.⁹¹ The breathtaking effect of the poem's climax surely owes much to this process. The focal images—the flood, the carpenter in his tub, the axe and cord—are suddenly brought to our conscious attention, not from nowhere (with an effect of mere surprise and chance), but from the semiconscious storage of previous acceptance, unanticipated, perhaps, but inevitable. It is this solidity of detail, along with the characterization interlaced intimately with it, that gives the ingenious plotting its overpowering substantiality.

In this remarkably self-contained world of facts, no room is left for abstract, *a priori* formulations. The humor of the poem arises from the unequal conflict between fact and the few illusions that unhappily insist on themselves. The devastating victory of the norm is supported, in the manner of comedy, by reducing the "errors" to caricature. The error of religion—to pass over the error of not wedding one's "simylitude" (3228)—is represented by the credulous, illiterate carpenter. His knowledge of Scripture is from mystery plays, seen "ful yoore ago" (3537). Noe (Noah) for him is "Nowel." His piety is all spells and asseverations; he is of that self-satisfied, unthinking persuasion that expresses itself in saws and goes by precedents:

> "This world is now ful tikel, sikerly.   [3428]
> I saugh to-day a cors yborn to chirche
> That now, on Monday last, I saugh hym wirche."

> "Help us, seinte Frydeswyde!   [3449]
> A man woot litel what hym shal bityde.
> This man is falle, with his astromye,
> In som woodnesse or in som agonye.
> I thoghte ay wel how that it sholde be!
> Men sholde nat knowe of Goddes pryvetee.
> Ye, blessed be alwey a lewed man
> That noght but oonly his bileve kan!
> So ferde another clerk with astromye;
> He walked in the feeldes, for to prye
> Upon the sterres, what ther sholde bifalle,
> Til he was in a marle-pit yfalle;
> He saugh nat that."

He is gulled by a clerk, and by his belief in "Goddes pryvetee."

The error of clerk Nicholas is faith in intellect and in the sufficiency of wit:

> "A clerk hadde litherly biset his whyle,   [3299]
> But if he koude a carpenter bigyle."

His quite enormous sufficiency, conveyed in the opening description (3199 ff.), is already touched with irony in the epithet "hende." It is fascinating to watch this term, which means "gracious" and "ready-handed" and "clever" and

226

"comely" and "near at hand," sharpen as the poem progresses.[92] It becomes a signal of his defeat. He has already solved the ethic of the poem, assault, when his cleverness elaborately overextends itself and leads to Absolon's assault on him.

Faith in Love is the heresy most elaborately dealt with in the poem, and it is most elaborately caricatured. Linguistic analysis has shown how much the Oxford idiom of love is the idiom of English rather than of French romance.[93] It is the native version of the imported heresy that is parodied here. More congenial to the setting, it is also funnier than Continental love would have been, for it is exposed to the laughter of the sophisticated, who know better, as well as of the Miller's kind, who know worse. But it remains crushingly conventional, and the stylistic vehicle for the comedy of love is the farrago of convention and naked instinct that is Absolon's courtship of Alisoun:

> "I wol go slepe an houre or tweye,   [3685]
> And al the nyght thanne wol I wake and pleye."
> Whan that the firste cok hath crowe, anon
> Up rist this joly lovere Absolon,
> And hym arraieth gay, at poynt-devys.
> But first he cheweth greyn and lycorys,
> To smellen sweete, er he hadde kembd his heer.
> Under his tonge a trewe-love he beer,
> For therby wende he to ben gracious.
> He rometh to the carpenteres hous,
> And stille he stant under the shot-wyndowe—
> Unto his brest it raughte, it was so lowe—
> And softe he cougheth with a semysoun:
> "What do ye, hony-comb, sweete Alisoun,
> My faire bryd, my sweete cynamome?
> Awaketh, lemman myn, and speketh to me!
> Wel litel thynken ye upon my wo,
> That for youre love I swete ther I go.
> No wonder is thogh that I swelte and swete;
> I moorne as dooth a lamb after the tete.
> Ywis, lemman, I have swich love-longynge,
> That lik a turtel trewe is my moornynge.
> I may nat ete na moore than a mayde."
> "Go fro the wyndow, Jakke fool," she sayde.

The French lover "rometh" perhaps, but he does not "swelte and swete," nor does he catch up on his sleep before a sleepless night. The courtly delicacy of speech and of toilette⁶⁴ have become in this small-town, provincial version the anal-retentive, squeamish spotlessness registered in Absolon's portrait (3312 ff.) and punished with terrible aptness at the end.

The delectable Alisoun sets in motion the lovemaking of the poem, and her celebrated portrait answers to several versions:

> Fair was this yonge wyf, and therwithal   [3233]
> As any wezele hir body gent and smal.
> A ceynt she werede, barred al of silk,
> A barmclooth eek as whit as morne milk
> Upon hir lendes, ful of many a goore.
> Whit was hir smok, and broyden al bifoore
> And eek bihynde, on hir coler aboute,
> Of col-blak silk, withinne and eek withoute.
> The tapes of hir white voluper
> Were of the same suyte of hir coler;
> Hir filet brood of silk, and set ful hye.
> And sikerly she hadde a likerous ye;
> Ful smale ypulled were hire browes two,
> And tho were bent and blake as any sloo.
> She was ful moore blisful on to see
> Than is the newe pere-jonette tree,
> And softer than the wolle is of a wether.
> And by hir girdel heeng a purs of lether,
> Tasseled with silk, and perled with latoun.
> In al this world, to seken up and doun,
> There nys no man so wys that koude thenche
> So gay a popelote or swich a wenche.
> Ful brighter was the shynyng of hir hewe
> Than in the tour the noble yforged newe.
> But of hir song, it was as loude and yerne
> As any swalwe sittynge on a berne.
> Therto she koude skippe and make game,
> As any kyde or calf folwynge his dame.
> Hir mouth was sweete as bragot or the meeth,
> Or hoord of apples leyd in hey or heeth.
> Wynsynge she was, as is a joly colt,

Long as a mast, and upright as a bolt.
A brooch she baar upon hir lowe coler,
As brood as is the boos of a bokeler.
Hir shoes were laced on hir legges hye.
She was a prymerole, a piggesnye,
For any lord to leggen in his bedde,
Or yet for any good yeman to wedde.

This is not merely a dead convention vivified.[95] So much has been said of the naturalness and realism of it that I may here speak one-sidedly for the effect of the convention itself. The form is still rhetorical *effictio*, and still preserves the convention of the inventory, disarrayed indeed, but listing at every turn the categories of the archetype: the fairness, the eye, the bent brows, the hue, the voice, the mouth, the carriage, the silken costume, the jewelry, the accomplishments. And each category is filled by a superlative. The similes are the similes that apply in the Oxford context, just as Absolon's gifts of spiced ale and piping hot waffles apply. In Oxford it is a brunette rather than a blonde, plucked brows rather than natural, embroidery of black silk rather than of gold, pearls of latten, not precious stones. The convention domesticated carries still some of its original idealizing power. Its function is manifold. I feel in this description, especially where it deals with such unsuspicious images as the "newe perejonette tree," an outright, unqualified sympathy with the character, a response in the poet himself similar in some respects to his sympathy with the Wife of Bath. The literary effect is as if to present Alisoun as the one precious illusion in the poem. Here the milleresque philosophy finds its one ideal, and allows itself its one large formulation:

In al this world, to seken up and doun,   [3252]
There nys no man so wys that koude thenche
So gay a popelote or swich a wenche.

She was a prymerole, a piggesnye,   [3268]
For any lord to leggen in his bedde,
Or yet for any good yeman to wedde.

On another level the portrait is comic in the way that Absolon is comic. It matches perfectly (to the sophisticated audience) the gaucherie of his "lovelongynge." This is a small-town heroine, whose brows *are* plucked, whose eye *is* lecherous, whose forehead shines—from washing after work (3310 f.). Finally, on the level of terms like "weasel," "loins," "gore," "colt," and "pig's-eye," the portrait describes the delectable little animal who is not to be won by a protracted, artificial wooing.

The strands of imagery that I have rather painfully disentangled are of course twisted solidly together in the poetry. Images like "morne milk," "wolle . . . of a wether," "hoord of apples," contribute to more than one strand. The silky black and white of Alisoun's ensemble, if it is not piquantly noncommittal, may contribute to all. "Loins" and "gore" in this context have literary-parodic as well as sexual associations.[96] The humor of Absolon's discovery of the animal is prepared by his misguided attention to the ideal. For the Miller (whose views are presumably being reflected here, though the feeling is possibly too fine for him) the animalism and the ideality must be intertwined. As it does with the Carpenter's religion and Nicholas' cleverness, however, the poem's lusty naturalism bluntly triumphs over the illusion of Love, leaving Alisoun unscathed, perhaps, but not undiscovered.

There is nothing in the fabliau tradition that dictated the introduction of courtly conventionalism in the *Miller's Tale*. Chaucer had no need to encumber himself with the "dreary," "artificial," "hackneyed" form, save the need of meaning. Here he actually realized a potency of the fabliau that is not quite realized in any fabliau of the French tradition. In *Du Clerc qui fu repus*, in *D'Aloul*, in the *Dit de la gageure*, the fragments of courtly convention are inoperative.[97] In the *Miller's Tale* they serve perspective, affording the fabliau a mordantly pointed comment, from below, on the futility of love *paramours*.

ii. The *Merchant's Tale*

In the *Merchant's Tale* the structure of comparisons and relationships is essential to the theme. Without this structure the poem would not merely lack perspective; it would hardly be a poem at all. It is decidedly negative in feeling, and depends for its meaning on a rich backdrop of references. These are sometimes only implied, sometimes sketched in with dashing brevity; it is very much a poem in which the single line and the single image carry enormous weight. It is prickly with small ironic allusions. Fitting to the trickiness of the poem—and to the indelicacy of its subject matter—criticism has been slender, but excellent. Tatlock's analysis of the dramatic and psychological elements, and Sedgewick's description of the multiplex structure, between them bring to light most of the values and relationships juggled here; there are several acute studies of the poem's irony besides, and a very useful evaluation of its heritage from romance and fabliau.[98] After referring the reader to these (in the note just indicated), there remains to me less of fresh description than of rearranging to fit my theme what has already been well said of the poem's style elsewhere.

In dealing with the literature of courtly love it is sometimes difficult to distinguish "style" proper from dramatic action. Courtly action is itself so stylized that under some literary circumstances, as in the *Miller's Tale,* a few characteristic motions will serve to suggest the whole system. Of the richly elaborate rhetoric of courtliness, more is withheld than given. The same is true of the *Merchant's Tale.* The "courtly" love of squire Damyan and May, and some aspects of the old knight January's dotage on his young wife, are represented in an almost perfunctory way, and more in action than in poetic elaboration. This is not because courtliness is less than a central feature of the poem: it is more important here than in the *Miller's Tale.* Part of the reason is rather in the sheer virtuosity of the treatment itself. As in the *Nun's Priest's Tale,* Chaucer has become so sure of his materials that he can play with them, and in this play he often gives up patient and safe elaboration for the fireworks of rapid allusion. A corollary of the extraordinary mobility of style and tone in the two tales is their frequent use of matter—subjects, conventions, even diction—that has been given its full context in other tales. But neither poem is a latter-day *House of Fame,* and in the *Merchant's Tale* the thinness of the courtly style also serves the meaning, lending courtly idealism to the process of bitter negation that is the Merchant's fashioning of life.

The feeling of the poem is quite different from those of others which come to a negative judgement on courtly love. It deals in negation, not by comparison alone, but by perversion. In the *Troilus* courtly love is revealed, by comparison with naturalism, to be impractical, naïve, shortsighted; but its idealism preserves for it an indestructible intrinsic value. In the *Miller's Tale* the courtliness is at least innocent, parochial, harmlessly misplaced. In the *Merchant's Tale* we have courtliness without innocence or idealism. The "courtly" action is propelled by egotism and sensuality. The naturalism that is played against this courtliness is similarly bled of value. In the "bisynesse" of Pandarus, the gusto of the Wife of Bath, the unreflective animalism of Alisoun, there is a substantial honesty, a fulfillment of nature that Chaucer famously delights in. But the naturalism of the *Merchant's Tale* is not honest. Conversely, it is tricked out with the courtliness and with piety in an ugly, hypocritical disguise. The two attitudes in this unpitying adjustment thus reduce each other to something worse than a moral nullity.

Negation, perversion, are characteristic of the narrative tone. The Narrator of the *Troilus* is sympathetic, and the irony of the poem arises much in spite of his efforts. The *Miller's Tale,* as if in sympathy with the poem's ruling hostility to generalization, has very little overt narrative comment. But here the narrator, as in the *Reeve's Tale,* is both prominent and unsympathetic. The *Merchant's Prologue* is unusually important in establishing the narrator's attitude—he is savagely disappointed in his two months' marriage. His long preamble in praise of marriage (1267–1392) takes from this context a sarcastic reversal of meaning, supported internally by a few spaced barbs:

> For who kan be so buxom as a wyf?   [1287]
> Who is so trewe, and eek so ententyf
> To kepe hym, syk and hool, as is his make?
> For wele or wo she wole hym nat forsake;
> She nys nat wery hym to love and serve,
> Thogh that he lye bedrede, til he sterve.

> A wyf is Goddes yifte verraily;   [1311]
> Alle othere manere yiftes hardily,
> As londes, rentes, pasture, or commune,
> Or moebles, alle been yiftes of Fortune,
> That passen as a shadwe upon a wal.
> But drede nat, if pleynly speke I shal,
> A wyf wol laste, and in thyn hous endure,
> Wel lenger than thee list, paraventure.

> The hye God, whan he hadde Adam maked,   [1325]
> And saugh him al allone, bely-naked,
> God of his grete goodnesse seyde than,
> "Lat us now make an helpe unto this man
> Lyk to hymself"; and thanne he made him Eve.

> Housbonde and wyf, what so men jape or pleye,   [1389]
> Of worldly folk holden the siker weye;
> They been so knyt ther may noon harm bityde,
> And namely upon the wyves syde.

His commentary on the action preserves by turns extravagantly and impatiently this sarcastic acceptance. The brazen, unscrupulous May is fifteen times called "fresshe May." January is "noble":

> Somme clerkes holden that felicitee   [2021]
> Stant in delit, and therfore certeyn he,
> This noble Januarie, with al his myght,
> In honest wyse, as longeth to a knyght,
> Shoop hym to lyve ful deliciously.

His housynge, his array, as honestly
To his degree was maked as a kynges.
Amonges othere of his honeste thynges,
He made a gardyn . . .

Their marriage, with Lust on his side and Greed on hers, is "made al siker
ynogh with hoolynesse" (1708). She is "his paradys, his make" (1822). Criseyde
succumbs to the combined power of Troilus' "worthynesse" and Pandarus'
energy. Alisoun succumbs to Nicholas' pleasant violence. May, on the other
hand, just succumbs. The comment on her response to Damyan's "cardboard"
symptoms of courtly love is:

> Lo, pitee renneth soone in gentil herte!   [1986]

She loves him "benyngnely" (2093). She grants him her "verray grace" (1997).
 The narration does not rest with this perverted diction. It can become highly
rhetorical, using apostrophe, *descriptio, exclamatio,* heroic simile, machinery in-
digenous to a *Knight's Tale*. The time descriptions are heightened with astrology in the very manner of Chaucer's high style. But with celebration of these
"worthy folk," and with some internal irony of its own, the rhetoric is always
dyspeptic:

> Al ful of joye and blisse is the paleys,   [1712]
> And ful of instrumentz and of vitaille,
> The mooste deyntevous of al Ytaille.
> Biforn hem stoode instrumentz of swich soun
> That Orpheus, ne of Thebes Amphioun,
> Ne maden nevere swich a melodye.
> At every cours thanne cam loud mynstralcye,
> That nevere tromped Joab for to heere,
> Nor he Theodomas, yet half so cleere,
> At Thebes, whan the citee was in doute.

> Hoold thou thy pees, thou poete Marcian,   [1732]
> That writest us that ilke weddyng murie
> Of hire Philologie and hym Mercurie,
> And of the songes that the Muses songe!
> To smal is bothe thy penne, and eek thy tonge,
> For to descryven of this mariage.
> Whan tendre youthe hath wedded stoupyng age,
> Ther is swich myrthe that it may nat be writen.

Assayeth it yourself, thanne may ye witen
If that I lye or noon in this matiere.

O perilous fyr, that in the bedstraw bredeth!   [1783]
O famulier foo, that his servyce bedeth!
O servant traytour, false hoomly hewe,
Lyk to the naddre in bosom sly untrewe,
God shilde us alle from youre aqueyntaunce!
O Januarie, dronken in plesaunce
In mariage, se how thy Damyan,
Thyn owene squier and thy borne man,
Entendeth for to do thee vileynye.
God graunte thee thyn hoomly fo t'espye!

Were it by destynee or aventure,   [1967]
Were it by influence or by nature,
Or constellacion, that in swich estaat
The hevene stood, that tyme fortunaat
Was for to putte a bille of Venus werkes—
For alle thyng hath tyme, as seyn thise clerkes—
To any womman, for to gete hire love,
I kan nat seye; but grete God above,
That knoweth that noon act is causelees,
He deme of al, for I wole holde my pees.
But sooth is this, how that this fresshe May
Hath take swich impression that day,
For pitee of this sike Damyan,
That from hire herte she ne dryve kan
The remembrance for to doon hym ese.[99]

When the narrator stands farther back to display his characters more fully,
the effect is devastating. Though the description in the poem is sketchy, it is
famous for its graphic ugliness, the more ugly for the romantic context. The
wedding night is introduced with the imagery of epithalamium; then we turn
to watch January priming himself with aphrodisiacs.[100] It takes only a small
suggestion of tender lyricism to make doubly revolting his actual lovemaking:

This Januarie is ravysshed in a traunce   [1750]
At every tyme he looked on hir face;
But in his herte he gan hire to manace
That he that nyght in armes wolde hire streyne

234

Harder than evere Parys dide Eleyne.
But nathelees yet hadde he greet pitee
That thilke nyght offenden hire moste he,
And thoughte, "Allas! O tendre creature,
Now wolde God ye myghte wel endure
Al my corage, it is so sharp and keene!
I am agast ye shul it nat susteene.
But God forbede that I dide al my myght!
Now wolde God that it were woxen nyght,
And that the nyght wolde lasten evermo.
I wolde that al this peple were ago."

And Januarie hath faste in armes take   [1821]
His fresshe May, his paradys, his make.
He lulleth hire, he kisseth hire ful ofte;
With thikke brustles of his berd unsofte,
Lyk to the skyn of houndfyssh, sharp as brere—
For he was shave al newe in his manere—
He rubbeth hire aboute hir tendre face,
And seyde thus, "Allas! I moot trespace
To yow, my spouse, and yow greetly offende,
Er tyme come that I wil doun descende."

Thus laboureth he til that the day gan dawe;   [1842]
And thanne he taketh a sop in fyn clarree,
And upright in his bed thanne sitteth he,
And after that he sang ful loude and cleere,
And kiste his wyf, and made wantown cheere.
He was al coltissh, ful of ragerye,
And ful of jargon as a flekked pye.
The slakke skyn aboute his nekke shaketh,
Whil that he sang, so chaunteth he and craketh.
But God woot what that May thoughte in her herte,
Whan she hym saugh up sittynge in his sherte,
In his nyght-cappe, and with his nekke lene;
She preyseth nat his pleyyng worth a bene.

May visits the lovesick Damyan in a scene from romance:

This Damyan, whan that his tyme he say,   [1936]
In secree wise his purs and eek his bille,

In which that he ywriten hadde his wille,
Hath put into hire hand, withouten moore,
Save that he siketh wonder depe and soore,
And softely to hire right thus seyde he:
"Mercy! and that ye nat discovere me,
For I am deed if that this thyng be kyd."
This purs hath she inwith hir bosom hyd,
And wente hire wey; ye gete namoore of me.
But unto Januarie ycomen is she,
That on his beddes syde sit ful softe.
He taketh hire, and kisseth hire ful ofte,
And leyde hym doun to slepe, and that anon.
She feyned hire as that she moste gon
Ther as ye woot that every wight moot neede;
And whan she of this bille hath taken heede,
She rente it al to cloutes atte laste,
And in the pryvee softely it caste.

The invitation to the garden is the stylistic climax of the poem. The garden
is like that of the Rose, only more fair. The blind, jealous, lecherous old man
bids his completely unfeeling wife to come out and play there. His song is a
parody of the Song of Songs. To give January this, the most lyrical and most
sacred allusion[101] in the poem, was at once the supreme twist of the narrative's
bitterness and of the poet's virtuosity:

"Rys up, my wyf, my love, my lady free!   [2138]
The turtles voys is herd, my dowve sweete;
The wynter is goon with alle his reynes weete.
Com forth now, with thyne eyen columbyn!
How fairer been thy brestes than is wyn!
The gardyn is enclosed al aboute;
Com forth, my white spouse! out of doute
Thou hast me wounded in myn herte, O wyf!
No spot of thee ne knew I al my lyf.
Com forth, and lat us taken oure disport;
I chees thee for my wyf and my confort."

The turtle's voice prompts me to recall Absolon at Alisoun's window:

"What do ye, hony-comb, sweete Alisoun,   [3698]
My faire bryd, my sweete cynamome?

236

> Awaketh, lemman myn, and speketh to me!
> Wel litel thynken ye upon my wo,
> That for youre love I swete ther I go.
> No wonder is thogh that I swelte and swete;
> I moorne as dooth a lamb after the tete.
> Ywis, lemman, I have swich love-longynge,
> That lik a turtel trewe is my moornynge.
> I may nat ete na moore than a mayde."

The tales of the Miller and the Merchant have much in common. Their plots and collections of characters are similar, and in a large sense their stylistic materials are the same. The poetic strategy in each is to play off an elevated attitude against blunt naturalism to expose a blindness. Some of their stylistic differences I have tried to show in passing. There is a difference in the quality of the styles seen separately, and thus also in the nature of each style's context. There is a difference in the range implied by the use of each style: one naturalism describes a norm generally accepted within the world of the tale, another reveals ugly, personal idiosyncrasy. There are differences in the relation between narrator and style and in the distribution of styles among the characters: other things being equal, what expresses a curable naïveté in a young clerk expresses a repulsive, inescapable self-deception in an old knight. And these are, I am sure, only a few of the variables by which the mixed style in Chaucer supports so many and various meanings.

But the variety is not limitless. Though each poem of this class may have its conclusion, each through its complex style also asks with rather special insistence the Chaucerian and late medieval question, "What is this world? what asketh men to have?" These poems are problematical in the way that the *House of Fame*, the *Parliament*, the *Troilus*, and the *Canterbury Tales* are problematical. The poem most kaleidoscopic in style, the *Nun's Priest's Tale*, is the one in which Chaucer revels most in the problem itself.

iii. The *Nun's Priest's Tale*

The *Nun's Priest's Tale*, much like the *House of Fame*, turns over a world of material, yet leaves an impression that is more of an inherent quality than of a specific teaching. It is above all brilliant, varied, a virtuoso performance. Though it contains a nugget of fable morality, its theme, like that of the earlier poem, is not found in the usual places, or expressed in the usual terms. The difference from the *House of Fame*—to pass over many resemblances, as between the Eagle and the Cock—is that here a theme so much more patently exists.

Though the poem is as complex as the other, it is not confused. Formerly the poet scrambled among his materials; here he sees through them. So the *Nun's Priest's Tale* not only epitomizes the *Canterbury Tales;* it fittingly serves to cap all of Chaucer's poetry. And so I put it last.

It is fitting, too, that a poetry so much involved with the French tradition should base its most representative poem on the *Roman de Renart.* I have no sympathy with the theories of common, primitive sources and isolated versions. Chaucer's "source" for the mock-heroic development of the tale can have been nothing less than the *Roman* itself.[102] No separate animal fable or collection of fables could have presented the tale of the Cock and the Fox to him in an aura at once so cosmic and so comic. The *Manciple's Tale* is a creditable example of what Chaucer might do with an isolated moral fable. The *Nun's Priest's Tale* is greatly more expansive than fable because the *Renart* is supremely so. The Nun's Priest's disrespect is equaled in breadth only by that of his equally un-beneficed French brothers, and it is secretly defended like theirs (as I guess) by an equal acceptance of the fundamental articles of faith. The humor of the *Nun's Priest's Tale* does not come at all as near to singeing its subjects; but this is the difference between the skirmishes preceding the war and the festive fireworks commemorating it in peace.

The tale will betray with laughter any too-solemn scrutiny of its naked argument. If it is true that Chauntecleer and Pertelote are rounded characters, it is also true that they are chickens. To ask which one of them has the better in their scholarly debate over dreams is to be too solemn; it is to assume that chickens, too, are concerned with scholarship. The serious point is more in the anomalous fact of the chicken debate itself than in its outcome. The tale has recently been welcomed into the Marriage Group, but it says little about marriage that it does not unsay. With what marriage, indeed, can it be said to deal? The marriage of Chauntecleer in the varying lights of the poem is courtly and bourgeois, monogamous and polygamous, incestuous, and unsolemnized, a relationship of paramours. The tale seems to have an irreducible core of antifeminism, but by similar tokens it is feminist too:

> But sovereynly dame Pertelote shrighte,   [3362]
> Ful louder than dide Hasdrubales wyf,
> Whan that hir housbonde hadde lost his lyf,
> And that the Romayns hadde brend Cartage.
> She was so ful of torment and of rage
> That wilfully into the fyr she sterte,
> And brende hirselven with a stedefast herte.

The most deliciously ambiguous line in Chaucer is the Nun's Priest's "I kan noon harm of no womman divyne" (3266). Even the theme of Pride, which comes closer to the mark,[103] is confounded finally by the tone of the poem:

> Bifel that Chauntecleer in al his pryde, [3191]
> His sevene wyves walknyge by his syde . . .

The difference between this and animal fable is that this cannot long be taken more seriously in one direction than in the other. Fable respects the boundary between animal fiction and the human truth it illustrates. But the whole spirit of this poem is to erase or at least to overleap the boundaries: animal and human, fiction and truth severally join and separate, change partners and flirt here. The one constancy in the poem is this shifting of focus, the Chaucerian multiple perspective which itself virtually constitutes the theme.

With the *Parliament,* the *Troilus,* and many of the *Tales* behind us, there is no difficulty in recognizing the deliberate and controlled art with which Chaucer manipulates his materials. In the *House of Fame* the transformation of Dante's golden Eagle into a loquacious pedant, the sequence of Dantean rhetoric and colloquial dialogue, leaves one in doubt between irony and inconsistency, art and chance.[104] The superior clarity of the *Nun's Priest's Tale* at such points is owing to a more sensitive knowledge of the potency of the materials, a surer sense of their meanings in combination, and so a bolder hand in their management. The rhetoric of the Nun's Priest, like the Merchant's and the Pardoner's, is boldly rhetorical, artistically overdone. Chauntecleer's scholarship is overwhelmingly, deliciously pedantic. The opening description of the poor widow and her farm is notably compact and pointed in meaning. Its careful impression of temperance and simple sufficiency, its husbanding of sensory effect, evokes an archetypal humility. The cock's magnificence breaks out amid this carefully restrained setting with the best Chaucerian effect: it expands, climbs, brightens, then bursts like a rocket into a shower of color.

> A yeerd she hadde, enclosed al aboute [2847]
> With stikkes, and a drye dych withoute,
> In which she hadde a cok, hight Chauntecleer.
> In al the land of crowyng nas his peer.
> His voys was murier than the murie orgon
> On messe-dayes that in the chirche gon.
> Wel sikerer was his crowyng in his logge
> Than is a clokke or an abbey orlogge.
> By nature he knew ech ascencioun

> Of the equynoxial in thilke toun;
> For whan degrees fiftene weren ascended,
> Thanne crew he, that it myghte nat been amended.
> His coomb was redder than the fyn coral,
> And batailled as it were a castel wal;
> His byle was blak, and as the jeet it shoon;
> Lyk asure were his legges and his toon;
> His nayles whitter than the lylye flour,
> And lyk the burned gold was his colour.

The transition from rhetoric and heroics back to the naturalism of the farm has the same candid shock effect; it is, indeed, much the same shift of perspective as when the squabble in the *Parliament* interrupts the gentle pleadings of noble lovers:

> O woful hennes, right so criden ye,   [3369]
> As, when that Nero brende the citee
> Of Rome, cryden senatoures wyves
> For that hir husbondes losten alle hir lyves;
> Withouten gilt this Nero hath hem slayn.
> Now wole I turne to my tale agayn.
> This sely wydwe and eek hir doghtres two
> Herden thise hennes crie and maken wo,
> And out at dores stirten they anon,
> And syen the fox toward the grove gon,
> And bar upon his bak the cok away,
> And cryden, "Out! harrow! and weylaway!
> Ha! ha! the fox!" and after hym they ran,
> And eek with staves many another man.
> Ran Colle oure dogge, and Talbot, and Gerland,
> And Malkyn, with a dystaf in hir hand;
> Ran cow and calf, and eek the verray hogges,
> So fered for the berkyng of the dogges
> And shoutyng of the men and wommen eeke,
> They ronne so hem thoughte hir herte breeke.

Not all the stylistic transitions have so thunderous an effect, nor are the various subjects that in turn occupy the field given equal elaboration. Exemplum and authority take almost two hundred verses in the debate between cock and hen; beauty is tested in a single image:

> "Madame Pertelote, so have I blis,   [3158]
> Of o thyng God hath sent me large grace;
> For whan I se the beautee of youre face,
> Ye been so scarlet reed aboute youre yen,
> It maketh al my drede for to dyen."

The complicated optics of the poem can hold a number of views simultaneously; or it can shift from one to the next and back with lightness and rapidity:

> Wommennes conseils been ful ofte colde;   [3256]
> Wommannes conseil broghte us first to wo,
> And made Adam fro Paradys to go,
> Ther as he was ful myrie and wel at ese.
> But for I noot to whom it myght displese,
> If I conseil of wommen wolde blame,
> Passe over, for I seyde it in my game.
> Rede auctours, where they trete of swich mateere,
> And what they seyn of wommen ye may heere.
> Thise been the cokkes wordes, and nat myne;
> I kan noon harm of no womman divyne.

It can produce a continuous band of overlapping views, as when Chauntecleer's magnificence passes into courtly love, and thence by the way of dreams and medical science into a most unromantic, domestic familiarity: "For Goddes love, as taak som laxatyf" (2943). Whatever the mode of altering and manipulating perspective, however, the fact of manipulation is always clear.

The context that confirms each particular stylistic device in its mock heroics is very broad. The plot of the poem, the description of the narrator, the dramatics of the pilgrimage frame, and the very sequence of the tales here all contribute to the one process of multiplying contradictions. The rich, jolly, secular Monk, with the fine horse and clinking bridle bells,[105] will relate nothing but a series of tragedies:

> Tragedie is to seyn a certeyn storie,   [1973]
> As olde bookes maken us memorie,
> Of hym that stood in greet prosperitee,
> And is yfallen out of heigh degree
> Into myserie, and endeth wrecchedly.

The Nun's Priest, whose "foul and lene" horse bespeaks a poverty much fitter for gloom, and whose anonymity prepares us for nothing more, tells a superbly humane tale, perhaps the best of all. The plot is tragic, until it ends happily. It is an allegory of the Fall—leaving Man, somewhat wiser, still in possession of his paradise, or his chicken yard. The tale's proximate literary context is not limited to the *Monk's Tale*. It easily extends itself, through "wommanes conseil," to the *Tale of Melibee*.[106] Through tragedy, eloquence, heroics, science, court flattery, courtly love, domesticity, dreams, scholarship, authority, antifeminism, patient humility and rural hullabaloo, there is scarcely a Chaucerian topic that is excluded from its purview and its criticism.

Unlike fable, the *Nun's Priest's Tale* does not so much make true and solemn assertions about life as it tests truths and tries out solemnities. If you are not careful, it will try out your solemnity too; it is here, doubtless, trying out mine. Some very great institutions lose importance in it, and some very humble ones are made magnificent. But considering Chaucer's reputation for satire and irony, the criticism in the tale needs less demonstration than does the wise conservatism that goes with it. The critical temper of the poem, unlike that of the *Merchant's Tale,* which is supported by a similar configuration of styles, produces no negative effect, but a continuously humane suggestion of the relativity of things. The shifting style and the succession of topics never rest long enough to serve a single view or a single doctrine or an unalterable judgment. Other tales adopt norms, then uncover differences according to their lights. This tale celebrates the normality of differences. If you take its humble, Griselda-like opening setting to represent a norm against which magnificence is satirized, you must reckon with the fox hunt that later turns the widow's dale and grove into a bedlam. Nor can you say that Chauntecleer and chickens in one perspective are not truly magnificent. None of the targets of the poem's parodies are demolished, or even really hit at the center. There are senses in which the solemnities of courtly love, science, marriage, authority, eloquence, tragedy, the Monk, and the *Tale of Melibee* are funny, but the *Nun's Priest's Tale* does not make us feel that they are always funny. That would be the philosophy of the Cook, a fool who sees life as a continuous jape: "But God forbede that we stynte heere . . ."[107] The tale quite literally fulfills its prologue, which promises a merry tale *after* heaviness; it offers no conclusion but that sublunary values are comically unstable. The only absolute virtue that its reading educes is an enlightened recognition of the problem of perception itself, the virtue of seeing:

> "For he that wynketh, whan he sholde see,   [3431]
> Al wilfully, God lat him nevere thee!"

The *Nun's Priest's Tale* is supremely Chaucerian in its poise before an overwhelming question. "What is this world?" That there is an absolute answer one can feel in the tacit security behind the Priest's humor, and in his sermonic conclusion:

> But ye that holden this tale a folye, [3438]
> As of a fox, or of a cok and hen,
> Taketh the moralite, goode men.
> For seint Paul seith that al that writen is,
> To oure doctrine it is ywrite, ywis;
> Taketh the fruyt, and lat the chaf be stille.
> Now, goode God, if that it be thy wille,
> As seith my lord, so make us alle goode men,
> And brynge us to his heighe blesse! Amen.

His relativism is itself relative, and has its free play, after all, because he is talking about *this* world, not the other. But his piety is not, any more than are Chaucer's palinode and retraction, the main feature of his story. In the *Nun's Priest's Tale,* as altogether in the mature Chaucer, we are compelled to respect the conservative conclusion because the question has been so superbly well confronted. The tale's wit is, in little, the Chaucerian criticism; its forbearance is the Chaucerian tolerance. The Chaucerian mixed style illuminates the tale's microcosmic contradictions, just as it expresses, in large, the great capaciousness of Chaucer's humane vision.

VII

chaucer and the
fifteenth century

In the history of the literature in English, Chaucer is an anomaly. He has no
significant predecessors. His historical position could be plotted by reference to
his contemporaries Gower, Langland, and the "Pearl" poet, and to Lydgate and
the Scottish Chaucerians. But among the contemporaries, only Langland is
comparable to him in realism and in complexity of style; the most Chaucerian
of the others, William Dunbar, writes a full century later. Most of his followers
see him only as the poet of high style:

> The noble rethor Poete of breteine
> That worthy was the laurer to haue
> Of peetrie and the palme atteine
> That made firste to distille and reyne
> The golde dewe droppis of speche and eloquence
> In-to our tounge . . .[1]

---

[1] For notes to chapter vii see page 272.

Chaucer's most illustrious admirer, Edmund Spenser, looks back to him from a distance of two centuries, and emulates him only faintly. English literature, then, for whatever the reasons, hardly provides us with a rich historical context for Chaucer's work, and it tends to promote a false idea of the novelty of his realism. In the preceding chapters I have suggested that Chaucer's position in literary history makes fuller sense if we consider him as belonging to that international, Gothic tradition of which French is the central literature. The earlier French tradition shows better than the English that Chaucer's realism is medieval, not modern or "Renaissance." It shows that his mixture of styles, rather than embodying some presumably advanced revolt from convention, is an expression of the very ambivalence of his culture, that it is the style of the period. Here I should like to indicate briefly and generally how the French tradition after Chaucer bears out these conclusions. The French literature of the fifteenth century does not of course descend from Chaucer. The two belong, however, to the same tradition, and Chaucer's historical position is defined as well by the final phases of the tradition as by its beginnings.

By 1400 the high Gothic mode in every field had passed into a phase that is variously called "late," "baroque," "decadent," "flamboyant."[2] Late Gothic art represents an unbalance, a conflict, or a disintegration of elements that the high Gothic had held in momentary poise, and it has its own ostentatiousness which accentuates the lack of coherence. The fifteenth century saw, on the one hand, the continuation of the courtly tradition in a last stand of extravagant display. The age self-consciously perpetuated chivalry in social rituals, with processions and tournaments, the creation of knightly orders and cults of love. In literature, correspondingly, the tradition of romance and erotic allegory goes on unabated, and the courtly lyric is worked out in ever more diverse and sophisticated forms. As in England "the golde dewe droppis of speche and eloquence" are highly prized, so in France a school of grands rhétoriqueurs carries the practice of verbal ornament to ridiculous lengths. It is an age of extreme conventionalism in art. On the other hand, it is also an age of realism. Irrespective of whether the powerful, commercially interested middle class, despite its aping of the nobility, forced a material view of things, or whether it was rather the nobility who now became aware of the shortcomings of chivalric idealism,[3] the fact is that the art of the period shows an extraordinary interest in everyday reality. Naturalism comes into its own in sculpture and painting. In literature the satiric-realistic tradition thrives, full of genre scenes and of intimate detailing of familiar speech and action. The earlier "bourgeois" frankness becomes more bold, with boisterousness, rawness, a crude sensualism and an impudent profanity.

These two sides of fifteenth-century culture exist together in varying relationships. In art, depending on the date, the field, and the man, naturalism can conceal a still highly worked symbolism, and chivalric ceremony can disguise a basic materialism and opportunism. Very often the mixture of styles is overt, based on the feudal distinction of class or just on transiency of mood. Whatever the manner of combination, however, an exaggerated Gothic dualism can be said to be a main trait of the style of the period. "All of the authors," it has been suggested, "have in some way or other the naturalistic view and the symbolic tradition as coördinates of their style."⁴

The decadence of late Gothic art, its excesses and defects of taste and form, is attributable to a loss of purposeful direction in the culture. Late medieval feudalism, whether courtly or religious, jealously preserved its forms and symbols, but could not perpetuate in depth its idealism. Late medieval realism, rapidly advancing in its capacity to see a naturalistic world and to represent it in art, was slow to acquire its own transcendentalism. The Renaissance was to recompose both motives in a new synthesis, but meanwhile transalpine culture seems to have been without moral underpinnings. Its symbolism is often merely gaud, its ceremony empty, its rhetoric only decorative. Its religion is incongruously stretched between new ecstasies of mysticism and a profane, almost tactile familiarity with sacred matters. Its sense of fact is often spiritless or actually morbid. For all its boisterous play, the age is profoundly pessimistic; it is preoccupied with the irretrievable passage of time, with disorder, sickness, decay, and death.

Chaucer is eligible to be classed as a late Gothic poet for his range, for his mixture of styles, and for occasional passages in the fifteenth-century mood.⁵ The *House of Fame* and the *Anelida* have the elaborateness and pointlessness, and some of the pessimism, of the later poetry. Chaucer's sentimental handling of maternal love and of little children is more of the fifteenth century than of earlier times. The unfinished *Cook's Tale* promises to have been the rawest of Chaucer's works. But these brushes with the possible dangers of his artistic and moral position serve to sharpen our notion of where Chaucer, in the main body of his works, actually stands. The feudal pageantry of the *Knight's Tale* could have, but did not, become the gratuitous and empty ceremonialism of the later *Jehan de Paris* and *Le Petit Jehan de Saintré*. The poem remains intensely moral; and its sense of chaos is bounded by a felt sense of order. Chaucer's Wife of Bath might have been given the decay of the flesh and the pessimism of Villon's *belle heaulmiere*.⁶ Instead she has vitality and inextinguishable morale. No work of Chaucer's could more easily have become a document of decadence than his *Pardoner's Tale*. It contains the depth of cynicism, the dwelling on fleshly corruption and death, the flamboyant rhetoric, the circumstantial realism, the vulgarized allegory, the crudity, and the tastelessness of the late Gothic style. Yet none of these traits is finally gratuitous or uncontrolled. Each is held in perspective: circumscribed by the larger scheme of the *Tales,* subsumed in the characterization of the Pardoner, bounded by the amicable ending, redeemed by the admission,

> And Jhesu Crist, that is our soules leche, [916]
> So graunte yow his pardoun to receyve,
> For that is best.

The tale, while it explores the outermost limits of the medieval moral order, still proclaims the integrity of that order. This is the main difference between Chaucer and the literature of the French tradition in its decadence.

He is, then, supremely an artist of his own age. He does not announce the Renaissance, at least not any more than do medieval humanism and Gothic realism generally. He is not "modern": nowhere does he assert seriously and as final the primacy of realism in art, or the primacy of man or of matter in the universe. He is medieval. Nevertheless, his historical position is unique. His characteristic achievement as an artist is the holding together and seeing in relationship to each other of the wide range of values, some of them antithetical, which had once made up the richness and poise of medieval civilization, and were now already making for its break-up. He is, indeed, the culminating artist of the French tradition. No other poet in France or England, endowed with the variety, the disparity, the disorder of late medieval culture, sees it so clearly, embraces it so grandly, and masters it so well. In Europe Chaucer is the last medieval whose world is wide, yet still intelligible, viable, and one.

notes

ABBREVIATIONS

BD	Book of the Duchess	NPProl, -T, -Ep	Nun's Priest's Prologue,
C	Chaucer		Tale, Epilogue
CFMA	Les Classiques Français du	OED	Oxford English Dictionary
	Moyen Age	PardProl, -T	Pardoner's Prologue, Tale
ClT	Clerk's Tale	ParsT	Parson's Tale
CT	Canterbury Tales	PF	Parliament of Fowls
CYT	Canon's Yeoman's Tale	PhysT	Physician's Tale
EETS	Early English Text Society	PMLA	PMLA: Publications of the
ELH	ELH: A Journal of English		Modern Language Associa-
	Literary History		tion of America
FrankT	Franklin's Tale	PriT	Prioress's Tale
GProl	General Prologue	ReeveT	Reeve's Tale
HF	House of Fame	RES	Review of English Studies
JEGP	Journal of English and Ger-	Romaunt	Romaunt of the Rose
	manic Philology	RR	Romanic Review; Roman
KnT	Knight's Tale		de la Rose
LGW	Legend of Good Women	SATF	Société des Anciens Textes
MancProl	Manciple's Prologue		Français
MerchT	Merchant's Tale	2NT	Second Nun's Tale
MillT	Miller's Tale	ShipT	Shipman's Tale
MLT, -Intro, -Ep	Man of Law's Tale, Introduc-	SP	Studies in Philology
	tion, Epilogue	SummT	Summoner's Tale
MonkProl, -T	Monk's Prologue, Tale	TC	Troilus and Criseyde
MLN	Modern Language Notes	UTQ	Univ. of Toronto Quarterly
MLQ	Modern Language Quarterly	WBProl, -T	Wife of Bath's Prologue, Tale
MLR	Modern Language Review	ZRP	Zeitschrift für Romanische
MP	Modern Philology		Philologie

BIBLIOGRAPHICAL NOTE

For Chaucer I use the *Complete Works*, ed. F. N. Robinson (Boston, Houghton Mifflin, 1933). In the second and subsequent citations of most books and articles, I use an abbreviated title; the first citation may be found by reference to the Index, under the author's name.

NOTE TO THE PAPERBACK EDITION

Since technical considerations prevent changes in the text and notes for this edition, I should like to call attention here to a few particularly relevant works either overlooked or not available at the time of original publication. Per Nykrog's *Les Fabliaux* (Copenhagen, 1957), is an important work, and (with G. Stillwell's article in *JEGP*, LIV [1955]) makes a stronger case than mine for courtly elements in the fabliaux. Vittore Branca, *Boccaccio medievale* (Florence, 1956) and Giuseppe Billanovich, *Restauri boccacceschi* (Rome, 1947) make virtually certain the fictional status of Boccaccio's romantic autobiography. Ralph Baldwin's *The Unity of the Canterbury Tales* (Copenhagen, 1955) anticipates several of my observations in chapter VI. W. Clemen's *Der junge Chaucer* has now been revised and translated as *Chaucer's Early Poetry* (London and New York, 1964). Robinson's 1933 edition of Chaucer has been superseded by a second edition (1957).

INTRODUCTION

Pages 1–10

[1] John Livingston Lowes, *Convention and Revolt in Poetry* (Boston, Houghton Mifflin, 1919) pp. 49, 51. On the implications of the concept of organic development as applied to history see J. Huizinga, *Wege der Kulturgeschichte*, German trans. Werner Kaegi (Munich, 1930), pp. 20–32, 58–60.

[2] *Geoffrey Chaucer and the Development of His Genius* (Boston, Houghton Mifflin, 1934), chap. iv.

[3] *Convention and Revolt*, pp. 98–100. See chap. vi, sec. 4, i, of the present work.

[4] See Ruth Crosby, "Oral Delivery in the Middle Ages," *Speculum*, XI (1936), 88–110; *idem*, "Chaucer and the Custom of Oral Delivery," *Speculum*, XIII (1938), 413–432. She cites (p. 414, n. 2), for instance, Chaucer's *Squire's Tale*, v. 235: "As knowen they that han hir bookes herd."

[5] Chaucer's lifetime (1340–1400) spans a period of change from French to English usage in official and upper-class England. In this connection Trevisa's translation of Higden's *Polychronicon* is often quoted, here from Robert Dudley French, *A Chaucer Handbook*, 2d ed. (New York, Crofts, 1947), p. 340. Higden in 1363 had complained that "Children in scole, ayenst the vsage and manere of alle othere naciouns beeth compelled for to leue hire owne langage, and for to construe hir lessouns and here thynges in Frensche, and so they haueth seth the Normans come first into Engelond. Also gentil men children beeth i-taught to speke Frensche from the tyme that they beeth i-rokked in here cradil..." In 1385 Trevisa could add: "now ... in alle the gramere scoles of Engelond, children leveth Frensche and construeth and lerneth an Englisch." English was officially permitted as the language of the law courts in 1362. In the following year the declaration of the summons opening Parliament was for the first time made in English. The earliest English proclamation of the city of London was issued in 1384. The earliest known will in English is of 1387. But English was not commonly used in legal, civic, and official documents until well into the fifteenth century. On the whole subject see Oliver Farrar Emerson, "English or French in the Time of Edward III," in his *Chaucer Essays and Studies* (Cleveland, 1929), pp. 271–297; Kathleen Lambley, *The Teaching ... of the French Language in England* (Manchester, 1920), pp. 3–25; R. W. Chambers, *On the Continuity of English Prose* (an extract from his introd. to Harpsfield's *Life of More*) EETS (London, 1932), pp. lxxxi–xc, cx–cxv.

[6] The pioneer work is Margaret Schlauch, "Chaucer's Colloquial English: Its Structural Traits," *PMLA*, LXVII (1952), 1103–1116.

[7] On Italian see Natalino Sapegno, *Il Trecento*, in *Storia letteraria d'Italia* (Milan, 1934), esp. pp. 74–76. In Latin the case is by the nature of things not so clear-cut. The medieval Latin equivalent of a "bourgeois" tradition is to be seen variously in comedy, goliardery, and satire, and in epistolary and expository prose. On the two prose styles see Ernst Robert Curtius, *European Literature and the Latin Middle Ages*, trans. Willard R. Trask, Bollingen Series, XXXVI (New York, 1953), pp. 148–151; on the "low" style see *ibid.*, pp. 386–387, n. 17.

[8] Cf. Curtius, *European Literature*, pp. 383–385.

[9] *Chaucer the Maker* (London, Faber & Faber, 1951), p. 19.

[10] *Some Versions of Pastoral* (London, Chatto & Windus, 1935), chap. ii.

[11] *The Well Wrought Urn* (New York, Reynal & Hitchcock, 1947), p. 80.

NOTES TO CHAPTER II

THE COURTLY TRADITION

Pages 11–57

[1] Some detailed accounts are: Gunnar Biller, *Etude sur le style des premiers romans français en vers (1150–1175), Göteborgs Högskolas Arsskrift,* XXII (Göteborg, 1916); Friedrich Schürr, *Das altfranzösische Epos* (Munich, 1926); Hennig Brinkmann, *Zu Wesen und Form mittelalterlicher Dichtung* (Halle, 1928); Helmut Hatzfeld, "Literarisches Hochmittelalter in Frankreich," *Tijdschrift voor Taal en Letteren,* XXV (1937), 81–123, 145–183; Erich Auerbach, *Mimesis: The Representation of Reality in Western Literature,* trans. Willard R. Trask (Princeton, 1953), chap. vi.

[2] See Reto R. Bezzola, *Le Sens de l'aventure et de l'amour* (Paris, 1947), pp. 81–86; Auerbach, *Mimesis,* pp. 134–136; Antoinette Fierz-Monnier, *Initiation und Wandlung: Zur Geschichte des altfranzösischen Romans . . .* [Studiorum Romanicorum Collectio Turicensis, V] (diss. Zürich, 1951), pp. 81–83.

[3] See J. Huizinga, *The Waning of the Middle Ages* (London, Arnold, 1934), pp. 182–188, 195–199; Brinkmann, *Wesen und Form,* pp. 81–90; Richard McKeon, "Rhetoric in the Middle Ages," in *Critics and Criticism,* ed. R. S. Crane (Chicago, 1952), pp. 260–296; D. W. Robertson, Jr., "Some Medieval Literary Terminology . . . ," *SP,* XLVIII (1951), 669–692; and esp. Edgar de Bruyne, *Etudes d'esthétique médiévale,* 3 vols. (Bruges, 1946), II, 14–49, 204–216, 313–343. On rhetoric see, further, chap. vi, sec. 2, of the present work.

[4] Cf. Auerbach, *Mimesis,* pp. 130–131; Bezzola, *Sens de l'aventure,* pp. 76–77.

[5] See Ch.-V. Langlois, *La Société française au XIIIᵉ siècle d'après dix romans d'aventure* (Paris, 1911); Karl Young, "Chaucer's 'Troilus and Criseyde' as Romance," *PMLA,* LIII (1938), 61–62. Realism in romance is taken up in sec. 3, *post.*

[6] See Edmond Faral, *Recherches sur les sources latines des contes et romans courtois du moyen âge* (Paris, 1913), pp. 307–388. Here is a precious passage on English romance from A. B. Taylor, *An Introduction to Medieval Romance* (London, Heath Cranton, 1930), p. 215: "The tower of Troyes is stated to have been built by Julius Caesar; Morgan la fée is described as wife to Julius Caesar, mother of Oberon the fairy-king, and grandmother of Alexander the Great; Huon of Bordeaux converts the Emperor of the Medes and Persians and enlists him as an ally against the Saracens in Palestine; an ally of the Trojans against the Greeks, called Polydamas, is described as the lover of the Queen of the Amazons; and King Arthur is visited by one Segramore, son of the King of Hungary and grandson of the Emperor of Constantinople."

[7] The relationship between courtly love and Christianity is a difficult and warmly debated subject. On the love religion see C. S. Lewis, *The Allegory of Love* (Oxford Univ. Press, 1936), pp. 18–22, 29. Further references, in a convenient résumé of the theories of the origin of courtly love, will be found in Theodore Silverstein, "Andreas, Plato, and the Arabs: Remarks on Some Recent Accounts of Courtly Love," *MP,* XLVII (1949–50), 117–126. See below, n. 49.

[8] Guillaume de Lorris and Jean de Meun, *Le Roman de la Rose,* ed. Ernest Langlois, 5 vols., SATF (Paris, 1914–1924), v. 636. On the other-world landscape in French romance generally see Oliver M. Johnston, "The description of the Emir's Orchard in Floire et Blancheflor," *ZRP,* XXXII (1908), 705–710; Faral, *Recherches,* pp. 369–372. On the tradition of the Earthly Paradise see Arturo Graf, *Miti, leggende e superstizioni del medio evo* (Turin, 1925), pp. 1–175; Edith G. Kern, "The Gardens in the *Decameron* Cornice," *PMLA,* LXVI (1951), 505–523.

⁹ The Middle English translation, *The Romaunt of the Rose*, is from the edition of F. N. Robinson, *The Complete Works of Geoffrey Chaucer* (Boston, Houghton Mifflin, 1933).

¹⁰ *Roman de la Rose* 1323–1410 (*Romaunt* 1349–1438).

¹¹ *Roman de la Rose* 876–901 (*Romaunt* 888–915). Cf. Alain de Lille's description of Nature, *The Complaint of Nature*, trans. Douglas M. Moffat, Yale Stud. Engl., XXXVI (New York, 1908), pp. 11–18; the Latin text is in Migne, *Patrologia Latina*, CCX, cols. 435–439.

¹² *Roman de la Rose* 1537–99, 1615–70 (*Romaunt* 1567–1629, 1649–1705).

¹³ See Otto Söhring, "Werke bildender Kunst in altfranzösischen Epen," *Romanische Forschungen*, XII (1900), 491–640.

¹⁴ See Edmond Faral, *Les Arts poétiques du XIIᵉ et du XIIIᵉ Siècle* (Paris, 1924), pp. 75–81.

¹⁵ Jean Renart [?], *Galeran de Bretagne*, ed. Lucien Foulet, CFMA (Paris, 1925), vv. 1282–85.

¹⁶ Cf. Brinkmann, *Wesen und Form*, pp. 2–10; De Bruyne, *Etudes d'esthétique*, II, 173–188.

¹⁷ *Eneas*, ed. J.-J. Salverda de Grave, 2 vols., CFMA (Paris, 1925–1929), vv. 7859–8020, 8445–8662.

¹⁸ *Eneas* 1677–1856.

¹⁹ Cf. Alfons Hilka, *Die direkte Rede als stilistisches Kunstmittel in den Romanen des Kristian von Troyes* (Halle, 1903), p. 86.

²⁰ Cf. Biller, *Etude sur le style*, p. 166; F. M. Warren, "Some Features of Style in Early French Narrative Poetry (1150–70)," *MP*, III (1906), 529–538; Hilka, *Die directe Rede*, pp. 144–150.

²¹ See C. Muscatine, "The Emergence of Psychological Allegory in Old French Romance," *PMLA*, LXVIII (1953), 1165–1179.

²² Chrétien de Troyes, *Cligès*, ed. Wendelin Foerster, 4th ed. (Halle, 1921), vv. 475–523, 626–872, 4410–4574; cf. *Eneas* 8953–80. The courtly sophistic is seen at its worst, perhaps, in the prose tract of Andreas Capellanus, *De Amore* (ed. Amadeu Pagès [Castelló de la Plana, 1930], trans. John Jay Parry [Columbia Univ. Press, 1941]), e.g., from the lips of a lady in amatory conversation: "When the conclusion of this assumption is disproved, you will be refuted" (Parry, p. 47).

²³ Aimon de Varennes, *Florimont*, ed. A. Hilka, *Gesellschaft für romanische Literatur*, XLVIII (Göttingen, 1933), vv. 8948–9036; Chrétien de Troyes, *Der Karrenritter [Lancelot]*, ed. Wendelin Foerster (Halle, 1899), vv. 1109–37.

²⁴ See Rita Lejeune-Dehousse, *L'Œuvre de Jean Renart*, Bibliothèque de la Faculté de Philosophie et Lettres de l'Université de Liége, LXI (Liége and Paris, 1935), pp. 144–159, 372.

²⁵ Chrétien de Troyes, *Yvain*, ed. T. B. W. Reid (Manchester, 1942), vv. 1288–99.

²⁶ *Eneas* 8073–81, 8085–94, 8099–8100, 8125–26, 8233–34, 8242–44, 8925–36.

²⁷ See Erhard Lommatzsch, "Darstellung von Trauer und Schmerz in der altfranzösischen Literatur," *ZRP*, XLII (1923), 20–67.

²⁸ See his *Allegory of Love*, pp. 112–136.

²⁹ Ernest Langlois, *Origines et sources du Roman de la Rose* (Paris, 1891), p. 57.

³⁰ Cf. *Romaunt* 1730–33:

> And therwithall such cold me hente
> That, under clothes warm and softe,
> Sithen that day I have chevered ofte.

1319: A! Lord, they lyved lustyly!
1641: For sithen [have] I sore siked …

³¹ "Many people, misled by the platitudinous allegory produced in ages to which allegory is a toy … are disposed to think that in turning to Guillaume de Lorris we are retreating from the real world into a shadowy world of abstractions. … Do not let us be deceived by the allegorical form. That, as we have seen, does not mean that the author is talking about non-entities, but that he is talking about the inner world—talking, in fact, about the realities he knows best."—*Allegory of Love*, pp. 114–115, q.v.

³² "Uncouthly," i.e., 'strikingly,' 'marvelously'; perhaps translating *cointement*, which Langlois records as a variant.

[33] I do not refer to his palinode (*De Amore*, III), but to sections of the first two books in which his style or his very text betrays him. One may cite the generally sophistical character of the dialogues in Book I, the section on the love of nuns (I. viii, ed. Pagès, p. 129), and his vacillating treatment of *amor purus* and *amor mixtus* (I. vi. H, II. vi; ed. Pagès, pp. 105–106, 156; trans. Parry, pp. 122–123, 167).

[34] Lewis suggests (*Allegory of Love*, pp. 122, 136) that Guillaume, in view of the introduction of Raison, might have ended his unfinished poem with a palinode, a refutation of Love. Since this is all guesswork, I may point out that the introduction and rejection of Raison is a commonplace in the psychology of the romances; Muscatine, "Emergence of Psychological Allegory," pp. 1174–1178. Jean de Meun, who was doubtless a better judge than any modern could be, preserves the fiction of his continuing of the original allegory, after having given Raison considerably more to say, by ultimately awarding the Lover his Rose. And would it not have been uncharacteristically ironic of Guillaume to have finally repudiated Love in the face of the dedication to "Rose" at the opening of the poem, and of the later passage (3508–10) in which he anticipates from her some reward? It is difficult to conceive of the poet's leading his audience through such intricate and sophisticated passages as the shooting of Amor's arrows (1681–1880; cf. 1867–8: "S'en i ot cinc bien encrotees, Qui jamais n'en seront ostees") only to reward their attentions with a refutation. The seriousness of Andreas Capellanus' palinode has been widely questioned; see, e.g., H. Hatzfeld in *Symposium*, II (1948), 287–288. But there are interesting interpretations of both the *De Amore* and the *Roman de la Rose* as anticourtly, Christian works. See M. Gorce, O.P., ed., *Le Roman de la Rose* (Paris, 1933), pp. 21–22; D. W. Robertson, Jr., "The Doctrine of Charity in Medieval Literary Gardens," *Speculum*, XXVI (1951), 36–39, 40–43; *idem*, "The Subject of the *De Amore* of Andreas Capellanus," *MP*, L (1953), 145–161.

[35] See, in addition to the sources already cited, Curtius, *European Literature*, esp. pp. 383–385.

[36] The parallel between erotic and religious experience in the age and culture has been widely noted; I refer here, however, to no rigid correspondences between the Lover and the worshiper of God, but rather to a general tension that now appears in both spheres, variously described as between phenomenalistic and idealistic, personal and impersonal, worldly and spiritual concerns. For religion, the twelfth-century type is Saint Bernard. The situation in the thirteenth century is discussed below, chap. iii, sec. 3. See Friedrich Heer, *Aufgang Europas: Eine Studie zu den Zusammenhängen zwischen politischer Religiosität, Frömmigkeitsstil und dem Werden Europas im 12. Jahrhundert*, 2 vols. (Vienna and Zürich, 1949), esp. pt. I, 182–235; Eduard Wechssler, *Das Kulturproblem des Minnesangs* (Halle, 1909), esp. chap. vii.

[37] On the troubadours see, e.g., Leo Spitzer, *L'Amour lointain de Jaufré Rudel et le sens de la poésie des troubadours*, Univ. of North Carolina Studies in the Romance Languages and Literature, V (Chapel Hill, 1944), a study in which the equilibrium between religious and secular, idealist and sensual impulses in the poetry is finely analyzed, and D. W. Robertson, Jr., "*Amors de Terra Lonhdana*," *SP*, XLIX (1952), 566–582, in which Rudel's poetry is interpreted in terms of its "commonplace Christian symbolism." On the Italians see Karl Vossler, *Die philosophischen Grundlagen zum "süssen neuen Stil"* (Heidelberg, 1904), esp. pp. 61–64; Giulio Bertoni, *Il Duecento*, 2d ed., in *Storia letteraria d'Italia* (Milan, 1930), pp. 246–264; Sapegno, *Trecento*, pp. 11–35.

[38] See Etienne Gilson, "La Mystique de la grâce dans la *Queste del Saint Graal*," *Romania*, LI (1925), 321–347.

[39] *Galeran* 3775–995; *Perceval*, ed. A. Hilka (Halle, 1932), vv. 168–394; *Cligès* 4290–334. It would be useless to try to classify too rigidly the gracefully formal style of courtly social intercourse, in which the "natural" idiom and action are at the same time conventional. Many "realistic" scenes of this kind do not have the meaning function that we can usually ascribe to realism in romance. See, e.g., Jean Renart, *Le Roman de la Rose ou de Guillaume de Dole*, ed. Rita Lejeune (Paris, 1936), vv. 970–1223; *Le Roman du Castelain de Couci*, ed. M. Delbouille, SATF (Paris, 1936), vv. 113–290; cf. Auerbach, *Mimesis*, pp. 131–132.

One should mention here, too, that the anticourtly motive is also expressed in romance through a convention of formal ugliness, caricature, which derives from the *vituperatio* of ancient epideictic oratory; see Faral, *Arts poétiques*, pp. 76–77; Curtius, *European Literature*, p. 182 n. Thus the *vilain* is conventionally described as being superlatively ugly; see, e.g., *Yvain* 288–308, *Roman de la Rose* 2920–24; cf. *Aucassin et Nicolette*, ed. Hermann Suchier, 8th ed. (repr. New York, 1936), piece 24.

[40] As Flourentine in the *Roman de la Violette*, Alexandrine in *Guillaume de Palerne*, Sipriane in *Florimont*, the old woman in *Eracle*, Imeine in *Ipomedon*, Lunete in *Yvain* (discussed *post*).

[41] Cf. the satiric tirades quoted by Joseph Bédier, *Les Fabliaux*, 5th ed. (Paris, 1925), p. 360.

[42] Lewis, *Allegory of Love*, pp. 124, 365.

[43] *Yvain* 1589–2037.

[44] *Roman de la Rose* 9452 ff., where Ami tells the Lover of the change after marriage:

> Or se claime seigneur e maistre
> Seur li, que sa dame ot clamee
> Quant ele iert par amour amee.
> —Amee?—Veire.—En quel maniere?
> En tele que se senz priere
> Li comandast: "Amis, sailliez";
> Ou: "Cete chose me bailliez,"
> Tantost li baillast senz faillir,
> E saillist s'el mandast saillir . . .

Cf. *Yvain* 2022 ff.

[45] So Gustave Cohen, *Chrétien de Troyes et son œuvre* (Paris, 1931), p. 314.

[46] Cf. Elise Richter, "Die künstlerische Stoffgestaltung in Chrestien's Ivain," *ZRP*, XXXIX (1917–1919), 388–390; Bezzola, *Sens de l'aventure*, pp. 80–84.

[47] Geoffrey of Vinsauf, *Documentum de Arte Versificandi*, par. 145 (ed. Faral, *Arts poétiques*, p. 312).

[48] Cf. Eleanor Prescott Hammond, *English Verse between Chaucer and Surrey* (Duke Univ. Press, 1927), p. 31: "Knowledge of Chrétien on Chaucer's part has not been demonstrated; but no student of literature can read the dialogues between Troilus and Pandarus without turning again to Chrétien's Yvain and pondering the conversations between the hesitating widow and her sprightly maid. Nor can a student refrain from drawing the spiritual comparison, whether contact between the two writers be proved or not."

[49] See Gustave Charlier, " 'L'Escoufle' et 'Guillaume de Dole,' " in *Mélanges . . . à M. Maurice Wilmotte*, 2 vols. (Paris, 1910), I, 92–96; Lejeune-Dehousse, *Jean Renart*, pp. 325–349, 368–375; Ingeborg Dubs, *Galeran de Bretagne: Die Krise im französischen höfischen Roman* [Studiorum Romanicorum Collectio Turicensis, III] (diss. Zürich, 1949), pp. 154–172; Fierz-Monnier, *Initiation und Wandlung*, p. 204; Albert Pauphilet, "Aucassin et Nicolette," in his *Legs du moyen âge* (Melun, 1950), chap. viii.

[50] Paul Meyer, ed., *Le Roman de Flamenca*, 2d ed. (Paris, 1901), p. iv.

[51] The dialogue in full (vv. 3949–5721): "Hai las!" "Que plains?" "Mor mi." "De que?" "D'amor." "Per cui?" "Per vos." "Qu'en pucs?" "Garir." "Consi?" "Per gein." "Pren li." "Pres l'ai." "E cal." "Iretz." "Es on?" "Als banz." "Cora?" "Jorn breu et gent." "Plas mi." [Trans. Hilda F. M. Prescott, *Flamenca* (London, Constable, 1930), pp. 78–113: "Alas!" "For why?" "I'm dying." "What of?" "Of love." "For whom?" "For you." "And I—?" "Heal me!" "How?" "By a means." "Take it!" "I have!" "What means?" "You'll go." "And where?" "To the baths." "When?" "Soon, for my joy." "Gladly."]

[52] *Flamenca* 4123–4301 (trans. Prescott, pp. 81–85).

THE BOURGEOIS TRADITION

Pages 58–97

[1] The standard work on the subject is Joseph Bédier, *Les Fabliaux*, 5th ed. (Paris, 1925); see on chronology, genres, and social setting, pp. 40–42, 359–364, 371–376; on style, pp. 341–357. For shorter treatments of the fabliau see Walter Morris Hart, "The Narrative Art of the Old French Fabliaux," in *Kittredge Anniversary Papers* (Boston, 1913), pp. 209–216; [Ch.] Guerlin de Guer, "Les Fabliaux," *Revue des Cours et Conférences*, XXVIII: 1 (1926–27). 325–350; Auerbach, *Mimesis*, chap. ix, esp. pp. 208–212. On sermon style see G. R. Owst, *Literature and Pulpit in Medieval England* (Cambridge, 1933), pp. 23–40. On the drama see G. Cohen, *Le Théâtre en France au moyen âge* (Paris, 1948), esp. pp. 69–101; Grace Frank, *The Medieval French Drama* (Oxford, 1954), esp. pp. 211–236. Owing to some uncertainty about the conditions of performance, it is not possible to distinguish absolutely between the mime (dramatic monologue or dialogue) and the few secular "plays" of the thirteenth century. See Edmond Faral, ed., *Mimes français du XIII⁹ siècle* (Paris, 1910), pp. viii–xv; *idem*, ed., *Courtois d'Arras*, CFMA (Paris, 1922), pp. iii–iv. Of the pre-Chaucerian literature of this tradition in English very little is extant. We can make inferences about the nature of the early English popular drama from the fifteenth-century manuscript versions of the mystery plays, many of which were written in earlier times or are clearly based on earlier tradition; see John Edwin Wells, *A Manual of the Writings in Middle English 1050–1400* (New Haven and London, 1916), pp. 548, 552–553, 557, 563. For narrative poetry we must rely almost entirely on the French. Bédier, *Les Fabliaux*, pp. 37–38, counts 147 French fabliaux extant, of what can logically be inferred to have been a production of thousands. Of those we have, six are in Anglo-Norman. But there are only two fabliaux, along with one animal tale, a fragment of an interlude, and a "humorous romance" to represent what may have been a sizable production of "Humorous Tales" in English; see Wells, *Manual*, p. 177.

[2] Bédier in 1925 counts 147 fabliaux extant. Of the 72 which are localizable, 38, or more than half, come from the North (*Les Fabliaux*, p. 43). The two best playwrights of the bourgeois tradition, Adam de la Halle and Jean Bodel, are Artesians. On the poetry of and about commerce see G. Schilperoort, *Le Commerçant dans la littérature française du moyen âge* (Groningen, 1933), pp. 27–116.

[3] Although for several fabliaux more recent editions exist, for convenience I refer here, as later, to volume and page of A. de Montaiglon and Gaston Raynaud, *Recueil général et complet des fabliaux des XIII⁹ et XIV⁹ siècles*, 6 vols. (Paris, 1872–1890).

[4] I, 16; I, 226; IV, 53. Cf. the practical function of the winter scenery in *Le Roman de Renart*, ed. Ernest Martin, 3 vols. (Strasbourg and Paris, 1882–1887), Branche III, vv. 1–3, 377–82, 435, which prepares us for the trick played on Isengrin.

[5] See, e.g., I, 172; I, 114; IV, 83; I, 239; IV, 194–97; V, 40; VI, 47. The piece *De l'Oustillement au villain* (II, 148–56), while not a fabliau itself, gives an excellent sense of the physical world of the fabliau.

[6] I disagree with both the count and the conclusions of L. A. Haselmayer, "The Portraits in Chaucer's Fabliaux," *RES*, XIV (1938), 310–314. Haselmayer sees "a vigorously defined tradition of conventional representation in the French *fabliaux*" (p. 313), but cites only seven portraits of any kind. I should add the four referred to in my text immediately below. Thus in the 157 pieces in the Montaiglon-Raynaud collection (of which 141 are fabliaux), there are some eleven portraits; of these only five use the catalogue method and the conventional courtly descriptive traits. Two (II, 94–96;

III, 5–6) appear in "fabliaux" which are predominantly courtly in style, and thus do not enter into our reckoning of the traits of the bourgeois tradition; three (II, 48; III, 237–38; VI, 180–81) occur in fabliaux of mixed style. To these five one can hardly add the portrait in *Du Fevre de Creeil* (I, 231–32), which begins to describe Gautier in conventional, courtly terms, but soon turns to a long description of his genitalia. There are a number of minor conventional touches elsewhere (e.g., II, 19; IV, 169). I shall discuss the incursion of courtly elements in the fabliau in sec. 2 following. Meanwhile, it seems clear that there is nothing resembling "a vigorously defined tradition of conventional representation" in the fabliaux as far as the formal portrait is concerned.

⁷ See, e.g., vv. 708–11, Alfred Jeanroy, ed., CFMA (Paris, 1925), and the partial explanation by Michel Dubois in *Romania*, LV (1929), 256–258.

⁸ See Faral, *Mimes*, pp. 6–28, 34–51; Charles H. Livingston, "The Fabliau 'Des Deux Anglois et de l'Anel,' " *PMLA*, XL (1925), 217–224; Hermann Albert, *Mittelalterlicher englisch-französischer Jargon*, Studien zur Englischen Philologie, LXIII (Halle, 1922). Aside from Anglo-French in the *Roman de Renart* (ed. Mario Roques, CFMA [Paris, Champion, 1948], I, 2392–2580, 2858–3034), there is a passage of comic Franco-Italian gibberish (ed. Martin, Va, 457–94). The one romance which contains comic Anglo-French dialect is the late thirteenth-century *Jehan et Blonde*. See Hermann Suchier, ed., *Œuvres poétiques de Philippe de Remi, sire de Beaumanoir*, SATF (Paris, 1885), II, 415–416. Here it is used to satirize an overbearing English nobleman, the Duke of Gloucester.

⁹ See particularly the fabliaux *De Sire Hain et de Dame Anieuse* (I, 98 ff.), *Le Chevalier confesseur* (I, 186–87), *Du Prestre et du chevalier* (II, 79–81), *Du Bouchier d'Abevile* (III, 238–39), *Du Clerc qui fu repus* (IV, 50), *De Boivin de Provins* (V, 62–63), *Les .IIII. Souhais Saint Martin* (V, 202), *A Peniworth of Witte*, E. Kölbing, ed., "Kleine Publicationen aus der Auchinleck-HS.," *Englische Studien*, VII (1884), 113–117. Cf. The Wakefield *Noah*, ed. J. Q. Adams, *Chief Pre-Shakespearean Dramas* (Boston, 1924), vv. 190–230; *Roman de Renart* I (ed. Roques) 2741–51, 3115–3206, Va (ed. Martin) 256–63.

¹⁰ See the fabliaux *Des Trois Avugles de Compiengne* (I, 75–76), *Du Prestre et des .II. ribaus* (III, 59–64), *Des .III. Dames de Paris* (III, 146–50); and the following plays: Bodel, *Jeu de Saint Nicolas* 595–959, 1078–1190, 1314–84; *Courtois d'Arras* 96–426; Adam le Bossu [Adam de la Halle], *Le Jeu de la feuillée*, ed. Ernest Langlois, 2nd ed., CFMA (Paris, 1923), vv. 905–1099. Lists of similar scenes in the English mystery plays are given by Julius Haller, *Die Technik des Dialogs im mittelalterlichen Drama Englands* (Worms a. Rh., 1916), pp. 78–79; and by Ola E. Winslow, *Low Comedy as a Structural Element in English Drama* (Chicago, 1926), pp. 4–10.

¹¹ See *Richeut*, ed. I. C. Lecompte, *RR*, IV (1913), 261–305.

¹² Bédier, *Les Fabliaux*, pp. 376–385; cf. Lucien Foulet, *Le Roman de Renard* (Paris, 1914), pp. 496–535.

¹³ The poem opens with a diatribe against evil speech, and the poet here makes the assertion, "Ja vilain mot n'entreprendrai / En oevre n'en dit que je face . . ." (V, 244–45).

¹⁴ Cf. Bédier, *Les Fabliaux*, pp. 35–36, 364–365.

¹⁵ The chemistry of the bourgeois attitude is so powerful here as to convert at least one conventional trait of courtly scenery to practical use. The April morning dew allows the rich *vilain* to follow his high-born wife's tracks through the garden, to where the ground gives evidence of her misconduct (I, 256–57).

¹⁶ Something of the same situation obtains in the drama; there is some comic-ironic use of courtly diction in the *Jeu de St. Nicolas*, but its effects are incidental and local. See Lucien Foulet, "Les Scènes de taverne . . . dans le *Jeu de Saint Nicolas*," *Romania*, LXVIII (1944–45), 430. I have not seen, on the other hand, any criticism which relates artistically the sacred and profane matter in such plays. The fifteenth-century English *Second Shepherds' Play* of the Towneley Cycle seems to be one of the earliest in which humor and seriousness are artistically related. See John Speirs, "The Mystery Cycle (I): Some Towneley Cycle Plays," *Scrutiny*, XVIII (1951), 111; Francis J. Thompson, "Unity in The Second Shepherds' Tale [sic]," *MLN*, LXIV (1949), 302–306.

¹⁷ Cf. Huizinga, *Wege der Kulturgeschichte*, pp. 143–144.

[18] See Foulet, *Roman de Renard*, pp. 215, 338–342; Ulrich Leo, *Die erste Branche des Roman de Renart nach Stil, Aufbau, Quellen und Einfluss*, Romanisches Museum, XVII (Greifswald, 1918), pp. 74–117.

[19] *Le Roman de Renart, Première Branche*, ed. Mario Roques, CFMA (Paris, Champion, 1948), vv. 1498–99 (ed. Martin, 1438–39).

[20] Foulet, *Roman de Renard*, pp. 180, 214–215; M. Wilmotte, "L'Auteur des Branches II et Va du Renard et Chrétien de Troyes," *Romania*, XLIV (1915–1917), 258–260.

[21] Cf. Foulet, *Roman de Renard*, p. 179, on Branche II: "C'est partout, sous la bonne humeur du récit, le même respect pour les institutions féodales, le même vif intérêt pour les formes de la procédure." The deepening vein of satire in the later branches of the *Renart* relates it to the fabliau and goliardic traditions. It is not until we come to the adaptations of the cycle in the late thirteenth and early fourteenth centuries that Reynard becomes clearly the vehicle for outright social protest.

[22] Roques, ed., *Roman de Renart*, I, pp. xi–xii.

[23] Bédier, *Les Fabliaux*, pp. 359–370.

[24] Huizinga, *Wege der Kulturgeschichte*, pp. 142–144.

[25] The principal recent studies are Gérard Paré, *Les Idées et les lettres au XIII° siècle: Le Roman de la Rose* (Montreal, Université, 1947), superseding his *Le Roman de la Rose et la scolastique courtoise*, Publications de l'Institut d'Etudes Médiévales d'Ottawa, X (Paris and Ottawa, 1941); and Alan M. F. Gunn, *The Mirror of Love: A Reinterpretation of "The Romance of the Rose"* (Lubbock, Texas, 1952). For shorter treatments see Gorce, *Roman de la Rose*, pp. 9–65; Lewis, *Allegory of Love*, pp. 137–156. The typical nineteenth-century view is embodied in Langlois, *Origines*, esp. pp. 93–100; see also refs. in Gunn, *Mirror of Love*, pp. 11–16.

[26] The symposium aspect has been treated at length by Gunn, *Mirror of Love*, pp. 317 ff.

[27] Gunn, reading the whole poem as an allegory of the progress of youth to maturity, sees a kind of experiential filiation among all the views it expresses; this, and the fact that all the arguments turn on a central subject, love, give them relatedness and unity. See *Mirror of Love*, pp. 141–198, and *passim*. Paré, while neglecting the integration of Guillaume's *Amor* into Jean's scheme, gives a fine idea of the moral (to him, immoral) unity of the poem; see *Les Idées et les lettres*, pp. 313–321.

[28] The speeches, with minor interruptions, are located as follows: Amor, *Roman de la Rose* 2077–2764; Raison, 4229–7184; Ami, 7283–9999 (Jealous Husband, 8467–9360); Faus Semblant, 11006–976; Duenna, 12740–14546; Nature, 16729–19405; Genius, 19505–20667.

[29] Translated from Paré, *Les Idées et les lettres*, pp. 283–284.

[30] Cf. *Roman de la Rose* 21551–82.

[31] *Roman de la Rose* 6945–7184.

[32] *Roman de la Rose* 4403–20, 4545–58, 5763–88, 6943–78; cf. Paré, *Les Idées et les lettres*, p. 318; Gunn, *Mirror of Love*, pp. 148, 202–203.

[33] See, on medieval naturalism, Walter Goetz, "Die Entwicklung des Wirklichkeitssinnes vom 12. zum 14. Jahrhundert," *Archiv für Kulturgeschichte*, XXVII (1937), 33–73; Lynn White, Jr., "Natural Science and Naturalistic Art in the Middle Ages," *American Historical Review*, LII (1947), 421–435, and the references therein. Comprehensive discussions of the style of the art of the period, in a large cultural context, are given by Max Dvořák, "Idealismus und Naturalismus in der gotischen Skulptur und Malerei," *Historische Zeitschrift*, CXIX (1919), 1–62, 185–246 (see esp. pp. 8, 14–16, 38–42, 195–199, 207–210); and Arnold Hauser, *The Social History of Art*, trans. Stanley Godman, 2 vols. (New York, 1952), I, 232–244. Although each of these commentators has a special approach to the period, all agree on the emergence of naturalism in the thirteenth century in many parallel fields of culture.

[34] Goetz, "Entwicklung des Wirklichkeitssinnes," pp. 41–43; Jean de Meun's anticipation of the worldly and antichurchly ideology underlying the politics of Philip IV's reign is suggested by Franz Walter Müller, *Der Rosenroman und der lateinische Averroismus des 13. Jahrhunderts* (Frankfurt, 1947), pp. 14–15, 21, 24–27.

[35] White, "Natural Science," pp. 429–430.

[36] Gorce, *Roman de la Rose*, pp. 13–14, 45–58; Müller, *Rosenroman*, pp. 4–27; Paré, *Les Idées et*

les lettres, pp. 321–327. On Jean's naturalism as a development of the neoplatonic "principle of replenishment" see Gunn, *Mirror of Love*, pp. 205–255.

[37] See Paré, *Les Idées et les lettres*, pp. 298–299 n. The most extreme case for Jean's Averroism is made by Müller, *Der Rosenroman*.

[38] See vv. 870–912 (ed. Martin).

[39] Indeed, the diction is comparable. See *Roman de la Rose* 12932–44, quoted with Chaucer's version, p. 85 of the present work.

[40] Cf. *Roman de la Rose* 19369–98, 6945–7184.

[41] *Complaint of Nature*, trans. Moffat, p. 42.

[42] *Canterbury Tales, General Prologue* 731–742; cf. *Roman de la Rose* 15159–94.

[43] Faral ed., *Mimes*, vv. 55–81. The following translation is from Edward B. Ham, "The Rutebeuf Guide for Mediaeval Salescraft," *Studies in Philology*, XLVII (1950), 22.

[44] Ed. Charles H. Livingston, *Le Jongleur Gautier le Leu*, Harvard Studies in Romance Languages, XXIV (Cambridge, Mass., 1951), pp. 165–183.

[45] See, e.g., *Roman de la Rose* 12751, 12784, 13007, 13041–42, 13150–52, 13336–40, 13598, 13602, 14668–70.

[46] It should be noted that there are other excursions into satiric realism in the poem, as for example the antifeminist diatribe of Genius, vv. 16323–706, which contains a lively bedside monologue (16402–536) illustrating how a wife worms secrets out of a husband. Diatribes containing dramatically elaborated exempla are not uncommon in the medieval satiric tradition; cf. the speech of the nagging wife in St. Jerome, *Adversus Jovinianum*, ed. J. P. Migne, *Patrologia Latina*, XXIII, col. 276, and its versions in Eustache Deschamps's *Miroir de mariage*, ed. Gaston Raynaud, *Œuvres complètes de Eustache Deschamps*, IX, SATF (Paris, 1894), vv. 1594–1606, and Chaucer's *Wife of Bath's Prologue* 235–42. The speech of Jean's Jealous Husband is technically just such an exemplum. The point to be made here is that Genius' diatribe remains just that; it is unmotivated, unrelated to the speaker and the action. (Could it be that it means allegorically that successful procreation [Genius] must depend not only on nature—the speech is addressed to Nature, but not applied to her,—but also on a recognition of the intractability of the female?) It represents the sheer inertia of the satiric tradition, whereas the other monologues we are discussing represent a reshaping of it, in which the diatribe and its contained exempla are organized into a new congruence with the personality of the speaker, and taken a step away from simple satire. It is only in this light that one can accept Lewis' remark concerning the Duenna's speech (*Allegory of Love*, pp. 146–147), that "it would argue great ignorance of good satiric writing to put it in the first rank." It is in a way not satiric at all.

[47] *Roman de la Rose* 12889, 13088, 13127, 13174, etc. Her self-conscious remark: "Car sage fame n'a pas honte / Quant bone auctorité raconte" (13921–22) may be owing to the language of Horace (13924) rather than to the fact of quoting him.

[48] *Roman de la Rose* 8561, 8612, 8719, 8759, 9009, 9188.

[49] See *Roman de la Rose* 7307–18, 10285–306.

[50] Cf. Gunn, *Mirror of Love*, pp. 159–161.

[51] *Roman de la Rose* 11269–517.

[52] See Rudolf Hirzel, *Der Dialog*, 2 vols. (Leipzig, 1895), II, 384–385.

[53] See *Roman de la Rose* 7153–77; Robertson, "Some Medieval Literary Terminology," pp. 670–677.

[54] Huizinga, *Waning of the Middle Ages*, p. 217, notes a similar case in Deschamps's *Miroir de mariage*: "The author sometimes puts exalted truths into the mouth of Folly and Desire, though their part is that of the devil's advocate."

[55] *Roman de la Rose* 12390–91, 12547–49, 12730–32.

[56] The *chanson de mal mariée* is a lyric which often has a monologue as its basis and deals with the lament of a dissatisfied spouse. In the twelfth and thirteenth centuries it is semiaristocratic in tone and not satirical. See Alfred Jeanroy, *Les Origines de la poésie lyrique en France au moyen âge* (Paris, 1925), pp. 84–100; Helen Estabrook Sandison, *"The "Chanson d'Aventure" in Middle English*

(Bryn Mawr, 1913), pp. 11–12, 51, 55; F. L. Utley, *The Crooked Rib* (Columbus, 1944), pp. 40–41. Utley suggests a close relationship between the *chanson de mal mariée* and the genre, represented by the Duenna's and the Wife of Bath's monologues, which he calls the "confession, the medieval origin of which is obvious enough" (p. 41). But all the *chansons* cited by him on pp. 40–41 appear to be later than the *Wife of Bath's Prologue*. It appears, then, as Miss Sandison (pp. 53–56) suggests with respect to Dunbar's *Tua Mariit Wemen and the Wedo*, that the satirical *chanson* is influenced by the Wife of Bath and the Duenna, and not *vice versa*. There is no adequate treatment of the confession as a literary form in medieval literature; the dissertation of George M. Rutter, "Confessions in Medieval Literature" (Harvard, 1928), is substantially a listing by types.

[57] This is undeniably the tradition in which she belongs. The best treatment, with an acute and elaborate analysis of the Duenna and her predecessors, is that of Joseph de Morawski, ed., *Pamphile et Galatée* by Jehan Bras-de-Fer (Paris, 1917), pp. 90–155, esp. 115–130; see also Luigi Foscolo Benedetto, *Il "Roman de la Rose" e la letteratura italiana*, Beihefte zur Zeitschrift für Romanische Philologie, XXI (Halle, 1910), 36–42.

[58] Cf. Morawski, *Pamphile*, p. 122: "Cette idée de descendre dans le passé d'une vieille, de mettre en contraste sa jeunesse et sa vieillesse et d'éveiller notre pitié pour l'une, tout en nous inspirant le dégoût pour l'autre, n'est pas, à vrai dire, une innovation de Jean; son mérite personnel consiste plutôt à avoir su combiner harmonieusement les différents traits, plus ou moins traditionnels, dont s'était précisé, au cours des siècles, le portrait de la vieille."

NOTES TO CHAPTER IV

CHAUCER'S EARLY POEMS

Pages 98–123

[1] The best account of the literary characteristics and historical significance of the early poems is that of Wolfgang Clemen, *Der junge Chaucer: Grundlagen und Entwicklung seiner Dichtung*, Kölner Anglistische Arbeiten, XXXIII (Bochum-Langendreer, 1938). The most appreciative criticism of the poems is in the articles of Bertrand H. Bronson, *"The Book of the Duchess* Re-opened," *PMLA*, LXVII (1952), 863–881; "Chaucer's Hous of Fame: Another Hypothesis," Univ. of California Publications in English, III, No. 4 (1934), 171–192; "In Appreciation of Chaucer's Parlement of Foules," Univ. Calif. Publ. English, III, No. 5 (1935), 193–223; "The Parlement of Foules Revisited," *ELH*, XV (1948), 247–260. For the chronology see R. D. French, *Chaucer Handbook*, p. 392. New reasons for putting *HF* before *PF* are adduced by Robert A. Pratt, "Chaucer Borrowing from Himself," *MLQ*, VII (1946), 262–264.

[2] See G. L. Kittredge, "Guillaume de Machaut and *The Book of the Duchess*," *PMLA*, XXX (1915), 1–24.

[3] This is, for instance, the implication of Lowes, *Chaucer*, pp. 84–93; cf. George Lyman Kittredge, *Chaucer and His Poetry* (Harvard Univ. Press, 1915), p. 54, where "contemporary French fashions of allegory and symbolism and pretty visions" are contrasted with "the language of the heart."

[4] *Œuvres de Guillaume de Machaut*, ed. Ernest Hoepffner, 3 vols., SATF (Paris, 1908–1921), as follows: *Remede de Fortune*, vv. 3889–4012; *Jugement dou Roy de Behaingne* 1185–1223; *Fonteinne Amoureuse* 89–188; *Dit dou Lyon* 1537–78; and *Voir Dit*, ed. P. Paris (Paris, 1875), *passim*.

[5] Hoepffner ed., *Œuvres de Machaut*, I, lvii–lix; II, x–xi; III, xxxix.

[6] *Navarre* 37–540.

[7] Cf. Auerbach, *Mimesis*, p. 216; Kern, "Gardens in the *Decameron*," pp, 522–523.

[8] Gaston Raynaud ed., *Œuvres de Deschamps*, XI, 378.

[9] See, for instance, Kittredge, *Chaucer*, pp. 66–68; Lowes, *Chaucer*, pp. 122–123.

[10] See *MLT* 554–74; *Lancelot* 447–48.

[11] Bronson, "Book of the Duchess," esp. pp. 871–872, 879–881.

[12] For this important commonplace of Chaucer criticism see Clemen, *Der junge Chaucer*, pp. 49, 155–156, 178–183.

[13] *BD* 240–69. In fairness to the Narrator, we must note that he says he made this offer "in my game" (238), jokingly, and yet seriously: "And yet me lyst ryght evel to pleye—" (239).

[14] Ovid, *Metamorphoses* XI, 592–632; Statius, *Thebaid* X, 84–136; *Ovide moralisé* XI, 3431–3515, ed. C. de Boer, 5 vols. (Amsterdam, 1915–1938), Vol. IV (Verhandelingen der Koninklijke Akademie van Wetenschappen te Amsterdam, Afdeeling Letterkunde, Nieuwe Reeks, XXXVII), pp. 201–203. John Gower's version, later than Chaucer's, has little color; see *Confessio Amantis* IV, 2927–3123, in his *Works*, ed. G. C. Macaulay, 4 vols. (Oxford, 1899–1901), II, 380–385. Froissart does not tell the story of Ceyx and Alcyone, and gives only an insignificant account of the awakening of Morpheus; see *Paradys d'Amour* 23–28 in his *Œuvres: Poésies*, ed. A. Scheler, 3 vols. (Brussels, 1870–1872), I, 2.

[15] This situation has generated a whole spectrum of interpretations. For adverse comment see Lewis, *Allegory of Love*, p. 170; J. S. P. Tatlock, *The Mind and Art of Chaucer* (Syracuse, 1950), p. 30. Favorable comment sometimes sees the Narrator as consistently naïve: Lowes, *Chaucer*, pp. 124–125; Howard Rollin Patch, *On Rereading Chaucer* (Cambridge, Mass., 1939), p. 33. Sometimes it straddles the issue, making contradictory statements: Kittredge, *Chaucer*, pp. 48–53, 70; Clemen, *Der junge Chaucer*, pp. 57–59. And sometimes, starting with the Narrator's tact within the dream, it sees him as consistently mature and sophisticated, even in the prologue: Bronson, "Book of the Duchess," pp. 863–864, 869–877; James R. Kreuzer, "The Dreamer in the *Book of the Duchess*," *PMLA*, LXVI (1951), 543–547. An intermediate reading, which sees the Narrator as more awestruck than either stupid or sophisticated, is offered by Donald C. Baker, "The Dreamer Again in *The Book of the Duchess*," *PMLA*, LXX (1955), 279–282.

[16] Raymond Preston, *Chaucer* (London and New York, Sheed & Ward, 1952), p. 39.

[17] *Der junge Chaucer*, pp. 106–108.

[18] "Hous of Fame," pp. 184–187.

[19] *Chaucer*, p. 74.

[20] Bronson, "Parlement . . . Revisited," p. 260.

[21] "Appreciation," pp. 198, 203–211.

[22] *PF* 183–210.

[23] Clemen, *Der junge Chaucer*, pp. 190, 200–201; Bronson, "Appreciation," pp. 216–219. Cf. Gardiner Stillwell, "Unity and Comedy in Chaucer's *Parlement of Foules*," *JEGP*, XLIX (1950), 473.

[24] "Appreciation," p. 219.

[25] See R. E. Goffin, "Heaven and Earth in the 'Parlement of Foles,' " *MLR*, XXXI (1936), 493–499; R. M. Lumiansky, "Chaucer's *Parlement of Foules*: A Philosophical Interpretation," *RES*, XXIV (1948), 81–89. Cf. Stillwell, "Unity and Comedy," pp. 473–474, 478; Bronson, "Appreciation," p. 201.

[26] No poem will prove anything about another, but in the absence of better explanation, the comparison will have to do. At any rate, I lean no more heavily on *HF* here than Chaucer does. Much of the same reading was running through his head when he composed the two poems. Each contains, for instance, a temple of Venus. Pratt, "Chaucer Borrowing," pp. 262–263, shows that the invocation to Venus in *PF* is probably adapted from *HF*. More germane to the issue, the motif of the guided journey in recompense for the Narrator's labors is common to both. The promise of love tidings, made by the Eagle in *HF*, is fulfilled by Africanus in *PF* (112, 168). The Ciceronian view of the littleness of the earth as seen from above is strikingly secularized in *HF*, into travelogue material (907; cf. Clemen, *Der junge Chaucer*, p. 124). I suggest, then (*post*), that its seriousness in *PF* does not yet extend beyond the characterization of the Narrator.

[27] Cf. Bronson, "Appreciation," pp. 199–202; Goffin, "Heaven and Earth," pp. 497–499.

261

TROILUS AND CRISEYDE

Pages 124–165

[1] There have been many comparisons of the two poems. Among the most important are: Karl Young, *The Origin and Development of the Story of Troilus and Criseyde*, Chaucer Society (London, 1908), with elaborate analysis of the sources of the *Filostrato* and of other sources of the *Troilus*; Hubertis M. Cummings, *The Indebtedness of Chaucer's Works to the Italian Works of Boccaccio*, Univ. of Cincinnati Studies, Ser. II, Vol. X (Cincinnati, 1915), pp. 50–122; Mario Praz, "Chaucer and the Great Italian Writers of the Trecento," *Monthly Criterion*, VI (1927), 24–34, 153–156; N. E. Griffin, intro. to *The Filostrato of Giovanni Boccaccio*, ed. and trans. Griffin and A. B. Myrick (Philadelphia, 1929), pp. 95–107; C. S. Lewis, "What Chaucer Really Did to *Il Filostrato*," *Essays and Studies by Members of the English Association*, XVII (1932), 56–75; Karl Young, "Chaucer's 'Troilus and Criseyde' as Romance," *PMLA*, LIII (1938), 40–56; Thomas A. Kirby, *Chaucer's "Troilus": A Study in Courtly Love*, Louisiana State Univ. Stud., XXXIX (University, La., 1940), pp. 121–284; Sanford B. Meech, "Figurative Contrasts in Chaucer's *Troilus and Criseyde*," *English Institute Essays, 1950* (New York, 1951), pp. 57–88. On Chaucer's use of a French translation see R. A. Pratt, "Chaucer and Le Roman de Troyle et de Criseida," *SP*, LIII (1956), 509–539.

[2] Henri Hauvette, *Boccace* (Paris, 1914), pp. 87–88; Vincenzo Pernicone, "Il 'Filostrato' di Giovanni Boccaccio," *Studi di Filologia Italiana*, II (1929), 77–86.

[3] This is put more strongly by Francesco De Sanctis, *History of Italian Literature*, trans. Joan Redfern, I (London, 1930), 311: ". . . it is a page from the secret history of the Neapolitan court, a portrait of that bourgeois, mediocre life, halfway between the rough ingenuity of the people and the ideal feudal or chivalric life." Cf. Pernicone, "Il 'Filostrato,'" pp. 126–127.

[4] *Il Filostrato*, ed. V. Pernicone, in *Scrittori d'Italia*, CLXV (Bari, 1937), Pt. II, st. 124–127; VI, 31.

[5] There are occasional passages in which a particular mundanity or colloquialism might seem to the modern reader jarring in its context. See, e.g., II, 135; III, 68; V, 20; VI, 7; VII, 101. Usually the context shows that these are not felt to be jarring by Boccaccio.

[6] For relatively intimate details of the physical setting, and of realistic look or "business," see II, 120; III, 26, 28; IV, 22, 77, 100, 114; V, 51; VI, 23.

[7] Carlo Grabher, *Boccaccio* (Turin, Unione Tipografico, 1945), p. 69.

[8] *History*, p. 312.

[9] *Filostrato* VII, 93–99.

[10] When I first set forth this general view of the importance of the ironic contrasts in the poem ("The Form of Speech in Chaucer," diss. Yale, 1948), it had already been partly anticipated by John Speirs, "Chaucer: (I) 'Troilus and Criseyde,' " *Scrutiny*, XI (1942–43), 84–108 (repeated in his *Chaucer the Maker* [London, 1951], see esp. pp. 51–52, 73–79); it has since been strikingly affirmed by Meech, "Figurative Contrasts," pp. 58–63.

[11] Emile Legouis, *Geoffrey Chaucer*, trans. L. Lailavoix (London, Dent, 1913), p. 133.

[12] "What Chaucer Really Did," p. 59. Lewis's thesis is amplified by Young, " 'Troilus' as Romance."

[13] *Allegory of Love*, pp. 177–182.

[14] *Allegory of Love*, pp. 172–173.

[15] Since the turn of the century the poem has been prevailingly called a realistic novel, or read as one. See the references in Young, " 'Troilus' as Romance," pp. 38–40. The rediscovery of conventionalism in the *Troilus* by Lewis and Young (above, note 12) indisputably exposes wide areas

in the poem that naturalistic criticism has ignored, and shows the naturalistic point of view to be quite inadequate. On the other hand, neither Lewis nor Young seems to me to produce a satisfactory synthesis. Both in turn underplay the poem's realism, Young by making of it, without regard to its antiromantic poetic effect, a characteristic of romance itself.

[16] See Ian Watt, "Realism and the Novel," *Essays in Criticism*, II (1952), 376–396; for a similar view of conventionalism and naturalism in the drama see S. L. Bethell, *Shakespeare and the Popular Dramatic Tradition* (London, 1944), pp. 22–24.

[17] *Shakespeare*, pp. 26–29, 63–67, 108–112.

[18] The functions of the Narrator as a character in Chaucer have been classified and commented upon by H. Lüdeke, *Die Funktionen des Erzählers in Chaucers epischer Dichtung*, Studien zur Englischen Philologie, LXXII (Halle, 1928), esp. chap. iv. Lüdeke directs attention to the artistic form and function of Chaucer's Narrator, especially in *TC* (p. 134), but the scheme of his work precludes critical study of the relationship between the Narrator and the meaning of any given poem. We are similarly led to the edges of this problem by Crosby, "Chaucer and the Custom of Oral Delivery," pp. 413–432; and by B. H. Bronson, "Chaucer's Art in Relation to His Audience," in *Five Studies in Literature*, Univ. Calif. Publ. English, VIII, No. 1 (1940), esp. pp. 31–37.

[19] *Chaucer*, pp. 122–23.

[20] *Roman de la Rose* 12487–540.

[21] *Roman de la Rose* 2265–2576 (*Romaunt* 2387–2716).

[22] Thus Chaucer gets his cue for the Narrator's unwittingly realistic appraisal of Troilus from the *Filostrato*:

Quinci diceva molte altre parole [I, 57]
piangendo e sospirando, e di colei
chiamava il nome . . .
. . .
mercé non trova, ma tutte eran fole
e perdiensi ne' venti, ché a lei
nulla ne pervenia . . .

[Then he spoke many other words, weeping and sighing, and he called her name . . . he found no sympathy, for they were all idle tales, lost in the wind, and none came to her.] Cf. I, 41, 48.

[23] Cf. *TC* V, 1849–55, where the archaism of the courtly love story merges with the pagan, historical quality of the Troy background:

Lo here, of payens corsed olde rites,
. . .
Lo here, the forme of olde clerkis speche
In poetrie, if ye hire bokes seche.

[24] Cf. Pernicone, "Il 'Filostrato,' " p. 121: ". . . un grande scetticismo sovrapposto ad un elevatissimo sentimento di amicizia e ad una pseudo-coscienza morale." A convenient summary of the diverse critical opinions on Chaucer's Pandarus will be found in Kirby, *Chaucer's "Troilus,"* pp. 177–187.

[25] *BD* 30–43. The awakening of the love-tossed Pandarus by the "cheterynge" of the swallow (*TC* II, 50–70) is perhaps a reminiscence of the awakening of the Narrator by the birds in *BD* 291–297.

[26] *The Poet Chaucer* (Oxford Univ. Press, 1949), p. 65.

[27] *TC* II, 1555–III, 231; III, 594 ff.; *Filostrato* III, 21–30. Cf. R. K. Root, ed., *The Book of Troilus and Criseyde by Geoffrey Chaucer* (Princeton, 1945), pp. xxix–xxx.

[28] Gautier d'Arras, *Eracle* [ca. 1163], ed. E. Löseth, *Œuvres de Gautier d'Arras*, Vol. I (Paris, 1890), vv. 4032–4687. For some suggestive parallels in motif and diction cf. *Eracle* 4064–4102, and *TC* I, 589–95, 687–96; *Eracle* 4103–25, and *TC* I, 857–58, 680–84, 757–59; *Eracle* 4141–48, 4160–89, and *TC* I, 792–819; *Eracle* 4199–4221, and *TC* I, 860–79.

[29] Montaiglon-Raynaud, *Fabliaux*, V, 6–12; II, 18.

[30] *Florimont* [1188], 9133-73.

[31] *Guillaume de Palerne* [*ca*. 1200], ed. H. Michelant, SATF (Paris, 1876), vv. 1718-21, 2802-76. For further parallels cf. *G. de P.* 1671-88, and *TC* III, 117-23; *G. de P.* 1703-07, and *TC* III, 183-89; *G. de P.* 2805-10, and *TC* III, 71-74. Young has a discussion of other "scenes of bedroom intrigue" from romance in *Origin and Development*, pp. 151 ff.

[32] *Allegory of Love*, p. 180.

[33] On his syntax see Schlauch, "Colloquial English," esp. p. 1116.

[34] *TC* II, 624-648 (quoted in part *supra*).

[35] As an index of Chaucer's naturalization of the Italian, I note that of the five entrances quoted below, only four are in the *Filostrato*. Of these, the entrance of Pandarus at the beginning of *TC* II, and 150 lines of the magnificent dialogue ensuing, are based on *Filostrato* II, 34-35, in which there is no dialogue at all. The other three are based on *Filostrato* II, 79, 108-109, 128, in which there are only nine lines of dialogue.

[36] *TC* I, 561; IV, 428; cf. II, 267-73.

[37] *TC* II, 368, 377.

[38] On abduction, *TC* IV, 526-638; on Fortune, *TC* I, 841-54; III, 1625-38; IV, 383-92, 600-603.

[39] *TC* III, 239-403; *Filostrato* III, 5-17.

[40] *TC* IV, 344-92, 822-24; V, 1731-43.

[41] Cf. *TC* II, 1355-58; IV, 872-75.

[42] Cf. Speirs, *Chaucer*, pp. 57, 73, 75-79; and Meech, "Figurative Contrasts," pp. 66-67: "Troilus, the ideal lover, must be poet as well as warrior. His vein is that of the romantic, a vein of pure poetry ... The pragmatic confidant is as consistently prosaic in his imagination as the lover is poetically inspired, prosaic, however, in lively fashion. His is the sharp realistic figure...."

[43] See note 50, below.

[44] *TC* III, 988, 1057.

[45] Lewis, *Allegory of Love*, p. 196.

[46] The mechanics of this situation can be simply stated in terms of the definition of H. W. Fowler, *A Dictionary of Modern English Usage* (Oxford Univ. Press, 1946), s.v. "irony": "Irony is a form of utterance that postulates a double audience, consisting of one party that hearing shall hear & shall not understand, & another party that, when more is meant than meets the ear, is aware both of that more & of the outsiders' incomprehension." The audience, then, is the second party to the separate but often concurrent incomprehensions of Troilus and Pandarus. The question of comprehension or incomprehension in a symbolically or conventionally represented figure like Troilus does not, of course, involve his intrinsic characterization, and would not easily arise in a purely conventional context. His comprehension is demanded—and thus his incomprehension is produced— by his periodic appearance in a naturalistic context. With Pandarus, as with Bottom in Fairyland, the situation is just the reverse.

[47] Cf. *Filostrato* I, 15: "come a colei che mai nessuno avere / n'avea potuto..."; and *Fil.* V, 14; "tosto si dovea permutare, / e lui per nuovo amante abbandonare"; *Fil.* VI, 8: "da sì alto e grande intendimento / tosto la volse novello amadore."

[48] *TC* II, 651. The whole setting of the episode, not in the *Filostrato*, is reminiscent of *Eneas* 8031-84. Cf. Robinson, ed., *Chaucer*, p. 931.

[49] See also *TC* II, 91, 213, 264 f., 407, 447 f., 505, 1142, 1154-86; III, 566-68; and especially where the dialogue itself reflects concurrent action: II, 276 f., 293, 302 f., 1254. This degree of reflection of the physical aspects of a situation in direct discourse is foreign to the courtly style; cf. the other instances in Chaucer: *BD* 749; *ShipT* 106, 426; *SummT* 1752; *MancProl* 35-37; *CYT* 664.

[50] On the convention of the inner debate, see chap. ii, sec. 1, *supra*. The monologues of Criseyde on false felicity and jealousy (III, 813-40, 988-1050) and that of Troilus on free choice (IV, 958- 1078) must similarly be read as conventional, not naturalistic. Particularly the first and last, with their scholastic idiom, are ridiculous if read otherwise. They are so far removed from the level of the dramatic situation that Pandarus (present to each) responds to neither. Their connection with

the speaker is abstract. That Criseyde experiences a sense of the mutability of happiness, and Troilus a sense of the determination of things, we may admit; but the speeches must be taken as impersonal comments on the action, Chaucer's formulation, not his characters'. The reading of this form and of the lyric monologue as naturalism involves some questionable characterizations. Kittredge, *Chaucer*, p. 133, attributes to Criseyde "the excellent mental habit of looking at a subject or a proposition from several points of view"; W. C. Curry, "Destiny in Chaucer's *Troilus*," *PMLA*, XLV (1930), 153, gives Troilus a "naturally philosophical mind"; Bronson, "Book of the Duchess," p. 866, makes the Man in Black "adept in the fashionably sophisticated language of paradox and metaphor." On the same issue in Shakespeare see Bethell, pp. 62–75.

⁵¹ See *Filostrato* IV, 165, quoted in chap. v, sec. 1, of the present work.

⁵² Robinson omits the comma after *youre*.

⁵³ The philosophical (as distinct from the literary) relationship of the epilogue to the poem has been well expounded a number of times. See, e.g., James Lyndon Shanley, "The *Troilus* and Christian Love," *ELH*, VI (1939), 271–281; D. W. Robertson, Jr., "Chaucerian Tragedy," *ELH*, XIX (1952), 1–37; Theodore A. Stroud, "Boethius' Influence on Chaucer's *Troilus*," *MP*, XLIX (1951), 1–9.

⁵⁴ See, e.g., *TC* II, 1271–74, 1757; III, 1319–20, 1373–93, 1681–94.

⁵⁵ Usually seen as a post-Victorian Aristotelian "tragic flaw." Kittredge, *Chaucer*, p. 135: "Cressida is . . . fatally impressionable and yielding"; Lewis, *Allegory of Love*, p. 185 (cf. 189–190): "the ruling passion of his heroine . . . is Fear"; Root, ed., *Troilus*, p. xxxii: "[she] has from the beginning of the story a fatal weakness—the inability to make a deliberate choice." The search for a flaw of character has been extended to Troilus, too; here it clearly illustrates the tendency of the Aristotelian reading to become a "realistic," psychological reading of the whole poem. See Joseph S. Graydon, "Defense of Criseyde," *PMLA*, XLIV (1929), 141–177, where the catastrophe is attributed to Troilus' "stupidity and instability of character" (p. 149). This thesis would at first appear excessively naïve. It has been severely attacked by Joseph M. Beatty, "Mr. Graydon's 'Defense of Criseyde,'" *SP*, XXVI (1929), 470–481, and by J. Milton French, "A Defense of Troilus," *PMLA*, XLIV (1929), 1246–1251, on the ground that Graydon ignores the element of convention in Chaucer's handling of Troilus. But there is something to be said for Graydon. On the one hand he correctly senses the irony in the handling, on the other his consistency of approach makes clear, if unwittingly, the absurdity of reading the whole poem as a naturalistic document.

⁵⁶ *TC* V, 92–196, 687–1099, 1421–30, 1587–1631; cf. *Filostrato* VI, 1–34; VII, 105.

⁵⁷ Cf. *TC* I, 553 and V, 412–13.

⁵⁸ *Chaucer*, p. 79; cf. Robertson, "Chaucerian Tragedy," p. 33.

⁵⁹ On his power of speech see *TC* V, 95, 798, 804, 946–51, 1010–11, 1033; on tactics cf. V, 99–105 and II, 267–73; on idiom, gesture, and circumstance cf. V, 108, 852–58 and II, 150 ff.; V, 144, 152 and II, 290, 293.

⁶⁰ See V, 1023–29 (with the preceding heightened description). Cf. Arthur Mizener, "Character and Action in the Case of Criseyde," *PMLA*, LIV (1939), 78.

⁶¹ The critical problem is well analyzed by Mizener, "Character and Action," pp. 65–66, and *passim*. The theory presented here, it will be seen, follows upon Mizener's critique of the psychological approach, but with different results. His hypothesis is "that for Chaucer a character consisted in a group of unchanging fundamental qualities, and that the relationship between such a character and the events of the narrative was one of congruence rather than of cause and effect. . . . Chaucer's chief interest was in the action rather than in the characters" (p. 67). The psychological approach registers the ambiguity of Criseyde in various ways; see, e.g., R. K. Root, *The Poetry of Chaucer*, 1st ed. (Boston, Houghton Mifflin, 1906), p. 115: "he has conveyed a superficial impression that his heroine is a virtuous woman seduced by treachery, and has then in the sequel shocked and surprised us by her ready yielding to Diomede, all the while giving in his narrative the true interpretation of her character, which shall resolve all seeming inconsistency. One is tempted to ask, however, whether this artistic duplicity is not too successful in its attempt to mislead, and whether in consequence Criseyde has not proved to many readers a hopeless enigma"; Kittredge, *Chaucer*, p. 126: "Cressida

is marvellously subtilized, baffling alike to us and to herself"; W. P. Ker, *Essays on Medieval Litera-ture* (London, Macmillan, 1905), p. 85: "There is nothing in the art of any narrative more beautiful than Chaucer's rendering of the uncertain, faltering, and transient moods that go to make the graceful and mutable soul of Cressida"; cf. Kirby, *Chaucer's "Troilus,"* p. 235-237.

Notes to Chapter VI

THE CANTERBURY TALES

Pages 166–243

[1] Robert A. Pratt and Karl Young, "The Literary Framework of the Canterbury Tales," in *Sources and Analogues of Chaucer's Canterbury Tales*, ed. W. F. Bryan and Germaine Dempster (Univ. of Chicago Press, 1941), p. 19.

[2] Cf. Pratt and Young, "Literary Framework," pp. 1-3, 9-13; Kittredge, *Chaucer*, pp. 147-150.

[3] Arnold Hauser, *The Social History of Art*, trans. Stanley Godman (New York, Knopf, 1952), I, 272-273; cf. Dagobert Frey, *Gotik und Renaissance* (Augsburg, 1929), p. 38.

[4] Kern, "Gardens in the *Decameron*," p. 522.

[5] Charles R. Morey, *Mediaeval Art* (New York, Norton, 1942), p. 259.

[6] "The Literary Form of the Prologue to the *Canterbury Tales*," *MP*, XLIX (1952), pp. 173-174: "What a writer finds in real life is to a large extent what his literary tradition enables him to see and to handle.... A literary form ... is a scheme of experience recognized in the tradition ... It is, moreover, a scheme that directs the discovery of material and detail and that orders the disposition of the whole."

[7] "Chaucer's Prologue to Pilgrimage: The Two Voices," *ELH*, XXI (1954), 6.

[8] Hoffman, "Chaucer's Prologue," p. 16.

[9] A similar situation in Shakespeare is discussed by Bethell, *Shakespeare*, p. 46: "the imagery, often clearly contemporary and 'out of period,' assures continuity of sharp contrast between the his-torical material and the contemporary experience with which it is brought into active relationship. The co-presence of such contrasting elements renders doubly impossible any mere illusion of actu-ality: ... at the same time the historical element distances and objectifies what is contemporary, and the contemporary element gives current significance to an historical situation."

[10] For the Latin see *ShipT* 435, *PardProl* 314, *MonkProl* 1892, 1906; for the rest, see respectively *PardProl* 304-17, *MLIntro* 35-38, *ClerkProl* 5-18, *MancProl* 99-102, *MLIntro* 16-32.

[11] The extreme positions, here somewhat simplified, are those of Kittredge, *Chaucer*, p. 155: "... the Pilgrims do not exist for the sake of the stories, but *vice versa*. Structurally regarded, the stories are merely long speeches expressing, directly or indirectly, the characters of the several persons"; and Lüdeke, *Funktionen des Erzählers*, p. 139: "Fast alle Geschichten der CT sind altes episches Gut, das vorhanden war, bevor Chaucer an seine Pilger dachte. In jeder dieser Erzählungen war der Ton, in welchem sie vorzutragen war, mehr oder weniger durch den Stoff bestimmt."

[12] Lüdeke, *Funktionen des Erzählers*, p. 143, concludes that within the tales (with the exception of the dramatic monologues) there is little more characterization of the narrator than Chaucer had reached in his previous work. For an excellent characterization of the Canterbury Narrator see E. Talbot Donaldson, "Chaucer the Pilgrim," *PMLA*, LXIX (1954), 928-936.

[13] The most important studies of rhetoric for our purposes are Faral, *Arts poétiques*; J. M. Manly, "Chaucer and the Rhetoricians," *Proceedings of the British Academy*, XII (1926), 95-113; Traugott Naunin, *Der Einfluss der mittelalterlichen Rhetorik auf Chaucers Dichtung* (Bonn, 1929); J. W. H. Atkins, *English Literary Criticism: The Medieval Phase* (Cambridge, 1943); Curtius, *European Litera-ture*, esp. pp. 62-202.

[14] Faral, *Arts poétiques*, pp. 87–88; Atkins, *Criticism: Medieval*, pp. 107–108.

[15] Curtius, *European Literature*, pp. 180–202; Faral, *Arts poétiques*, pp. 75–84, 70–72. For examples of rhetorical prescriptions see, for the portrait, Geoffrey of Vinsauf, *Poetria Nova*, vv. 554–99 (ed. Faral, pp. 214–215); for place description, Matthew of Vendôme, *Ars Versificatoria*, I, 109–11 (ed. Faral, pp. 147–149); for apostrophe, Geoffrey of Vinsauf, *Poetria Nova*, vv. 264–460 (ed. Faral, pp. 205–211); idem, *Documentum*, II, 2, 24–28 (ed. Faral, pp. 275–277).

[16] "Chaucer and the Rhetoricians," p. 97.

[17] "Chaucer and the Rhetoricians," pp. 110, 111.

[18] Naunin, *Rhetorik*, p. 53: "Es ist zuzugeben, dass die Rhetorik einen grossen Einfluss auf Chaucer ausgeübt hat. . . . Aber eine allmähliche prozentuale Abnahme können wir nicht feststellen. Denn einerseits zeigt schon das erste Werk, B. D. [*Book of the Duchess*], grosse Verstösse gegen die Regeln der Rhetorik und eine nicht übermässige Benutzung ihrer speziellen Vorschriften, und andererseits finden wir auch in seinen letzten Werken noch viel Rhetorik. Chaucer hat jedoch die Rhetorik nicht immer auf gleiche Weise verwendet. In seinen frühen Dichtungen hebt sie noch mehr aus der Erzählung heraus, während sie in den späteren enger mit ihr verwächst." See also Veré L. Rubel, *Poetic Diction in the English Renaissance* (New York, 1941), pp. 22–23, n. 27.

[19] Atkins, *Criticism: Medieval*, p. 114.

[20] The ensuing remarks are adapted and slightly condensed from my "Form, Texture and Meaning in Chaucer's *Knight's Tale*," *PMLA*, LXV (1950), 911–929. For fuller bibliography and more minute documentation the reader is referred thereto. I must also refer here to three essays, published earlier but unknown to me at the time of first writing, which anticipate and are at least partly confirmed by the present interpretation: W. H. French, "The Lovers in the *Knight's Tale*," *JEGP* XLVIII (1949), 320–328; H. S. Wilson, "*The Knight's Tale* and the *Teseida* Again," *UTQ*, XVIII (1949), 131–146; and most important, William Frost, "An Interpretation of Chaucer's Knight's Tale," *RES*, XXV (1949), 289–304.

[21] See, respectively, H. N. Fairchild, "Active Arcite, Contemplative Palamon," *JEGP*, XXVI (1927), 285–293; J. S. P. Tatlock, *The Development and Chronology of Chaucer's Works* (London, 1907), pp. 232–233.

[22] J. R. Hulbert, "What Was Chaucer's Aim in the *Knight's Tale?*" *SP*, XXVI (1929), 375, 380, 385.

[23] Root, *Chaucer*, pp. 169, 171–172.

[24] See Walter Clyde Curry, *Chaucer and the Mediaeval Sciences* (Oxford Univ. Press, 1926), pp. 124–126.

[25] See Robert A. Pratt, "Chaucer's Use of the *Teseida*," *PMLA*, LXII (1947), 615, n. 60.

[26] Pratt, "*Teseida*," pp. 617–620.

[27] In the supernatural signs, KnT 2265–67, 2333–40, and particularly Saturn's speech, KnT 2453 ff., where the nature of Arcite's death is forecast.

[28] Cf. Frost, "Interpretation," p. 293: "Much of the beauty of the Knight's Tale . . . resides in a certain formal regularity of design"; p. 299: "The recurrent occasions of life for people of such condition as this are ceremonious, their actions at such times being imbued with the piety of ancient ritual"; p. 300 (quoting KnT 2847–49: "This world nys but a thurghfare ful of wo . . ."): "The sentiment is a commonplace . . . it nevertheless has power in the Knight's Tale because that poem, although its plot is concerned with success in love and its setting pictures aristocratic splendours, presents on the whole such an abiding and various image of 'every wordly soore.' "

[29] Curry, *Mediaeval Sciences*, pp. 130–139, shows that the physiognomies of Lygurge and Emetrius, in line with the precise astrological correspondences of the poem, are respectively those of "Saturnalian" and "Martian" men. Curry asserts (p. 120) "that the real conflict behind the surface action of the story is a conflict between the planets Saturn and Mars." But this is to mistake the cosmic symptoms for the disease itself.

[30] Cf. Frost, "Interpretation," pp. 294, 297–298.

[31] Agnes K. Getty, "Chaucer's Changing Conceptions of the Humble Lover," *PMLA*, XLIV (1929), 210–212.

[32] See W. H. French, "Lovers," p. 327; Wilson, *"Knight's Tale,"* pp. 142–143; and my article in *PMLA*, LXV, 925.

[33] It should be noted that Saturn's role is purely Chaucer's addition to the story, as are also many of the unfortunate exemplary figures in the temple descriptions; see Pratt, *"Teseida,"* p. 618. Frost, "Interpretation," p. 300, points out the functionalism of these descriptions.

[34] See Frost, "Interpretation," pp. 302–304; Charles A Owen, Jr., "Chaucer's *Canterbury Tales:* Aesthetic Design in Stories of the First Day," *English Studies,* XXXV (1954), 49–56.

[35] The principal study is that of J. Burke Severs, *The Literary Relationships of Chaucer's Clerkes Tale,* Yale Studies in English, XCVI (Yale Univ. Press, 1942). This contains excellent texts of Chaucer's two main sources (earlier printed in *Sources and Analogues,* pp. 296–331), and a textual comparison between them and the *Tale.* The Petrarch text is translated by French, *Handbook,* pp. 291–311. Important progress toward a proper appreciation is made by James Sledd, "The *Clerk's Tale:* The Monsters and the Critics," *MP,* LI (1953), 73–82, in clearing away many of the critical misconceptions that have surrounded the poem. Speirs, *Chaucer,* pp. 151–155, makes some good but lamentably brief comments.

[36] On the history of the story see Severs, *Literary Relationships,* pp. 3–32; Elie Golenistcheff-Koutouzoff, *L'Histoire de Griseldis en France au XIVᵉ et au XVᵉ siècle* (Paris, 1933), pp. 115–150; Käte Läserstein, *Der Griseldisstoff in der Weltliteratur,* Forschungen zur Neueren Literaturgeschichte, LVIII (Weimar, 1926).

[37] *ClT* 540 ff., 925–38, 995–1001.

[38] *ClT* 254: "gemmes, set in gold and in asure"; 388: "an hors, snow-whit"; 1117: "clooth of gold."

[39] Cf. *ClT* 253–73, 372–92, 778–82, 984, 1114–27.

[40] Cf. *ClT* 281–87 and 1009–15; 365 and 1051; 372–85 and 1114–20; 449–55 and 617–23; 569–72, 680–83, and 1094–96.

[41] See Severs, *Literary Relationships,* pp. 233–237.

[42] The pathetic in Chaucer is most notably displayed in *PriT, MLT, PhysT,* and the Hugelino episode in *MonkT* 2407–62. For resemblances in tone or substance cf. *ClT* 547–60 and *MLT* 826–61; *ClT* 209–22, 428–41, 1079–99 and *PhysT* 5–10, 39–58, 105–14, 231–53.

[43] *Chaucer,* p. 153.

[44] Ed. Severs, *Literary Relationships,* p. 254 (*Sources and Analogues,* p. 296).

[45] *Literary Relationships,* pp. 234–235. Severs' conclusion on Chaucer's adaptation is partly as follows (p. 247): "His own chief contribution seems to have been a heightening and intensification of the contrasts . . . a crueler sergeant, a more unfeeling marquis, a more submissive (though not less real) Griseldis . . ."

[46] Speirs, *Chaucer,* p. 154, comments on the latter passage as follows: "The 'oxes stalle' taking up the resonance from previous lines

But hye god som tyme senden can
His grace in-to a litel oxes stalle

half-consciously recalls the manger in which the infant Christ was laid. The 'markis' calling the peasant girl partially seems God calling the soul; her act of obeisance to her feudal lord seems almost an act of worship. The waterpot also, in such a context, dimly awakens Biblical virgin-at-the-well associations. The pomp of the marriage that follows partially suggests the souls' espousals." Cf. Sister Mary Raynelda Makarewicz, *The Patristic Influence on Chaucer* (Washington, 1953), pp. 197–198. Chaucer's *ABC,* to the Virgin Mary, is a convenient index of his religious imagery; with particular regard to *ClT,* see vv. 169–178.

[47] See Walther Küchler, "Ueber Herkunft und Sinn von Boccaccios Griselda-Novelle," *Die Neueren Sprachen,* XXXIII (1925), 263–265.

[48] Cf. Sledd, *"Clerk's Tale,"* pp. 74–75.

[49] See the excellent study by J. R. R. Tolkien, "Chaucer as Philologist: *The Reeve's Tale,"* in *Transactions of the Philological Society* (London, 1934), pp. 1–70.

[50] J. M. Manly, *Some New Light on Chaucer* (New York, 1926), p. 106, cites half a dozen terms from the *Friar's Tale* to show that Chaucer thereby consciously lays the scene in the North. His case is rather poor. The horses' names, "Brock" and "Scott," and the command "hayt" have been found in East Anglia and Yorkshire; see Walter W. Skeat, ed., *The Complete Works of Geoffrey Chaucer*, 2nd ed., Vol. V (Oxford, 1900), p. 328. The words "tholed," "caples," and "lixt" (for "liest") are commonly found in Midland and Southern texts. See *OED*, s.vv. "thole," "caple," "lie."

[51] "Chaucer as Philologist," p. 3.

[52] See chap. iii, sec. 1, *supra*.

[53] *Secunda Pastorum*, ed. George England, *The Towneley Plays*, EETS, Extra Ser., LXXI (London, 1897), vv. 201–16. The Southern forms Mak uses are "ich be" for "I am" and the plurals "goyth" and "doyth." The date of the play is uncertain; I take it to have been written in the second quarter of the fifteenth century. See Mendal G. Frampton, "The Date of the Flourishing of the 'Wakefield Master,'" *PMLA*, L (1935), 631–660.

[54] See *OED*, s.v. "disparage, I." Chaucer's use here is incorrectly listed as the first example of sense 2: "To bring discredit or reproach upon; to dishonor, discredit," etc. But cf. *WBT* 1067–69:

> "My love?" quod he, "nay, my dampnacioun!
> Allas! that any of my nacioun
> Sholde evere so foule disparaged be!"

[55] *MerchT* 1685–87.

[56] Wayne Shumaker, "Alisoun in Wander-Land," *ELH*, XVIII (1951), 79–80, collects the details "which distinguish her from other lusty women": "At the time of her marriage she was not simply 'young,' but twelve years old. She had not 'several' husbands, but five, not to speak of other company in youth. Of the five, two were bad and three good, rich, and old. Her fifth husband was named Jankyn and had once been a clerk at Oxford. She was on good terms with her niece and had a gossip whose name was the same as her own. The occasion on which she and Jankyn had such fine dalliance in the field that she was moved virtually to propose to him came during a Lent. Jankyn's age when she admired his clean legs as he walked behind her fourth husband's bier was twenty, she then being forty or older. Her deafness was caused by the same man's having struck her on the ear after she had torn a leaf from one of his books. If we add to these and other similarly precise bits of information given us by Alys herself the further details provided earlier by the *General Prologue*—the location of her home, her florid complexion, the color of her hose, the hugeness of her hat, the nature of her dentition, the excellence of her wimpling, and so on,—the portrait which finally emerges is remarkable for its roundness and the vividness of its coloring." On the Duenna see chap. iii, sec 3, *supra*.

[57] *Chaucer*, p. 239.

[58] See Dorothy Everett, "Chaucer's 'Good Ear,'" *RES*, XXIII (1947), 207; and on the Wife's syntax otherwise, Schlauch, "Colloquial English," *passim*.

[59] *WBProl* 44b–44f, 89–90, 130–32, 136, 149, 198–99, 418, 447, 510, 608, 618.

[60] Shumaker, "Alisoun," p. 87. Shumaker (p. 88) comments on the implications of this fact: "The Authorities are omnipresent in Chaucer, in his most deeply serious works as well as in his most lighthearted and raucous stories. They are one mark of his 'medievalism,' his deference to the ideal notions we were given the impression he had abandoned. And having said so much, I must follow the line of argument to the end and assert that nowhere in the *Canterbury Tales* does Chaucer commit himself utterly to an exploration of the implications of personality."

[61] *FrankT* 1355–1456. See Germaine Dempster, "Chaucer at Work on the Complaint in the *Franklin's Tale*," *MLN*, LII (1937), 16–23; James Sledd, "Dorigen's Complaint," *MP*, XLV (1947), 36–45.

[62] See William Witherle Lawrence, *Chaucer and the Canterbury Tales* (New York, 1950), pp. 124–125 and n. 12; Robert A. Pratt, "The Order of the *Canterbury Tales*," *PMLA*, LXVI (1951), 1158–1159.

[63] See chap. iii, sec. 3, *supra*.

[64] Jerome, *Adversus Jovianum*, I, 47, in Migne, *Patrologia Latina*, XXIII, col. 277 (*Sources and Analogues*, p. 211). Cf. *Roman de la Rose* 8667–77; *Miroir de Mariage* 1553–75.

[65] I, 48, in Migne, *Patrologia Latina*, XXIII, col. 279 (*Sources and Analogues*, p. 212).

[66] Cf. "I woot" and "ye knowe," *WBProl* 27, 29, 55, 63, 90, 99, 200.

[67] Cf. *WBProl* 34, 59–62, 71–72, 115–17, 123, 129–32.

[68] See chap. iii, p. 88 *supra* and note 46.

[69] Jerome, *Adversus Jovianum*, I, 47, in Migne, *Patrologia Latina*, XXIII, col. 276 (*Sources and Analogues*, p. 211).

[70] French, *Handbook*, pp. 327–332, gives a brief résumé of the scholarship, including the quotation from Tyrwhitt. See also Thomas R. Lounsbury, *Studies in Chaucer*, 3 vols. (New York, 1892), II, 389–390, 500–502 (on Chaucer's skepticism); Kittredge, *Chaucer*, p. 17 ("contemporary anecdote"); S. Foster Damon, "Chaucer and Alchemy," *PMLA*, XXXIX (1924), 782–788 (Chaucer "a serious student of alchemy"); Paull F. Baum, "The Canon's Yeoman's Tale," *MLN*, XL (1925), 152–154; Robinson, ed., *Chaucer*, pp. 15–16. Curry, *Chaucer and the Mediaeval Sciences*, pp. xix–xxi, issues a useful *caveat* against reading Chaucer's scientific attitudes in his artistic works. Chaucer's interest, he says, "was evidently centered in the personality of the Canon's Yeoman . . ."

[71] Thus I follow Speirs, *Chaucer*, p. 197: ". . . the misguided effort . . . exposes itself as a scientific specialist drive, uncontrolled by humane intelligence as to ends, such as we have grown familiar with as a phenomenon of our own day"; and Preston, *Chaucer*, p. 282: "The evils of competition and applied science, after six centuries, are more completely out of control . . . and of this progress Chaucer observed the beginnings."

[72] This division is recognized by Damon, "Alchemy," p. 783, and Baum, "Canon's Yeoman's Tale," pp. 152–153.

[73] *CYT* 748, 786–89, 819.

[74] See John Read, *The Alchemist in Life, Literature and Art* (London, 1947), pp. 23–24.

[75] See M. Berthelot, *La Chimie au moyen âge*, I (Paris, 1893), pp. 238–239, 281, 344–345; Arthur John Hopkins, *Alchemy Child of Greek Philosophy* (New York, 1934), pp. 213–215; and the illustrative materials printed by John Webster Spargo in *Sources and Analogues*, pp. 691–698.

[76] See Manly, *New Light*, p. 246.

[77] *CYT* 705, 861, 916–19, 984, 1158–59, 1302–03.

[78] See, e.g., *ParsT* 333; *Boece* III, met. 9. On the medieval aesthetic of ugliness see De Bruyne, *Etudes d'esthétique*, II, 215–216; III, 110–112, 268, 273–274.

[79] On the alchemical inventory see Berthelot, *La Chimie*, pp. 14–15; note that the alchemical texts and criticisms printed by Spargo in *Sources and Analogues* occasionally fall into rhetorical cataloguing of "dirty things," e.g., Petrarch (p. 693): "omnis angulus habebit pulves, & lebetes, & phialas olentium aquarum; herbas praeterea peregrinas; & externos sales, & sulphus, & distillatoria, & caminos"; Robert of York (p. 698): "quicunque dixerunt, quod haec ars est ex ovis, ungulis animalium, urina, sanguine, felle, spermate, & similibus & aliis etiam mineralibus diminutis combustibilis corruptibilis & nihil venientibus . . . quod esset ex capillis & ovis, arsenicis, & sulphuribus & rebus immundis & sordidis, ita quod quidam ex infirmitate suae rationis fecerunt eam, & ex stercore et urina, & hoc absit a sapientibus Dei gloriosi & sublimis." On the *parade* see P. Abrahams, "The Mercator-Scenes in Mediaeval French Passion-Plays," *Medium Aevum*, III (1934), 112–123; on the *Herberie* see above, chap. iii, sec. 3. To this tradition also belongs the Pardoner's preliminary sales talk, *PardT* 347–88.

[80] "The Clerical Status of Chaucer's Alchemist," *Speculum*, XVI (1941), 107.

[81] *Inferno* XX, 38.

[82] *CookProl* 4360.

[83] See sec. 4, iii, *post*.

[84] See, e.g., C. Hugh Holman, "Courtly Love in the Merchant's and the Franklin's Tales," *ELH*, XVIII (1951), 241–252; Wayne Shumaker, "Chaucer's *Manciple's Tale* as Part of a Canterbury Group," *UTQ*, XXII (1953), 147–156; on *2NT* and *CYT*, sec. 3, iii, *supra*.

[85] The term was apparently coined by Eleanor P. Hammond, *Chaucer: A Bibliographical Manual*

(New York, 1908), p. 256, to describe a small "class of narratives"; its prominence in criticism is owing to G. L. Kittredge, "Chaucer's Discussion of Marriage," *MP*, IX (1912), 435–467, and his *Chaucer*, chaps. v and vi. The existence of the group has since been questioned and defended. A bibliography of the problem is contained in the notes of Lawrence, *Chaucer*, pp. 121–144.

[86] See, respectively, *KnT* 1761, *MerchT* 1986, *SqT* 479 (cf. *LGW* F503); and *KnT* 2779, *MillT* 3204.

[87] *MLT* 288–94; *NPT* 3355–61.

[88] See Germaine Dempster, *Dramatic Irony in Chaucer* (Stanford, 1932), and Charles A. Owen, Jr., "The Crucial Passages in Five of the *Canterbury Tales*," *JEGP*, LII (1953), 294–311, where this and other sources of irony are taken up.

[89] E. M. W. Tillyard, *Poetry Direct and Oblique*, rev. ed. (London, 1948), p. 92, in one of the few requisitely serious discussions of the poem.

[90] See Paul E. Beichner, "Absolon's Hair," *Mediaeval Studies*, XII (1950), 222–233. Fr. Beichner provides a virtual history of "Absolon" in the Middle Ages.

[91] The interested reader may verify these recurrences in John S. P. Tatlock and A. G. Kennedy, *A Concordance to ... Chaucer* (Washington, 1927).

[92] See Paul E. Beichner, "Chaucer's Hende Nicholas," *Mediaeval Studies*, XIV (1952), 151–153.

[93] See E. T. Donaldson, "Idiom of Popular Poetry in the *Miller's Tale*," in *English Institute Essays, 1950* (New York, 1951), pp. 116–140.

[94] Expounded in the *Roman de la Rose* 2099–2174 (*Romaunt* 2223–88); but the whole of the God of Love's lecture is of more than passing interest in connection with Absolon.

[95] So Lowes, *Convention and Revolt*, pp. 98–100.

[96] Donaldson, "Idiom," pp. 131–132.

[97] See chap. iii, sec. 2, *supra*.

[98] J. S. P. Tatlock, "Chaucer's *Merchant's Tale*," *MP*, XXXIII (1936), 367–381; G. G. Sedgewick, "The Structure of *The Merchant's Tale*," *UTQ*, XVII (1948), 337–345; Dempster, *Dramatic Irony*, pp. 46–58; Owen, "Crucial Passages," pp. 297–301; Margaret Schlauch, "Chaucer's *Merchant's Tale* and Courtly Love," *ELH*, IV (1937), 201–212.

[99] See also *MerchT* 1869–89, 2057–71, 2107–15, 2125–31, 2219–36.

[100] *MerchT* 1795–1812.

[101] The common religious-allegorical meaning of the Biblical passage, and thus the irony arising here, are expounded by Robertson, "Doctrine of Charity," pp. 43–45: "For the doting knight, May represents what the lady in the *Canticum* represents to the faithful: she is his Holy Church, his Blessed Virgin, his refuge from the transitory world."

[102] The issue is described by J. R. Hulbert in *Sources and Analogues*, pp. 645–646. I. C. Lecompte, "Chaucer's *Nonne Prestes Tale* and the *Roman de Renard*," *MP*, XIV (1917), 737–749, argues persuasively for the adequacy of *Renart*, Branche II, as source; but he need not have stopped short of Ia, nor, indeed, of the whole collection.

[103] See Speirs, *Chaucer*, p. 186; for other recent criticisms see J. Burke Severs, "Chaucer's Originality in the *Nun's Priest's Tale*," *SP* XLIII (1946), 22–41; R. M. Lumiansky, "The Nun's Priest in *The Canterbury Tales*," *PMLA*, LXVIII (1953), 896–906; Mortimer J. Donovan, "The *Moralite* of the Nun's Priest's Sermon," *JEGP*, LII (1953), 498–508; Owen, "Crucial Passages," pp. 305–309. Milton Miller, "Definition by Comparison," *Essays in Criticism*, III (1953), 369–377, does not analyze the poem, but uses it in a very Chaucerian way to illustrate some fine general statements about Chaucer.

[104] See chap. iv, sec. 2, *supra*.

[105] In *MonkProl* and *NPProl* Chaucer quite deliberately recalls items from the Monk's portrait in *GProl* 165–207.

[106] The parody of the *Monk's Tale* is noted by Samuel B. Hemingway, "Chaucer's Monk and Nun's Priest," *MLN*, XXXI (1916), 479–483. On the Fall see Donovan, "*Moralite*," esp. p. 508; Speirs, *Chaucer*, pp. 188–193. On the *Melibee* see Lumiansky, "Nun's Priest," pp. 902–903. Lumiansky suggests that the description of the Nun's Priest by the Host in *NPEp* is broadly ironic, that the Nun's Priest is really frail and scrawny. This, if true, would be thoroughly in accord with

271

the poem's contradictory spirit. But I do not see how, short of dramatic performance, an irony depending so much on our actually seeing the character can be communicated in a narrative poem.

[107] *CookProl* 4339.

NOTES TO CHAPTER VII

CHAUCER AND THE FIFTEENTH CENTURY

Pages 244–247

[1] From John Lydgate, *The Life of Our Lady* (1409–1411), quoted in Caroline F. E. Spurgeon, *Five Hundred Years of Chaucer Criticism and Allusion (1357–1900)*, Chaucer Society, Ser. 2, No. 48, Pt. I (London, 1914), p. 19.

[2] Franco-Burgundian art, literature, and culture of the late Middle Ages have been the subject of several excellent studies. The oversimple generalizations presented here are based largely on the observations of Huizinga, *Waning of the Middle Ages;* Auerbach, *Mimesis,* chap. x; Italo Siciliano, *François Villon et les thèmes poétiques du moyen âge* (Paris, 1934); Henri Focillon, *Art d'occident* (Paris, 1938); Erwin Panofsky, *Early Netherlandish Painting,* 2 vols. (Cambridge, Mass., 1953); Helmut Hatzfeld, "Geist und Stil der flamboyanten Literatur in Frankreich," *Estudis Universitaris Catalans,* XXII (1936; Homenatje a Antonio Rubió i Lluch, III), 137–193. Walter F. Schirmer brings the English fifteenth century into this sphere; see "Das Ende des Mittelalters in England," in his *Kleine Schriften* (Tübingen, 1950), pp. 24–39.

[3] Cf. Auerbach, *Mimesis,* pp. 248–249; Huizinga, *Waning of the Middle Ages,* p. 115.

[4] Hatzfeld, "Geist und Stil," p. 185.

[5] Among the principal critics of Chaucer, Clemen seems to be the only one who has been alert to the comparison. See *Der junge Chaucer,* esp. pp. 27–28, 142, 148–149, 170–172, 180, 201; cf. Hatzfeld, "Geist und Stil," pp. 163, 184.

[6] See François Villon, *Le Testament,* vv. 453–532 (in his *Œuvres,* ed. A. Longnon, 4th ed., rev. Lucien Foulet, CFMA [Paris, 1932], pp. 26–29).

index

INDEX

275

romance, 15, 17; in courtly style, 60; in fabliau, 60, 66; of characters in *RR* of Jean, 94; concreteness of in *C*, 103; in *HF*, 113, 114; in *PF*, 116; in *Filostrato*, 126, 127; in *TC*, 158; seasonal, in *GProl*, 169, 170; a rhetorical figure, 173; in *KnT*, 176–189 *passim;* in *ClT*, 192; in *C*, 197; in *MerchT*, 234; in *NPT*, 239–240. See also *Descriptio*

Dialect: in mime, 64, 201; in *ReeveT*, 199–204; in *FriarT*, 269; in *Second Shepherds' Play*, 201–202; in *Jehan et Blonde*, 257; in *Renart*, 257

Dialogue: in *Eneas*, 12; in romance, 19–21, 49; courtly, 24; in *RR* of Guillaume, 39; colloquial, in *Eneas*, 42–43; dramatic, in *Yvain*, 48–50; formal, in *Yvain*, 51–52; central action in *Flamenca*, 55; in fabliau, 64; in *BD*, 106–107; in *PF*, 111–112, 118; in *Filostrato*, 127; in *TC*, 142–145, 156–157; little in *KnT*, 177, 181; in *C*, 197; in *HF*, 239

———in monologue: in romance, 22; in *Eneas*, 12; in *Yvain*, 50–51; in *Flamenca*, 55–57

Dickens, C., 65

Diction: in romance, 14; in *RR* of Guillaume, 37–38; of Lover in *RR* of Guillaume, 160; in fabliau, 64; in *RR* of Jean, 76, 78–79, 83, 88–90; in Alain de Lille, 78; in Machaut, 99; in *BD*, 102; in *HF*, 109, 113; in *PF*, 116–118, 119; in *ClT*, 195; in *ReeveT*, 204; in *MillT*, 226–227; in *MerchT*, 231, 232–233. See also Idiom

Didacticism, convention in med. lit., 92

Digression: in *RR* of Jean, 73; convention of, 93

Diomede, 163

Discourse, direct: in *Eneas*, 19–25, 28; in romance, 19–29; in *RR* of Guillaume, 39–40; in courtly trad., 40; in *BD*, 102; in *KnT*, 177, 187. See also Dialogue; Monologue

Dit de la gageure, 68, 230

Doctrine in *WBProl*, 207–213 *passim*, 223, 230

Don Quixote, 96, 137

Donaldson, E. T., 266, 271

Donovan, M., 271

Drama, medieval, 58, 64, 167, 168, 219, 226

Dream: in *RR* of Guillaume, 31, 100; in Machaut, 99; in *BD*, 101, 102, 103, 104, 107; psychology in *BD*, 102; in *HF*, 108, 114; in *PF*, 115, 121; in *TC*, 158; tradition of, and opening of *CT*, 169

Dream of Scipio, 115, 120, 121

Dryden, John, 29

Dubois, M., 257

Dubs, I., 255

Duenna, 31, 72–77 *passim*, 82–88, 91–96 *passim*, 130, 137, 140, 141, 205, 206, 259

Dunbar, William: 244; *Twa Mariit Wemen*, 260

Dvořák, M., 258

Eagle, 110–113, 142, 146, 237, 238, 239

Effictio. See Portrait

Emerson, O. F., 251

Empson, W., 8

Eneas: 19–30 *passim*, 42–43, 111, 154, 253 (edition); experiment in, 12; lack of theme, 13

English literature, medieval, 5, 6, 168, 227, 244–245, 252, 256

Epic, 6, 12, 13, 69, 70, 127. See also *Chanson de geste* and individual authors

Epistle against Jovinian, 71, 207, 208, 259

Eracle. See Gautier d'Arras

Escoufle, L', 15, 54, 137

Everett, D., 269

Exemplum: 91, 93, 186, 200, 206, 210–211, 240, 259; in *HF*, 110

Fable, 58, 59, 237, 238, 239, 242

Fabliau: 58, 59–69, 72, 75, 94, 95, 96, 140, 198, 203, 212–213, 224, 230, 256 (edition); English, 7, 256; C's treatment of, 198–200, 204. See also individual titles and topics

Fairchild, H., 267

Faral, E.: *Recherches*, 252; ed. *Arts Poétiques*, 253, 255, 266, 267; *Mimes*, 256

Faus-Semblant, 73, 90–94, 96, 137, 207

Fevre de Creeil, Du, 257

Fierz-Monnier, A., 252, 255

Figurative language in fabliau, 60–61

Flamenca, 5, 47, 55–57, 70, 131, 165, 255 (edition)

Floire et Blancheflor, 125

Florimont, 26, 140, 253, 255

Focillon, H., 272

Formula: in *KnT*, 177; in *WBProl*, 211, 212

Fculet, L., 257, 258

Fowler, H. W., 264

Frame of *CT*, 168–171, 222–223, 241

Frampton, M., 269

Francis, St., 72, 196, 197

Frank, Grace, 256

Franklin's Tale, 111, 207

French, J. M., 265

French, R. D., *Handbook*, 251, 260, 268, 270

French, W. H., 267, 268

French language in England, 251

Frey, D., 167, 266

277

fabliau, 62–63, 170; in *BD*, 102; of Criseyde, 154; in *GProl*, 169–171, 173, 200; in *RR* of Guillaume, 33, 34–35, 170, 255; a rhetorical figure, 173; in *KnT*, 180–182; of Absolon, 228; convention of ugliness, 255; in *Yvain*, 255; in *Aucassin*, 255; of Monk, 271

Pratt, R. A.: "C Borrowing," 260, 261; "*Roman de Troyle*," 262; "Framework," 166, 266; "*Teseida*," 267, 268; "Order of *CT*," 269

Praz, M., 262

Prescott, H. F. M., trans., 56, 255

Preston, R., 108, 261, 270

Prestre et d'Alison, Du, 140

Prestre et des .II. ribaus, Du, 62, 257

Prestre et du chevalier, Du, 69, 257

Prioress, 170

Prioress' Tale, 192, 223, 268

Privilège aux Bretons, 64

Prudence, 94

Quatre Souhais Saint Martin, Les, 257

Raynaud, G., 101, 256, 259, 260

Read, J., 270

Realism, "figural," 14

Realism (style), discussed *passim*

Reeve, 199, 200–201, 203, 222

Reeve's Prologue, 199

Reeve's Tale, 7, 198–204, 223, 224

Renart, Jean: *L'Escoufle*, 15, 54, 137; *Galeran de Bretagne*, 18, 54, 253; *Guillaume de Dole*, 15, 54, 254

Renart, *Roman de*. See *Roman de Renart*

Renaut de Beaujeu, *Bel Inconnu*, 54–55

Rhetoric: as lit. instrument, 1, 4; "high style," 6, 173; med. trad. of, 3, 6, 14, 54, 173; in *Eneas*, 12; classical, 14, 173; in lyric monologue, *Yvain*, 53; avoided in fabliau discourse, 64; in *RR* of Jean, 79; in *BD*, 101, 103, 107; in *HF*, 108; in *Filostrato*, 126; in *TC*, 130, 134; of Pandarus, 139, 145; in *GProl*, 170; of Host, 171; in *CT*, 173–175; textbooks, 173, 174; Manly on, 174; C's use of, 174–175; in *KnT*, 177, 180, 189; in Petrarch's tale of Griselda, 191; in *ClT*, 192, 193–194; in *CYT*, 214, 223; in *NPT*, 222, 239, 240; in *MLT*, 222; in *MerchT*, 233–234; C's reputation for, 244; late medieval, 245–247; in *PardT*, 247

———figures of: catalogue, 17, 121; rhet. question, 24; apostrophe, 26, 135, 173, 233; anaphora, 53; *contentio*, 134; *descriptio*, 173,

194–195, 233; *exclamatio*, 173, 233; *conduplicatio*, 173; *subjectio*, 173; *dubitatio*, 173; *digressio*, 174; *expolitio*, 174; *circumlocutio*, 174; *occupatio*, 177; *pronominatio*, 180; *comparatio*, 222; *vituperatio*, 255. *See also* Portrait; Exemplum; Formula; Invocation

Rhythm: in romance, 14; in speech of Venus (*RR*), 37; in song of Male Bouche (*RR*), 44; of speech in *Yvain*, 49; in fabliau, 64; of monologue in *RR* of Jean, 89; in *HF*, 108; in *PF*, 119; of Pandarus' speech, 142; in *ClT*, 192; in dramatic monologue, 205; in *WBProl*, 206, 210

Richeut, 65, 257

Richter, E., 255

Robert of York, 270

Robertson, D. W., Jr.: "Terminology," 252, 259; "Andreas," 254; "Doctrine of Charity," 254, 271; on Rudel, 254; "Tragedy," 265

Robinson, F. N., 264, 265, 270

Roman de la Rose, 5, 142, 167, 172, 215, 252 (edition), 270. *See also* Guillaume de Lorris; Jean de Meun

Roman de la Violette, 255

Roman de Renart, 5, 59, 69–70, 77–78, 238, 256 (ed. Martin), 257 (ed. Roques)

Roman de Thebes, 11, 12, 14

Roman de Troie, 13, 125

Romance: 11–57 and *passim*; devel. of, 11–13, 54–55, 57. *See also* individual authors and topics

Romaunt of the Rose, 16–17, 18, 27, 31–39 *passim*, 44, 253, 263, 271

Root, R. K., 176–177, 263, 265, 267

Roques, M., 257, 258

Rubel, V., 267

Rutebeuf, *Herberie*, 63, 79–81, 94, 219

Rutter, G., 260

Saint Piere et du jougleur, De, 64, 68–69

Sandras, E., 6

Sapegno, N., 251, 254

Schilperoort, G., 256

Schirmer, W., 272

Schlauch, M., 251, 264, 269, 271

Second Nun's Tale, 172, 192, 216–217

Second Shepherds' Play, 257, 269

Secunda Pastorum, 257, 269

Sedgewick, G., 230, 271

Setting: in romance, 15–17, 252; in courtly trad., 40; in fabliau, 60; in Machaut, 99; in *BD*,